Theology in a Suffering World

In this book, Christopher Southgate proposes a new way of understanding the glory of God in Christian theology, based on glory as sign. Working from the roots of the concept in the Hebrew Bible, *Theology in a Suffering World: Glory and Longing* shows that 'glory' is not necessarily about beauty or radiance, but is better understood as a sign of the unknowable depths of God. Southgate goes on to show how John and Paul transform the concept of glory in the light of the Cross. He then explores where glory may be discerned in the natural world, including in situations of pain and suffering. In turn, glory is explored in the poetry of R. S. Thomas and the writings of the Jewish mystic Etty Hillesum. Finally, the book considers what it might mean for Christians to be 'transformed from one degree of glory to another': that might mean becoming a sign of the great sign of God that is Christ, and conforming their longing to God's longing for the Kingdom to come.

Christopher Southgate is Associate Professor in Interdisciplinary Theology at the University of Exeter. Trained originally as a biochemist, he is still involved in origin-of-life research and is known in the science–religion debate for his edited textbook and his monograph on suffering in evolution, *The Groaning of Creation* (2008). This book is a sequel to *Groaning*, but it also builds on Southgate's career as a poet, in which he has won a Hawthornden Fellowship and published eight collections, and his experience as principal of a theological training scheme and as a spiritual director and retreat conductor.

Theology in a Suffering World

Glory and Longing

CHRISTOPHER SOUTHGATE

University of Exeter

CAMBRIDGE
UNIVERSITY PRESS

CAMBRIDGE
UNIVERSITY PRESS

University Printing House, Cambridge CB2 8BS, United Kingdom

One Liberty Plaza, 20th Floor, New York, NY 10006, USA

477 Williamstown Road, Port Melbourne, VIC 3207, Australia

314–321, 3rd Floor, Plot 3, Splendor Forum, Jasola District Centre,
New Delhi – 110025, India

79 Anson Road, #06–04/06, Singapore 079906

Cambridge University Press is part of the University of Cambridge.

It furthers the University's mission by disseminating knowledge in the pursuit of
education, learning, and research at the highest international levels of excellence.

www.cambridge.org
Information on this title: www.cambridge.org/9781107153691
DOI: 10.1017/9781316599945

© Christopher Southgate 2018

First published 2018

Printed and bound in Great Britain by Clays Ltd, Elcograf S.p.A.

A catalogue record for this publication is available from the British Library.

Library of Congress Cataloging-in-Publication Data
NAMES: Southgate, Christopher, 1953– author.
TITLE: Theology in a suffering world : glory and longing / Christopher Southgate,
University of Exeter.
DESCRIPTION: 1 [edition]. | New York : Cambridge University Press, 2018.
IDENTIFIERS: LCCN 2018011111 | ISBN 9781107153691 (hb)
SUBJECTS: LCSH: Glory of God–Christianity. | Suffering–Religious aspects–Christianity.
CLASSIFICATION: LCC BT180.G6 S68 2018 | DDC 231/.4–dc23
LC record available at https://lccn.loc.gov/2018011111

ISBN 978-1-107-15369-1 Hardback

Contents

Acknowledgements

I thank Orion Books for permission to reproduce copyright material from *R. S. Thomas: Collected Poems 1945–1990* (Dent, 1993) and Bloodaxe Books for permission to reproduce copyright material from *R. S. Thomas: Collected Later Poems 1988–2000* (Bloodaxe, 2004).

Versions of sections of the argument of this book first appeared in 'Divine Glory in a Darwinian World', *Zygon* 49 (2014), 784–807, and in 'The Orientation of Longing' in *Issues in Science and Theology: Do Emotions Shape the World?* edited by D. Evers et al. (Springer, 2016), 73–86.

This book began as the 2014 Sarum Lectures, and I thank the Lectures' Trustees for their invitation and support and the Trustees of the South West Ministry Training Course for sabbatical leave (and splendid colleagues there for covering for my absences).

The book has been strengthened by many presentations, especially at the 2014 European Society for the Study of Science and Theology; the 2015 International Society for Science and Religion; the 2016 American Academy of Religion; the 2016 Conference 'Exploring the Glory of God' at St John's College, Durham; and the 2016 Greenbelt Festival, also at the Catholic University of Lyon; Copenhagen University; the Durham Centre for Catholic Studies; the Theology and Religion Seminar at the University of Exeter; the Jerusalem Chamber Seminar at Westminster Abbey; the University of St Mark and St John (Plymouth); Truro Theological Society; in classes for the South West Ministry Training Course; at training days for the Dioceses of Exeter and Gloucester; and at meetings of New Zealand Christians in Science at Auckland and Christchurch.

My interest in semiosis stems from my long and generative collaboration with Dr Andrew Robinson, which I value enormously.

Beyond that, I am very grateful indeed to many colleagues who have advised on the manuscript at various stages, including Drs Richard Burridge, David Catchpole, Jason Fout, Christopher Gill, David Horrell, Daniel Pedersen, Bethany Sollereder, Francesca Stavrakopoulou, David Tollerton, G. C. Waldrep, Carys Walsh, Megan Warner, and Vernon White, also my invaluable research assistant Katherine Manley Frost. I also thank my editor at Cambridge University Press, Beatrice Rehl, and her staff.

I take sole responsibility for the final content, its adventures, eccentricities, and errors.

I dedicate the book with great affection to my wife Sandy, without whose love none of these adventures would have been possible.

Abbreviations

CD   Barth's *Church Dogmatics*
GL   von Balthasar's *The Glory of the Lord*
MP   von Balthasar's *Mysterium Paschale*
TD   von Balthasar's *Theo-Drama*
TL   von Balthasar's *Theo-Logic*

Full details are given in the Bibliography.

Bible Quotations

Quotations from the Bible are occasionally from the King James Bible (KJV). Unless otherwise attributed, all quotations are from the New Revised Standard Version (NRSV). Quotations from the Septuagint (LXX) are from Sir L. C. L. Brenton, *The Septuagint Version in Greek and English* (Grand Rapids, MI: Zondervan, 1970).

Introduction

This is a world of great beauty, physical intricacy and biological diversity, in which humans sometimes act with goodness, and occasionally with real heroism. It is also a world in which creatures inflict on each other considerable trauma through such behaviour as predation and parasitism, and a world in which natural phenomena such as the movement of tectonic plates cause enormous extents of suffering. Human beings, moreover, routinely act selfishly, and sometimes with great cruelty.

So much seems obvious enough. It is the very grain of our experience of the world from day to day. My observation of much Christian preaching, and the theology that lies behind it, is that in response to ugliness and suffering in the world, it still gives 'the ancient Christian answer'[1] that all these evils can be traced to the sin of the first humans. As I have shown in recent writing (along with many other theologians writing in dialogue with science),[2] this answer is now implausible in terms of chronology. We can be confident from the fossil record that both predation and disease pre-dated the human species by millions of years.

The conclusion that primeval human sin directly caused the suffering inflicted by animals on each other was always dubious theologically, as being a direct challenge to the goodness of God. Why would a good God

---

[1] J. Polkinghorne, 'Pelican Heaven', *Times Literary Supplement*, April 3 2009, 31.

[2] C. Southgate, *The Groaning of Creation: God, Evolution and the Problem of Evil* (Louisville, KY: Westminster John Knox Press, 2008), chapter 2; also e.g., A. R. Peacocke, *Theology for a Scientific Age: Being and Becoming – Natural, Divine and Human* (London: SCM Press, 1993), 248.

allow one act of disobedience to cause suffering in so many creatures? I have also contested the notion that any rebellious power or mysterious force is responsible for all the disvalues[3] in the natural world.[4] That notion is problematic both theologically and scientifically. Theologically, because that would be to accord more power to a force opposed to God than the Christian tradition has typically been willing to accede.[5] It would be to suggest that God set out to create straw-eating lions and was unable to do so. Scientifically, because the difficult but fascinating conclusion to be drawn from evolutionary science is that it is the same process – evolution driven at least in part by natural selection – that gives rise to both the values of beauty, diversity and ingenuity in creation, and to the disvalues of suffering and extinction.[6] Further, it is the same processes that cause so much 'natural evil' among humans – earthquakes, tsunamis, volcanic eruptions, hurricanes and typhoons – that made the world so extravagantly fruitful for life.

All of this runs counter to any simplistic theology that associates all goodness and beauty with God and all violence, cruelty, and suffering with rebellion either by humans or other powers opposed to God. Instead, it suggests that God, as the creator of the world, is deeply implicated in the causal structures that lead to such disvalues. Not only through the fact of having brought the world into existence, but also through having created processes to which disvalues were intrinsic.

However, I also recognise that gradually humans evolved the power of self-conscious freely choosing agency. This was the emergent power to make (while still somewhat constrained by genetic and environmental factors) both loving choices, out of a life of self-giving love,[7] and also evil choices. Those choices are real, and I discuss them further in Chapter 4. What they do not account for is the general suffering of the non-human world as part of the evolutionary process (as opposed to specific ecological harms that humans have subsequently committed), and harms

---

[3] The term 'disvalue', when applied to the natural world, stems from an important analysis by H. Rolston, III, 'Disvalues in Nature', *The Monist* 75 (1992), 250–78.

[4] C. Southgate, 'Re-Reading Genesis, John and Job: A Christian's Response to Darwinism', *Zygon* 46 (2011), 370–95.

[5] Moreover, a range of texts in the Hebrew Bible suggests that predation exists within the creative providence of God; see, e.g., Psalm 104.21, Job 38.39–41.

[6] On the reality of suffering among non-human creatures, see Southgate, *Groaning*, 3–4. On extinction as disvalue, see ibid., 14–15.

[7] Southgate, *Groaning*, chapters 4 and 6, and Chapter 5 of this book.

directly attributable to the natural processes through which the Earth functions as a life-bearing planet.

Writing well before those processes came to be understood through the work of Darwin and his successors, that extraordinary visionary William Blake already poses the sharp questions that must bother Christians about the ambiguity of the world. In his poem 'The Tyger' Blake asks, 'what art, what anvil' formed tigerness? Did he who made the Lamb make the tiger? And perhaps most difficult of all, did God 'smile his work to see', though that work gives rise to a life of subtle stalking and terrible, flesh-tearing violence?[8] My conclusion, arrived at after a great deal of pondering, is that God's was the 'art', God's the 'anvil' (if so the process of natural selection may be termed), and that God does indeed smile on God's work in the tiger, even while lamenting and suffering with the struggle and trauma of the prey animal.[9]

The present study is in a way the complement to my previous book, *The Groaning of Creation*. In that book I was concerned with the enterprise of theodicy. I sought to answer the question how, given the reasoning just presented (especially in relation to the suffering of non-human creatures) can Christians continue to hold to the goodness of God? I provided a 'compound theodicy' in respect of 'evolutionary evil', including the following theological moves: constraint on the ways God could create a fruitful world; compassionate divine accompanying of each suffering creature; a final state of consummation from which all suffering had been removed; and a human vocation to act as partners, even co-redeemers, in the ultimate liberation of creation.[10]

I am concerned in the present project not so much with *explaining* the co-existence of the disvalues in creation with the goodness of God as with *facing up to* and *relating to* an ambiguous world, and seeking to explore and relate to its Creator and Redeemer.[11] So I am in need of a language for expressing how we might read God's ways with this ambiguous world, and how we might better understand the human call to respond to God.

---

[8] W. Blake, *Poetry and Prose of William Blake*, ed. G. Keynes (New York: Random House, 1946), 72–3.

[9] Southgate, *Groaning*, chapter 4.   [10] Ibid., chapters 1, 3–5, 7.

[11] This is a real challenge for much Christian worship. As Walter Brueggemann writes: Worship that is always 'happy, positive and upbeat ... is destructive because it requires persons to engage in enormous denial and pretense about how life really is.' *Finally Comes the Poet: Daring Speech for Proclamation* (Minneapolis, MN: Fortress Press, 1989), 47.

This language has to be capable of encompassing God's creating of this ambiguous world, God's great reconciling act in Christ, and the final promise of an eschatological state from which all struggle and suffering have been eliminated.

That of course is a massive task, and even great systematic treatments ultimately seem, as Aquinas came to know, 'like straw', in the face of the task of speaking of God. This present modest study seeks first to face honestly the ambiguities of the world as God created it, and second to propose a set of lenses through which God's ways with an ambiguous world may be explored.

DISCOURSE ON DIVINE GLORY

In this book I re-present an ancient theological concept as a vehicle for speaking of God's self-communication to the world. This vehicle is *the concept of divine glory*. That may seem an odd choice as a way of engaging with ugliness bound up with beauty, but I suggest it is a very generative choice, for the following reasons:

1. Divine glory has about it an inalienable element of mystery, which is very important in seeking to find language to address God's ways with a suffering world. Glory is not something that will ever be neatly reducible to a straightforward proposition. Glory is always more, and other, and more dangerous.

2. The root from which is derived the principal term for divine glory in the Hebrew Bible, *kavōd*,[12] is associated with weight, importance, significance, rather than beauty or radiance.[13] Glory is therefore a discourse that can encompass the ambiguity of the world, and the ugliness of creaturely suffering, and face the possibility of God's involvement in, and even responsibility for, that suffering.[14]

---

[12] Variously transliterated with the consonants kbd or kvd, and with various accenting of the vowels.

[13] David Brown associates *kavōd* with 'a "weight" or what overwhelms ... light or darkness might thus have very similar effects. Both brilliant light and impenetrable darkness might "weigh" or "press down" on the human observer in similar ways, creating awe or fear.' *Divine Generosity and Human Creativity: Theology through Symbol, Painting and Architecture* (London: Routledge, 2017), 82–3.

[14] The greatest modern exponent of the theology of glory, Hans Urs von Balthasar, makes in effect the same move when he distances himself from 'aesthetic theology', which might explain away tragedy and death within an overall teleology, in favour of a theological aesthetics. Such an aesthetics cannot allow itself to 'exclude the element of the ugly, of the

Glory is as Jason Fout has said 'prominent in first-order discourse about God',[15] but it is not a term that is well understood. Christopher Morgan notes that it is 'one of the hardest Christian terms to define'.[16] I want to suggest that the concept goes well beyond the familiar connotation of bright and beautiful light, and that it can convey the apprehension of ambiguity in the world that is my concern here.

When the seraphim in Isaiah 6 cry out that the whole earth is full of God's glory, that acclamation can be understood as the earth being full of the importance of God, the weight of the divine reality. The term *glory* is not simply testament to the beautiful aspects of the world. Indeed the vision of Isaiah is full of smoke and dread. And in the New Testament, Christ comes into his full glory at his 'hour', which is seen by the writer of the Fourth Gospel as beginning with Christ's Passion.[17] So divine glory encompasses not only light and radiance but also pain and suffering, degradation and death.

It seems to me therefore that the language of glory (as distinct from beauty)[18] provides a vehicle for speaking honestly of the ambiguity of the created world and of human experience under God. Also, glory in the Scriptures is typically something apprehensible (usually by sight though occasionally by another sense[19]), therefore something that can be contemplated.[20] Through that contemplation, that search, more can be understood of the God who is ultimately mysterious and always beyond our understanding.

It remains to ask – what understanding of glory, a notoriously elusive concept, is both faithful to its use in Scripture and in the best of modern theology, and is also able to contain the ambiguity of the natural world,

---

tragically fragmented, of the demonic, but must come to terms with these': *The Glory of the Lord: A Theological Aesthetics,* Vol. 1, Seeing the Form, transl. E. Leivà-Merikakis, ed. J. Fessio, S.J. and J. Riches (Edinburgh: T&T Clark, 1982), 460.

[15] J. Fout, *Fully Alive: The Glory of God and the Human Creature in Karl Barth, Hans Urs von Balthasar and the Theological Exegesis of Scripture* (London: Bloomsbury T&T Clark, 2015), 26.

[16] C. W. Morgan, 'Towards a Theology of the Glory of God' in *The Glory of God,* ed. C. W. Morgan and R. A. Peterson (Wheaton, IL: Crossway, 2010), 153–87, at 156.

[17] John 3.14; 12.23. See Chapter 2 for further exploration of this theme in John.

[18] See Chapter 1 for further discussion of the distinctions between glory and beauty.

[19] See, e.g., Sir 17.13 'their ears heard the glory of his voice'.

[20] Carey Newman, insisting that *kavōd* in the Hebrew Bible 'cannot be reduced to a light phenomenon' continues that *kavōd,* 'when used in reference to Yahweh, is best semantically defined as revealed, visual, divine presence'. C. C. Newman, *Paul's Glory-Christology: Tradition and Rhetoric* (Leiden: Brill, 1992), 137, n. 7.

the suffering of Christ on the Cross, and the eventual Christian hope for the redemption of all things?

As I shall show in Chapter 2, the biblical witness to the glory of the Lord begins (canonically) with various appearances to the Hebrews in the wilderness. That glory is described as being 'in the cloud' (Ex 16.10), 'like a devouring fire on the top of the mountain' (24.17), and later filling the tabernacle (40.34), and appearing at the tent of meeting (Nm 14.10).

In interpreting texts of this kind, and in contemplating the natural world, seeking to understand something of God, there seem to me to be three basic options, three ways of expressing the relation of apprehensible indications of deity both to the divine and to the material. The first is a naïvely realist one, which sees deity directly and unreservedly expressed in physical manifestations. On this understanding Yahweh literally was the 'devouring fire' in texts such as Exodus 24.17.[21] That understanding may indeed represent an important early strand in Hebrew tradition, may indeed lie behind the introduction of the weightiness term *kavōd* as a way of expressing divine presence. However, such a local, physical under-standing of God clearly struggles to incorporate transcendence, the sense that the divine *kavōd* is important across the whole world (as in Is 6.3), and that that importance in turn reflects something profoundly ineffable, something beyond human comprehension. The creator-creature distinc-tion is necessarily compromised in such a naïve view. To the extent that this naïve realism may have been present in early expressions of Hebrew religion, it is countered (and necessarily so) by the apophatic instinct that emerged in the tradition, and which we see in texts such as Exodus 33.18–21, 1 Kings 19.11–12, and Ezekiel 1.28, and eventually in a reluc-tance even to write the divine name.

The second possibility is a Platonic metaphysics, in which the material is a copy of a more perfect spiritual world. In such a scheme 'the ideal is attained by jettisoning and devaluing material existence while the soul seeks unity with the Infinite'.[22] This is a very compelling scheme – hence its huge influence on Western thought ever since Plato. But this matter-spirit hierarchy is not, in the last analysis, the scheme to which the Incar-nation points us. Felix Ó Murchadha notes that at the Incarnation:

---

[21] Though the texts themselves often undercut such naïve realism, Exodus 24.17 reads 'The *appearance* of the glory of the Lord was *like* a devouring fire'; cf. also Ezekiel 1.28: 'This was the appearance of the likeness of the glory of the Lord'.

[22] S. M. Garrett, *God's Beauty-in-Act: Participation in God's Suffering Glory* (Eugene, OR: Pickwick Books, 2013), 121.

worldly hierarchies are undermined: the Word has become flesh, the immortal dies, the most high is as a slave. Such an incarnational logic ... stands opposed to a sacred logic, which still governs Plato's texts ... Christianity is profane precisely in its refusal of that logic.[23]

One danger of a Platonic scheme within Christianity is, as James K. A. Smith notes, that of making 'materiality and embodiment a kind of "necessary evil"',[24] rather than something primordially affirmed good, and of which the goodness is reaffirmed in the Incarnation. Such schemes, then, will always tend to be' 'overweighted' towards the transcendent and treat the material only as instrumental.

That brings us to what I see as the third major possibility – that of a semiotic scheme, in which the material world – not as a sort of expedient but as a necessary outworking of the character of God – carries *signs* of the divine reality. In an important survey of the glory of the Lord in the Hebrew Bible, Carey Newman stresses that the Lord is not localized where the glory of the Lord (*kavōd Yahweh*) is seen; rather, the latter only appears at the 'periphery or edge' of 'where Yahweh is thought to be'.[25] Newman continues, 'Yahweh is never said to be located in *kavōd*'.[26] The glory functions rather as a sign of the divine. This is an insight of the first importance to an incarnational, sacramental faith.[27] In a helpful little article on sacramentality, Patrick Sherry draws on von Balthasar's essay on prayer, in which von Balthasar contrasts a Platonist spirituality, which will really desire directness of spiritual engagement with God, with one that accepts the mediating role of signs in the material world.[28]

Those signs are, however, not rightly discerned by everyone – even in respect of the Incarnate Christ, *the* great sign of the nature of God, the writer of the Fourth Gospel can note that 'he came to what was his own, and his own people did not accept him' (Jn 1.11).[29] Even the ultimate

---

[23] F. Ó Murchadha, *A Phenomenology of the Christian Life: Glory and Night* (Bloomington, IN: Indiana University Press, 2013), 6. As Garrett observes, the goodness of creation is always in question in a Platonic scheme; *God's Beauty-in-Act*, 121.

[24] J. K. A. Smith, *Speech and Theology: Language and the Logic of the Incarnation* (London: Routledge, 2002), 176.

[25] Newman, *Paul's Glory-Christology*, 21.   [26] Ibid., 23.

[27] As David Jones recognised in his essay 'Art and Sacrament', *Epoch and Artist: Selected Writings*, ed. H. Grisewood (London: Faber and Faber, 1973), 143–79.

[28] P. Sherry, 'The Sacramentality of All Things', *New Blackfriars* 89 (2008), 575–90.

[29] Cf. also Simeon's prophecy in Luke 2.34: 'This child is destined for the falling and rising of many in Israel, and to be a sign that will be opposed'.

demonstration of love, on Calvary, can be rejected, as Luke describes it being rejected by one of the two thieves (Lk 23.39).[30]

I pursue the question of how the natural world may be contemplated, and how that contemplation relates to the various objections to the enterprise of natural theology, in Chapter 3. But first I propose a way of construing divine glory as providing a language for this semiotic understanding of God's self-communication to the world.

DIVINE GLORY AS SIGN

My principal understanding of divine glory is as follows:

1. Because the depth of the divine reality is utterly beyond human knowing, and because glory is always represented in the Bible as something apprehensible, I propose that *the apprehension of divine glory is typically the perception of a sign or array of signs pointing beyond itself to the unknowable depths of the reality of God.*
2. That sign, being a self-communication of the divine nature, *always calls for a human response.*[31]

There is of course a Plato-influenced ontology at work in this scheme, in the sense that the material acts as sign of what transcends both the material and the human comprehension. What I seek to avoid, however, is the implicit or explicit denigration of the material that can be a feature of Platonic schemes. So Simone Weil, one of the most important theological Platonists of the twentieth century, associates 'gravity' with the risk of 'baseness',[32] whereas I use 'weight' or 'depth' of reality to connote

---

[30] As Douglas Dales points out, writing of the theology of Michael Ramsey, the differing response of the thieves 'reveals the power of divine love, and its agony in weakness, unable to force repentance, but able to save to the uttermost those who turn to God': *Glory: The Spiritual Theology of Michael Ramsey* (Norwich: Canterbury Press, 2003), 29.

[31] So also Richard R. Melick, Jr., 'The glory of God is the self-revelation of his character (being) and the visible and energetic (power) presence of God ... God's glory, then, is always dynamic. It produces a response from those who witness it.' 'The Glory of God in the Synoptic Gospels, Acts and the General Epistles': *The Glory of God*, ed. C. W. Morgan and R. A. Peterson (Wheaton, IL: Crossway, 2010), 79–106, at 80.

[32] S. Weil, *Gravity and Grace*, transl. E. Crawford and M. von der Ruhr (London: Routledge, 2000 [1952]), 2.

what can be partially explored through contemplation (humble and faithful interpretation of signs) but ultimately transcends comprehension.[33]

I propose then a new interpretative strategy for approaching the concept of glory in the Scriptures and in the contemporary world. In work on ecological reading of the Pauline epistles,[34] colleagues and I articulated the concept of a 'hermeneutical lens', a way of reading texts and events to bring out issues of contemporary importance. In the current book, *our principal lens for reading divine glory will be as a sign of the divine reality*. In Chapter 2 this lens is used to interpret biblical texts on glory. In Chapter 3 signs of God in the natural world are read in terms of glory.

In Chapter 2 I seek to show that a semiotic reading of biblical texts on glory emphasizes helpfully both what is revealed and what is concealed in the manifestation of divine glory. The texts on divine glory in Exodus are particularly telling in this regard. At the same time they show that this interpretation of divine glory has to be more flexible than a straightforward semiotic interpretation, because sometimes the reference of the term is more directly to the divine essence, rather than to a sign of God's nature. Also, application of our lens to the ministry and Passion of Christ, in particular through the reading of the New Testament's most explicitly semiotic text, the Fourth Gospel, enables us to see glory even within darkness, pain and degradation. And further application of the lens to the life of the believer, as explored in the Pauline letters, suggests possibilities for the Christian's participation in the divine semiosis (Chapter 5).

It is important to clarify what type of interpretative strategy this is. Horrell et al. write that:

a kind of acknowledged circularity is necessarily intrinsic to a fruitful hermeneutic: *hermeneutical lenses are at one and the same time products of the tradition and the means for its critical rereading and reconfiguration.* Equally crucial, however, is the impact of the relevant contemporary context in generating the particular priorities which shape the formulation of hermeneutical lenses.[35]

---

[33] An understanding influenced by the apophatic tradition that stems from the work of Pseudo-Dionysius the Areopagite. For an introduction to this tradition, see D. Turner, *The Darkness of God: Negativity in Christian Mysticism* (Cambridge: Cambridge University Press, 1995).

[34] D. G. Horrell, C. Hunt, and C. Southgate, *Greening Paul: Rereading the Apostle in a Time of Ecological Crisis* (Waco, TX: Baylor University Press, 2010).

[35] Horrell et al., *Greening Paul*, 43, emphasis in original. We also make there the important point that any given hermeneutical lens will bring some aspects of the object of study into focus, while leaving others blurred. Ibid., 42.

The contemporary context shapes this hermeneutical lens in two important ways. First, it includes the analysis of semiotic categories developed by C. S. Peirce,[36] and helpfully re-explored in recent work by my colleague Andrew Robinson.[37] Application of these categories to a semiotic reading of glory will lead in the course of the book to some new ways of expressing God's interaction with the world. Second, the natural sciences, especially evolutionary biology and plate tectonics, force us to acknowledge God's involvement as creator in processes that occasion great suffering. This leads to a requirement for a richer understanding of the mystery of the divine reality than is seen in much Christian theology, which has, as I began by indicating, a tendency to 'cherry-pick' what it shows off from the ways of God with the world.

For the Christian, such a semiotic understanding of divine glory as I am advancing here comes easily, because Christ functions as the quintessential example of such a sign of the divine reality. So in John 1.14 KJV 'we beheld his glory', which is described as being 'as of the only begotten of the Father, full of grace and truth'. In other words, 'we' saw the weightiness, the importance, the 'significance' of Jesus.[38] The author of the Fourth Gospel saw this importance as being that of an utterly reliable sign of the character of God – so that to see the Son is to see the Father (Jn 14.9), to know of God's character that though it is beyond our knowing, it is full of grace and truth.[39]

A related thought is expressed by Paul at 2 Corinthians 4.6, when he writes: 'For it is the God who said, "Let light shine out of darkness",

---

[36] See T. L. Short, *Peirce's Theory of Signs* (Cambridge: Cambridge University Press, 2007).

[37] A. Robinson, *God and the World of Signs: Trinity, Evolution, and the Metaphysical Semiotics of C. S. Peirce* (Leiden: Brill, 2010); A. Robinson, *Traces of the Trinity: Signs, Sacraments and Sharing God's Life* (Cambridge: James Clarke, 2014).

[38] David Jones quotes Maurice de la Taille to the effect that Jesus at the Last Supper 'placed himself in the order of signs' ('Art as Sacrament', 179). But what the Johannine Prologue seems to suggest is that Jesus did this throughout his ministry. For Rowan Williams, Christ reveals 'the divine character, the inner integrity of God', 'Theology in the Face of Christ', unpublished lecture given on 4 October 2004, rowanwilliams.archbishopof canterbury.org.

[39] As Frances Young puts it, writing of the thought of Gregory of Nyssa, 'the hidden Father [is] made luminously manifest in the infinite icon of [Christ's] beauty': *God's Presence: A Contemporary Recapitulation of Early Christianity* (Cambridge: Cambridge University Press, 2013), 173. To say this is not to seek to reduce the complexity of Christ's life, or to oversimplify the character of God. As I note further in Chapter 5, Jesus could be stern, seemingly impossibly demanding, even (at first) excluding of the needy as in the story of the Syrophoenician woman in Mark 7. In speaking of him as a sign of the Father we should not, I believe, flatten out or seek to explain away these difficulties.

who has shone in our hearts to give the light of the knowledge of the glory of God in the face of Jesus Christ.'[40] Christ is the perfect sign of the Godness of God, and to look upon Christ is to see all we can see of that Godness. To return to the Fourth Gospel, the Prologue ends with the resonant claim that 'No one has ever seen God. It is God the only Son, who is close to the Father's heart, who has made him known' (Jn 1.18).[41]

And the coming of this perfect sign asks of us a response, which in the Johannine Prologue is to believe 'in his name' (Jn 1.12). The Incarnation manifests divine glory, the human Jesus as sign of the divine nature, but a sign that both reveals and conceals. As von Balthasar notes: 'The one God, who is invisible by nature, ... appears while not appearing and enters visibility while at the same time remaining a ground that rests in itself.'[42]

Two further observations will help us at this stage. First, Newman's perception that the *kavōd Yahweh*, the particular technical term used in the Hebrew Bible for the glory of the Lord, 'does not denote, at least in the first instance, a character or an attribute of Yahweh'.[43] Neither is the meaning of the *kavōd Yahweh* exhausted by '"fire" or "brightness"'.[44] Glory is not like beauty or majesty or power, though these attributes may be used as images of the character of glory.[45] Rather glory is, I want to

---

[40] I return to 2 Corinthians 3–4 in detail in Chapter 5.

[41] In describing the Incarnate Son as the quintessential sign of the Godness of God, I am not seeking to move away from classical Chalcedonian formulations of Christology, but rather to point up an insight particularly suggested by the Johannine and Pauline texts just cited, and to explore the additional dimensions that semiotic insights might offer. See Chapter 5 for further discussion of the type of sign of God that Jesus may be understood to have been.

[42] von Balthasar, *GL1*, 609.

[43] Newman, *Paul's Glory-Christology*, 24. Fout comes to the same conclusion from exploring the section on glory in K. Barth, *Church Dogmatics*, Vol. 2, Part 1, The Doctrine of God, transl. T. H. L. Parker, W. B. Johnston, H. Knight, J. L. M. Haire, ed. G. W. Bromiley and T. F. Torrance (Edinburgh: T&T Clark, 1957). (Fout, *Fully Alive*, 37; for more on this passage in Barth, see Chapter 1). Von Balthasar: 'This glory (*Herrlichkeit*) of God's is ... precisely what constitutes *the* distinctive property of God, that which from all eternity distinguishes him from all that is not God; this is his wholly other-ness, which he can communicate only in such a way that, even as it is communicated, it remains his and only his': H. U. von Balthasar, *The Glory of the Lord: A Theological Aesthetics*, Vol. 6, Theology: The Old Covenant, transl. B. McNeil C.R.V. and E. Leivà-Merikakis, ed. J. Riches (Edinburgh: T&T Clark, 1991), 10 (emphasis mine).

[44] Newman, *Paul's Glory-Christology*, 24.

[45] In Barth, according to Fout, the principal images are honour, light and beauty (*Fully Alive*, 37).

suggest, *a sign of the Godness of God*. The German theological word for glory, 'Herrlichkeit', helps us here. It could be rendered literally in English as 'lordliness'. The *kavōd Yahweh* connotes a manifestation of the Lord, through movement or presence.[46] What I want to insist throughout this study is that divine glory is not (necessarily) about light or radiance, or yet fame, but about whatever shows us the Godness of God.[47] Both parts of that last clause are important – glory is about 'the Godness of God', but is also about 'what shows us'. Glory is about that Godness communicated to and for the creation.[48]

My second observation at this stage is that the sort of sign that Jesus is of the Godness of God is in many ways a disturbing one.[49] As I noted, the Fourth Gospel makes clear that Jesus' ministry of signs culminates in his making of himself the ultimate sign; at his 'hour' he is 'lifted up' for the healing of the world. In other words, Jesus' signification of God culminates in his Resurrection, yes, but also in his Passion.[50] The Godness of God is – as Jürgen Moltmann and others have stressed – a God enduring the agony of crucifixion for the life of the world.[51] Glory, then, may be associated with all those elements that make the Passion of Christ so profound and disturbing for us – abandonment, pain, silence, innocent suffering stretched to extremes.

This project, then, does not seek to take all the light and beauty out of divine glory, but it does seek to offer a richer and more profound picture than is sometimes given. The language of glory provides a way of talking about the Godness of God, with which the creation is 'charged',[52] without reducing the mysterious divine to one or a small set of God's attributes. It avoids a theology that praises and gives thanks to God for all the good

---

[46] Newman, *Paul's Glory-Christology*, 20–4.   [47] Cf. Fout, *Fully Alive*, 146.

[48] Ibid., 28: 'God's glory is expressed in God's acts in and for the creation, not merely in being for Godself.'

[49] In Rowan Williams' study of C. S. Lewis's Narnia writings, Williams makes the fascinating point that by using the allegorical figure of Aslan, the great lion, Lewis is able to convey something of the 'strangeness and wildness' of the Saviour: *The Lion's World: A Journey into the Heart of Narnia* (London: SPCK, 2012), chapter 3. In reflecting – as Christians very properly must – on the humanness of the Christ, and on his grace and truth, we should not lose sight of the strangeness and, yes, wildness, of the only-begotten of the Father.

[50] For further analysis, see Chapter 2.

[51] J. Moltmann, *The Crucified God: The Cross of Christ as the Foundation and Criticism of Christian Theology*, transl. R. A. Wilson and J. Bowden (London: SCM Press, 1974).

[52] See later in this chapter, and Chapter 3, for further examination of this term, borrowed from Gerard Manley Hopkins' poem 'God's Grandeur' in *Poems and Prose: Selected with an Introduction and Notes by W. H. Gardner* (Harmondsworth: Penguin, 1953), 27.

things that happen, without acknowledging God's involvement in disvalues and suffering. This book explores the limits of discourse on divine
glory, pressing into the most difficult areas, like the Indian Ocean tsunami
(Chapter 3), or the experience of Holocaust victim Etty Hillesum in a
Nazi transit camp (Chapter 4) because the most difficult areas form the
best test of new understandings.

This is not a definitive study of every biblical text on glory.[53] And my
proposal that our starting point for understanding God's glory should be
semiotic has to be nuanced in the light of texts in which 'glory' seems to
speak more directly of the divine essence (Chapter 2). I acknowledge too
that there are exceptions to the reading I propose. There are three texts
in Exodus 14 in which *kavōd* seems to have a more 'secular' sense of
'reputation', when Yahweh 'gains glory' by triumphing over Pharaoh.[54]
There are hints of the same understanding in the 'glorification' language
in the Fourth Gospel. These are the sorts of emphasis that are 'blurred' by
the particular hermeneutical lens being adopted here.

The other most plausible understanding of divine glory is in terms
of honour. In their different ways Newman, Fout and Haley Goranson
Jacob are all attracted to this sense of the word.[55] Where I differ from
their emphasis on honour is principally that I am concerned with how
divine glory *functions*, rather than trying to arrive at too static a sense of
what it might *be*. I take this question up further in Chapters 1 and 2 as
I explore the spectrum of meanings that the concept of divine glory
embraces. There I explore the insight that some texts, especially Exodus
33.18f., seem to suggest a meaning of divine glory close to a restatement
of the identity of God, or the essence of God's nature. So *divine glory
needs to be understood on a spectrum from sign to essence*. It is at the
'essence' end of the spectrum that my interpretation comes closest to the
construing of divine glory as honour.[56]

My understanding of glory also stresses the importance of creaturely
response – a remarkable aspect of divine self-communication as depicted

---

[53] Nor do I go into the very fascinating traditions about glory in the early Church, and in the
evolution of Judaism. So, the remarkable tradition of the 'Shekinah glory' in Rabbinic
and mystical tradition, as a way of speaking indirectly of the indwelling of God, also falls
outside my scope.

[54] Exodus 14.4, 17, 18.

[55] Newman, *Paul's Glory-Christology*, 146–52; Fout, *Fully Alive*, chapter 5; H. Goranson
Jacob and N. T. Wright, *Conformed to the Image of His Son: Rethinking Paul's Theology
of Glory in Romans* (Downers Grove, IL: IVP Academic, 2018).

[56] See Chapter 2 for further discussion.

in the Scriptures is that the creature is not utterly overwhelmed[57] but has a quantum of freedom of response. Even in the utterly awesome vision of Isaiah in the Temple, the prophet, deeply aware of his own sin and profound inadequacy, yet offers himself in freedom (Is 6.8). I take up the question of the Christian's response to glory in Chapter 5.

In this study I explore the outworking of my understanding. In Chapter 1, I clarify the concept of divine glory, and relate it to Peirce's theory of signs. I then compare the concept of divine glory with that of beauty, and go on to relate divine glory to the human experience of wonder. I then test my understanding in relation to texts in the Hebrew Bible and the New Testament, focusing especially on Exodus, Isaiah and Ezekiel, and the Gospel of John (Chapter 2).[58] In Chapter 3 I explore the claim of Isaiah 6.3 that the whole earth is full of the divine glory, pressing that claim in terms of our contemplation of the natural world. As promised, I push the question as to whether divine glory can be discerned in hard and disturbing cases – the 2004 tsunami, the hunting eagle, the malarial mosquito. As this is clearly an exercise in a form of natural theology, I also include an exploration of how this approach relates to recent writing in that field.

THREE-LENSED SEEING

Christians naturally reach for contemplation of the Cross as a way of engaging with the suffering in the world. Such a contemplative lens opens up a view of glory in which what we see of the struggles in the natural world – profoundly rich and important though the picture is – can be seen in relation to the sense of God's depth of engagement with all suffering.[59] *Gloria mundi*, what the not-yet-completely redeemed world discloses of its creator, must be appropriated and understood in the context of *Gloria crucis*, of the gift – made possible by the character of the creation – of the Incarnate Christ and his self-surrender on the Cross. But what I stress here is the importance of what I term 'three-lensed seeing', in which these two views in counterpoint are combined in a triptych with an eschatological perspective, the creation as it will be in its transformed state. *Gloria mundi*, what the not-yet-completely redeemed world discloses of its creator, must be appropriated and understood in the context of *Gloria crucis*,

---

[57] This is a very important emphasis for Fout; see *Fully Alive*, chapter 5.
[58] I reserve treatment of Pauline texts for Chapter 5.
[59] J. McDaniel, *Of God and Pelicans: A Theology of Reverence for Life* (Louisville, KY: Westminster John Knox Press, 1989); Southgate, *Groaning*, chapters 3 and 4.

of all we see of God in the Passion of Christ – and this in turn opens up and is informed by what one might term *Gloria in excelsis*, the eschatological song of the new creation, in which creaturely flourishing will be attained without creaturely struggle.

I proceed in Chapter 4 to stress that true discernment of glory involves facing up, as much as is humanly possible, to the way things really are – bearing reality, to paraphrase T. S. Eliot. I explore how glory may be seen in the 9/11 Memorial in New York, in the face of Christ in Piero della Francesca's haunting painting of the Resurrection, and in the work of the poet R. S. Thomas. I also consider the extraordinary witness of the Dutch Jewish intellectual Etty Hillesum, who could find life glorious even in the camp from which she was transported to Auschwitz.

Finally, returning to the New Testament, I explore in Chapter 5 what it might mean for followers of the crucified, glorified One to be 'transformed from one degree of glory to another' (2 Cor 3.18). My discussion of glory leads finally into reflections on longing – divine and human, and exploration of the thought that coming more truly into the image and likeness of God, being transformed from one degree of glory to another, entails conforming our longings to God's longing, for humans' full participation in the ways of justice, love and peace.

This book does not attempt to be a comprehensive survey of the theme of divine glory. That would be a massive task, beyond both my compass and my intention. Rather I pursue what might be regarded as a research programme in the Christian contemplation of the world, designing a new hermeneutical lens for reading divine glory, and thereby proposing a hypothesis about how divine glory may most helpfully be understood. The effectiveness of the reading of texts and events with this lens forms a test of the hypothesis, and to test it to the full, I choose events that form the most difficult cases for its application. Ultimately, such a research programme will need to be evaluated according to its agreement with data (understood in terms of Scripture, tradition, reason and experience), its coherence, scope and fertility.[60] I attempt a brief evaluation of this kind in the Conclusion.

Two things will, I hope, be clear from this introduction. First, that my exploration of divine glory starts from an attempt to be honest about the complex mixture of value and disvalue that presents itself to a Christian

---

[60] See I. G. Barbour, *Religion and Science: Historical and Contemporary Issues* (London: SCM Press, 1998), 113, for the use of these criteria in evaluating a framework in religious thought.

contemplating the world that God has created and is in the process of redeeming. Second, that in exploring my understanding of glory, I have deliberately chosen the hardest types of cases, not out of perversity, but because severe testing is the most rigorous way to examine the durability of an approach. So the reader should not expect an uplifting journey full of lightness, but a struggle to 'bear reality' in as authentic a way as possible, and discern within it signs of the God who gave that reality its existence.

This book has something in common with the attempt of Richard Harries in his study *The Beauty and the Horror*. Like me, he writes a book 'that tries to avoid cheap polemics and easy answers, taking seriously all the time the very understandable objections that might be made against the perspective from which it is written'.[61] Like Harries, I am on a quest to 'find God in such a contradictory world'.[62] This is both an exploration of the ambiguities of the world God has made and an effort to explore the underexplored subject of divine glory. It differs from a theodicy in that it is not an effort to establish a set of propositions that defend the goodness of God. Rather it is an effort to engage with the reality of God's creation and revelation using the resources of Scripture, tradition, reason and experience, in a way that aims at honest contemplation of how things really are.

I acknowledge that I write out of a particular faith tradition and cultural context. Although my explorations span the natural sciences, poetry and mysticism as well as biblical and systematic theology, all of this is done within the context of the English-speaking academic world and the Christian theology of the early twenty-first century, and that informs my positions and choices in all sorts of ways both consciously and unconsciously. All I can do is acknowledge my own limitations and constraints.

In a relatively short book, I attempt first-order discourse about God in dialogue with not only biblical studies and academic theology, but also with evolutionary biology, art, poetry, and mysticism. I am aware of the huge ambition of such a project, but hope my adventures will be suggestive for readers with a wide range of interests, as well as advancing the specific academic conversations to which this book seeks to contribute.

---

[61] R. Harries, *The Beauty and the Horror: Searching for God in a Suffering World* (London: SPCK, 2016), 9.
[62] Ibid., 7.

Glory as Sign, and The Relation of Glory to Beauty and Wonder

My treatment of divine glory stems from a conviction and a guess. The conviction is that the word 'glory' is used to mean very many different things, and, worse, it is used in Christian liturgy and theological discourse without any clear idea of what is meant. Gordon Fee in his commentary on 1. Corinthians has to abandon precision; he says 'to define this term is like trying to pick up mercury between one's fingers'.[1]

The guess is the one that I began to explore in the Introduction, that discourse on glory may be a helpful way to express our understanding of God's engagement with the ambiguities of the natural world and the complexities of the human spirit.

My task, then, is to offer a lens for interpreting afresh the concept of divine glory. This hermeneutical lens, arising itself from reflection on Scripture as well as our current context, leads, I shall claim, to generative readings of certain key scriptural passages concerned with glory, and also offers a way of speaking with honesty about God's ways with the world. This will include engagement with pain, absence, and silence as well as the more traditional connotations of glory - splendour, radiance, and eschatological triumph.

In this chapter I consider some important sources for a contemporary study of divine glory and the longing to which it leads. I refine the understanding of glory I proposed in the Introduction, and consider what

---

[1] G. Fee, *The First Epistle to the Corinthians* (Grand Rapids, MI: Eerdmans, 1987), 515–16. This is a particularly skilful analogy because mercury is the densest of all liquids. Its liquidness connotes its elusiveness; its density connotes the weightiness with which divine glory is associated.

contribution C. S. Peirce's taxonomy of signs might make to the under-standing divine glory as sign. Lastly, I reflect upon the relation of glory to praise, beauty, and wonder, making it clear why I do not include crea-turely praise within my understanding of God's glory, and why although I see wonder as an essential component of the human response to glory, I find necessary equations of glory with beauty unhelpful.

BALTHASAR, BARTH, AND C. S. LEWIS

The main precedent for contemporary studies of glory must of course be Hans Urs von Balthasar's massive theological aesthetics, *The Glory of the Lord*.[2] It is hard to write about divine glory without merely joining the voluminous secondary literature on von Balthasar.[3] I recognise his huge contribution – especially his insight that much of what has been explored in terms of the hearing and receiving of God's word, and thus growing into Christ, can be re-expressed in terms of the visual imagery of seeing the divine glory.[4] He writes:

at decisive places in Scripture God's 'glory' (*kabod*) manifests itself *before* God's word is heard ... Such glory without words is ... the apparition of him who, in his utter differentness, must be perceived in his reality and truth before his address can be heard.[5]

I also greatly appreciate von Balthasar's perception that kenosis between the Persons of the Trinity is to be regarded as an eternal property of God.

---

[2] See the Bibliography for full details.

[3] One might start on that literature from the commentaries of Aidan Nichols OP: *No Bloodless Myth: A Guide through Balthasar's Dramatics* (Edinburgh: T&T Clark, 2000); *Say It Is Pentecost: A Guide through Balthasar's Logic* (Edinburgh: T&T Clark, 2001); *The Word Has Been Abroad: A Guide through Balthasar's Aesthetics* (Edinburgh: T&T Clark, 1998).

[4] As Stephen Garrett puts it, for von Balthasar, 'God through his glory has revealed something about himself *before* he has said anything, making it clear that God ... must be perceived as he is before his words are heard. Such is the glory of God "without words"': *God's Beauty-in-Act: Participating in God's Suffering Glory* (Eugene, OR: Pickwick Pubs, 2013), 75, citing von Balthasar GL6, 11–12. Emphasis in original.

[5] H. U. von Balthasar, *The Glory of the Lord: A Theological Aesthetics*, Vol. 6, Theology: The Old Covenant, transl. B. McNeil C.R.V. and E. Leiva-Merikakis, ed. J. Riches (Edinburgh: T&T Clark, 1991), 12. Garrett, exegeting this point of von Balthasar's, says that this establishes the point that 'there is a measure of understanding necessary before perceiving subjects can respond to God's self-revelation.' Our response to the signs that are glory depends on our first recognising that 'God is God and we are not, for no-one can perform his or her part in God's theo-drama without knowing this fact first' (*God's Beauty-in-Act*, 75, n. 62).

This is very important in affirming that the mysterious God of creation is also the God of Christ's self-giving. For von Balthasar, the signification of the Godness of God is the revelation of what I have elsewhere called 'deep intratrinitarian kenosis'.[6] As Sarah Coakley explains,

> For von Balthasar ... the idea of kenotic self-surrender is too pervasive and important a characteristic of divine love to circumscribe its significance in christology alone; it is eternally true of the perichoretic and reciprocal interrelations of the persons of the Trinity, not something newly impressed on the divine by the events of the incarnation.[7]

A related emphasis on kenosis as finding its origin in the triune nature of God in Godself is found in Michael Ramsey (deriving in his case from the kenotic theology of Charles Gore). For Ramsey Jesus' self-abandonment 'is the experience in history of the self-giving of the eternal God'.[8] Thus, 'Christmas is as costly in self-giving as Good Friday.'[9]

This Trinitarian 'ur-kenosis' in von Balthasar dissolves the powerful dichotomy posed by Luther in his famous distinction between a *theologia gloriae* and a *theologia crucis*. Luther had asserted that our knowledge of God must centre on the foolishness of the Cross; inferences about God

---

[6] C. Southgate, *The Groaning of Creation: God, Evolution and the Problem of Evil* (Louisville, KY: Westminster John Knox Press, 2008), 158, nn. 22, 25. Garrett calls this 'the divine eternal kenosis of the Godhead', *God's Beauty-in-Act*, 82. This eternal kenosis, a concept deriving from Bulgakov, is called 'Ur-kenosis' by J. N. Martin, *Hans Urs von Balthasar and the Critical Appropriation of Russian Religious Thought* (Notre Dame, IN: University of Notre Dame Press, 2015). On the links between von Balthasar and Bulgakov, see Martin, *Balthasar*, 181–95.

[7] S. Coakley, Kenosis: Theological Meanings and Gender Connotations' in *The Work of Love: Creation as Kenosis,* ed. J. Polkinghorne (London: SPCK, 2001), 192–210, at 199. Cf. H. U. von Balthasar, *Theo-Drama: Theological Dramatic Theory,* Vol. 4: The Action, transl. G. Harrison (San Francisco: Ignatius Press, 1994), 323–4. For a discussion, see Garrett, *God's Beauty-in-Act,* 82–3. This 'deep intratrinitarian kenosis' in von Balthasar seems to some to place him dangerously close to tritheism – see *God's Beauty-in-Act,* 56, and references therein. For further criticism, see *God's Beauty-in-Act,* 154–7, where Garrett finds that von Balthasar's effort to retain divine impassibility in tandem with eternal kenosis lapses into incoherence. This tempts to me to respond that we should bite the bullet and accept, with scholars such as Jürgen Moltmann and Paul Fiddes, the real passibility of God. See, e.g., P. S. Fiddes, *Participating in God: A Pastoral Doctrine of the Trinity* (Louisville, KY: Westminster John Knox Press, 2000) for a telling discussion. Even von Balthasar concedes that 'there is something in God that can develop into suffering', *TD4,* 328.

[8] A. M. Ramsey, *The Gospel and the Catholic Church* (London: Longmans, Green, 1956), 24.

[9] Ibid.

from creation are insecure without the primary data of the *theologia crucis*.[10] The God behind the creation is the *deus absconditus*, the hidden God. As Howsare points out, this risks splitting the God of salvation from God in Godself.[11] But von Balthasar's ur-kenosis allows him to assert that the God of creation is in God's very nature the Triune God of self-giving love.[12] Both creation and Cross are outworkings of this essential nature. I explore the nuances of this further in Chapter 3.

What is attempted here, however, has very different emphases from von Balthasar's project. I am concerned with the semiotic aspects of God's glory. I explore how that shapes the reading of the biblical texts, and our contemplation of the natural world, as understood with the aid of contemporary science. And I draw on twentieth century poetry and mysticism from areas of faith not explored by von Balthasar. Finally, when I explore the implications of glory in the New Testament for the common life of Christian believers, I do so from a very different ecclesial background.

Behind von Balthasar lurks the yet more massive figure of Karl Barth, who ends Vol. 2/1 of *Church Dogmatics* by tackling 'The Eternity and Glory of God', and further explores 'The Glory of the Mediator' in Vol. 4/3, first half.[13] Barth offers fascinating reflections on glory as the self-declaration of God, or as Fout puts it, 'a self-referentially communicative dynamism'.[14] All aspects of this phrase are important. Divine glory is self-referential – it is 'elemental to who God is'. It is communicative, 'revealing and making Godself known to creation'.[15] It is dynamic – it makes an ongoing impact on whatever context it is manifested within; it is not merely a static expression of honour or reputation. I explore Barth's understanding of divine glory further later in the chapter. Barth's treatment is, however, limited by his characteristic insistence that natural

---

[10] So Kristine A. Culp, '[Luther] charged that when theology attends to "glory" – that is, to pretensions of power, not the rightful glory of God – and neglects suffering, it will misconstrue reality': *Vulnerability and Glory: A Theological Account* (Louisville, KY: Westminster John Knox Press, 2010), 117.

[11] R. A. Howsare, *Balthasar: A Guide for the Perplexed* (London: T&T Clark/Continuum, 2009), 89.

[12] Von Balthasar, *TD4*, 326. For a recent exploration in depth of this type of trinitarianism see B. Gallaher, *Freedom and Necessity in Modern Trinitarian Theology* (Oxford: Oxford University Press, 2016).

[13] Full details are in the Bibliography.

[14] J. Fout, *Fully Alive: The Glory of God and the Human Creature in Karl Barth, Hans Urs von Balthasar and the Theological Exegesis of Scripture* (London: Bloomsbury T&T Clark, 2015), 37.

[15] Ibid.

theology is a 'strangely sullen and even barbarous undertaking',[16] a judgment that hugely constrains his ability to see glory in the non-human world.

C. S. Lewis preached a famous sermon in 1941, 'The Weight of Glory'. This is actually an essay on longing – for that ultimate state of glory referred to 2 Cor 4.17. Somewhat off-puttingly, Lewis writes that:

> Glory suggests two ideas to me, of which one seems wicked and the other ridiculous. Either glory means to me fame, or it means luminosity. As for the first, since to be famous means to be better known than other people, the desire for fame appears to me as a competitive passion and therefore of hell rather than heaven. As for the second, who wishes to become a kind of living electric light bulb?[17]

Glory, then, is a very familiar, but somewhat embarrassing word, the meaning of which eludes us like mercury through the fingertips. In secular life it sits somewhat uneasily, imprecisely associated with a religious discourse that lurks only on the edge of most people's lives in the Britain of the second decade of the twenty-first century. And such a contemporary consciousness is profoundly suspicious of any human reputation that might earn, however briefly, the title 'glory'. The term is only advanced with any confidence in respect of achievement in sport – an Olympic title achieved against the odds, or a long-ago triumph wistfully recollected (England's 1966 win in the soccer World Cup sticks in the mind). To speak of any other type of human celebrity in terms of glory is at once to presume that this was or will be followed by a fall from grace. That goes to make the point that God's glory is something utterly different, not a matter of transient fame or fallible reputation, as is all human glory.

DIVINE GLORY AS SIGN FURTHER EXPLORED

Why equate divine glory principally with a sign of the divine reality, rather than with the reality itself? Well, glory is repeatedly associated in Scripture with theophany, with manifestation of the otherwise invisible

---

[16] K. Barth, *Church Dogmatics*, Vol. 2, Part 1, The Doctrine of God, transl. T. H. L. Parker, W. B. Johnston, H. Knight, J. L. M. Haire, ed. G. W. Bromiley and T. F. Torrance (Edinburgh: T&T Clark, 1957), 666.

[17] C. S. Lewis, *The Weight of Glory and Other Addresses* (Grand Rapids, MI: Eerdmans, 1949), 8. Note that even Lewis in this famous sermon, and despite its title, neglects the 'weightiness' connotations of the Hebrew *kavōd* which are such a profound starting point for our understanding of divine glory.

and ultimately unknowable God.[18] The ultimate unknowability of the divine is an important apophatic curb on the reach of our positive vision of God. Moreover, if divine glory could be equated with the reality of God *simpliciter*, then there would be no need for the term. It would be enough to speak of God without reference to glory. Brunner helpfully notes that glory 'designates something in God, and yet again something that does not mean God's being in Himself, but rather God's Being as it becomes visible in His revealed Presence for the eye of faith'.[19] This reminds us of the limitation in our apprehension in the divine reality. Diogenes Allen makes a similar move.[20] He thinks of glory as the presence of God in the world, related to divine immanence, while holiness he associates with divine transcendence. But Allen perhaps underrates the extent to which glory is semiotic – it is not just divine immanence, but rather immanence and transcendence manifest in a sign, discernible by (as Brunner says) the human interpreter, the eye of faith. I return to the complex and sometimes disturbing effort to make this discernment in Chapters 3 and 4.

The study of semiotics from C. S. Peirce onwards[21] shows that signs 'work' because of a relation between the sign and the object – between, for example, a theophany and the reality underlying it. But, crucially, the sign is not reducible to the 'object' it signifies (or vice versa)– theophanies, then, cannot be tidied away into neat propositions.

Theological reasoning, then, urges apophatic caution in not *equating* glory with divine reality. I have wrestled hard with this question of the

---

[18] I note George Savran's point that in no two visual theophanies 'is YHWH presented in the same fashion': *Encountering the Divine: Theophany in Biblical Narrative* (London: T&T Clark/Continuum, 2005), 7. Signs of God's nature are various, and variously interpreted by their chroniclers. See Isaiah 55.8–9 for a restatement of the utter unknowability of God's thoughts and ways.

[19] E. Brunner, *The Christian Doctrine of God. Dogmatics*, Vol. 1, transl. O. Wyon (London: Lutterworth, 1949), 286.

[20] He writes: 'The side [of God] that is present to us is the immanence of God as God manifests Godself to us. But the other side of the coin is always hidden from us, since God's infinite nature is forever beyond our comprehension or grasp': D. Allen, *Theology for a Troubled Believer: An Introduction to the Christian Faith* (Louisville, KY: Westminster John Knox Press, 2010), 12–13.

[21] For helpful modern accounts of Peircean semiotics, see T. L. Short, *Peirce's Theory of Signs* (Cambridge: Cambridge University Press, 2007), and A. Robinson, *God and the World of Signs: Trinity, Evolution, and the Metaphysical Semiotics of C. S. Peirce* (Leiden: Brill, 2010). For a more accessible account, see A. Robinson, *Traces of the Trinity: Signs, Sacraments and Sharing God's Life* (Cambridge: James Clarke, 2014).

ontological status of glory, and am helped by the understandings of Maimonides, who distinguished between cases where:

1. 'the glory of *Y.H.V.H.* is ... intended to signify the created light that God causes to descend in a place in order to confer honor upon it in a miraculous way'.[22] Maimonides here refers to Exodus 24.16 – the *kavōd Yahweh* abiding on Sinai - and Exodus 40.34 where it fills the tabernacle,

2. cases where 'the glory of *Y.H.V.H.* ... "is ... intended to signify [God's] essence and true reality"',[23] citing Moses' appeal and Yahweh's response at Exodus 33.18f.

3. cases where '*Glory* is ... intended to signify the honoring of [God] ... by all men ... For the true way of honoring Him consists in apprehending His greatness.'[24]

Maimonides concludes, 'Understand then the equivocality with reference to *glory* and interpret the latter in every passage in accordance with the context.'[25] Wise advice indeed.

In this account I distinguish sharply between creaturely glorification of God, Maimonides' third category, and divine glory itself. God's greatness *requires* no glorification. Praise is the proper response of the creature to the creator, but creaturely praise adds nothing to the divine glory. This is the vital distinction between human glory, which may be almost entirely manufactured out of the praise of others (as with a supermodel, a rock singer, or a sportsman overhyped on the basis of a single performance), and the divine glory in which there is no shadow of inflation or illusion. It may seem curious to distinguish so strongly between two uses of the same root word, between creaturely glorification and divine glory. But theology must so distinguish because this is a part of the way theologians seek to understand the distinction between creature and creator.

I set aside, then, creaturely praise, and return to Maimonides' first two senses of 'glory' – theophanic sign on the one hand, and direct expression of divine reality on the other. I fully endorse his conclusion that both senses must be considered, according to context. Indeed I suggest that the term 'divine glory', to retain its richness, cannot be equated either with the divine reality, or yet only with theophanies. *It must be allowed to roam*

---

[22] M. Maimonides, *The Guide of the Perplexed*, Vol. 1, transl. S. Pines (Chicago: University of Chicago Press, 1963), 156.
[23] Ibid.   [24] Ibid., 157.   [25] Ibid, emphasis in original.

along a spectrum of meaning between equation with the divine reality,[26] *and disclosure of that reality.*[27] This fluidity of meaning seems to me entirely appropriate to the mystery of the divine self-communication.[28] The term cannot ever collapse altogether into the ontological end of the spectrum (see my comment in the next paragraph on 'weight'). It remains, in C. W. Morgan's terms, 'the extrinsic manifestation of the intrinsic'.[29] But neither can it ever migrate so far in the direction of demonstration as to lose close connection with essential divine reality, because God's self-communication is utterly faithful to God's nature.

It may seem odd, having invoked the root meaning of *kavōd* as weight, to speak of it as sign, which ordinarily has a more indefinite connotation. But (at the risk of pedantry) weight is what is measured in physics, but it is a sign – albeit an extremely dependable one – of a more basic reality, that of mass. In our ordinary measures of mass we measure (in a range of ways) the attraction of a mass to the mass of the Earth. It is actually very difficult – within ordinary experimental physics - to imagine measuring mass directly. In respect of masses beyond the gravitational range of the Earth, we rely on their context to infer mass from indirect measurement. So also with the type of sign that is glory. It is an utterly reliable indicator of the deep reality of God, which we cannot 'measure' in any other way than through an outward manifestation. The difference, of course, is that God's self-manifestation is personal and deliberate, not an automatic outworking of a physical law.

---

[26] Such as Stephen J. Nichols finds in the work of Jonathan Edwards, seeing divine glory as interchangeable with 'God's essence and perfections'. 'The Glory of God Present and Past' in *The Glory of God*, ed. C. W. Morgan and R. A. Paterson (Wheaton, IL: Crossway 2010), 23–46, at 38. So also C. F. Evans, calling glory 'an eschatological term which comes nearest to denoting the divine life itself': *Resurrection and the New Testament* (London: SCM Press, 1970), 160.

[27] For Edwards, 'the glory of God speaks both to his internal glory, signifying what is inherent within God and to the external expression or communication of the internal glory.' Nichols, 'Glory', 40. This is a helpful way of expressing the spectrum of meaning I infer.

[28] Christopher W. Morgan explores seven senses of divine glory, confirming that the term must be allowed to take up a range of meaning. Morgan's first and second senses – God himself or an internal characteristic of God – refer to the ontological end of our spectrum; his third and fourth to God's presence or the display of God's attributes; his fifth and sixth to the eschatological anticipation of God's ultimate goal and the seventh to creaturely praise: 'Towards a Theology of the Glory of God' in *The Glory of God*, ed. C. W. Morgan and R. A. Paterson (Wheaton, IL: Crossway, 2010), 153–87 at 157–9.

[29] Ibid., 163.

PEIRCE'S TAXONOMY OF SIGNS

One test of the effectiveness of thinking of glory primarily in semiotic terms is whether consideration of the different types of sign is generative for the exposition of glory. Here I am much helped by the work of my colleague Andrew Robinson[30] on the classification of signs in the work of Peirce. Robinson shows that Pierce classified signs according to the nature of the sign in itself, the sign's relation to the object it signifies, and the sign's relation to the interpretant.

The nature of signs in themselves Pierce classified according to whether they are qualisigns, representing their objects by virtue of their sheer quality (the classic example being 'a colour-sample of paint or cloth'), sinsigns (singular occurrences, 'such as a leaf blown by the wind') or legisigns ('a sign replicated according to some rule for the purpose of signifying, as when a letter or word is written on a piece of paper').[31] Peirce also categorised signs according to the relation of the sign to the object – which can be that of an icon – a direct likeness – or an index, which 'represents its object by virtue of some direct relationship between the two such that the character that makes the index a sign would be lost if the object were removed'.[32] A simple example would be a pointing finger. The third category of sign-object relations is what Peirce called a symbol. Note that this is a specific and technical use of the term 'symbol', meaning that the sign-object relation was by convention. Scripture functions as a symbolic 'legisign' – Christians read it as sign of the divine reality because of the established convention that it *is* Scripture, 'God-breathed' (2 Tim 3.16).

In Chapter 2 I shall explore what sign-types can be discerned in the biblical passages on which I shall focus, and I shall extend that analysis in Chapter 3 when I consider signs in the natural world. Finally, in Chapter 5 I shall return to the notion of Jesus as qualisign, and what it might mean for the ordinary believer to seek to make her life a qualisign of that great qualisign.

In terms of Peircean semiotics, our spectrum of meanings of glory from theophany to ontology can be understood in terms of God's glory involving different types of signification. Towards the 'ontological end' of the spectrum, where what is perceived as glory connotes something very close to the divine essence, this connotation might be understood in Peirce's terms as a qualisign, functioning as a sign by dint of its sheer quality.

---

[30] Robinson, *God;* also *Traces.*   [31] Robinson, *God,* 39–40.   [32] Ibid., 119.

Taking up the example of a sample of paint, this is a sign of that colour by dint of its quality as perceived by the onlooker (the interpretant of the sign). In a sense, therefore, a qualisign would be as close to the object it signifies as a sign can ever get. One of Robinson's most creative moves is to propose that, while particular incidents in Jesus' life reflect a range of sign-types, the overall quality of his life represented the life of God by virtue of its sheer quality. The 'colour' of that life is what can be most truly known of the 'colour' of God's own life.[33] Whereas the other end of the spectrum – at which we find such signs of God as the heavy cloud in Exodus – will tend to be characterised by what Peirce would have called indexical signs, signs that point to their object. The great theophanies of the Hebrew Bible are typically 'sinsigns'– once-off occurrences. They might be thought of either as pointing to what is signified (indexes), or as icons, signs-by-likeness of the nature of God.[34] See Robinson's work for a much more developed discussion of Peirce's classification of signs and its relation to the acts and life of Jesus.[35]

In Peirce a sign always points to an object (the thing signified) and requires an interpretant in order to function as a sign. An instance of glory might or might not be interpreted (the classic instance of failure of inter-pretation being that poignant clause in the Prologue to the Fourth Gospel, 'his own people did not accept him' (Jn 1.11).

In Peircean semiotics it is also very important that signs may be fallible – they may not point truly or consistently to their object. This is very familiar from human 'glory'. The glory of celebrity, as we know so well in this celebrity-obsessed age, is, in the end, almost always found to be illusory. Political, sporting or artistic triumphs may point for a time to some exceptional powers in the individual(s) concerned, but may be very transient. Reputation is very often based on media manipulation.[36]

---

[33] Ibid., 123–8. This would tie in with such texts as Colossians 1.15 and Hebrews 1.3. See Chapter 5 for further development of this idea.

[34] See Chapter 2 for further discussion.

[35] Robinson, *God and Traces*. Fascinatingly, Gordon Fee, in reflecting on 1 Cor 2.10, the Spirit's searching 'even the deep things of God', says this: 'the Spirit of God becomes the link between God and humanity, the "quality" from God himself which makes the knowing possible': *First Epistle to the Corinthians*, 110. The activities of the Spirit could therefore be seen as manifestations of the deep things of God, manifestations, in the thesis of this book, of glory.

[36] Interestingly, the Greek word most often used for glory in the New Testament, *doxa*, carried with it in ordinary ancient Greek usage these associations of exaggerated or dubious signification. A word meaning 'opinion' came to be used by the biblical writers to connote the opinion that the world rightly and objectively ought to have – the correct interpretation of a sign, and therefore by extension the sign itself (cf. Barth, CD2/1, 641–3). See Chapter 2 for discussion of this semantic transition.

But there is no exaggeration or illusion in the reality of God. Nor does God deceive God's creatures. Therefore, God's self-communication through signs, which manifest the divine reality, needs to be taken as utterly faithful. Open to misinterpretation, yes, but in its signification utterly true of the divine reality to which it points. This is another example of the radical difference between creator and creatures.

FURTHER REFLECTIONS ON GLORY

Paul Ricoeur, drawing on the thought of Levinas, writes that 'Glory is not a phenomenon. It is not a theme. It cannot be called to appear in court. It is the unsaid of the unsaid.'[37] This is a reminder that the very term 'glory', which seems so much about the manifestation of the deity, is ultimately profoundly apophatic. The ultimate inexpressibility of God is 'expressed' even – perhaps particularly – in how theologians articulate the self-communication of the divine. It is often said that the classical attributes of God, such as omnipotence and omniscience, were in their original formulation apophatic theological statements. They were statements that any limit to God, for example to God's power, or knowledge, is a limit beyond our knowing or expression.[38] These statements, then, are not best thought of as positive philosophical propositions, as they are often assumed to be. That is all the more true, it seems to me, of statements about divine glory, which as we have seen are not statements about attributes but about *Herrlichkeit*, the lordliness or Godness of God.

This has an interesting outworking in regard to divine omnibenevolence. Again this may be understood as a term expressing the concept that whatever limit there might be to God's benevolence is beyond the limit of our knowing. But as we shall explore further in Chapters 3 and 4 – as indeed is the common experience of human beings from day to day – divine benevolence seems curiously, mysteriously constrained. In my work on theodicy I explore aspects of the nature of this constraint.[39] But in this work of doxology, glory-study, I seek to face, rather than

---

[37] P. Ricoeur, *Figuring the Sacred: Religion, Narrative and Imagination*, transl. D. Pellaurer, ed. M. Wallace (Minneapolis, MN: Fortress Press, 1995), 123.

[38] For a recent discussion of theologies of the classical divine attributes in relation to alternatives, see Garrett, *God's Beauty-in-Act*, 1–15.

[39] C. Southgate, 'Cosmic Evolution and Evil' in *The Cambridge Companion to the Problem of Evil*, ed. C. Meister and P. K. Moser (Cambridge: Cambridge University Press, 2017), 147–64.

to explain, this apparently constrained benevolence. I acknowledge to the full that creaturely suffering is part of the 'very good' creation, for the existence of which God is solely responsible. I acknowledge too that the God whom Christians meet in the Scriptures is not a neat set of philosophical attributes. This God meets creatures in a cosmic narrative of creation and redemption, not simply in propositions. The glory of this God cannot be called to appear in court. And part of the inexpressibility of this glory is that it involves not only the whole story of the creation as it has been up to now, but also the dynamic of incarnation and atonement by which God has entered irrevocably into that creation, and the ultimate consummation in which creaturely life will be drawn up into the life of God. Hence the need for the 'three-lensed seeing' I described in the Introduction.

I return to this theme of a threefold perspective on glory below. But for now I merely restate that when we encounter the term 'glory of God' we must expect that, according to context, its meaning may be found anywhere on a spectrum from pure sign to ultimate reality.[40]

The lay enquirer's journey in exploring this spectrum is typically from theophany to ontology. She begins by thinking about glory in terms of brilliant radiance, the 'devouring fire on the top of the mountain in the sight of the people of Israel' (cf. Ex 24.17), or the face of Jesus at the Transfiguration. Then she begins to understand about 'weight', that *kavōd* connotes 'that which constitutes the importance or value of a being, giving it privilege and honour because it belongs to it'.[41] She comes to interpret spectacular theophanic manifestations in terms of God's surpassing reality and importance. Thus, starting from glory as theophany, she begins to approach a more ontological understanding of glory, one that equates it more closely with divine being in itself.

In the discussion of glory in *Church Dogmatics 2/1*, we see Barth traverse the reverse path. First he talks of the ineffable excellence of all God's qualities, of glory as 'the self-revealing sum of all divine perfections'. Consider, however, the following sequence of quotations:

---

[40] God's self-communication can be *about* Godself – this is the semiotic end of the spectrum – or *of* Godself, which is the ontological end. (I thank Dr Fout for this insight.) To express this spectrum in relation to Jesus is to understand the ontological end of the spectrum as Jesus's glory *with* the Father and the semiotic as Jesus' glory *from* the Father, his functioning as a manifestation or sign of the Father.

[41] Barth, *CD2/1*, 642.

'It [glory] is God's being in so far as this is in itself a being which declares itself'.[42]

God 'not merely is all this [His attributes] and maintains Himself as all this, but ... demonstrates Himself as all this'.[43]

'It is obvious that in biblical usage this [God's self-declaration] is what is specifically meant when we speak of His glory, and not simply of His being.'[44]

'it is necessary and rewarding to ask specifically to what extent His glory is this outshining, this self-declaration'.[45]

'God's glory is the glory of His face ... God in person ... God who bears a name and calls us by name. God is glorious in the fact that He does this.'[46]

The great Swiss theologian starts with glory as ontology, and then in order to do full justice to the term, he finds himself talking more and more about God's self-declaration, of God showing God's face and calling us by name, hence more and more of glory as sign that invites response. Barth moreover makes clear how this self-communication must be distinguished from some generalised emanation of light by a surpassing light – God's self-declaration does not go out into empty space; rather God calls creatures by name.

Barth also says that 'God's glory is the answer evoked by Him of the worship offered Him by his creatures.'[47] This is the third sense proposed by Maimonides. However, that creaturely answering, that response of praise and worship, seems to me to come under the category of creaturely glorification, not of the divine glory itself. I prefer to separate the sign that is God's self-communication from the creaturely response, which adds nothing to God's all-sufficient Godness, though (through the power of the Spirit) it augments fellowship between God and creature.

One last observation about this spectrum of meanings of glory. Christians express God's ways with the world in terms of a narrative that has

---

[42] Ibid., 643.

[43] Ibid., 644. Note also K. Barth, *Church Dogmatics*, Vol. 4, Part 3, First Half: The Doctrine of Reconciliation, transl. G. W. Bromiley, ed. G. W. Bromiley and T. F. Torrance (Edinburgh: T&T Clark, 1961): 'The glory of God ... however, is the power of God Himself, grounded in His being as free love, to characterize, proclaim, and demonstrate himself as the One He is in all his competence and might' (47–8). In other words, an aspect of the Godness of God is God's power to communicate Godself in signs utterly faithful to that Godness.

[44] Barth, CD2/1, 646.   [45] Ibid.   [46] Ibid.   [47] Ibid., 647.

trajectory towards the eschaton. In that final state God will be all in all
(1 Cor 15.28); the earth shall be filled with the knowledge of the Lord
(Is 11.9; cf. also Hb 2.14). The whole of creation will be perfused with
the reality of God, and every creature's whole being will be response. The
believer's *doxa* will be perfectly attuned to that of God.[48]

So in establishing a spectrum of meanings from the semiotic to the
ontological, we should note that an important element in the Bible's use of
the term glory is anticipation of the eschaton, in which there will be no
more need for sign or theophany, for God will be with God's creatures in
a new and perfected way. That sense of anticipation is of course also
semiotic: it is a sign not so much of the fathomless reality of God in the
present moment, but of the promise of God that the creator-creature relation will ultimately be transformed, a sign of the new 'withness' in which
the Godness of God will be with the creature when 'he will wipe every tear
from their eyes. Death will be no more; mourning and crying and pain
will be no more, for the first things have passed away' (Rev 21.4).

THE IMPORTANCE OF HUMAN RESPONSE TO GLORY

My account of divine glory speaks of it as *sign that always invites response,*
indeed openness to transformation, on the part of the interpreter. Why
invitation to transformation, rather than transforming power in itself?
It is not my intention here to plumb the great theological conundrum
of predestination and human free will. I content myself with stating my
conviction that God works with real human choices to bring about God's
intentions. Richard Harries, writing of the biblical image of God the
potter and humans the clay, asserts the importance of the fact that we
are 'thinking, talking, feeling clay, able to suffer and argue back'.[49] Even
Jesus, in the temptations and again in Gethsemane, is shown as having the
choice not to follow his destiny, and in numerous other contexts in which
a great vocation is asked of someone, there is a real choice to be made.[50]

---

[48] This is the sense in which we should take 1 Corinthians 2.7 – 'God's wisdom, secret and
hidden, which God decreed before the ages for our glory'. See Fee, *First Epistle to the
Corinthians,* 106, who notes parallel texts in 1 Thessalonians 2.12; 2 Thessalonians 1.10;
Romans 8.17, 8.29–30.

[49] R. Harries, *The Beauty and the Horror: Searching for God in a Suffering World* (London:
SPCK, 2016), 111.

[50] Fout is likewise concerned that accounts of divine glory not overwhelm human agency
(*Fully Alive,* 25, n. 39). Indeed, his concern goes further, into the human component
in the reception of revelation. This takes us into the intricate question of how this

In this account I shall be exploring both theophany, in its usual sense of a divinely imparted sense-impression evoking awe and wonder, and the sort of sustained contemplation that requires the trained eye of faith to discover anew from the details of the natural world that 'the whole earth is full of [God's] glory' (Is 6.3).

In theophanies God very evidently takes the initiative; in the second case the contemplative 'does most of the work', though he/she is utterly dependent on the work of the Holy Spirit to make authentic seeing possible. But in all cases the divine sign *invites* response. It contains within it the possibility that the witnesses to the theophany will not respond, or (as so often in the Exodus story) that the response of faithful obedience will not last. Equally, a sign of God always invites *response*. Barth describes God's self-declaration as 'a sovereign, irresistible event',[51] and so it must be, for no being could constrain the sovereign Lord's self-communication. But the reception of the self-declaration, the interpretation of the sign, always, I want to hold, involves an element of human agency, however much God might long for a particular response, however supremely attractive God's self-communication might be.

Von Balthasar notes that 'God only shows himself to someone, only enraptures him, in order to commission him'.[52] Glory is therefore always associated with the other theme I develop towards the end of this book, that of longing. God longs for the acceptance of whatever is God's offer, for response from those experiencing the glory, response that welcomes the transforming work of the Spirit, and hence makes possible a new degree of cooperation between God and human being in the realisation of that consummated state for which both God and believers long. I take up that theme of divine longing, and the human longing that can respond to the divine, in Chapter 5.

THE RELATION OF DIVINE GLORY TO BEAUTY AND WONDER

I end this chapter by considering why the focus of the book should be divine glory, not divine beauty as is often explored in this type of

---

divine-human semiosis works, when the divine sign needs human interpretation to operate, but the human interpretation is in turn a divinely given property. I take up this question in discussing 'instress' in Chapter 3.

[51] Barth, *CD2/1*, 644.

[52] H. U von Balthasar, *The Glory of the Lord: A Theological Aesthetics*, Vol. 2, Studies in Theological Style: Clerical Styles, transl. A. Louth, F. McDonagh and B. McNeil C. R. V., ed. J. Riches (Edinburgh: T&T Clark, 1984), 31.

theology. This section therefore explores how my understanding of glory relates to theologies that emphasise beauty rather than glory, and goes on to consider the place of wonder in the contemplation of creation, and behind that the contemplation of God.

Von Balthasar identifies glory with 'transcendental beauty'.[53] But glory as properly understood cannot be simply equated with beauty as the latter is commonly understood. For Tim Gorringe:

> Christ was from the beginning understood through Isaiah 53, the figure who 'had no beauty, that we should desire him', and the crucifixion was a standing reproach to a primarily aesthetic approach to life, any divinisation of beauty in itself.[54]

There is much celebration, in certain parts of the Christian tradition, of the beauty of creation, and the beauty of Christ the redeemer. (Sometimes the latter is conceived in physical terms – more often in moral terms.[55]) By these two – the beauty of God's creation and of the Incarnate Son, so the argument runs, can be glimpsed the beauty of God in Godself. But at once appeal to the beauty of creation runs into problems. In Chapter 3 we shall draw on the exclamation of the seraphim in Is 6.3: 'The whole earth is full of God's glory'. And insofar as the glory of God is to be found in the *whole* way the natural world is, that glory must in some measure be reflected even in what we do not tend to find beautiful, even in apparent ugliness, cruelty and waste, qualities in creation that – for some – lead to doubt of God. We must therefore, as Garrett says, 'avoid an aestheticism that conceives of God's beauty as ornamental, nostalgic and innocuous, signifying the beautiful as an escape from the pain and bane of our existence'.[56]

Richard Harries, considering the particularity of sheer existence, writes:

---

[53] H. U von Balthasar, *The Glory of the Lord: A Theological Aesthetics,* Vol. 1, Seeing the Form, transl. E. Leiva-Merikakis, ed. J. Fessio, S.J. and J. Riches (Edinburgh: T&T Clark, 1982). However, he also remarks that: 'Almost the only occasion on which scripture uses esthetic terms is when speaking of the mystery of the suffering servant, and then to deny their application'; also see von Balthasar, 'Revelation and the Beautiful' in *Explorations in Theology, Vol. 1: The Word Made Flesh,* transl. A. V. Littledale with A. Dru (San Francisco: Ignatius, 1989), 113.

[54] T. Gorringe, *Earthly Visions: Theology and the Challenges of Art* (New Haven, CT: Yale University Press, 2011), 42.

[55] P. Sherry, *Spirit and Beauty: An Introduction to Theological Aesthetics* (London: SCM Press, 2002), 73–5.

[56] Garrett, *God's Beauty-in-Act,* 120.

It is the beauty of existence as such, the fact that something might have existed, or might have existed differently, but there it is, as uniquely itself. The experience is also one of wonder and awe, but I use the word 'beauty' because this implies an evaluative element.[57]

But this is to conflate beauty with the goodness of existence. Many aspects of God's creation are deeply troubling. They are signs of God by virtue of being creatures, but it is hard to accord their existence a straightforwardly positive evaluation. We shall cite an example in Chapter 3 when we consider the malarial mosquito. Its intricacy of lifestyle should evoke wonder, but hardly a sense of beauty. We shall also see in Chapter 4 that glory can be found in silence, in absence, and under conditions of oppression, not traditional loci of the beautiful. So we must either accept that glory is not to be equated with beauty, or we must modify our idea of what, in its transcendent dimension, beauty is.

Garrett has a useful taxonomy of approaches to theological beauty. He begins with what he terms the 'transcendental/iconic'.[58] Beauty is perfect in God and God works it in the world through the Spirit, so that (quoting here John Milbank) 'to see . . . the beautiful is to see the invisible in the visible'.[59] My particular concern about this move, in the context of this study, is that as I go on to develop in Chapter 3, such a contemplation of the natural world, looking for beauty as sign-by-likeness of the creator God, risks an over-selective and partial apprehension of the creation.[60] Much of the natural world contains what we are inclined to regard as ugly and disturbing, yet that too is God's creation, and is a necessary counterpart of what we find beautiful,[61] and manifests something of the Godness of God.[62]

---

[57] R. Harries, *Beauty and the Horror*, 3–4.   [58] Garrett, *God's Beauty-in-Act*, 51–7.

[59] J. Milbank, G. Ward and E. Wyschgorod, *Theological Perspectives on God and Beauty* (Harrisburg, PA: Trinity Press International, 2003), 3.

[60] As David Bentley Hart says: 'beauty – conceived as a gracious stillness artificially imposed upon the surface of the primordial ontological tumult – mocks the desire for justice.' *The Beauty of the Infinite: The Aesthetics of Christian Truth* (Grand Rapids, MI: Eerdmans, 2003), 16. Yet he then seems to fall into his own trap when he goes on 'worldly beauty shows creation to be the real theatre of divine glory – good, gracious, lovely, and desirable, participating in God's splendor'. Ibid., 21.

[61] Southgate, *Groaning*, chapter 3. The appeal to beauty in creation carries with it a trap, which is to be led to ascribe to forces other than God those natural events that we find profoundly disturbing. Such dualism erodes the Christian doctrine of God as sovereign and creator *ex nihilo*, and divides up our experience in a way that is both theological and scientifically incoherent. A tougher brand of seeing is necessary to rightly contemplate glory in the natural world.

[62] See Chapter 4 for defence of a distinction between the disvalues in the non-human creation on the one hand, and freely chosen human harms on the other.

In respect of the arts I would be the first to admit the power of the subjective response to beauty, and its capacity to move the spirit towards an apprehension of God. At very important moments in my life, Mozart's *Requiem* and Eliot's *Four Quartets* have both functioned in that way. But those moments are not only in danger of over-subjectivism, but in respect of the natural world can reflect partial and deficient contemplation. Rowan Williams shows that the classic definition of beauty as *id quod visum placet*[63] (Aquinas) must involve a recognition that what pleases the vision varies according to circumstance.[64] Williams goes on to note that in the thought of Jacques Maritain, on which he is drawing, beauty is 'a kind of good, but not a kind of truth'.[65] Beauty, then, pleases; glory may not please, because it is tied inexorably to what is most deeply, and very often uncomfortably, true. Williams again:

> what Maritain is, I think, cautioning against is any suggestion that the sensation of being in the presence of the desirable gives you any information about how the world actually is or about what is humanly to be done about it. Given that the human will is spectacularly fallible and self-deceiving, a judgement of beauty cannot as such be morally or metaphysically illuminating.[66]

Garrett's second category is the 'anthropocentric', based on the experience of the redeemed community of God, an approach he finds in Edward Farley, but clearly regards as unsatisfactory.[67] My own experience also makes me dubious. Years of membership of a small Anglican parish church have taught me much about courage and unspoken devotion, but little about beauty, as ordinarily understood. And insofar as there is beauty in the redeemed life broken and poured out for others, that surely draws us into Garrett's third category, the 'Christological'.

In this category Garrett puts von Balthasar.[68] A Christological grounding enables von Balthasar to escape from the problem of subjectivism. What is beautiful is the Christ-form, whether or not we might happen to find it so. In *The Glory of the Lord,* von Balthasar meditates on this very enigmatic category of *form*. Brendán Leahy explains that:

---

[63] 'That which pleases the vision'.

[64] R. Williams, *Grace and Necessity: Reflections on Art and Love* (London: Continuum, 2005), 11.

[65] Ibid., 12.   [66] Ibid., 12–13.   [67] Garrett, *God's Beauty-in-Act,* 53–4.

[68] Also Bentley Hart, although Garrett remarks that Hart 'ironically has little to say about what beauty actually is, ascribing beauty to God often because God's self-revelation is intrinsically pleasing'. Ibid., 54, n. 130.

Form means a totality of parts and elements, grasped as such, existing as defined as such, which for its existence requires not only a surrounding world but ultimately being as a whole. More than the parts we see and make out, it is the outer manifestation or expression of an inner-depth. It *is* this mysterious inner-depth in manifestation and expression.[69]

For von Balthasar, 'Admittedly, form would not be beautiful unless it were fundamentally a sign and appearing of a depth and fullness that, in themselves and in an abstract sense, remain both beyond our reach and our vision.'[70] As Garrett notes, 'form' both points to invisible mystery and is the mystery's apparition; it therefore both reveals and veils[71] – very much what attracted me to the discourse of glory.[72]

The crucial form for von Balthasar is the Christ-form. Here von Balthasar draws on Barth's sense that 'The beauty of God' in 'the beauty of Jesus Christ' appears therefore precisely in the crucified, but the crucified, precisely as such, is the one risen. Von Balthasar's justification for calling the paschal mystery beauty is that 'its effect on human souls is analogous to the effect worldly forms of beauty have on souls'.[73] The supreme example of form, then, is God's appearing in Christ – whatever is Christic, then, including the horror of the Passion, is beautiful because it is an aspect of this overarching form, in which 'all have meaning and are held together in him'.[74]

But this leaves von Balthasar, it seems to me, with the converse problem. At the centre of the Christian Gospel is the Passion of Christ, a story of sustained human cruelty, emptying Jesus of any physical beauty and pushing him even to the cry of dereliction (Mk 15.34), with its sense of the terrible absence of the Father. Even if the Passion is taken to be exemplary of the beauty of moral strength and sinlessness, of 'ecstatic outgoing love for the other',[75] it is full of pain, and is followed by a time of mysterious silence. This time of Good Friday and Holy Saturday, so important to

---

[69] B. Leahy, 'Theological Aesthetics' in *The Beauty of Christ: An Introduction to the Theology of Hans Urs von Balthasar*, ed. B. McGregor, OP, and T. Norris (Edinburgh: T&T Clark, 1994), 23–55, at 31, emphasis in original.

[70] Von Balthasar, *GL1*, 118.

[71] Garrett, *God's Beauty-in-Act*, 66, quoting von Balthasar, *GL1*, 151.

[72] See Chapter 3 for further discussion of 'form' in von Balthasar.

[73] K. Mongrain, *The Systematic Thought of Hans Urs von Balthasar: An Irenaean Retrieval* (New York: Crossroad, 2002), 67.

[74] Garrett, *God's Beauty-in-Act*, 54.

[75] J. S. Begbie, 'Beauty, Sentimentality and the Arts' in *The Beauty of God: Theology and the Arts,* ed. D. J. Treier, M. Husbands and R. Lundin (Downers Grove, IL: IVP Academic, 2007), 45–69, at 63.

von Balthasar and his 'theo-drama', is so far from anything that would be subjectively adjudged beautiful in any ordinary sense that the term comes to seem very awkward, so theologically particular as to part company with all its ordinary force. In a sense Christ suffered 'beautifully', as R. S. Thomas seeks to maintain in his Calvary poem 'The Musician', drawing on a concert by Kreisler.[76] But the (relative) failure of that poem is the failure of that terminology.[77] There was no pleasingness to the eye, no *id quod visum placet*, on Calvary. To say that the Passion of Christ evokes in us the same feelings that beautiful objects do would be to risk sanitising that Passion, tidying it into an acceptable human category (as too many atonement theories have done). But if Christians stay with Christ's actual experience, if they contemplate it honestly and seek to bear its reality[78] as fully as they can, then they recognise in it the associations that Gorringe notes with the last of the Songs of the Suffering Servant, Is. 52–3, which as we shall see in our treatment of the Fourth Gospel are so important for John's identification of the Cross with glory (Chapter 2). The Servant, 'lifted up', 'glorified',[79] is 'so marred … in appearance, beyond human semblance' (Is 52.14). In looking on Christ, we see that ugliness, distortion, pain, and apparent abandonment seem intrinsic to the Christian story, and that engagement with that story cannot be only on the basis of those feelings that beautiful objects evoke.

Theologians of beauty acknowledge these things, and offer phrases like 'terrible beauty',[80] or 'broken beauty',[81] or advocate a shift from a worldly to a divine aesthetic. Von Balthasar writes: 'If the Cross radically puts an end to all worldly aesthetics, then precisely this end marks the decisive emergence of the divine aesthetic'.[82] And Barth can write: 'in this self-revelation [beauty in the crucified], God's beauty embraces death as well as life, fear as well as joy, what we might call the ugly, as well as what we might call the beautiful'.[83]

---

[76] R. S. Thomas, *Collected Poems 1945–1990* (London: J. M. Dent, 1993), 104.

[77] Interestingly D. Z. Phillips, in his theological study of R. S. Thomas, also sees that poem as a failure: *Poet of the Invisible God: Meaning and Mediation in the Poetry of R. S. Thomas* (London: Macmillan, 1986), 45–6.

[78] I take up the theme of the bearing of reality more fully in Chapter 4.

[79] See the analysis of John 12 in the light of Isaiah 52.13 LXX given in Chapter 2.

[80] Sherry, *Spirit*, 30–1. The phrase is found in the poetry of both Yeats and Rilke.

[81] E. J. Walford, 'The Case for a Broken Beauty: An Art Historical Viewpoint' in *The Beauty of God: Theology and the Arts,* ed. D. J. Treier, M. Husbands and R. Lundin (Downers Grove, IL: IVP Academic, 2007), 87–109.

[82] Von Balthasar, *GL1*, 460.   [83] Barth, *CD2/1*, 665.

This expanded understanding of beauty still makes me uneasy. It moves a long way from common-sense understandings of beauty (and indeed from Aquinas' classic definition).[84] Moreover, there seems to me to be at least an element of circularity in saying:

- to understand the nature of the divine, one must look to the beautiful.
- but we must define the beautiful in terms of the Passion of the divine Son.[85]

Garrett himself calls God's beauty *'the fittingness of the incarnate Son's actions in the Spirit to the Father's will'*. He continues, *'This fittingness radiates God's glory'*.[86] While I find this helpful, it serves for me to reinforce glory as prior to beauty. Garrett's formulation could be reframed to point out that there is an exquisite fittingness in the way the Son, in the power of the Spirit, expresses himself in life and death as the perfect sign of the loving will of the Father. The beauty of this is the perfection of this signification, of glory as I understand it in this book.

At the same time 'fittingness', though it has merit in parsing out the economy of salvation, seems a very limited way of speaking about God. It almost smacks of the aesthetician measuring God. The Godness of God seems rather to transcend any notions humans can construct of fittingness. Beyond fittingness there is an extravagance to the character of God's ingenuity in creation, God's passionate love in redemption, and God's extraordinary generosity and forbearance in awaiting humans' growth into freedom. Beyond the limits of our perception of beauty we receive signs of the divine – not reducible to or digestible within a human aesthetic – which I have been calling glory.

As I noted, the principal word for glory in the Hebrew Scriptures is *kavōd*, a word deriving from a root meaning weight, substance. What is

---

[84] I recognise that I am in this a child of modernity, in Milbank's terms. He writes: 'Before modernity, the sublime was an aspect of beauty itself – the terrible aspect that is the wounding excess of the visible that pierces our everyday defences.' Milbank et al., *Theological Perspectives*, 3. But I do not think it is necessarily helpful to wrench the meanings of words back into past eras, and I am also struck by Aquinas's willingness to detach beauty from goodness and by the absence of any hint of the terrible sublime from *id quod visum placet*. See later in this chapter for discussion of wonder, which is another way of speaking of what pierces our everyday defences.

[85] Cf. N. O'Donoghue: 'how do I judge the beauty of the form of Christ unless by way of my inner idea or sense of the beautiful? Either Christ shatters my conception of the beautiful or he fulfils it.' 'Theology of Beauty' in *The Analogy of Beauty: The Theology of Hans Urs von Balthasar,* ed. J. Riches (Edinburgh: T&T Clark, 1986), 1–10, at 7.

[86] Garrett, *God's Beauty-in-Act,* 16, emphasis in original.

genuinely glorious (in human terms) is what is most substantial, most real and lasting. What is glorious in divine terms is whatever is a sign of the depths of the divine reality, the uttermost of the real. This uttermost must always be mystery to us, and as Allen reminds us, 'we do not solve mysteries; we enter into them. The deeper we enter into them, the more illumination we get'.[87] And this illumination by divine glory always invites a response.

As subtle a thinker as von Balthasar is very well aware of this, and therefore entitles his theological aesthetics *The Glory of the Lord*, and explicitly distinguishes it from an aesthetic theology. As Noel O'Donoghue notes in a penetrating critique of von Balthasar, the concept of 'glory' comes to predominate over that of beauty as *The Glory of the Lord* unfolds.[88] Indeed von Balthasar himself confirms this in a short essay looking back at his work – he writes that:

What is involved is primarily not 'beauty' in the modern or even in the philosophical (transcendental) sense, but the surpassing of beauty in 'glory' in the sense of the splendour of the divinity of God himself as manifested in the life, death, and resurrection of Jesus and reflected, according to Paul, in Christians who look upon their Lord.[89]

Barth writes:

God is not beautiful in the sense that he shares an idea of beauty superior to Him, so that to know it is to know Him as God. On the contrary, it is as He is God that He is also beautiful, so that He is the basis and standard of everything that is beautiful and of all ideas of the beautiful.[90]

Thus, Barth returns us to the sheer Godness of God, and what can be known of it. This Godness is so often disturbing rather than delighting – either in its appalling power as in the Exodus or its apparent weakness at Calvary – that I continue to hold that glory, as sign of the Godness

---

[87] D. Allen, *Temptation* (Princeton: Caroline Press, 1986), 18. Note that the metaphor of light steals back in, but not necessarily brilliant, radiant, showy light, but the light gained by exploration into mystery.

[88] N. O'Donoghue, 'Appendix: Do We Get beyond Plato? A Critical Appreciation of the Theological Aesthetics' in *The Beauty of Christ: An Introduction to the Theology of Hans Urs von Balthasar*, ed. B. McGregor OP and T. Norris (Edinburgh: T&T Clark, 1994), 253–66, at 257 n. 1.

[89] Hans Urs von Balthasar, 'Another Ten Years – 1975', transl. J. Saward, in *The Analogy of Beauty: The Theology of Hans Urs von Balthasar*, ed. J. Riches (Edinburgh: T&T Clark, 1986), 222–33, at 224.

[90] Barth, CD2/1, 656.

of God, is a much more helpful theological category than beauty with which to engage.

A further sense in which glory is to be preferred to beauty in examining God's ways with the world concerns what I have called three-lensed seeing – the need to consider every event in relation to *Gloria mundi*, signs of the creative activity of God, *Gloria crucis*, signs associated with God's self-giving in the Passion and death of Christ, and *Gloria in excelsis*, God's bringing of all of creation to consummation. The patterns of predation in the world may show both beauty in the skills of the predator but ugliness in the distress, trappedness, and suffering of the prey animal.[91] Could such an event be described as beautiful? Overall, I suggest not, despite its 'fittingness', its part in the ingenuity and intricacy of God's creation – *Gloria mundi*, and God's co-suffering with the suffering creature,[92] which might speak to 'the eye that sees' of *Gloria crucis*.[93]

A further fundamental problem with a theology of beauty per se is that it only takes the thinker to the vast divide between God and creature. Garcia-Rivera writes that:

The category of Glory, however, reveals a theological aesthetics. Beauty's Glory crosses the divine chasm between Creator and creature and shines forth in the creature's sign of the abyss.[94]

I take this to mean that creaturely beauty can, if associated with glory, be a real sign of the Creator. But as Garcia-Rivera goes on, 'Conceiving this crossing [of the Creator-creature abyss] is both at the heart of theological aesthetics and its greatest problematic'.[95]

The abyss is only crossed by divine self-communication, by the Godhead giving a sign of the divine life that invites the believer into communion. This is central to my thesis. Glory, insofar as it is apprehensible by the creature, should not be equated simply with the divine reality. It is always divine self-communication, which yet does not exhaust the depths

---

[91] I give in Chapter 3 the example of a golden eagle tracking down a mountain hare.

[92] Southgate, *Groaning*, chapters 3 and 4.

[93] There are hints of this multilensed seeing in Begbie, 'Created Beauty', but because of his strong Fall-based sense of the disorderedness of the world, his view is perhaps overskewed towards the eschatological lens.

[94] A. Garcia-Rivera, *The Community of the Beautiful: A Theological Aesthetics* (Collegeville, MN: The Liturgical Press, 1999), 14.

[95] Ibid., 14–15.

of the divine being.[96] That is why I tend to construe glory in this study as a sign of what lies beyond it, albeit – given the graciousness and faithfulness of God – an utterly trustworthy sign.

The category of glory, broadly understood and taking in account its Hebrew roots, allows us to talk both of that richness of revelation and of the depths of reality of which it speaks, without having to default either into depicting God as a list of philosophical propositions, or yet into a theology based on a too-easy synthesis of the biblical witness. So I invite the reader to accept that glory is not to be equated with beauty, and is a richer and more realistic category by which to name (as inadequately as we necessarily do) the signs God gives us of God's nature

Having established that glory is to be preferred to beauty in efforts to characterise God's ways with the world, I now turn to consider *the relation of glory to wonder*. Clearly in the classic Hebrew Bible theophanies wonder is expressed at its most extreme, in terms of amazement. Awe, and its companion emotion fear, is a strong element of the human response. I would extend this to say that the response to any sign of the divine reality, any manifestation of glory, will necessarily contain an element of wonder. This must be so because these signs necessarily extend the human imagination beyond the human understanding. I claim therefore that across all the manifestations of glory to which we shall attend, wonder is the primary, pre-reflective response. This may be accompanied by awe as described previously. That sense would be particularly marked when the sign experienced is eloquent – as theophanies are – of the littleness and fragility of human life, so limited in its security, its grasp of space, its span of time. But wonder can be evoked also by the microscopic and cosmic workings of the natural world, which do not necessarily threaten human life.[97] Indeed what is being observed may be the very processes that make human life possible. I discuss further in Chapter 3 those signs of the divine reality that are found in the intricacy of the Creator's ingenuity and power.

---

[96] Cf. von Balthasar: 'The finite intellect has no means, either inside or outside itself, to get an immediate glimpse of God; it remains dependent upon the sign language of the things through which God speaks it': *Theo-Logic: Theological Logical Theory*, Vol. 1: Truth of the World, transl. A. J. Walker (San Francisco: Ignatius Press, 2000), 234.

[97] Cf. M. Midgley: 'It is an essential element in wonder that we recognize what we see as something we did not make, cannot fully understand, and acknowledge as containing something greater than ourselves. This is not only true if our subject matter is the stars; it is notoriously just as true if it is rocks or nematode worms.' *Wisdom, Information and Wonder: What Is Knowledge For?* (London: Routledge, 1991), 41.

Kelly Bulkeley defines wonder as 'the feeling excited by an encounter with something novel and unexpected, something that strikes a person as intensely real, true, and/or beautiful'.[98] The response of wonder at elements of the created world, or the manifestation of the divine reality attested in Scripture, *may* be followed by evaluation of the event as beautiful, as pleasing to the vision. Interestingly, mountain landscapes have shifted markedly in aesthetic evaluation, from being thought ugly and savage in the pre-modern period to being revered by the English Romantics as indexes of the sublime. Those landscapes evoked wonder, and awe, before they were thought beautiful. That is an indication of why I consider that wonder should be seen as a primary, pre-reflective response, whereas the assignment of beauty is something more culturally determined.

There is a link here with the earlier discussion of the Cross, which I asserted could not easily be included in the category of the beautiful. It was, nevertheless, so the New Testament suggests by its strong associations with the last of the Servant Songs in Deutero-Isaiah,[99] an event by which all were 'astonished' (Is 52.14). The centurion's response as recorded in Mk 15.39, however understood, confirms that the Crucified Jesus was an object of wonder. Jesus was wondered *at*, in the manner of his dying.

But there is a second phase to wonder, which may be thought of as wondering 'that', after wondering 'at'. The centurion's response perhaps inches towards this. He wonders at the manner of Christ's giving up his spirit; he begins to wonder that such a man has been handed over to the powers to which he himself is in service. Wondering *that*, the reflective phase of wonder, is very important in the scientific and poetic contemplation of the natural world that we consider in Chapter 3.[100] It also has a key place in the types of contemplation we consider in Chapter 4.

---

[98] K. Bulkeley, *The Wondering Brain: Thinking about Religion with and beyond Cognitive Neuroscience* (London: Routledge, 2005), 3.

[99] Especially in John 12, as I discuss in Chapter 2.

[100] To paraphrase Sophia Vasalou, wonder is both a gasp at the extraordinary and also an iterated, organised practice: 'Introduction' in *Practices of Wonder: Cross-Disciplinary Perspectives,* ed. S. Vasalou (Cambridge: James Clarke, 2012), 1–15. Chris Impey writes of 'the vital spark of wonder that drives the best science', quoted in W. P. Brown, *The Seven Pillars of Creation: The Bible, Science and the Ecology of Wonder* (New York: Oxford University Press, 2010), 5; see also C. Deane-Drummond, *Wonder and Wisdom: Conversations in Science, Spirituality and Theology* (West Conshohocken, PA: Templeton Foundation Press, 2006); J. Moltmann, *Science and Wisdom,* transl. M. Kohl (London: SCM Press, 2003), 141–7.

There I consider forms of attention to world and to God that face up to the brutalities of which humans are capable, despite being created in God's image. Where glory is still perceived, and wondered at, this is followed by wondering that such a state of affairs can be part of God's providence. Again, to wonder at God's apparent absence, as we find in the poems of R. S. Thomas, is to wonder that such an absence can be experienced as having the pressure of presence (a wondering that occupied Thomas for probably the last thirty years of his life).

I claimed earlier that signs of the depth of the divine reality always call for a human response. I shall explore responses as we survey types of experience of glory. The response of fear and unworthiness is familiar from the biblical theophanies; another type of response is that deeper 'wondering that', which for Barth was essential to theology,[101] and which is also the mainspring of scientific enquiry, and much artistic and mystical exploration.

Wondering *that*, in all its forms, will tend to be accompanied by longing *that* – wondering that God allows such injustice to persist will be accompanied by longing that God's Kingdom may come, that there may be a time in which all those unbearable injustices and inequalities might be resolved.[102] Exploration of this theme of longing in Chapter 5 is what brings the book to a close.

A distinction may be made between the different roles of wonder in science, the arts, and the contemplation of God. It might be said that the role of wonder in science is to evoke inquiry, and the aim of the inquiry is to close down the sense of wonder, by developing comprehensive explanations of phenomena, explanations that do justice to the data and relate them to the regularities of the universe.[103] This is in effect the picture offered by Richard Dawkins in his study of wonder *Unweaving the Rainbow*.[104] Of course, in practice, as Dawkins would surely concede,

[101] K. Barth, *Evangelical Theology: An Introduction*, transl. G. Foley (New York: Holt, Rinehart and Winston, 1963), chapter 6.
[102] See S. Jones, *Trauma and Grace: Theology in a Ruptured World* (Louisville, KY: Westminster John Knox Press, 2009), chapter 9, for an account of the importance of wonder in recovery from trauma.
[103] An approach that goes back to Aristotle's *Metaphysics*, according to Savalou, 'Introduction', 7.
[104] R. Dawkins, *Unweaving the Rainbow: Science, Delusion and the Appetite for Wonder* (London: Allen Lane, 1998). See the critique of Dawkins in A. McGrath, *The Reenchantment of Nature: Science, Religion and the Human Sense of Wonder* (London: Hodder and Stoughton, 2002), chapter 8.

the inquiry always proves open ended.[105] But there is a sense in which wonder is the initial catalyst but not the goal of scientific inquiry. Wondering *at* is a very necessary starting point. Wondering *that* is to be replaced by explaining *that*. Such an approach to the world attracts a severe critique from Lisa Sideris.[106] She refers to 'serial wonder' as 'the force that drives ongoing discovery and successive puzzle-solving [in science]'[107] but complains that it 'expresses intolerance for mystery and the unknown'.[108] Lucid as this critique is, it is not my experience of doing science or working with scientists. Good science seems to me rather to be characterised by ongoing surprise that the reality of the world is not as 'commonsensical' as most people imagine,[109] by a sense of the immensity of what remains unknown, and by a healthy respect for that unknown, rather than intolerance.

The role of the artist, in contrast to that of the scientist, has been described as '"estranging" objects to rescue them from "automatized perception" and to replace mere recognition with sight'.[110] Works of art keep open a window onto wonder, and prevent its being closed down.[111]

One intriguing aspect of religious wonder is that the contemplation of that which is wondered at *increases* the wonder.[112] Or to put it another way, intensive wondering *that* leads back into an enhanced wondering *at* – and on in an iterative process.[113] Here is another link with longing – encounter with God increases, rather than dissipating, the believer's longing. Because both wonder and longing, when their focus is God, draw the human spirit towards what is infinite and infinitely mysterious, wonder

---

[105] Dawkins would be less ready, I suspect, to concede the force of questions that evoke human wonder but to which science can never give answers, especially the question: Why is there something and not nothing?

[106] L. H. Sideris, *Consecrating Science: Wonder, Knowledge, and the Natural World* (Oakland, CA: University of California Press, 2017).

[107] Ibid., 16. This reference to puzzle solving echoes T. S. Kuhn's description of 'normal science' in *The Structure of Scientific Revolutions* (Chicago: University of Chicago Press, 1962). Kuhn never makes clear in that book where the thinking behind a new paradigm comes from when the profession is locked into the old. Perhaps a sense of wonder going beyond the 'serial' is part of the answer.

[108] Sideris, *Consecrating*, 171.

[109] See L. Wolpert, *The Unnatural Nature of Science* (London: Faber and Faber, 1992).

[110] Savalou, 'Introduction', 5.

[111] One important element in this within my own art form, poetry, is the maintenance of ambiguity as a device to prevent semantic closure.

[112] See Barth, *Evangelical Theology*, 64–5 on this contrast between scientific and religious wonder.

[113] I thank Dr Fout for this observation. See Chapter 3 for further consideration of the contemplation of the natural world.

can only increase, longing can only increase, until such time as both are slaked by the transformed relationship to God that is promised at the eschaton when we shall 'see face to face' (1 Cor 13.12). Until then believers wonder at signs of the divine reality, and that is the process of contemplating glory. Closely bound up with that semiosis is believers' longing for that transformed relationship that transcends both hurt and crying, and that partial discernment that is all they can currently aspire to.

As I go on to develop in Chapter 3, my contention here is that authentic contemplation can draw powerfully on the resources of science, which so helpfully takes us beyond mere sense-impressions, but also on those of poetry and the arts, with their ability to frame moments of experience in all their richness and ambiguity, and those of mysticism, with its emphasis on a reaching for transcendence that can never be grasped. This is not, however, a form of contemplation reserved only for specialists. A stress on the primacy of the pre-reflective response of wonder as an essential element in the discernment of glory reminds us that the beginnings of this discernment are present to every human (cf. Rom 1.20). Also that all humans have opportunities to open themselves more fully to the response of wonder. And growing as a human being is (in part) about that opening to a fuller wondering at, where possible to a fuller wondering that, and also to a more wholehearted longing that. So it is my belief that this analysis, technical as it is in places, nevertheless contains the seeds of a proposal that can enrich human life, even (or perhaps especially) in the age of suffering in which we find ourselves.

CONCLUSION

This chapter has developed my understanding of glory on a spectrum from sign to essence. I have begun my analysis of how Peirce's semiotics may be applied to the study of glory, and explained why I find the concept of divine glory richer and more generative than that of divine beauty. Lastly, I have suggested that wonder is an essential element in the contemplation of glory. In the next chapter I go on to test my understanding of glory on the biblical sources.

2

Glory in the Scriptures

As I indicated in the Introduction, my approach to the understanding of divine glory is as follows:

1. Because the depth of the divine reality is utterly beyond human knowing, and because glory is always represented in the Bible as something apprehensible, I propose that *the apprehension of divine glory is typically the perception of a sign or array of signs pointing beyond itself to the unknowable depths of the reality of God.*
2. That sign, being a self-communication of the divine nature, *always calls for a human response.*

I went on to explain in Chapter 1 that *this semiotic understanding of glory has to be nuanced by recognising a spectrum of reference in the terminology of divine glory, from 'pure' sign to something much closer to divine essence.* This spectrum may be understood to collapse at the eschaton when God will be all in all.

GLORY IN THE BIBLICAL TEXTS

I now explore the ways in which this understanding of divine glory, in terms of a spectrum of meanings from semiosis to ontology, is consonant with plausible readings of the biblical texts on divine glory. Readers who are biblical scholars should be clear that I am not so much inferring this understanding from the sacred texts as proposing a hermeneutical strategy, and testing its effectiveness through readings of relevant texts, assessing their effectiveness in terms of consistency and generativity of interpretation.

My approach is not principally about pinning down what divine glory refers to in any given text; the reference is ultimately the Godness of God, and therefore beyond adequate expression. Von Balthasar: 'only the entire biblical revelation mediates in a total form what God wanted to communicate to us of his glory'.[1] Rather my approach stresses the *mode* of the divine self-communication, and that this mode is typically semiotic. This is, I hold, the best way to understand how reference to glory 'works'. I try to read the biblical texts in a Ricoeurian second naïveté,[2] recognizing the context-dependent character of those texts, and that the canon[3] contains strata of understanding that shift in emphasis over time,[4] but wanting to receive from the writers (and editors) what they believed to have been seen and heard in God's self-communication to God's people, and to test the helpfulness of my hypothesis about divine glory in leading to generative readings of these texts.

The interpretative approach adopted here is based on an hermeneutical lens,[5] or rather in this case a set of three lenses – *Gloria mundi*, the glory of God's creation; *Gloria crucis*, the glory of the Cross, and all suffering that brings the Passion of Christ into view; and *Gloria in excelsis*, the glory of the promised consummation of the world. These three lenses generate overlapping 'images', in the form of readings of the sacred texts. Reflection on certain key texts, especially in Exodus and John, confirms the value of a semiotic understanding of glory. In Exodus, the glory of the Lord is typically represented as a striking physical vision which yet does not exhaust the divine reality – it rather signifies the Lord's presence with 'his' people, while retaining a strong sense of the mystery and otherness of God. In John, the glory of Jesus is seen by the 'we' of the Prologue as an utterly reliable sign of the Father. Jesus' glorification, the consummation of his life as sign, comes at his 'hour', an hour both of degrading death and triumphant resurrection. However, we shall see that careful reading

---

[1] H. U. von Balthasar, *The Glory of the Lord: A Theological Aesthetics*, Vol. 6, Theology: The Old Covenant, transl. B. McNeil C.R.V. and E. Leivà-Merikakis, ed. J. Riches (Edinburgh: T&T Clark, 1991), 416.

[2] P. Ricoeur, *The Symbolism of Evil*, transl. E. Buchanan (Boston: Beacon, 1969), 351–2.

[3] Itself different between different Christian churches.

[4] I do not however even try to enter the very complex debates as to the dates at which Hebrew Bible texts originated and how and when they reached their final form.

[5] See D. G. Horrell, C. Hunt and C. Southgate, *Greening Paul: Rereading the Apostle in a Time of Ecological Crisis* (Waco, TX: Baylor University Press, 2010), Chapter 2 for further discussion of hermeneutical lenses.

of Exodus 33.18f. confirms the importance of an 'adjustable' lens system, through which glory-texts can be read on a spectrum from the purely semiotic to the more strongly ontological.

As I noted in the Introduction, seeing through lenses is a very helpful metaphor for textual interpretation in that it brings some aspects of objects into focus, while leaving other aspects blurred. I accept this limitation of my method, and accept also that other choices of lenses – glory as honour, glory as radiance, and the inclusion of praise as the giving of glory – would give a different interpretative picture. The validity of my choice of lenses may be judged by the consistency of its results with scriptural exegesis, by the generativity of the readings produced, and by the insights gained by applying the lenses to other contexts.

I test out my understanding of divine glory by surveying the scriptural references to the term, focusing on the principal term for God's glory in Biblical Hebrew, *kavōd*,[6] and the Greek word that translated it in the Septuagint and New Testament, *doxa*.[7] This is not a comprehensive survey, but one that seeks to identify and reflect upon the most important texts for our understanding of divine glory.

GLORY IN THE HEBREW BIBLE

The noun form of the root *kvd* occurs first in the biblical canon at Genesis 31.1, when the sons of Laban complain that Jacob has been stealing their father's *kavōd*, his substance, his material wealth (in the form of his flocks of sheep). The terms are those of financial defrauding or embezzlement, with little or nothing in the way of larger connotation. So humans, in this thought-world, have *kavōd*, weight of possession.

---

[6] See P. de Vries, *The Kābôd of YHWH in the Old Testament with Particular Reference to the Book of Ezekiel* (Leiden: Brill, 2016), for the first full English-language study of this word since 1966. De Vries also makes a careful study of the synonyms of *kavōd*. His conclusions about those other words do not alter the analysis presented here.

[7] George B. Caird notes that 44 Hebrew roots are translated in the Septuagint (LXX) by the Greek word *doxa* and its cognates. However, he claims that 'For the study of doxa in the LXX, the root kbd is more important than the other forty-three put together'. 'The New Testament Conception of Doxa' (D.Phil. Thesis, Oxford University, 1944), 52. See later in the chapter for a discussion of the choice of *doxa* to translate *kavōd*. It may be objected that I have taken a 'dictionary' approach of the sort no longer in fashion in biblical studies. But for a defence of this approach to the topic of glory see Rowan Williams, 'Theology in the Face of Christ', unpublished lecture given on October 4, 2004, rowanwilliams.arch bishopofcanterbury.org

The sense of weight can also be applied figuratively to the burden of an illness, or to oppression by a ruler.[8]

The second reference takes us a little further. Genesis 45.13 speaks of Joseph's *kavōd* in Egypt. At one level this is only his 'substance', as before. But in the context of the overall story there is something here of 'splendour', 'reputation' – *kavōd* as a sign of status as well as a bank balance. Maybe there is also a subtext that behind his *kavōd* in Egypt it's still just the same old Joseph, the cocky youngest brother, the youth thrown in a slave pit.

What of *kavōd* used of God? This must be acknowledged to be in the first instance a projection from the human world. The very physical sense of weightiness, importance, substance in the physical realm is transferred to the realm of the divine. For Rumrich '[t]he finite *kabod* of creatures complements and testifies to the infinite *kabod* of God'.[9] As Fout notes, 'When used of God, *kabod* assumes a more expansive meaning, referring to God's "presence", "splendour", or "that which makes God impressive to" humanity, or "the force of [God's] self-manifestation."'[10] De Vries uses the term 'hypostasis' to describe 'an independent form of the appearing of YHWH'.[11] This is 'the revelation of the inner being of YHWH'.[12]

---

[8] C. Dohmen, 'kāḇēḏ' in *Theological Dictionary of the Old Testament*, Vol. VII, ed. G. J. Botterweck, H. Ringgren, and H.-J. Fabry, transl. D. E. Green (Grand Rapids, MI: Eerdmans, 1995), 13–17, at 14.

[9] J. P. Rumrich, *Matter of Glory: A New Preface to* Paradise Lost (Pittsburgh, PA: University of Pittsburgh Press, 1987), 58.

[10] J. A. Fout, *Fully Alive: The Glory of God and the Human Creature in Karl Barth, Hans Urs von Balthasar and the Theological Exegesis of Scripture* (London: Bloomsbury T&T Clark, 2015), 147–8.

[11] De Vries, *Kābôd*, 57. De Vries never develops what he means by 'hypostasis'. But J. T. Strong quotes a definition: 'a quality, epithet, attribute, manifestation or the like of a deity which through a process of personification and differentiation has become a distinct (if not fully independent) divine being in its own right'. Clearly this has affinities with a sign of a full divine reality (and also with Logos Christology), though I would want to demythologise the localisations that Strong proposes – Yahweh as 'the enthroned divine king', and the domain of his *kavōd* 'the unclean regions of the earth'. Strong, 'God's kābôd: The Presence of Yahweh in the Book of Ezekiel' in *The Book of Ezekiel: Theological and Anthropological Perspectives*, ed. M. S. Odell and J. T. Strong (Atlanta: Society of Biblical Literature, 2000), 69–95, at 72. Strong also makes a useful link with the concept of an 'image' in Ancient Near Eastern thought, as 'a manifestation of the divine presence; yet at the same time it preserved the divine transcendence', at 77. The link between image and glory is explored in Chapter 5.

[12] De Vries, *Kābôd*, 117.

The hypothesis of this book is that references to divine glory are typically best understood as being to a sign or array of signs, which point beyond themselves to the underlying reality of God. The most familiar example of this signification is bright light, reflecting the awe and wonder evoked by beholding the blinding brilliance of the divine nature. However, as Newman insists, the meaning of *kavōd Yahweh* is not 'exhausted by "fire" or "brightness"';[13] as we have seen, the meaning of the root underlying the term *kavōd* connotes weight. Weight is a sign of substance, enduring reality. 'True glory, therefore, concerns something weighty, sober and grave.'[14] The receiver of theophany is both frightened and attracted, drawn closer and yet made more aware of 'the potentially lethal nature of encountering YHWH'.[15]

There is a danger of oversimplifying this very complex issue. That *kavōd* had the root meaning of weight does not prevent divine glory in the Hebrew Bible from being much associated with light, albeit often veiled by mysterious cloud.[16] This association with effulgent light is very marked in Isaiah 60 and subsequent apocalyptic usage. I discuss later in the chapter the remarkable choice of the LXX translators to use the Greek *doxa* to translate *kavōd*.[17] That *kavōd* lies behind the LXX and New Testament use of *doxa* does not altogether empty *doxa* of its associations with reputation, or lustre. Again, the association with radiance is unmistakably present in some texts (very particularly in one of the texts I shall examine in detail in Chapter 5, 2 Cor 3.18). What then *is* the importance of the connotation of weightiness?

First, the association with weight, or substance, acts as a corrective to the simple association of glory with light, or yet beauty. It also reminds us of the very concrete nature of Hebrew terminology – theophanies in the

[13] C. C. Newman, *Paul's Glory-Christology: Tradition and Rhetoric* (Leiden: Brill, 1992), 24.
[14] Rumrich, *Matter*, 16.
[15] G. Savran, *Encountering the Divine: Theophany in Biblical Narrative* (London: T&T Clark/Continuum, 2005), 10.
[16] M. Weinfeld, 'kābōd' in *Theological Dictionary of the Old Testament*, Vol. VII, ed. G. J. Botterweck, H. Ringgren, and H.-J. Fabry, transl. D. E. Green (Grand Rapids, MI: Eerdmans, 1995), 22–38. I note that de Vries disagrees with Weinfeld as to whether the derivation of *kavōd* in terms of weight still resonates when the noun is used of Yahweh; rather de Vries considers that 'the *kavod* of YHWH is understood as an effulgence of fire and light' in *Kābôd*, 353. In my view de Vries overstresses his 'light' theory, overinfluenced perhaps by sources such as Trito-Isaiah. See later in the chapter on Isaiah 6.
[17] In the vast majority of cases. See Newman, *Paul's Glory-Christology*, 142, for a list of exceptions.

Hebrew Bible are very physical. A real bush really burns; a cloud forms in the real shape of a pillar. So on the one hand the weightiness of divine glory emphasizes the profoundly physical character of Hebrew Bible theophany: on the other the imagery of weight is 'freighted' with metaphor. Weight is not literal – as in obesity(!) – but is strongly associated with the idea of importance. So the Exodus theophanies of the *kavōd Yahweh* connote 'massive' importance. The presence of Yahweh in 'his' *kavōd* is the most important aspect of the physical world that could be apprehended – it speaks at once to the utter transcendence of a God who can only be glimpsed in theophany, also to the extraordinary capacity of the physical world to bear those manifestations, and to God's determination to manifest Godself to the people in apprehensible (albeit terrifying) form.

Another aspect of this subject is the Hebrew instinct to apophasis. The Exodus accounts range all the way from the (highly anomalous) depiction of the direct communion between the Lord and the seventy elders (Ex 24.9–11), to a doubt as to whether the *kavōd* of Yahweh can even be directly apprehended, at least in a one-to-one encounter (Ex 33.18–23). On the latter account, which I take to be more typical of the instinct not to be able to speak directly of the Godhead (cf. 1 Kgs 19, Is 6, Ez 1), what is of overriding importance, and connotes the presence of the transcendent Lord of the universe, is itself only at most an oblique communication of that presence.

I now consider the accounts of divine *kavōd* in Exodus, one of the most important loci for the concept in the Hebrew Bible. Propp reminds us of the physicality of the term as it applies to human beings, and how the metaphor transfers into speech about God. He writes,

Prominent, too, is the word *kbd*, connoting heaviness, glory, wealth and firmness ... Moses suffers from *heavy* mouth (4:10) and arms (17:12); Pharaoh's *firmness* of heart (7:14; 8:11, 28; 9:7, 34; 10:1) makes Israel's labor *heavy* (5:9).[18]

He continues

Yahweh in response sends *heavy* plagues (8:20; 9:3, 18, 24; 10:14) so that he may be *glorified* over Pharaoh (14:4, 17, 18). The culmination is the descent

---

[18] W. H. C. Propp, *Exodus 1–18: A New Translation with Introduction and Commentary* (New York: Doubleday, 1998), 36, emphasis in original. Writing on 7.14 Propp notes that kbd connotes weight, something hard to move – a kābēd heart would be difficult to sway. 'In 4.10 Moses' "heavy" mouth and tongue hinder his speaking the divine word; in 7.14 Pharaoh's "heavy" heart prevents him from heeding it' (Ibid., 323).

of Yahweh's fiery *kābôd* 'Glory', described as a '*heavy* cloud,' first upon Sinai and later upon the Tabernacle (19:16; 24.16–17; 29:43; 33:18, 22; 40:34–38; cf. 16.7–10).[19]

For Propp, 'Yahweh's "Glory" is the portion of his essence visible on the terrestrial plane. In [the Priestly source] P it appears as a fire (24.17), most often shrouded in cloud.'[20] Thus:

Fire represents Yahweh's danger, purity and intangibility, as well as his brightness. As first creation, light is of all things closest to God. The image of God as fire wrapped in cloud evokes both a thunderhead and true combustion – especially the sacred fire in whose smoke sacrifices ascend to heaven.[21]

But note that the imagery is as much of darkness of cloud as it is of light or fire. Importantly in discussing the most intimate and 'revealing' passage in Yahweh's journey with the people of Israel in Exodus, Propp writes of Exodus 24.17, 'The text says what the Glory looked like to the Israelites, not what it actually was. This coyness in describing the Glory is still more marked in Ezekiel 1.'[22] Even so, the LXX translators feel the need to modify the text, writing 'God is not seen, only the place where he stood' and changing 'they beheld God' to 'they appeared in the place of God'.[23]

I now turn to one of the most fascinating passages on glory in the whole of Scripture.

[18] Moses said, 'Show me your glory, I pray.' [19] And he said, 'I will make all my goodness pass before you, and will proclaim before you the name, "The LORD"; and I will be gracious to whom I will be gracious, and will show mercy on whom I will show mercy. [20] But', he said, 'you cannot see my face; for no one shall see

---

[19] Ibid., 36. I note the very interesting analysis by K. Nielsen, *Incense in Ancient Israel* (Leiden: Brill, 1986), 82–5. While conceding the idea of the cloud/smoke associated with God's glory 'may be of an ultimately mythological origin' (84), he goes on to suggest that the pillar of cloud that 'represents Yahweh ... [and] is a sign of his presence' nevertheless 'cannot be explained as a memory of a natural phenomenon of the desert ... The idea of the presence in the incense cloud was projected back to the wilderness' (85). This is a big claim, and seems to limit both the theophanic powers of Israel's God, and the people's capacity to carry early mythic material over into later tradition.

[20] Propp, *Exodus 1–18*, 595. For the importance of the visual, as opposed to the merely oral, manifestation of God in the P account, see T. B. Dozeman, *Commentary on Exodus* (Grand Rapids, MI: Eerdmans, 2009), 578.

[21] Propp, *Exodus 1–18*, 595.

[22] W. H. C. Propp, *Exodus 19–40: A New Translation with Introduction and Commentary* (New York: Doubleday, 2006), 299.

[23] S. Terrien, *The Elusive Presence: Toward a New Biblical Theology* (Eugene, OR: Wipf and Stock, 2005 [1978]), 135.

me and live.' [21] And the LORD continued, 'See, there is a place by me where you shall stand on the rock; [22] and while my glory passes by I will put you in a cleft of the rock, and I will cover you with my hand until I have passed by; [23] then I will take away my hand, and you shall see my back; but my face shall not be seen.' (Ex 33.18–23)

Moses, having already spoken to God 'face to face' (33.11) 'makes one final supreme request that Yahweh should reveal himself in a fuller way than hitherto; only in the very depths of God can a final solution to the people's sin be found'.[24] In response to Moses' request God speaks of his *tûb*, his 'goodness, wealth, beauty or splendour'.[25] God proclaims God's name, linking this passage with the theophany at the burning bush. Johan Ferreira in his survey of the use of *kavōd* in the Hebrew Bible notes that 'If we interpret the answer of Yahweh to Moses affirmatively God responds positively to Moses' request', then 'God's *kavōd* 'is seen in his goodness; and in the book of Exodus God's goodness is his saving activity on behalf of his people.'[26]

Walter Moberly comments that 'The precise nuance of [Kavod], which in general means God's majesty, those qualities that call forth worship, must be determined from the context … in v. 22 … it is effectively synonymous with God himself, for the context is describing Yahweh himself passing by.'[27] Moberly continues, 'Moses sought not only that Yahweh's "face" should go with the people but that he might see Yahweh's glory. This latter was partially granted.'[28] For Fout, 'God's glory in this passage is presented primarily in terms of honour, reputation and identity'[29] though he admits that glory 'eludes easy categorization'.[30] Where Fout chooses to stress honour and praiseworthiness, I see mystery and depth – God does show 'intimacy and patience with God's servant'[31] but the main thrust of this exchange with Moses is that what can be shown is only a hint of the depths of the divine reality.

This is a *crux interpretum* for my understanding of the relation between divine glory and the divine nature. If Moses' request is altogether granted, then the divine glory is identified with, indeed reducible to, the

[24] R. W. L. Moberly, *At the Mountain of God: Story and Theology in Exodus 32–34* (Sheffield: JSOT Press, 1983), 76.
[25] Fout, *Fully Alive*, 152, n. 30.
[26] J. Ferreira, *Johannine Ecclesiology* (Sheffield: Sheffield Academic Press, 1998), 141–2.
[27] Moberly, *Mountain*, 76.   [28] Ibid., 106.   [29] Fout, *Fully Alive*, 155.   [30] Ibid.
[31] Ibid.

divine goodness and splendour. God is *tûb* through and through.[32] The divine *kavod* is a sign of that goodness.[33]

But if the request is not granted, then the *kavōd* is not functioning as a sign as it does in the earlier Exodus theophanies. Moses has seen all those signs. The *kavōd* of the Lord here rather connotes something it would be too terrible to see, the sheer Godness of God in its essence.[34] Interestingly, the passage then subverts the usual assumption that in the Hebrew Bible auditory communication takes precedence over the visual, and supersedes it where both are present. Here Moses listens to God but is not granted the ultimate visual experience he craves.

My own view is that we must presume that God's response is not altogether positive, but contains a necessary element of concealment. 'My glory you may not see.' Moses, the greatest of all the prophets in the Hebrew Bible, and the one who comes closest to reflecting the divine life to his people, has already spoken to God face to face. Now he is depicted as longing to see the divine glory, the actual *kavōd*, the sheer weightiness of the reality of God,[35] undisguised by cloud or other veiling. Fascinatingly, God turns this request aside – the sign that is offered is a partial one – for that is all humanity can bear.[36] For Moberly,

the fact that Moses is only permitted a partial or limited vision of God is probably intended to relate to the revelation of the moral character of God so as to convey

---

[32] Interestingly the LXX of Exodus 33.19 adopts this view, by translating *tûb* as *doxa*. Sir L. C. L. Brenton, *The Septuagint Version: Greek and English* (Grand Rapids, MI: Zondervan, 1970), 116.

[33] For B. S. Childs goodness is identified with glory at v.22, but he concedes that Moses' 'request to have God reveal himself in an unmediated form is ... denied'. *Exodus: A Commentary* (London: SCM Press, 1974), 595–6, quotation on 595.

[34] For Terrien 'the inner characteristic of the transcendent Godhead' (*Elusive Presence*, 146). Occasionally in the Old Testament 'glory' is straightforwardly a title for God, as at Jeremiah 2.11, Psalm 106.20LXX.

[35] Williams calls the *kabôd* of Yahweh 'the inner "resource" of God, that which grounds and informs God's substantial, objective presence, a presence which is fleetingly uncovered in theophanies in the Hebrew Scriptures but whose full manifestation in the world awaits the last days'. 'Theology in the Face'.

[36] So U. Cassuto, 'It is possible for you to hear the voice of the Lord speaking to you as one hears that of his friend (v. 11), but as far as seeing is concerned, that is to say, in regard to the comprehension of the Divine attributes, there is a boundary that man cannot cross.' *A Commentary on the Book of Exodus*, transl. I. Abrahams (Jerusalem: The Magnes Press, The Hebrew University, 1967), 435. Also see Savran, *Encountering*, 88–9 – nowhere else does Yahweh graciously and protectively prepare the human being for theophany. Savran confirms that Moses' request is not granted (215). Rather what Moses is given consists of 'the revelation of divine attributes, aspects of character rather than ocular representation' (216).

the meaning that the revelation of the grace and mercy of Yahweh in 33:19, 34:6f. is but a glimpse of the divine character and that the fulness is yet more extensive and profound.[37]

What is shown is goodness; what is withheld is the terrible wild otherness of God.[38] I note that von Balthasar also regards God as refusing Moses' request.[39]

Barbara Brown Taylor reflects that:

The God of Moses is not the grandfatherly type, a kind old deity who can be counted on to take the kids exciting places without letting them get hurt. The God of Moses is holy, offering no seat belts or other safety features to those who wish to climb the mountain and enter the dark cloud of divine presence. Those who go assume all risk and give up all claim to reward. Those who return say the dazzling dark inside the cloud is reward enough.[40]

Even so, these encounters leave Moses' face shining so brightly with reflected glory that the people cannot bear to look on him.[41] On the shining of Moses' face Moberly notes that:

Now the implication is that the Israelites see the glory of Yahweh in the face of Moses. As Moses was not able to see the face of Yahweh, so the Israelites can hardly endure to look on the face of Moses (v. 30); though insofar as Moses is man and not God, and the glory is reflected, they are able to behold him.[42]

This is very important for our reading in Chapter 5 of 2 Corinthians 3, and for consideration of how glory 'works' in the economy of salvation. The sign of God that is the manifestation of God's glory can cause the human being who says 'yes' to God, who is willing to draw near, to become him or herself a sign of the divine reality. The quintessential example of human willingness is the 'yes' of Jesus, supremely expressed in Gethsemane, but in every believer there is the opportunity for a 'yes' that is transformative, and makes of that human life a sign of glory.

---

[37] Moberly, *Mountain*, 80.
[38] Hinted at in that extraordinary passage Exodus 4.24–6, in which the Lord, having commissioned Moses, seeks his life on the road. De Vries: 'there is a close relationship between the goodness and the *kavōd* of YHWH, but they cannot be fully related'. *Kāvôd*, 130.
[39] Von Balthasar, *GL6*, 38.
[40] B. B. Taylor, *Learning to Walk in the Dark* (New York: HarperOne, 2014), 58.
[41] Dozeman: 'Thus the appearance of the divine glory will both conceal and reveal God to Moses, sparing his life yet invading his face with divine light.' *Exodus*, 731.
[42] Moberly, *Mountain*, 106.

More than that, as Fout helpfully points out, the human response to God can also be one of faithful questioning.[43] The most famous example of this is perhaps Abraham before the gates of Sodom (Gen 18.22–33). The 'yes' to the divine can be accompanied by questioning (the most significant New Testament example being Jesus' prayer in Gethsemane (Mk 14.32–9). The questioning does not prevent the person of faith being a sign of the divine glory, a sign of a sign[44] – if anything, I would suggest, the biblical witness is that the questioning within the 'yes' strengthens the human signification of divine glory. The human being close enough to God to put questions in integrity and worshipfulness can be a particularly effective sign of the ways of God with the world.

To return to Exodus 33.18f., what is bearable of the divine reality – what indeed is central to faith and to becoming part of the redemptive work of God – is goodness, but divine glory is something more, more mysterious, less bearable.[45] There is a link here with my observations in Chapter 1 in relation to Ricoeur. That of God which cannot be called to appear in court may indeed be far from bearable.

I side with Maimonides, as quoted in Chapter 1, in seeing Exodus 33.18f. as an instance of where *kavōd* is 'intended to signify [God's] true essence and true reality'.[46] This is glory as its most ontological, in the terms in which I framed the spectrum of meaning by which I am understanding divine glory. The inference of such a reading is indeed that this glory is more than Moses can bear. Godness remains ultimately mysterious.

Gregory of Nazianzus makes a fascinating reading of this text, according to Christopher Barina Kaiser. For Kaiser, 'What Moses saw, according to Gregory ... was neither the Father ... nor the Son ..., but the divine energy that is reflected in all of creation.'[47] This reading (which for Kaiser is a regrettable dilution of the physicality of the kyriocentric visions that propelled early Christology) offers an interesting further refinement to the thesis presented here. Even in what Maimonides regards as the classic example of divine glory understood ontologically,

---

[43] Fout, *Fully Alive*, 3.   [44] See Chapter 5 for further exploration of this concept.

[45] Cassuto has God say 'you may know that I am compassionate and gracious ... but the decision to act according to these virtues is at all times in My discretion, and it is impossible for you to know when, or if, I shall act thus.' *Commentary,* 436.

[46] M. Maimonides, *The Guide of the Perplexed,* Vol. 1, transl. S. Pines (Chicago: University of Chicago Press, 1963), 156.

[47] C. B. Kaiser, *Seeing the Lord's Glory: Kyriocentric Visions and the Dilemma of Early Christology* (Minneapolis, MN: Fortress Press, 2014), 285.

the most that can be seen is only the divine *energaiai* ('energies'), not the ineffable divine *ousia* ('being'). A text that might support such an understanding of the ontological sense of glory is Romans 6.4b: 'just as Christ was raised from the dead by the glory of the Father', where glory is not so much sign as *instrument* of the irresistible divine purpose. But insofar as the *energaiai* constitute a faithful sign of God's nature, while leaving the *ousia* forever mysterious, we can therefore hold that even at its most ontological, the divine glory remains only a partial disclosure of deity.[48]

In a very careful survey of the uses of *kavōd* in the Hebrew Bible, Carey Newman concludes that the *kavōd Yahweh* represents a technical term, a special way of talking of Yahweh's presence. It is associated especially with movement, or appearance. It is not exhausted by fire or brightness, nor does it 'denote, at least in the first instance, a character or attribute of Yahweh.'[49] As I remarked in the Introduction, *kavōd* is about the sheer Godness of God as manifest in the created world.

The *kavōd Yahweh* has a particularly important place in the texts identified by commentators as the P tradition, and in Isaiah, Ezekiel, and Psalms.[50] The Temple becomes the special earthly home of God's *kavōd* (Pss 26.8; 63.2), but that *kavōd* fills the whole earth (Is 6.3; Pss 19.1, 72.19). The Psalmist repeatedly pleads for a universal theophany (Pss 57.6, 12; 96.3; 96.7; 108.6; 113.4). As well as association with the place of worship, be it tabernacle or temple, there is a strong connection between *kavōd* (used in various senses) and the king (e.g., Ps 21.5).[51]

---

[48] Gregory concludes: 'sketching God's inward self from outward characteristics, we may assemble an inadequate, weak and partial picture'. Quoted in F. Young, *God's Presence: A Contemporary Recapitulation of Early Christianity* (Cambridge: Cambridge University Press, 2013), 393.

[49] Newman, *Paul's Glory-Christology*, 24. Cf. also de Vries, *Kābôd*, 363. For Dozeman, 'the Glory of Yahweh introduces a safeguard between God and humans that was absent from the original theophany of Exodus 19.16–19, allowing God to take up residency on earth in a qualified and thus in a less direct and dangerous form' (*Exodus*, 590).

[50] I do not want to enter the debate about which texts contain early material and which are the product of exilic or postexilic reflection, but merely direct the reader to Newman's discussion (*Paul's Glory-Christology*, chapter 3). He links the *kavōd*-experiences recorded of the Exodus and conquest periods with those in the Temple by remarking that 'the same God who led, guided, and conquered … has provided a way of regular worship; the author of deliverance-guidance-conquest now authors a regular avenue of blessing' (44).

[51] Newman, *Paul's Glory-Christology*, 44–52. Earlier Newman postulates that the spatial localization of the *kavōd Yahweh*, and its association with royalty, were important in the transition from the first phase of Israelite worship, inspired by wilderness experiences, to the second phase, based on the Temple (41–2). It is hard to resist the notion that this second phase represents an attempt to domesticate the wild and terrible God of the Sinai experiences. But the vision of Isaiah 6 in turn dramatically undomesticates the Lord!

Indeed, one way to characterise the interaction of God with human beings in the Old Testament is that signs of the divine reality are various and transient. In God's pursuit of closer relationship, they may be created or adopted by God, but may also be set aside. A very striking case, always chilling to read, is the near-sacrifice of Isaac, who as Terrien points out is 'the only sign [to Abraham] of the trustworthiness of God'.[52] Terrien continues, 'The sign of purity of faith was love at any cost for a God who conceals his Godhead in appearance of hostility.'[53] Israel's religion, then, is 'based on the courage to face the abyss of being, even the abyss of the being of God, and to affirm ... the will to gamble away not only one's own ego but even one's hope in the future of mankind'.[54] God substitutes a ram, itself a proleptic sign of how glory will be expressed in the salvation of the world. Ten chapters later the Lord wounds 'Israel', even as 'he' blesses him, at the ford of Jabbok (Gen 32.22–32). Terrien again: 'in the end, a God who is resisted and fought against will reaffirm life.'[55]

One of the great psalms to mention glory is Psalm 29. I quote here the central section, verses 3–9:

> [3] The voice of the Lord is over the waters;
>   the God of glory thunders,
>   the Lord, over mighty waters.
> [4] The voice of the Lord is powerful;
>   the voice of the Lord is full of majesty.
> [5] The voice of the Lord breaks the cedars;
>   the Lord breaks the cedars of Lebanon.
> [6] He makes Lebanon skip like a calf,
>   and Sirion like a young wild ox.
> [7] The voice of the Lord flashes forth flames of fire.
> [8] The voice of the Lord shakes the wilderness;
>   the Lord shakes the wilderness of Kadesh.
> [9] The voice of the Lord causes the oaks to whirl,
>   and strips the forest bare;
>   and in his temple all say, 'Glory!'

Note that it is the tree-stripping, wilderness-shaking God who is described as 'the God of *kavōd*' – it is to this tremendous natural force, undomesticated and undomesticable, that the Temple worshippers cry 'Glory!'.[56]

YHWH there is 'the terrifying God who fills Isaiah with the feeling of inadequacy and uncleanness'. H. Ringgren, 'qdš', in *The Theological Dictionary of the Old Testament*, Vol. XII, ed. G. J. Botterweck, H. Ringgren, and H.-J. Fabry, transl. D.W. Scott (Grand Rapids, MI: Eerdmans, 2003), 530–43, at 535.

[52] Terrien, *Elusive Presence*, 82.   [53] Ibid., 83.   [54] Ibid., 83–4.   [55] Ibid., 91.

[56] For further on this psalm, see de Vries, *Kābôd*, 196–8.

Notoriously, the people express to the prophet Samuel their desire to
have the sort of sign of divinity that other nations have, in the form of a
king.[57] The Lord grants their request, though even as 'he' does so, 'he'
indicates what an unsatisfactory sign a king can be (1 Sam 8.11–18).
Instead the people must make do with transient contact with their
Lord, sometimes through a mediator (e.g., Ex 19–20), sometimes through
indirect signs, especially the Law,[58] and the tradition of prophecy[59], but
following them even into exile (Ez 1).

A particularly fascinating theophany in the Hebrew Bible – not using
the term *kavōd* but with 'heavy' implications of it, is the dramatic story of
Elijah on Horeb (1 Kgs 19. 9–18). Three great physical manifestations –
wind, earthquake, and fire – all plausible signs of the awesome power of
God (as I discuss further in Chapter 3) are ruled out as theophanies. Elijah
is not to be given the sort of sign of the divine reality that Moses knew on
a mountain. Then comes a fourth manifestation, translated in the NRSV
as 'a sound of sheer silence'. Very tellingly it is this *silence* to which Elijah
responds.[60] This is the sign of the reality of God's presence that calls him
to wrap his face in his mantle (lest the thick darkness of glory dazzle him?)
and go out to the entrance to the cave, where he hears the divine address.
Sign and response, but note the paradoxical nature of the sign.

It is noteworthy that the divine *kavōd* could leave the holy places
of Israel. The First Book of Samuel notes its association with the ark
(4.21–22), which was captured by the Philistines. Walter Brueggemann
in his *Ichabod toward Home*[61] sees in this passage (which he takes to be
early) a foreshadowing of exile, and indeed of the transition from Cross to
Resurrection. He translates '*ichabod*' as 'where is the glory?' – a question
that might indeed have been on the lips of one of Ezekiel's contemporaries
going into exile, or on the lips of Christ's disciples after the Crucifixion.

---

[57] Here is where the Genesis 1 teaching that *all* human beings are created in the image and
likeness of God (1.26–7), not just the king, is particularly striking.

[58] An indexical sign replacing the icons of theophany. See Chapter 5 for the implications of
this for 2 Corinthians 3.

[59] Cf. S. S. Tuell: The people experience God through Ezekiel writing a book and telling
them his vision – 'text has replaced temple as the locus of divine presence'. 'Divine
Presence and Absence in Ezekiel's Prophecy' in *The Book of Ezekiel: Theological and
Anthropological Perspectives*, ed. M. S. Odell and J. T. Strong (Atlanta: Society of
Biblical Literature, 2000), 97–116, at 97.

[60] See Chapter 4 for further exploration of the relation between glory and silence, and the
appearance of divine absence.

[61] W. Brueggemann, *Ichabod toward Home: The Journey of God's Glory* (Grand Rapids,
MI: Eerdmans, 2002).

And the answer for Brueggemann, reading 1 Samuel 5, is 'heavy' under the covering of darkness, showing up the Philistine deity Dagon for only the idol that he is,[62] destroying the health of those who belittled the great sign of the holiness of Yahweh that is the ark, allowing the exiled people to find a new song, and ultimately harrowing hell.

In Chapter 1 I discussed the application of Peirce's categorisation of signs. The ark can be seen as what Peirce would have called a symbolic legisign, a sign related to its object, the holiness of God, by a convention (albeit one thought to be divinely established) acting in a lawlike fashion over time. The sign is closely associated with the *kavōd*, and when the sign is abused, the weight of the reality of which it is symbolic descends on the abusers. Psalm 24 celebrates the ark's triumphant return to Jerusalem, and 1 Kings 8 its installation in the new Temple, followed by the coming to dwell of the divine *kavōd* (cf. also 2 Chr 5.13–14).[63]

Famously the *kavōd Yahweh* leaves the Temple in Ezekiel (9.3, 10.4, 10.18–19),[64] only to return at the end of the book. So the prophets associate glory with judgment of the people's sin (e.g., at Is 3.8, Jer 2.11).[65] The reality of God is such that turning against divine holiness and wisdom leads to consequences. The prophets also link glory strongly with the promise of transformation (Hb 2.14, Zec 2.5, Is 40.5, 60.1–2).[66]

My core interpretation of divine glory – as sign of the deepest truth about reality, presencing that invites transformation – fits well with a classic theophany such as that at the burning bush (Ex 3.1–4.17) – even though *kavōd* is not mentioned in this passage. There God's invitation is accompanied by awesome divine command, that Moses remove his shoes, but it is still invitation – Moses could have declined the vocation he received. It will be clear too that my understanding of glory is close to that of a theology of sacrament, broadly conceived. Thus, John Macquarrie writes of the burning bush, 'in and through the particular being of this bush, Moses became aware of Being itself, the mysterious power of ultimate creative Being, the Ground of all particular beings.'[67] I explore the link between glory and sacrament in Chapter 3.

---

[62] Interestingly, in the Hebrew Bible the word *kavōd* is never used of idols.

[63] Williams points us to the proximity of 2 Chronicles 5.13–14 to 6.1, 'God is one who "dwells in thick darkness": 'Theology and the Face'.

[64] A possibility foreseen in Hosea (see Newman, *Paul's Glory-Christology*, 58). For an extended analysis of Ezekiel 8–11, see de Vries, *Kābôd*, 267–85.

[65] Newman, *Paul's Glory-Christology*, chapter 4.   [66] Ibid.

[67] J. Macquarrie, *A Guide to the Sacraments* (London: SCM Press, 1997), 9.

Mention of that passage in which Moses receives his call, having beheld a great and mysterious sign of the Godness of God, and heard a mysterious version of the divine name, takes me to the important association of *kavōd* with vocation. The glory of the Lord is intimately associated with three of the great call-narratives of the Hebrew Bible – Isaiah 6, Isaiah 40, and Ezekiel 1.[68] Isaiah 40 commissions the prophet to prepare the people for a mighty universal theophany; 40.5 prophesies that the glory of Yahweh will be revealed. Deutero-Isaiah goes on to elucidate what that *kavōd* is – that of the only God, the lord of the universe, the author of weal and woe alike (45.7).

But it is the other two narratives that particularly interest us here, because they give more detail – however allusive and mysterious – as to the form of the divine *kavōd*. I begin with Isaiah 6 (which has a parallel in the commissioning of Micaiah in 1 Kings 22). The mysterious vision accorded to the prophet is followed by his overhearing the song of the seraphim. 'Holy, Holy, Holy is the Lord of hosts; the whole earth is full of his glory' (v. 3). Otto Kaiser writes:

Whereas the first part of the heavenly song of praise hymns God's inner, hidden being, which is nevertheless powerful and strong in will, the second half praises the power by which he sustains and underlies the world, his *kābōd*, his honour and glory. Whereas in his innermost being God remains hidden from man in profound concealment for all but a few moments, in the everyday world man is not without a testimony to his presence. God's 'weightiness', God's glory, fills the whole earth with a living power. All reality proclaims him who created, sustains, and governs it. Thus heaven and earth, and day and night, tell us of his glory (Ps. 19.1f.).[69]

But this is not, Kaiser goes on, mere

rationalist natural theology. For man is blind to the glory of God to which all reality bears witness, until he is convinced of his holiness. But God's glory and God's holiness are always recognized simultaneously. Only someone who knows of his holiness also recognizes his glory. Consequently, one can follow Herntrich's comment on this passage, which in its turn follows the Württemberg divines

---

[68] Newman, *Paul's Glory-Christology*, 68–75.

[69] O. Kaiser, *Isaiah 1–12: A Commentary*, transl. R. A. Wilson, 2nd ed. (London: SCM Press, 1963), 78. Note that de Vries, who disputes the connotation of 'weightiness', claims that 'We must understand the garment of YHWH as a garment of light' but it is by no means clear why, when the text is silent on this point. *Kābôd*, 147.

Oetinger and Bengel in saying that God's 'holiness is his hidden, concealed glory ... But his glory is his holiness revealed.'[70]

Similarly S. H. Widyapranawa affirms that 'Holiness and glory (*kabod*) are closely connected with each other. Glory is the external manifestation of the divine essence which is holiness.'[71] So also Brevard Childs, noting that this terminology of glory is:

a special biblical idiom ... What Isaiah saw was the glory (*kābôd*) of God, that is, his outer manifestation. The picture is dynamic and in motion. Very shortly just the tip of his robe envelops the entire temple ... His glory is his disclosed holiness; his holiness is his inner glory (Oetinger, Bengel). Holiness in the Old Testament is not an ethical quality, but the essence of God's nature as separate and utterly removed from the profane.[72]

This is very helpful, as we consider what divine glory as sign might be a sign *of*. The answer is both simple and fathomless – it is a sign of holiness, of the utter distinctiveness and untouchability and incomprehensibility of God.[73] And, interestingly, holiness is equated by Childs, and those he cites, with God's 'inner glory'. So a single sentence expresses the spectrum we have been constructing – (outer) glory is disclosed holiness, it is manifestation, it is sign – albeit faithful sign – of God's utterly other Godness. 'Inner glory' is equated with holiness and thus with the divine essence – the other end of our spectrum of meanings of divine glory. This essence is the glory that in Exodus 33 Moses was not permitted to see, glory that brings death to human beings, and causes even heavenly watchers to cover their faces.[74]

Interestingly, this passage in Isaiah is one of the very few in the Bible that speaks of the Lord God being seen directly 'high and lifted up' (6.1), even if the vision is then immediately deflected to smoke[75] and seraphim.

---

[70] Kaiser, *Isaiah*, 78–9. For further discussion of strategies in natural theology, see Chapter 3.

[71] S. H. Widyapranawa, *The Lord Is Savior: Faith in National Crisis: A Commentary on the Book of Isaiah 1–39* (Grand Rapids, MI: Eerdmans, 1990), 32.

[72] B. S. Childs, *Isaiah* (Louisville, KY: Westminster John Knox Press, 2001), 55.

[73] For an introduction to holiness in the Hebrew Bible, see J. G. Gammie, *Holiness in Israel* (Minneapolis, MN: Fortress Press, 1989). Emil Brunner puts it thus: 'As the Holy One, God is Wholly Other, the Incomparable, the Sole Reality ... He can never be fully understood by any creature ... but it is precisely His will that He should be known as the Wholly Other; that is His glory'. *Revelation and Reason*, transl. O. Wyon (London: SCM Press, 1947), 45.

[74] Kaiser, *Isaiah*, 74–6.

[75] Nielsen suggests that Isaiah's vision must have stemmed out of his participation in cultic ceremonies involving the burning of incense (*Incense*, 82). This seems to me altogether

Their song of praise confesses that 'the whole earth is full of his glory' (6.3). This to me illustrates very well the interpretation I am proposing of the word *kavōd* – that it connotes, typically, the signs of the divine, and that these signs pervade the cosmos.[76] I draw from the Isaiah 6 theophany two insights: that glory is the external manifestation of the holiness of divinity, and that God's glory pervades the whole cosmos. I take up that profoundly affirmative, though also awe-inspiring and troubling, verdict on the natural world in Chapter 3.

Brueggemann argues that the Temple cult attempted to domesticate the terrible glory of the Lord, as seen in the Ark narrative. The glory is now to be the object of quiet liturgical devotion. This is bound up also with the support for the monarchy, for a king who 'can implement the *kabod* in human form'.[77] Part of the force of the vision of Isaiah 6 might therefore be that this domestication cannot work, but that in time of political uncertainty (after Uzziah's death) Yahweh, whose *kavōd* is cosmic in reach, still searched for those who can respond to it authentically and cry 'here I am, send me'.

Beyond First Isaiah we see three very important developments in the Hebrew Bible's handling of the theme of divine glory. First, with the vision of Ezekiel the *kavōd* becomes associated with the *bodily* form in which Yahweh appears.[78] Second, the claim that the divine *kavōd* is localized in Israel's sanctuaries drops away. Aelred Cody writes:

As often in the Old Testament, but particularly in Ezekiel and in the priestly component of the Pentateuch, the divine glory is a form, luminous but normally veiled from the eyes of mortals, through which God appears without being seen directly. In the priestly texts of the Pentateuch, the glory is found only in the tabernacle in the desert, the fore-runner of the Temple in Jerusalem. Here it is

---

too naturalistic, limiting both the theophanic power of the Lord and the capacity of the prophet's imagination to receive it.

[76] Some commentators, however, seem to interpret this text more in terms of Maimonides' third category of meaning of glory, creaturely praise, when they translate it as 'The whole earth is full of His praise.' Maimonides himself cites Isaiah 6.3 in this way (*Guide*, 156–7). But the force of the passage seems to me overwhelmingly to suggest God's outward self-communication, rather than what God receives from creatures. De Vries again wants to interpret this in terms of light-imagery, the earth bathed in *kavōd*, as by the rising sun, and also to consider the possibility that an eschatological state is being described (*Kābôd*, 148–50), but his evidence on both counts seems thin.

[77] Brueggemann, *Ichabod*, 65.

[78] H. Wildberger, *Isaiah 1–12: A Commentary*, transl. T. H. Trapp (Minneapolis, MN: Fortress Press, 1991), 267.

unexpectedly visible to Ezekiel in pagan Babylonia. The spatial context of God's glory in this vision is not the sacred space of the Temple but the vast sweep of the created world.[79]

Third, from Deutero-Isaiah on there is a sense of the revelation of divine glory lying in the future.[80] This prepares the way for the use of the term in Jewish apocalyptic, which has been well analysed by Newman. He quotes Klaus Koch to the effect that: 'The catchword *glory* is used wherever the final state of affairs is set apart from the present and wherever a final amalgamation of the earthly and heavenly spheres is prophesied.'[81] This is in accord with my proposal in Chapter 1 that at the eschaton the sense of glory as sign will collapse into the sense of glory as divine essence. As Paul puts it, 'we' shall then see 'face to face' (1 Cor 13.12). This, incidentally, is our first link with the theme of longing, which will occupy us in Chapter 5. In apocalyptic, glory is something longed for, as the state of the blessed, as the presently unattainable heavenly Jerusalem.

For Ezekiel, only in God's graciousness did the divine glory reside in the temple 'as a visible sign of his presence'.[82] But God's true abode is in heaven (cf. 1 Kgs 8.22f.). The sign is only a sign – it does not comprehend all of God's greatness. Note that in the extraordinary vision in Ezekiel 1 it may be thought that it is the whole vision, not just the figure on the throne, that is the appearance of the likeness of God's glory.[83] Note too the circumspection with which the vision is described, 'This was the appearance of the likeness of the glory of the LORD' (Ez 1.28).[84]

Newman points us to the importance of throne visions in apocalyptic, under the 'pervasive' influence of Ezekiel 1.[85] The best known to most readers will be the vision in Daniel 7, of 'one like a son of man'. Here

---

[79] A. Cody, OSB, *Ezekiel: With an Excursus on Old Testament Priesthood* (Wilmington, DE: Michael Glazier, 1984), 26–7.

[80] But see my discussion, later in this chapter, of the Gospel of John for a very important connection with glorification in the last Servant Song of Deutero-Isaiah.

[81] Newman, *Paul's Glory-Christology*, 81.

[82] D. I. Block, *The Book of Ezekiel: Chapters 1–24* (Grand Rapids, MI: Eerdmans, 1997), 360.

[83] J. W. Olley, *Ezekiel: A Commentary Based on Iezekiēl in Codex Vaticanus* (Leiden: Brill, 2009), 243–4. De Vries notes the likely influence on Ezekiel 1 of both Isaiah 6 and Exodus 33. *Kābôd*, 364–5.

[84] De Vries: 'The description can in fact not be visualised. The glory speaks to one's imagination, but it is an imagination that cannot be fleshed out.' *Kābôd*, 365. He continues, 366: 'The more abundantly the *kavōd* of YHWH is described, the more its hiddenness is demonstrated.

[85] Newman, *Paul's Glory-Christology*, 93.

glory becomes a signifier of 'the exalted position of the special representative'.[86] For the Christian theologian this is a very important movement.
Ezekiel, remarkably, has a vision of the *kavōd Yahweh* in the form of a
human being. In Daniel this becomes a special representative, a type of
angelic figure who can bear the *kavōd* as a sign of his status as the
particular servant of the Ancient of Days. In both cases the sign that is
the *kavōd* has become associated with a human figure. But in Ezekiel 1,
as in Isaiah 6, this figure is a vision of the Godness of God, a sign of the
divine reality; in Daniel the figure is a sign of the divine *kavōd*, so in a
sense a sign of a sign of the divine reality.[87] This prepares the thought-
world in which the Fourth Gospel can write of Jesus possessing glory 'as
of the only-begotten of the Father' (Jn 1.14KJV).

But it is possible that just as influential on later thinking on glory are
the visions in the First Book of Enoch. Enoch too envisages a 'Son of
Man', one who 'is a man who possesses "glory" in a special degree
unknown in the Hebrew Bible. Glory designates the Son of Man as God's
representative, who will appear "in glory" in order to judge'.[88] But the
emphasis on throne-imagery – very possibly derived from Ezekiel 1 – must
have attracted to it the imagery of radiance, of brilliant beauty associated
with the most precious of materials, just as the eschatological longing in
apocalyptic must have concentrated minds on visions from which all
darkness had been dispelled.[89]

This imagery has come a long way from the pillar of cloud in the
wilderness, or yet the smoke of Isaiah 6. Part of the task of this book is
to keep in view those earlier theophanies, with all their mystery, their
darkness as well as their light.

An old but durable analysis of *kavōd* in the Hebrew Bible is found in
Millard Berquist's thesis of 1941.[90] Berquist's own understanding of the
divine *kavōd* is summarized when he considers the meanings the Greek word
doxa had to bear when it was used to translate divine *kavōd* in the LXX:

---

[86] Ibid., 99.
[87] Depending on how Ezekiel 8 and 10 are read, this figure in Daniel may be prepared for in
the figure the prophet meets at Ezekiel 8.2.
[88] Newman, *Paul's Glory-Christology*, 99, n. 48, drawing here on the work of Mowinckel.
[89] Ibid., 87: 'The signifying power of Glory extends far beyond the rather technical titu-
lar use; the word is plastic enough to refer to other aspects of the heavenly visions.'
Newman also thinks the title 'the Lord of glory', only present in the New Testament at
1 Corinthians 2.8, may derive from 1 Enoch (Ibid., 237.)
[90] M. J. Berquist, 'The Meaning of *Doxa* in the Epistles of Paul' (Ph.D. Thesis, Southern
Baptist Theological Seminary, 1941).

A summary term for the self-revelation of Jehovah in its various elements by actual or figurative manifestation

[a] term of ascription by which affirmation is given to such nature

Jehovah himself, being used as a designation of the Divine Being

Brilliance, splendor, brightness, glowing fire etc. of divine origin and significance, and even divine representation.

Specifically, God's manifestation of himself among men as savior and redeemer.[91]

The first, fourth, and fifth of these senses correspond to the understanding of glory as sign, the third to the other end of our 'spectrum', glory as essence, and the second is a helpful way to express the way in which divine glory evokes creaturely praise.[92] The last of Berquist's senses helps us by emphasizing that God's self-communication of Godself through signs, calling for response, is very often to communicate God's nature as redeemer.

Clearly there is an element of projection involved in taking a physical, human category and applying it to the numinous. So it is doubly interesting to see how this happens with the divine *kavōd*. It is connoted not by anything that can be straightforwardly comprehended, but by a cloud, by fire hidden by cloud, later by an indwelling of a place too holy for extended human presence. The honour or reputation attaching to human *kavōd* is likewise projected onto God, but it should be noted that in the Hebrew Bible divine *kavōd* never becomes a wholly abstract noun like honour or reputation. It always retains a concreteness and a sense of dynamism, rather than being a static-seeming attribute. It always retains the physical connotations associated with theophany. If anything the later visionary writings in Daniel and Enoch reinforce, rather than diluting, this sense of the physical. Indeed in the tradition that stems from Ezekiel's vision the physical manifestation of *kavōd* becomes associated more and more with a human form.

In relation to Peirce's categorization of signs, I suggest that the *kavōd Yahweh* in the Hebrew Bible was understood, effectively, as an iconic sign of the nature of God.[93] Whether visible as a dark cloud or a brilliant light, or yet (as in Ez 1) in the mysterious form of a human figure, the most vivid

---

[91] Berquist, 'Meaning', 49–50.
[92] A classic example being Psalm 29.2, 'Ascribe to the Lord the glory of his name.'
[93] It is because of their iconic character that accounts of them are usually accompanied by cautions and circumlocutions (as in Ez 1.28), so that the Lord is not being evoked too directly

manifestations of the *kavōd Yahweh* served not just as an index, pointing to God's presence, but signified God's reality more directly through their awe-evoking character. They may be thought of as signs-by-likeness of a reality different from either ordinary physical phenomena, or from the manifestations of the power and majesty of earthly potentates. Theophanies are typically what Peirce would have called sinsigns; they are singular appearances, not part of a system of signs.

Another important unpublished thesis on glory is that of George Caird. Caird wants to establish that the sense of divine glory that the New Testament takes over from the Hebrew Bible is fundamentally that of honour, and secondarily that of radiance (together with the praise and worship that these engender). But Caird, to my mind, wrenches the term 'honour' away from its ordinary sense in English. He paraphrases Psalm 19.1a, 'The heavens are telling the glory of God', as 'The work of creation is His honour',[94] and the seraphim's proclamation in Isaiah 6.3 as, 'His honour is the fullness of the whole earth'[95] – both distinctly odd-seeming readings.

Caird is right to invoke a Hebraic sense of 'honour'[96] very different from that of the English language even of the 1940s (let alone the far more honour-suspecting English of the twenty-first century). The Hebrew *kavōd* has a very concrete sense of 'weight' and 'importance'. So Caird's sense of what is primary about *kavōd* and its Greek translation is at the ontological end of our spectrum of meaning – a way of speaking of the Godness of God, with all its 'weight' and importance.

However, Caird's analysis seems to me misleading in two respects. First, in supposing that the more visual, theophany-related sense of divine glory is always about *radiance*, as opposed to a range of physical manifestations inspiring awe and dread. Second, in supposing that this more dynamic, self-manifesting, self-communicating sense of the glory of God is always secondary to glory understood as the fact of God's importance and Godness. These emphases in Caird are both connected to the way he seems to devalue the parts of the Exodus narrative he attributes to the P writer, regarding these as, in effect, as derivative insertions heavily influenced by Ezekiel.[97] And by the time of Ezekiel the sense of dazzling radiance is already much associated with visions of the divine. So Caird

---

[94] Caird, 'The New Testament Conception', 74.   [95] Ibid., 75.   [96] Ibid., 233.
[97] Ibid., 105f. Though I would claim that not only the Exodus theophanies, but also those of Isaiah 6 and Ezekiel 1 are intrinsically semiotic in character.

for all his impressive analysis misses the semiotic aspect of divine glory, and its association not just with honour and radiance but with mystery.

In the New Testament witness the Godness of God finds its ultimate sign in the face of Jesus Christ (2 Cor 4.6).[98] It is to that witness that we now turn, beginning from those early translations of the divine *kavōd* of the Hebrew Bible into the Greek of the LXX.

GLORY IN THE GREEK SCRIPTURES – THE WORD *DOXA*

We now come to the use of the term 'glory' in Greek, keeping in mind the connotations of *kavōd* that we have explored. The decision of the translators who produced the Septuagint to render *kavōd* by the Greek word *doxa*[99] is one of the most interesting interfaces between Hebrew and Greek in the whole of biblical translation.

At first sight the choice of *doxa* is a distinctly strange one. Greek concepts of glory begin not with *doxa* but with *kleos*, the Homeric word for glory. The core meaning of *kleos* is 'news', and hence the report that might be made of the hero, hence the undying fame that a hero might gain by great exploits, by *aretē* in the sense of warrior excellence.[100]

The translators of the Hebrew Bible into Greek used the word '*doxa*', which in common Greek parlance meant 'opinion', and from there 'reputation'. In philosophical discourse it could mean 'mere appearance' as opposed to *alētheia*, 'truth'.[101] This might at first sight seem a very curious juxtaposition with *kavōd*. The translator, in Kittel's words, 'taking a word for opinion, which implies all the subjectivity and therefore all the vacillation of human views and conjectures, he made it express something absolutely objective, i.e., the reality of God'.[102] Nevertheless, the use of *kavōd* in respect of God was 'a way of safeguarding the

---

[98] The controlling text in David F. Ford, *Self and Salvation: Being Transformed* (Cambridge: Cambridge University Press, 1999).

[99] 181 times, according to Fout, *Fully Alive*, 147, though note also Newman's point that on 20 occasions *kavōd* is translated by a different word. Newman, *Paul's Glory-Christology*, 142, n. 27.

[100] Often in violent struggle, see C. Taliaferro, 'Glory in Human Nature' in *The Ashgate Research Companion to Theological Anthropology*, ed. J. F. Farris and C. Taliaferro (Aldershot: Ashgate, 2011), 319–27, at 321.

[101] W. Jaeger, *Early Christianity and Greek Paideia* (Cambridge, MA: The Belknap Press, 1961), 55.

[102] G. Kittel, 'dokeō, doxa, doxazō, sundoxazō, endoxos, endoxazō, paradoxos' in *Theological Dictionary of the New Testament*, Vol. II, ed. G. Kittel and G. Friedrich, transl. G.W. Bromiley (Grand Rapids: Eerdmans, 1964), 232–55, at 245.

appearance of God ... the form in which he chooses to reveal himself'.[103] In other words, God only ever communicates Godself in part, by means of signs. And *doxa* 'with its connotation of some distance from reality, was apparently found to be a reasonable Greek equivalent of it'.[104]

Note that neither *kleos* nor *doxa* would be used of Greek deities, who being immortal had no need to transcend the limitations and finality of death by seeking enduring fame or reputation.[105] So the projection we noted previously in Hebrew theology – weightiness of human being extrapolated to the ultimate weightiness of God – is not found in Classical Greek religion. The Greek philosophers too remain by and large suspicious of *doxa* – true wisdom and true happiness are not to be found in it. Ancient Greek worship, too, would have avoided this term, if for a rather different reason. The cult tended to be very physical and concrete, oriented around the image of the deity. This is a far cry from the imageless worship insisted on in Exodus, which opens up the whole territory of signs of an unseen and unseeable God.

Suffice it to say that by the time of the New Testament *doxa* has acquired all the majesty and *terribilità* of the Hebrew *kavōd*.[106] For Bauckham *doxa* acquires in the Greek Bible the meaning 'visible splendor', 'which it never had in Greek before this'.[107] But Giorgio Agamben writes that, 'In the Bible neither *kabhod* or *doxa* is ever understood in an aesthetic sense: they are concerned with the terrifying appearance of YHVH, with the Kingdom, Judgment and the throne.'[108]

---

[103] A F. Segal, *Paul the Convert: The Apostolate and Apostasy of Saul the Pharisee* (New Haven, CT: Yale University Press, 1990), 52–3.

[104] A E. Harvey, *Renewal through Suffering: A Study of 2 Corinthians* (Edinburgh: T&T Clark, 1996), 52. Note T. B. Savage's point that the LXX translators of Isaiah use *doxa* for a range of properties of God other than those that the Hebrew writers explicitly termed 'glory', especially 'the awesome and visible majesty of God ... also ... his incredible strength', citing such verses as Isaiah 2.10, 24.14, 26.10, 40.26, 45.24. *Power through Weakness: Paul's Understanding of the Christian Ministry in 2. Corinthians* (Cambridge: Cambridge University Press, 1996), 114.

[105] I thank Professors Christopher Gill and Richard Seaford for this observation.

[106] George B. Caird: 'So complete was the semantic change which overtook *doxa* and *doxazō* because of their use in the LXX, that they simply assumed all the meanings and associations of the Hebrew words they had been used to translate.' 'The Glory of God in the Fourth Gospel: An Exercise in Biblical Semantics', *New Testament Studies* 15 (1968), 265–77, at 268.

[107] R. Bauckham, *Gospel of Glory: Major Themes in Johannine Theology* (Grand Rapids, MI: Baker Academic, 2015), 44.

[108] G. Agamben, *The Kingdom and the Glory: For a Theological Genealogy of Economy and Government (Homo Sacer II, 2)*, transl. L. Chiesa (with M. Mandarini) (Stanford, CA: Stanford University Press, 2011), 198. Interestingly Agamben goes on to note the

A good illustration in English of the ambiguities of the biblical terms *kavōd* and *doxa* can be found by considering the word 'grandeur'. This is a word that in its more *kavōd*-like form reminds us of the opening lines of Hopkins' poem 'God's Grandeur': 'The world is charged with the grandeur of God/It will flash out, like shining from shook foil.'[109] The magnificent reality of God imbues the world – that is the ontological reality lying behind creation.[110] But only sometimes do we get flashes, signs of that reality. The signs are physical, marvellously evoked by Hopkins by thinking of the flash of foil, and 'the ooze of oil crushed'. These are powerful similes for the essence of what underlies the world. We shall explore these signs in the natural world in much more depth in Chapter 3.

But the term grandeur can also evoke for us the Greek sense of *doxa* in terms of worldly reputation – human ceremonies like Queen Victoria's Diamond Jubilee. Grandeur seems perfectly adapted to a vanished world of pomp and crowned heads in procession. Such a ceremony was a sign of human power and solidarity, but a deeply flawed and misleading sign. It spoke of power that was insecurely founded on heredity, and solidarity that was insecurely founded on consanguinity. The follies of which such a system was capable are sternly rebuked by the *kavōd* of the Cenotaph, the great memorial to World War I in Whitehall in London, designed by Edwin Lutyens. This very plain block of Portland stone, narrowing in stages to an almost flat top, contains no triumphal decoration, only at each end a laurel wreath and the inscription 'The Glorious Dead'. It is, then, a monument to glory, a sign of a profound underlying reality, but one from which all the more dubious connotations of human *doxa* have been stripped away. It is a monument also lacking (at least to my eye) all beauty, and therefore a helpful illustration of the distinction between beauty and glory we explored in Chapter 1. In its monolithic-seeming, monosyllabic-seeming blockiness, it is a monument to a certain sort of earthly *kavōd*, to the weight of a single brute fact – that war takes human lives. Those lives are deemed 'glorious' in their deaths by the monument,

---

way the term 'Shekinah', literally the habitation or residence of God, became attracted to the 'kabod yahweh' in the Targumic process. So the Targum of Gen 28.16 replaces 'The Lord is in this place' with 'The Glory of the Shekinah is in this place' (Ibid., 200). There is a link here with the eschatological connotations of glory – it will be a sign of God's having come to dwell in the places of promise (cf. Is 4.5, 40.5; Hb 2.14).

[109] G. M. Hopkins, *Poems and Prose: Selected with an Introduction and Notes by W. H. Gardner* (Harmondsworth: Penguin, 1953), 27.

[110] The origins of 'grandeur' in the French suggest that connotation of substantiality that *kavōd* evokes in the Hebrew.

but without adornment or differentiation, without celebrity of any sort. The block of stone is a sign of a brute, inescapable fact.[111]

Newman, in puzzling over the choice of *doxa* to translate *kavōd*, argues that a great advantage of *doxa* was precisely it was not the technical language used of the epiphany of pagan deities.[112] He also notes that both *kavōd* and *doxa* have 'subjective' and 'objective' senses – they can reflect what is intrinsic to an entity ('subjective', in Newman's terms), and the response that is due to an entity (for Newman, 'objective'). To my mind 'subjective' and 'objective' here is a slightly awkward terminology, given that 'subjective' often means 'in the head of the subject', and therefore not necessarily 'objectively' true.[113] Perhaps a clearer terminology would be to distinguish first-person glory, that which is intrinsic to an entity, and second-person glory, that which is accorded to an entity by others. In respect of divine glory, recall that we are considering only first-person glory, since creaturely praise and honouring cannot add to the glory of God.

Newman then goes on to analyse the semantic fields of *kavōd* and *doxa*, and to discover that they have one field in common, that of honour.[114] Honour therefore becomes the dominant way in which Newman, and after him Fout, seek to understand the New Testament connotations of glory. Newman's analysis is a compelling one. Fout makes a case that honour is the most encompassing term by which to understand divine glory, beauty and light being subsidiary to this.[115] However in my view honour is too much of a God-directed, second-person term – it is what is accorded to God by worshippers, rather than the 'communicative dynamism' to which Fout appeals earlier in his text.[116] Fout makes appeal to the influential anthropological work of Bruce Malina on honour and shame.[117] But it is important to realise

---

[111] Interestingly, the sides of the Cenotaph are not quite vertical but converge towards a point three hundred metres above them – a very subtle architectural twist to the sign, added by Lutyens in the final construction of the monument. The monosyllabic sign points beyond itself, to an invisible transcendent.

[112] Newman, *Paul's Glory-Christology*, 152.

[113] So Caird, in an article on which Newman draws here, uses these terms in a different sense again, distinguishing between the subjective response to an entity and the objective cause of the response. 'The Glory of God', 267. Caird claims that 'outside the LXX *doxa* had only the subjective sense' (Ibid.).

[114] Newman, *Paul's Glory-Christology*, 157–63.   [115] Fout, *Fully Alive*, 146.

[116] Ibid., 37.

[117] B. Malina, *The New Testament World: Insights from Cultural Anthropology* (Louisville, KY: Westminster John Knox Press, 1993), chapter 2.

that Malina describes interactions concerning honour as taking place between social equals. A being of 'unequal, superior, exalted status, for example ... God' is 'socially barred from responding to challenges to their honor'.[118] God's honour is peculiar to Godself and distant from creatures (except through the medium of their praise). It is therefore so unlike the honour of human individuals as to make the term, in my view, unhelpful.

Majoring on honour, then, tends to throw the weight of the understanding of glory too much onto Maimonides' third category, the human response to the divine.[119] This is understandable in Fout, because he wants to explore that human response, and emphasise (as I would also do) that that response involves all our human faculties of learning and questioning, as well as obedience. It also accords with the strong stress Fout puts on the New Testament in his study, and therefore on *doxa* rather than *kavōd*.

Undoubtedly the New Testament texts involve the connotations of reputation, honour, that go with the use of *doxa*, but I do not see this as the most fundamental meaning of divine glory. That meaning lies for me on the spectrum we have been describing, between divine glory as (a) sign of the mystery of the divine reality and (b) a way of speaking of essence, of the sheer Godness of God.[120] It is in this latter sense that glory comes closest to the sense of 'honour', but there is still a problem with conflating the two.

We saw earlier that 'honour', like *kavōd* and *doxa*, *can* reflect first-person use, what is intrinsic to an entity. That sense seems to me to be ebbing out of the word 'honour' in modern English. Honour in this intrinsic, first-person sense is a term that used to be applied to certain positions – as in the title 'His Honour' accorded to English judges. That title differs interestingly from the title 'Honourable' used for English nobility and legislators. 'His Honour' implies what Newman calls the subjective meaning and I have termed the first-person sense[121] – the role of judge *possesses*, ipso facto, honour. 'Honourable' implies that the person should be *accorded* honour, and hence connotes the second-person sense. (The irony of that title, in British political exchange, will

---

[118] Ibid., 44.   [119] Maimonides, *Guide*, 156–7.

[120] Fout is closer to this understanding when he goes on to speak of 'the glory of the Lord as it is found in Scripture as being more encompassingly about God's presence and identity, richly described, specifically through God's covenant-commitments and God's acts' (*Fully Alive*, 146). This has much more of the outward-from-God sense that I see as primary.

[121] Though 'objective' in Caird's terms, as connoting the objective cause of the honouring.

not be lost on anyone who has heard a broadcast of *Prime Minister's Questions*.) But the first-person sense of honour, that which is intrinsic to the entity – as for example in the notion within the British system of titles that the monarch as sovereign is 'the font of honour' – seems to me to be fast dropping out of the language. Therefore to think of glory in terms of honour is in danger of admitting too many connotations from the second-person side, the honour accorded to a being by others.[122] The biblical witness, and especially the main connotations of *kavōd*, privilege the first-person side, the Godness of God in Godself.

I also consider that 'honour' does not convey the full register of the biblical *kavōd*, which must have been in the minds of the New Testament writers, even though they were working with a word of a different colour in *doxa*.[123] The divine *kavōd* is a much more mysterious term than 'honour' – it is associated in the very physical Hebrew imagination with light and fire, but also with cloud and thick darkness. Fout admits that he emphasizes honour as a way to understand glory 'in order to preserve the fullness and positive valence of [God's] identity'.[124] Fout goes on to acknowledge that he does not 'mean to *reduce kabod* or doxa to honour: glory is a rich term, in accord with the rich (i.e. simple yet fathomless) identity of the Lord'.[125] So he concedes that he is selecting one aspect of glory.

In a sense honour as an understanding of divine glory is both too intrinsic and not intrinsic enough. It is too intrinsic for the theophanic end of the spectrum of meanings of glory – glory as God's gracious self-communication of the Godness of God. (As I noted earlier, honour lacks a sense of dynamism; honour does not have sufficient of the connotation of self-manifestation, self-communication, for the semiotic end of the spectrum.) And at the other end of the spectrum, the ontological, the term 'honour' seems to lack the depth and mystery required to speak of the essence of the illimitably holy Godness of God. Moses does not, in my view, ask 'Show me your honour' on Sinai.

---

[122] Even in the biblical context, Malina's account of honour as 'a claim to worth that was publicly acknowledged' (*New Testament World*, 29) has a major second-person component. See also D. A. DeSilva, *Honor, Patronage, Kinship and Purity: Unlocking New Testament Culture* (Downers Grove, IL.: InterVarsity Press, 2000), 27f.

[123] Von Balthasar also questions the reduction of glory to honour (*GL6*, 26, n. 11) for the rather different reason that he wants to associate glory with the transmutation of the pagan word *charis* into the theological concept of grace (Ibid., 350). God makes present his salvation in the world, 'and thus precisely grace' (Ibid.).

[124] Fout, *Fully Alive*, 149.   [125] Ibid., 151, emphasis in original.

Another way to engage with this question is to consider what might be the opposite of glory. On the 'honour' interpretation of glory it would be shame, dishonour. But my spectrum of meanings for glory would suggest rather different opposites. At the ontological end of the spectrum, the opposite would be Godforsakenness, the absolute absence of the Godness of God. At the semiotic end, the opposite of glory, I suggest, would be futility, hopelessness, the 'vanity' of the author of Ecclesiastes, the lack of any sign of what transcends the ordinary cycle of living. The whole burden of Qoheleth's twisting, turning, aphoristic style is that human beings can gain no access to the divine reality – pattern and purpose and meaning, beyond the day-to-day rhythms of life and the seemingly arbitrary turns of destiny, have been specifically rendered inaccessible to humans (cf. Eccl 3.11).[126] The pursuit of any sign that might constitute glory is repeatedly rebuked as 'vanity' (Hebrew *hebel*; Greek *mataiotēs*). Qoheleth's is a glory-free world, and it therefore acts as a useful point of reference. Whatever can be glimpsed of glory in Scripture, in the natural world, in the arts, has escaped the black hole into which Qoheleth consigns all hope. Both of these senses of the opposite of glory can be found in that extraordinary study of glory, the Book of Job, where all efforts to find purpose and meaning are confounded, and the depths of Godforsakenness are met at the climax of the Book by the most austere and magnificent set of signs of the divine reality.[127]

I recognise that, like Fout, I approach the subject of glory from my own particular theological concerns – especially that of giving full semantic space to God's identity as the creator of a profoundly ambiguous creation – but more generally I am concerned to let the term 'glory' retain the widest, richest, range of meaning. Where the association of divine glory with first-person honour comes closest is at the ontological end of our spectrum of meanings of glory, where the emphasis is strongest on Godness in itself, as opposed to self-communicated signification of Godness. But even there I feel that interpreters who equate divine glory with honour are stretching the latter English word beyond its helpful compass.[128]

---

[126] So also W. P. Brown, 'the sage cannot detect a glimpse of divine expression ... As for creation's big picture, the sage has sapped all sense of wonder from it'. *The Seven Pillars of Creation: The Bible, Science and the Ecology of Wonder* (New York: Oxford University Press, 2010), 185.

[127] See Chapters 3 and 4 for further discussion of Job.

[128] Rather as we saw writers on beauty do in Chapter 1.

THE NEW TESTAMENT

I now survey the use of the term *doxa* for divine glory in the New Testament, leaving aside, for the present, Pauline texts, which are treated in detail in Chapter 5. I explore the use of *doxa* in the Synoptic Gospels, and then concentrate on the Fourth Gospel's revolutionary use of the term, which will be so important for the rest of the book. Chapter 5 will focus on how Paul too transforms the understanding of glory when he applies it to the working of the Spirit in the Christian community, especially in 2 Corinthians. This all-too-brief survey, which finishes with a look at the remaining New Testament texts, should not be taken as an effort to harmonise the writers' uses of the term; rather our task is to assess how their different nuances of *doxa* might or might not support reading the term through a semiotic lens.

As Melick notes, the Synoptic use of divine *doxa* is dominated by Luke's emphasis on the term, especially at the birth narrative and the Transfiguration; neither Mark nor Matthew uses the term in these contexts.[129] Note especially Luke 2.9 where the appearance of the glory of the Lord parallels that of the angel of the Lord.[130] This is as I would expect, since both are signs of the divine reality. Fascinatingly the verb used of the glory here is *perilampsein*, which Luke uses again at Acts 26.13 for Paul's account of his Damascus Road experience. The effect, as with so many theophanies, is to evoke fear.

Doxa also appears interestingly in the Song of Simeon (Lk 2.29–32). The destiny of the child held in the old man's arms is described as 'the glory of your people Israel'. This could be read as 'the perfect sign of what Israel, the called people of God, could be'.

The New Testament offers a disturbing picture of Satan as 'enthroned in glory, possessing all the kingdoms of the world'.[131] In Matthew and Luke, Satan tempts Jesus to perform three glorious signs, and as Wendy Farley points out, Jesus ends up performing a version of each of them.

---

[129] R. R. Melick, Jr., 'The Glory of God in the Synoptic Gospels, Acts and the General Epistles' in *The Glory of God*, ed. C. W. Morgan and R. A. Peterson (Wheaton, IL: Crossway 2010), 79–106, at 80–90.

[130] Ibid., 84. For Newman, 'Isaiah 6.3 (LXX) forms the basis of Luke 2.14' – in both cases the heavenly beings burst forth into praise. *Paul's Glory-Christology*, 173, n. 26. In the Scriptures and tradition angels are an important category of sign of the reality of God. However, angelology is too huge a subject to receive treatment in the present book.

[131] W. Farley, *The Wounding and Healing of Desire: Weaving Heaven and Earth* (Westminster John Knox Press, 2005), 99.

Jesus goes on to effect a miraculous feeding, to establish a kingdom, to overcome death. But in the frame in which Satan presents them, each of these signs would be false to the divine reality to which Jesus witnesses. This is important to the semiotic understanding of glory that is being explored here; it is not just a specific vision or a specific action that constitutes the sort of sign of the divine reality we are designating as glory; it is the context and indeed the intent of the action that must be included in the overall discernment of glory. Jesus' three great actions that correspond to the temptations are all performed out of 'divine yearning and zeal' (to borrow a phrase from Pseudo-Dionysius, quoted by Farley[132]); his refusal to act out of the mere display of power is also, in its way, an authentic display of glory.[133]

Luke alone makes explicit the link between the Transfiguration and glory. Matthew makes a connection with Sinai, with the shining of Jesus' face (Mt 17.2). But in Luke, Moses and Elijah appear 'in glory' (Lk 9.31).[134] Jesus by contrast is seen to *possess* glory in himself, when he is seen as he really is (9.32).[135] But as Terrien points out, 'He was the reflection of the glory of God, but the reflection of this glory led to Jerusalem and to his own death.'[136] Luke, fascinatingly, records that the disciples were then alone with Jesus, and they were silent (9.36). Some may sense a connection with the shorter ending of the Gospel of Mark, where the women, faced with the extraordinary revelation of the Resurrection, say nothing to anyone. But it is not resurrection that is being evoked here, but *glory*. The Transfiguration is the great sign, within the narrative of Jesus' ministry, that Jesus is not just the shining-faced new Moses, but one greater still, the beloved who will be sacrificed for the world, the ultimate sign of the self-giving love of God. It is also the great anticipation of Jesus' appearance at the Parousia.[137]

---

[132] Ibid.

[133] To put this in terms of our approach of 'three-lensed seeing', if Jesus had performed the actions to which he was being tempted, they would have been authentic manifestation of his role of a sign of the divine glory in creation (*Gloria mundi*) but they would not have been in accord with the kenotic self-giving that led to the Cross, and which – in von Balthasar's ur-kenotic scheme discussed in Chapter 1 – is intrinsic to the Godness of God (*Gloria crucis*).

[134] In an event which, fascinatingly, seems to be depicted by Luke as having occurred at night.

[135] Melick, 'Glory', 89.   [136] Terrien, *Elusive Presence*, 425.

[137] A. M. Ramsey, *The Glory of God and the Transfiguration of Christ* (London: Longmans, Green, 1949), 118.

In my proposal that the meaning of divine glory has to be seen on a spectrum from sign of the divine reality to what is conceivably knowable of the essence of that reality (even if that is 'only' the divine *energaiai* immanent in the world), I also concluded in Chapter 1 that at the eschaton those two meanings converge, for those immanent energies will so flood the world that 'God will be all in all.'[138] The whole New Testament, indeed, may be regarded as an anthology of the coming of that eschatological age in which the two senses of divine glory unite. So it is worth acknowledging the texts, especially in the Synoptics, that prophesy the Parousia of Jesus in imagery of glory.[139] This for the Synoptic Evangelists is a new depiction of Jesus the signifier, one in which all the power and majesty of the Father is expressed in the second coming of the Son. Divine messengers will then not make fleeting appearances, but will be a constant sign of the triumph of the Risen Christ.

The pervasive association of glory in the New Testament with the eschatological triumph of Christ in God should evoke in the Christian contemplative the response of *longing*. 'We do not yet see' (Heb 2.8) this final state of human beings in utterly harmonious partnership with God. Christians glimpse it, claim the promise of it, but it remains elusive, and believers should long for it. I take up the theme of human, and divine, longing in Chapter 5.

THE GOSPEL OF JOHN

The Fourth Gospel brings glory into a sharper focus than the Synoptics. For Richard Bauckham, glory is 'a key theme in the Gospel of John ... but it is rarely given extended exposition'.[140] He continues,

glory helps to explicate the relationship between the Sinai covenant ... and the incarnation and cross of Jesus. [Glory] is also a term John uses to penetrate the meaning of Jesus' ministry and miracles. Above all, glory is a theme that John uses, *very distinctively among the New Testament writers* to highlight, by paradox, the extraordinary nature of the love of God for the world in going to the lengths of Jesus' abject dying in the pain and shame of crucifixion.[141]

---

[138] Or in the imagery of the Hebrew Bible, 'the earth shall be filled with the knowledge of the glory of the Lord' (Hb 2.14).

[139] Mk 8.38 par. Mt 16.27, Lk 9.26; Mk 13.26 par. Mt 24.30, Lk 21.27, also Mt 19.28, 25.31.

[140] Bauckham, *Gospel*, 43.   [141] Ibid., 43. Italics mine.

Raymond Brown devotes a whole appendix in his magisterial commentary on John to the word *doxa*.[142] For him, God's *doxa* is 'a *visible* manifestation of His majesty in *acts of power*'.[143] The emphasis on divine power is interesting. It accords with the character of the signs around which the first half of the Gospel is structured. But, as Bauckham points out, at Jesus' hour, his *doxa* is manifested to the full in an act of power of a very particular and paradoxical kind, that of being lifted up in torture and pain. So the Godness of God, so often revealed in Scripture in acts of more conventional power, is also seen in the power of arms opened wide in atoning love, in 'the gift of eternal life to all believers'.[144]

For Bauckham however there is a prior revolution in the use of the term, before John's extraordinary association of glory with Passion, in that John declares in the Prologue that glory becomes visible, not hidden, when the Word becomes flesh and dwells among us (Jn 1.14).[145] Such glory is 'full of grace and truth', 'the radiance of the character of God'.[146] Craig Evans makes a persuasive case that Exodus 33–4 lies behind the second half of the Johannine Prologue (Jn 1.14–18).[147] We see v.17 balance Moses' contribution with that of Christ, but before that the key statement in v.14 that 'we beheld his [Christ's] glory' is intended as the definitive answer to Moses' longing in Exodus 33.18 to see the divine glory.[148] Jesus' intimacy with the Father at John 1.18 may be contrasted with Moses' oblique sight of God at Exodus 33.23.

Further, as Evans goes on to point out, God's glory comes to be seen in the tabernacle (Ex. 40.34, LXX *skēnē*): but the dramatic statement of the Johannine Prologue is that 'the word became flesh and dwelt (*eskēnōsen*) among us (Jn 1.14)'. Given that 'skēnos and skēnōma were often used for the tabernacle of the human body ... tabernacle imagery was uniquely able to capture the idea that people encountered God's Word and glory in the person of Jesus'.[149] Brown suggests that 'In Johannine thought

---

[142] R. E. Brown, S.S. *The Gospel According to John: Chapters 1–12* (London: Geoffrey Chapman, 1971), 503–4.

[143] Ibid., 503, italics in original.

[144] R. E. Brown, S.S. *The Gospel According to John: Chapters 13–21* (London: Geoffrey Chapman, 1971), 751.

[145] Bauckham, *Gospel*, 51. See the Introduction for the importance of this verse for my thesis.

[146] Bauckham, *Gospel*, 52.

[147] C. A. Evans, *Word and Glory: On the Exegetical and Theological Background of John's Prologue* (Sheffield, JSOT Press, 1993), 79, and references in n. 2 therein.

[148] So also Bauckham, *Gospel*, 49–51.   [149] Evans, *Word*, 82, quoting H. Koester.

Jesus during his lifetime was the tabernacle of God embodying divine glory'.[150] This seems to me to tally well with my semiotic understanding, since what is a tabernacle but a sign of the presence of a God whose holiness cannot be confined or localized? Jesus becomes that sign of the divine reality represented in the Hebrew Bible by God's indwelling of tabernacle and temple.

It may also be that Targumic expansion of Isaiah 6.1, 'I saw *the glory of* the Lord' (my italics to indicate what the Targumist added) lies behind John 1.14 – 'we beheld his glory'. Clearly the Isaianic vision is in the Evangelist's mind, since we see him applying it to the stubbornness of the people at John 12.38–41.[151] Yet for all the inspiration that comes from the Hebrew Bible, including its Greek translation and Targumic expansion, it seems that in John 'Jesus redefines glory, even the glory of God. In his own words and deeds he reveals God's glory' and very particularly 'in his death he covers himself with glory even as God gives him glory'.[152] This combination of glory with death is a radically new development.

It seems reasonable to associate John 1.14 – 'we have seen his glory, the glory as of a father's only son' – and John 3.16 – the extent of the Father's love is that he sent the Son. Richard Harries writes: 'the central thrust of [Jesus'] ministry ... was to be taken as a sign of the way God reaches out to include all of us'.[153] Jesus is the utterly reliable sign of the character of the Father, and hence of the Father's saving love in sending the Son, a love that comes to full expression at the Cross.[154]

Jesus' visible glory is evident throughout his ministry (cf. Jn 1.14, 2.11), which is perhaps why John has no need to record a scene of transfiguration.[155] Bauckham in his discussion of the first part of John, the so-called Book of Signs, notes that Jesus never seeks *doxa* from others,

---

[150] Brown, *John 13–21*, 781.   [151] Evans, *Word*, 162.

[152] D. Moody Smith, *The Theology of the Gospel of John* (Cambridge: Cambridge University Press, 1995), 122.

[153] R. Harries, *The Beauty and the Horror, Searching for God in a Suffering World* (London: SPCK, 2016), 87.

[154] So also Williams: 'God cannot be conceived as an eternal individual self, but as a life lived eternally in the "investment" in the other. Thus the believer perceives what I have called the interiority and integrity of God, the resource and solidity of divine life: what is indestructibly in God is this life-in-the-other. To see the freedom of God to be in the cross is to see *glory*, because it is to see how God's utterly non-negotiable presence and action can be real in the physical body of the tortured and dying Jesus'. 'Theology in the Face'.

[155] But see later in this chapter on W. H. Vanstone's view of this.

not does he seek to add to his own (Jn 5.41, 5.44, 7.18, 8.50, 8.54)[156] or love human *doxa* (12.43); he only seeks and loves the glory of God (5.44, 7.18, 12.43). 'Jesus, by seeking God's glory and not his own, actually incurs dishonor and disgrace in the eyes of humans but approval from God.'[157] So Bauckham, having in his study of glory in John effectively translated *doxa* by 'honour' up till then, recognizes that the term goes deeper. He says,

Arguably, there is a hint that by seeking only the glory of God, Jesus is revealing God's glory in the flesh. The radiance of God's character is displayed in Jesus' humility before God and his obedience to God. By centering his life not in himself but in God, Jesus reveals God.[158]

Or, in the terms in which I have been discussing glory, Jesus acts as the ultimate sign of the Godness of God. This is confirmed for Bauckham when he considers John 17.5, when Jesus prays 'Father, glorify me in your own presence with the glory that I had in your presence before the world existed.'[159] This is not mere honour, but 'the glory of God that no one can see on earth and live, the unveiled radiance of "who God is"'.[160]

One of the most troubling episodes in John's Book of Signs is Jesus' response to the news of Lazarus' illness at the opening to Chapter 11. Given the news that his beloved friend is ill, Jesus does not go to him, but responds that this illness is not *pros thanaton* (it does not 'lead to death' (NRSV), is not 'to end in death',[161] is not, to offer another translation, 'in the cause of death'. Rather it is 'for God's glory, so that the Son of Man may be glorified through it'. The resuscitation of the dead Lazarus is the last of the great signs that occupy Chapters 2–11. It is a sign that death does not have the victory, because of Jesus. It is a sign therefore of the reality of the God who sent his Son into the world 'that everyone who believes in him may not perish but may have eternal life' (Jn 3.16).

But note the chilling power of the story that is unfolding. There is no quick rescue, no easy route past the suffering. The reality of the God who

---

[156] Cf. Caird, citing some of these same passages: 'Jesus does indeed at an earlier period in his ministry contrast the *doxa* (recognition) which men seek from one another, and which blinds them to the reality of the true *doxa* (oneness with God) which he himself is content to receive as a gift at the hands of his Father': 'Glory of God', 270.

[157] Bauckham, *Gospel*, 58. Cf. S. M. Garrett, *God's Beauty-in-Act: Participation in God's Suffering Glory* (Eugene, OR: Pickwick Books, 2013), 103–4: judged from the wrong perspective the Suffering Servant is always misunderstood.

[158] Bauckham, *Gospel*, 58.   [159] Ibid., 59.

[160] Ibid., 59–60. I take up the implications of John 17 further in Chapter 5.

[161] Brown, *John 1–12*, 420.

created this world, and so loved it, is that the path of love is not away from death, but through it. Jesus' own reaction to the grief of the sisters is outrage 'at the hole death has torn in the very fabric of existence'.[162] God is the creator of a 'cruciform' world.[163] And the increase in Jesus' *doxa* makes the more inevitable and imminent the coming of his 'hour', when he will be lifted up, as the Father's eternal life-giving gift. As Brown comments: 'the writer [of the Fourth Gospel] has chosen to take *one miracle* and to make this the primary representative of all the mighty miracles of which Luke speaks [at Lk 19.37]'[164] – and therefore the focus of the Pharisees' enmity.[165] But even the resultant plot to kill Jesus turns out to contain the necessity of his sacrifice, as revealed to Caiaphas as high priest (Jn 11.50).

Raymond Brown calls the second half of the Gospel 'the Book of Glory'.[166] This in itself is very striking – it is not the first long section, the 'Book of Signs', that most speaks of glory, but the second, which leads inexorably to Jesus' 'hour'). This is the hour of Jesus being lifted up, the hour of the climax of his earthly glorification. As Bauckham confirms, the whole sequence of Jesus' humiliation, suffering, death and exaltation is his glorification.[167] That the writer of the Fourth Gospel seems to see glory in a violent and degrading execution is one of the main considerations that led me in Chapter 1 to stress the difference between glory and beauty, and emphasise that the reference of divine glory is something much more profound and troubling.

That said, there is a *crux interpretum* here – a radical difference between interpreters of the Fourth Gospel. Is the true glory of Christ as revelation of God to be found in exaltation, Resurrection and Ascension, with the Cross only the necessary prelude, or is the glory also in the humiliating death itself? Tord Larsson, in a helpful little essay, calls the former view 'traditionalist', and identifies it with Calvin, and among contemporary exegetes with John Ashton. The latter view he calls

---

[162] T. Gardner, *John in the Company of Poets: The Gospel in Literary Imagination* (Waco, TX: Baylor University Press, 2014), 109.

[163] Cf. H. Rolston III, *Science and Religion: An introduction* (Philadelphia: Templeton Foundation Press, 2006 [1987]), 144. Cruciformity is explored further in Chapters 3 and 5.

[164] Brown, *John 1–12*, 429.

[165] Cf. Caird: 'Jesus is said to be glorified by this sign partly because it is the last of the series and leads directly to his glorification on the Cross, partly because, like all the other signs, it is an occasion for his manifesting of his glory. But the glory of Jesus is the glory of God himself': 'Glory of God', 272.

[166] Brown, *John 1–12*, cxxxix.   [167] Bauckham, *Gospel*, 54.

'revisionist' and identifies with Luther, and in the twentieth century with Bultmann and D. Moody Smith. Larsson's own point is that this contemporary difference of emphasis goes all the way back to the patristic era.[168]

It is vital to my thesis in this book that I hold the 'revisionist' view, and accept Moody Smith's point that 'Jesus' death is the crucial moment of God's revelation.'[169] Thus,

the concept of glory (Greek: *doxa*) in the Fourth Gospel is intimately connected with revelation and with Jesus' death ... So Jesus redefines glory, even the glory of God ... The iconoclastic Jesus of the Synoptic Gospels overturns the conventions and expectations of his contemporaries, but the revolutionary Jesus of the Fourth Gospel goes even further by redefining in a thoroughgoing way what is meant by the glory of God.[170]

Inspection of the texts focusing on the 'hour' of Jesus' glorification (especially Jn 7.39, 12.16, 12.23, 13.31) and his being lifted up (3.14, 8.28, 12.32) confirms this view. These texts point to and converge on the Cross itself,[171] and John makes clear that the 'hour' is both one that Jesus sees as inevitable, the culmination of his mission, and also one by which he is deeply troubled, one from which he might pray to be saved (Jn 12.27). Brown says this: 'Since John conceives of passion, death and resurrection as the one "hour", John sees the theme of glory *throughout the whole hour.*'[172] So Moody Smith is right that Jesus' glorification includes the Cross, and thus redefines our understanding of divine glory.[173]

---

[168] T. Larsson, 'Glory or Persecution: The God of the Gospel of John in the History of Interpretation' in *The Gospel of John in Christian Theology*, ed. R. Bauckham and C. Mosser (Grand Rapids, MI: Eerdmans, 2008), 82–8.

[169] Moody Smith, *Theology*, 120. Richard Harries concludes the same: 'that glorification [of Jesus] consisted of the crucifixion, resurrection and going to the Father as part of one movement' (*Beauty and the Horror*, 84–5).

[170] Moody Smith, *Theology*, 121–2. So also Gardner, *John*, 117, 'The hour of his death – the hour in which God's deepest nature or glory will be revealed – is now here.'

[171] Williams writes, 'For John, Jesus' journey towards the cross is the record of a gradual unveiling of glory ... What is new in John ... is the focus upon John's association of glory in its fullness with the cross.' 'Theology in the Face'.

[172] Brown, *John 1–12*, 504, italics mine.

[173] Cf. also A. J. Köstenberger, 'The Glory of God in John's Gospel and Revelation' in *The Glory of God*, ed. C. W. Morgan and R. A. Peterson (Wheaton, IL: Crossway, 2010), 107–26, who also draws the same inference about the Johannine writings from looking at Revelation (122). So too Caird, in analysing John 13.31, 'if we ask what John means when he says that the Son of Man is glorified and God is glorified in him, one proper and accurate answer is that he means the Cross': 'The Glory of God', 266. For Frances Young, 'in this Gospel, the cross is the "hour of glory", to which the whole narrative moves': *God's Presence*, 40.

I develop my case further by showing that Jesus' lifting-up and glorification has to be linked to the last of the songs of the Suffering Servant in Deutero-Isaiah. In the centre of John 12 is a remarkable pair of sayings:

12.23b 'The hour has come when the Son of Man will be glorified.'

12.34b: 'How can you say that the Son of Man must be lifted up?'

The second saying is represented as the crowd's response to the first. Therefore 'to be lifted up' (*hupsothēnai*) is being paired with 'to be glorified' (*doxasthai*). These verbs, tellingly, are paired in Isaiah 52.13 LXX.[174] In the Hebrew text of Isaiah 52.13–14 NRSV the servant is 'exalted and lifted up, and shall be very high ... [but] there were many who were astonished at him – so marred was his appearance'. But the LXX has 'exalted, and glorified exceedingly ... so shall thy face be without glory from men, and thy glory shall not be honoured by the sons of men'.[175] So the link between being lifted up and being glorified is already there in the LXX of Deutero-Isaiah, as is the sense that human beings fail to respond to the sign that is the Servant's exaltation.[176]

Later in the chapter at 12.41 the author links the glory of Jesus with the vision of First Isaiah.[177] Evans writes:

according to the evangelist this 'glory' is the glory which the prophet Isaiah saw and of which he spoke (Jn 12.41). The coordination of the quotations of Isa. 53.1 (Jn 12.38) and Isa. 6.10 (Jn 12.40) suggests that what was *seen* was the 'glory' which the prophet beheld in his famous vision of Isaiah 6 and what was *spoken*

---

[174] Though Ashton is cautious about drawing too strong a link here. *Understanding the Fourth Gospel* (Oxford: Clarendon Press, 1991), 495, n. 25. This is in accord with his reluctance to see the climax of Jesus' glorification as the Cross.

[175] Brenton, *Septuagint*, 889.

[176] Caird notes that *hupsothēnai* is given a double meaning in John's Gospel. It is an act of cruel human beings; it is an act of God in which God exalts the Son. 'The exaltation or glorification of Jesus is his death.' 'The New Testament Conception', 339. Caird continues, 'Elsewhere in the New Testament the Servant Song is regarded as a description of the sufferings that must precede the glory of Jesus. To John it is a description of his glory. For the glory of him who is in the bosom of the Father is seen as its brightest when he is numbered with the transgressors and bears their iniquity in order that they may be numbered with him and bear his glory' (Ibid., 349). Cf. also J. M. F. Heath, 'Isa 52–3 engages attentiveness to a pattern of visual piety ... viewers of the Servant who died for them are astounded at his earthly appearance; some reject him, others see and understand his glory received from God. This was taken up in early Christianity, including by Paul and John, as a mode of interpreting Jesus' earthly form and differentiating faithful from unfaithful spectators.' *Paul's Visual Piety: The Metamorphosis of the Beholder* (Oxford: Oxford University Press, 2013), 234.

[177] Bauckham notes that the same Hebrew verb for 'lifted up' can be found in Isaiah 6.1 and 52.13. *Gospel*, 53.

were the words of the Suffering Servant Song. That is to say, when (or because) Isaiah saw God's *glory* he spoke about God's *servant*, who is none other than the *logos* who became flesh and tabernacled with us.[178]

So as the Gospel prepares to turn to the Passion, there is this twofold association of glory, with exaltation and with the suffering of the Cross, and the language is so skilfully fused that neither motif can be detached from the other. The sign of God, the life that is the manifestation of the divine glory, with the power of healing like the serpent in the wilderness (Nm 21.9), is a sign transformed by the sinfulness of human response; the sign becomes a human being grotesquely marred by bearing the world's cruelty.

Also in Pilate's saying 'Behold the man' there is a double sense, as Gardner relates. Pilate seems to say 'Behold, in this broken and humiliated figure, man in all his glory', to show us 'who man is, and [that] this is the "glory" he deserves.'[179] But as well, as Gardner continues, 'this is also true glory – embodied in this man who, having put aside all power and authority in order to gain back the world, is now being exalted in his humiliation. Can you see this?'[180] And Christians can, if they have eyes to see that what is without *doxa* from a human standpoint turns out to be the ultimate disclosure of the redemptive character of God.

The Fourth Gospel, then, culminates in the necessity for the Son to be 'lifted up', an image referring both to crucifixion and to exaltation. There is Moses-imagery, deriving from the serpent lifted up by Moses. But vitally importantly there is also an echo of the last servant song of Deutero-Isaiah, in particular Isaiah 52.13.

For Williams: 'The seeing of glory in the cross and the crucified is … a synoptic moment of grasping together unreserved love and unqualified pain and abandonment … as such it is the vision of glory, the inner resource, the inner logic, of God's life … Seeing God in the midst of Godlessness is to see glory.'[181]

Roy Harrisville surveys the twentieth century aspects of the tension in Johannine studies over the centrality of the Passion. He adduces two further lines of evidence in favour of the Passion as the climax of the Gospel. First, he notes that the only occurrence of a voice 'from heaven' in John is in response to Jesus' 'Gethsemane' moment at John 12.27-8.[182]

---

[178] Evans, *Word*, 180–1, italics in original.   [179] Gardner, *John*, 165.   [180] Ibid.
[181] Williams, 'Theology in the Face'.
[182] R. A. Harrisville, *Fracture: The Cross as Irreconcilable in the Language and Thought of the Biblical Writers* (Grand Rapids, MI: Eerdmans, 2006), 212.

The coming of the voice at that precise juncture acts as confirmation that this moment of the seed falling into the ground and dying is indeed the appointed hour of God's action. Second, Harrisville reminds us that John moves the timing of Jesus' death to coincide with the slaughter of the Passover lambs. It is the *death* that echoes the delivering act of God at Passover.[183]

I am also persuaded by the analysis of a scholar far removed from the 'guild' of biblical studies, the priest-theologian W. H. Vanstone. In his lucid little study *The Stature of Waiting*,[184] Vanstone divides the Fourth Gospel's account of Jesus' life into two – the ministry in which Jesus does the 'work' of the Father, and the time from his being 'handed over' to his death. The latter phase is 'night' (Jn 13.30), the time when Jesus is the passive recipient of the cruelty of the world. But Vanstone's point is that *both* of these phases are dimensions of Jesus' glorification. Jesus shows God's nature in a series of signs, beginning with the water into wine. This is as Vanstone says 'the performance by Jesus of the *works* of the Father'.[185] The outworking of these signs culminates, disturbingly, in Jesus' delay at going to his friend Lazarus, as we have noted.

But Vanstone goes on to note that Jesus 'was not yet glorified' (cf. Jn 7.39). There is a further phase, which is not 'one single event but ... a continuum which includes His passion and death, His resurrection and ascension and possibly also His gift of the Spirit at Pentecost'.[186] Vanstone continues:

so clear and consistent is John's vision of this continuum that the raising up or exaltation of Jesus upon the cross is already invested, in the eyes of John, with that same glory which other writers discern only when He is raised up from death and exalted into heaven.[187]

Indeed, there is a particular moment 'when the divine glory becomes powerfully evident in Jesus, so evident as to be perceived by man and to impress and overwhelm them[sic] ... [this is] precisely the moment when Jesus is handed over and enters into passion.'[188] The powerless soon-to-be prisoner speaks the words, 'I am he', *ego eimi* (Jn 18.5), and

---

[183] Ibid., 216.
[184] W. H. Vanstone, *The Stature of Waiting* (London: Darton, Longman and Todd, 1982).
[185] Ibid., 73.
[186] Ibid., 74. Vanstone recognizes importantly that Jesus' glorification is not to be equated with the Passion alone.
[187] Ibid.   [188] Ibid.

his soon-to-be captors draw back and fall to the ground.[189] Vanstone sees this as the Johannine version of the Transfiguration. If we accept this, note again how radically John has transformed a preexisting motif. The glory of Jesus with the Father is now located not in a mountain-top experience, in the classic 'territory' of theophany and divine power, but in utter vulnerability, on the verge of arrest that is bound to lead to torture and death. Vanstone again, 'It is as Jesus is handed over, as He enters into passion, that the ultimate dimension of the divine glory becomes manifest in Him and evident to men.'[190] The climax of Jesus' work as sign of the depths of divine reality is that God so commits Godself to the world as to be 'handed over' – not as misfortune or failure, but as the completion of the mission of the Son (as Jesus' final words confess).[191] For Vanstone this is what love, at its uttermost, means – complete offering of the self and waiting on the response of the other. This for Vanstone is 'the shape of the glory of loving'.[192]

It is worth mentioning that this emphasis of Vanstone differs from the general view of the Johannine Jesus, which is as Ashton summarises,

> No doubt he is portrayed as subject to human weaknesses, hunger, fatigue, grief; but these in no way diminish the extraordinary control he exercises over his own fate ... Master of his fate, captain of his soul, his head bloody but unbowed, he never had to confront either the fell clutch of circumstance or the bludgeonings of chance.[193]

Vanstone's point is that out of the Johannine Christ's complete control, such that his captors reel back at a word, comes his handing himself over for the life of the world. It is complete handing over, to fell clutches and bludgeoning of the most total and dehumanising kind. I can agree with Ashton that 'Paradoxical as it may seem, "the glory of Christ crucified" is an accurate summary of John's own vision.'[194] But not that:

> The evangelist is inviting his readers to *see past* their own memory or knowledge of Jesus' agonizing death to his triumph over the forces of evil ... so as to

---

[189] For Williams, 'it is not fanciful to see in the falling-back of the soldiers confronted with Jesus in Gethsemane a serious echo of Old Testament imagery such as that in II Chr': 'Theology in the Face'.

[190] Vanstone, *Stature*, 75.

[191] 'Jesus, in handing Himself over, in passing of His own will from action to passion, enacts and discloses that which, at the deepest level, is distinctive of divinity' (Ibid., 89).

[192] Ibid, 99.   [193] Ashton, *Understanding*, 141–2.

[194] J. Ashton, *The Gospel of John and Christian Origins* (Minneapolis, MN: Fortress Press, 2014), 193.

compress the events of Good Friday and Easter Sunday unto a single momentous happening, the defeat of the prince of this world and the victory of Christ.[195]

The structure of the Gospel, with its repeated anticipation of the 'hour' that Jesus himself dreads, and its long treatment of the events of the night of his betrayal and the day of his death, does not seem to accord with this supposed compression. And the reduction of the complex dynamic of atonement to a 'Christus-victor' view means minimising the influence of Isaiah 52–3 on the Evangelist, and also does not seem to tally with that famous verse: 'God so loved the world that he *gave* his only Son' (Jn 3.16). Not 'sent to effect victory', but 'gave' to endure death.[196]

I now broaden these theological reflections beyond a narrow focus on the Fourth Gospel. As the divine Son, Jesus revises Christians' understanding of the Godness of God by his kenotic acceptance of human form (Phil 2). Like the God of the Hebrew Bible he remains an object of wonder (Mk 1.27, 2.12, etc.); but he conveys the Godness of God in the washing of his disciples' feet (Jn 13),[197] in love of enemy (Mt 5.44), in mercy for his persecutors, in the 'handing over' of his Spirit (Jn 19.30). Rumrich in his study of *Paradise Lost* comments 'The perfection of the Son's exaltation occurs only after he drops to apparently the nadir of doxa.'[198] Milton's Satan attempts his own glorification – the Divine Son renounces all status and suffers martyrdom, and that proves, as the revolution wrought by the Fourth Gospel shows us, to be not the nadir but the climax of *doxa*.

In being lifted up, in degrading execution, Jesus is also glorified, and begins moreover his journey back to the Father.[199] So Gardner: 'To say, then, that when [Christ] is lifted up on the cross he will be "glorified" is to

---

[195] Ibid.

[196] For Young, 'God needs to make reparation for creating a world like this, otherwise there can be no atonement ... Human beings are reconciled to God by God taking responsibility for all the "gone-wrongness", entering into the depths of our darkness and transforming it from within'. *God's Presence*, 247. That is why for Young, the Cross is 'the hour of glory' (Ibid.). Cf. also A. J. Byers, 'For the Fourth Gospel, divine glory is most prominently manifested not in Isaiah's glorious vision but in the scene on Golgotha where the embodied Word was crucified.' *Ecclesiology and Theosis in the Gospel of John* (Cambridge: Cambridge University Press, 2017), 198.

[197] Ramsey, *Glory*, 69–70.   [198] Rumrich, *Matter*, 173.

[199] Evans, *Word*, 180; Moody Smith, *Theology*, 100. On John 13.31, see Caird, 'Glory of God', translating the verse 'Now the Son of God has been endowed with glory, and God has revealed his glory in him' (271). Caird thus rightly stresses the link between divine glory and divine self-communication, and downplays the significance of glorification by humans.

say that in his death, the grain of wheat falling to earth and dying, God's deepest nature will be made visible.'[200]

JESUS' DERELICTION, GLORIFICATION, AND RESURRECTION

I make what may seem the very surprising suggestion that the cry of dereliction at Mk 15.34, 'My God, my God, why have you forsaken me?' is also a manifestation of glory.[201] How can this be, when the 'cry' seems to be Jesus expressing the apogee of doubt, and even a sense that his mission, so confidently embraced, has ended in failure. The gap between Father and Son seems at its greatest and most troubling in this moment. And yet precisely because it so sticks out from the Evangelists' depictions of their respective versions of Jesus, the cry must be of particular importance.

What then about the divine reality does the cry of dereliction signify? Taken in isolation, it might seem to suggest that indeed Jesus had been mistaken. Ethically exemplary and spiritually valiant, but mistaken as to possessing that unique invulnerable closeness to God that would enable him to confront the authorities and powers of the world. But glory is more than theophany; it operates through arrays or networks of signs. Networks that build 'reputation' and contribute to a sense of essence. In the light of the other aspects of the network of signs of Jesus' nature and mission (a network made as Richard Burridge has noted[202] so much richer by our having four canonical gospels), we can interpret rather differently the sign that is the cry of dereliction. We can apprehend it both as the ultimate mark of the humanness of the Incarnate Son, and the ultimate sign (before the death itself) of the extremity of giving in the compassionate salvific heart of the Triune God.

It is at the 'cry' that the extent and cost of the divine self-giving is shown to the full, in the agony of the Son, and in the agony of the Father that mirrors it.

One could develop this idea by reference to Jesus' nature as fully divine and fully human. Jesus revises human notions of glory first by making a messianic entry into Jerusalem in humble circumstances and company,

---

[200] Gardner, *John*, 116.
[201] So also F. Ó Murchadha, *A Phenomenology of the Christian Life: Glory and Night* (Bloomington, IN: Indiana University Press, 2013), 113.
[202] R. A. Burridge, *Four Gospels, One Jesus: A Symbolic Reading* (London: SPCK, 1994).

then by withdrawing each evening to pray, forsaking the chance for extra attention and celebrity. And lastly because he 'sets his face' to be 'handed over'[203] – he follows a destiny that is the destruction of all celebrity, all beauty.[204] He transcends the human desire to inflate reputations and then undercut them. Rather, as von Balthasar puts it, 'in the uttermost form of a slave, on the Cross, the Son's glory breaks through, inasmuch as it is then that he goes to the (divine) extreme in his loving, and in the revelation of that love'.[205]

In terms of semiotic categories, the signification of God finds a new and radical iconism in the one sent out of the Father's love, and lifted up to draw all to himself (Jn 12.32). For Gardner, God glorifies Jesus 'by revealing the splendor and power of his giving of himself, and this glorifies the Father by revealing the depths of his love for mankind'.[206]

This emphasis on Jesus' passion as the climax of his glory poses the question as to the significance of the Resurrection. Bultmann felt that the Resurrection added nothing to John's message of the Cross[207] but Moody Smith is surely right to say that 'The resurrection allows Jesus' ministry and message to be seen for what they were and are.'[208] For von Balthasar, 'The "glory" of Christian transfiguration is in no way less resplendent than the transfiguring glory of worldly beauty, but the fact is that the glory of Christ unites splendour and radiance with solid reality, as we see preeminently in the Resurrection and its anticipation through faith in Christian life.'[209]

In terms of our model of glory as sign, the Resurrection forms a necessary lens through which this extraordinary sign of God's nature as love can be seen. It forms the third lens of three-lensed seeing, the glory that transcends creaturely death and therefore connects all creatures with that eschatological promise that God will wipe away every tear. In the signification of the divine reality that we are exploring as glory, the Resurrection forms the complement to the Cross. If the Cross shows us the utter vulnerability and self-giving of the Godhead in solidarity with creatures and for their redemption, the Resurrection shows us the capacity of God to reach even into the uttermost darkness, spiritual

---

[203] See the analysis of Vanstone, *Stature* earlier in this chapter.
[204] In the terms of Isaiah 53, as discussed in Chapter 1.
[205] H. U. von Balthasar, *Mysterium Paschale: The Mystery of Easter*, transl. A. Nichols (San Francisco, CA: Ignatius Press, 1990), 29.
[206] Gardner, *John*, 149.   [207] Moody Smith, *Theology*, 123.   [208] Ibid.
[209] Von Balthasar, *GL1*, 124.

and physical, and transform it.[210] It also shows us the ultimate irresistibility of that power.

The notoriously incomprehending disciples may have thought, in the hours after the crucifixion, that they were living after all not in the messianic story but in Ecclesiastes. Everything in which they placed their hope turns out to be vanity. All their efforts too are vanity, and they might better have passed their time eating, drinking and being merry (not that the itinerant rabbi on whom they had placed their hopes seems to have neglected these things).

It is interesting that in the Gospel of John, which has been our principal source in understanding the way divine glory functions in the life and death of the Incarnate Christ, the signs of the Resurrection are progressive. In John 20 we read:

[3] Then Peter and the other disciple set out and went towards the tomb. [4] The two were running together, but the other disciple outran Peter and reached the tomb first. [5] He bent down to look in and saw the linen wrappings lying there, but he did not go in. [6] Then Simon Peter came, following him, and went into the tomb. He saw the linen wrappings lying there, [7] and the cloth that had been on Jesus' head, not lying with the linen wrappings but rolled up in a place by itself. [8] Then the other disciple, who reached the tomb first, also went in, and he saw and believed; [9] for as yet they did not understand the scripture, that he must rise from the dead. [10] Then the disciples returned to their homes. [11] But Mary stood weeping outside the tomb. As she wept, she bent over to look into the tomb; [12] and she saw two angels in white, sitting where the body of Jesus had been lying, one at the head and the other at the feet. [13] They said to her, 'Woman, why are you weeping?' She said to them, 'They have taken away my Lord, and I do not know where they have laid him.' [14] When she had said this, she turned round and saw Jesus standing there, but she did not know that it was Jesus.

The first sign, as seen by the disciple Jesus loved, is simply a shocking absence – grave-clothes but no body. The second sign, seen by Peter, is that this is an ordered absence, no mere sudden and violent grave-robbery.[211] The third sign is the appearance of the angels to Mary Magdalene. (Fascinatingly, the divine messengers appear only to a woman.) Finally comes the appearance of the Risen Lord, but he is not recognised until he speaks. One way to understand this progressive vision is that the narrator seeks to convey that the fact of resurrection cannot be grasped

---

[210] Von Balthasar, *MP*, 68: 'from out of the emptiness of the death of God streams forth glory (*doxa*) and sounds the resurrection word'.

[211] Cf. B. Lindars, *The Gospel of John: New Century Bible Commentary* (Grand Rapids, MI: Eerdmans; 1972), 601.

all at once. Like the fact of death, it only gradually sinks in. But for our purposes here it is important to note that the first sign, in the Fourth Gospel, is an absence, and that mystery in itself is a profound sign of the divine power at work. Not until the third sign is there an association with brightness, in the clothing of the angels.

The signs of the Resurrection, and the appearances of the Risen Jesus, transform the disciples' vision, such that their eyes are opened and they can not only begin to see the new, eschatological future – seeing the world through the lens of *Gloria in excelsis*, as we have termed it – but they are also empowered to see through the lens of *Gloria crucis* – to begin to see how it might be that in the economy of God the grain of wheat must fall into the ground, in John's image, or in Luke's language it was 'necessary that the Messiah should suffer these things and then enter into his glory' (Lk 24.26), to see (or at least begin to try to interpret), the sign of God that is the glory of the Cross. As the history of atonement theory shows, interpretation of this great sign – the victorious self-sacrifice of the Christ, in which the work of the Incarnation culminates – is a profoundly difficult process. But we at least have this multiple lens (ground slightly differently by our different sources) by which to see into the glory.

Denys Turner points us to a fascinating suggestion of Bonaventure, that it is in contemplation of the broken, crucified Christ that we 'pass out of this world to the Father', that we encounter truly the unknowability of God. 'For he who loves this death can see God, for it is absolutely true that *Man shall not see me and live* (Ex 33,20)'.[212] The sign of God that is Christ is at its truest, its most utterly transparent of the divine reality, at Christ's death. So Jesus reveals that divine power is in Farley's words 'mind-bendingly strange'.[213]

Arguably, understanding of divine glory was revised again as Christianity became the official imperial religion, and became conformed to the glory of the emperors. Whitehead put it chillingly when he wrote, 'When the Western world accepted Christianity, Caesar conquered; and the received text of Western theology was edited by his lawyers ... The brief Galilean vision of humility flickered throughout the ages, uncertainly ... The deeper idolatry, of fashioning God in the image of the Egyptian, Persian and Roman imperial rulers, was retained.'[214]

---

[212] The close of Bonaventure's *Itinerarium*, as quoted in D. Turner, *The Darkness of God: Negativity in Christian Mysticism* (Cambridge: Cambridge University Press, 1995), 133.
[213] Farley, *Wounding*, 97.   [214] Ibid., 96.

THE REMAINDER OF THE NEW TESTAMENT

Christologically, the writer to the Hebrews makes a hugely important statement when he describes Jesus as the 'radiance of the glory', *apaugasma tēs doxēs* (of God) (1.3). Melick calls this the closest the New Testament gets to a definition of glory.[215] Enigmatic as this term *apaugasma* is, it must be regarded as congenial to the semiotic understanding I am developing here. Jesus functions as radiance of something that cannot quite be seen of itself without him, he is *the* sign of a reality beyond our comprehension. The parallel phrase, *charactēr tēs hupostaseos*, 'exact imprint of [God's] being' emphasizes the exact fidelity of the semiosis. And as Ramsey notes, in the thought of Hebrews 2.9 'death crowned with glory and honour', 'we are near ... to the Johannine doctrine of the identity of Cross and glory'.[216]

Words from the root *dox-* are interestingly prominent in the First Letter of Peter (thirteen occurrences in five chapters). The main thought is eschatological – glory is conferred on Jesus at his Resurrection (1.21), and will be revealed finally to great rejoicing (4.13); praise and glory are the eschatological reward of the believer (1.7, 4.13, 5.1, 5.4); God's eternal glory in Christ is the believers' calling, even though they suffer for a little while (5.10); God will be glorified even by the Gentiles at the final judgement (2.12). All this fits with my sense that at the eschaton glory as sign and glory as essence cohere in a God-filled state into which human beings can be drawn.

It is the more unusual expressions in 1. Peter that are worth some attention; 4.14 reads 'If you are reviled for the name of Christ, you are blessed, because the Spirit of glory, which is the Spirit of God, is resting on you.'[217] That believers who have dared to call themselves '*Christianoi*' are reviled is a sign of the Spirit resting on them. The author has adapted Isaiah 11.2LXX by making the verb 'rest' (*anapauetai*) present, not future. The believers are a prolepsis of the eschatological state to come, they are already the visible dwelling-place of God, the manifestation of the redeeming reality.[218] I take up the idea of the life of believers as a sign of Christ further in Chapter 5. 1 Peter 1.8 also sees glory as already

---

[215] Melick, 'Glory', 105. Cf. Newman, *Paul's Glory-Christology*, 189, n. 54.

[216] Ramsey, *Glory*, 44.

[217] For further analysis of this verse, and the echo of Isaiah 11.2LXX, see P. J. Achtemeier, *1. Peter: A Commentary on First Peter* (Minneapolis, MN: Fortress Press, 1996), 309.

[218] Cf. also W. Grudem, *The First Epistle of Peter: An Introduction and Commentary* (Leicester: Inter-Varsity Press, 1988), 102–4; 179–80.

conferred on the believers in the quality of the joy with which they are filled. This joy is described as *dedoxasmenē*, glory-filled, no doubt a reflection of the presence of the 'Spirit of glory' resting on them. Finally, the odd use of the plural *tas meta tauta doxas* in 1.11 may refer to successive stages in Jesus' glorification, successive stages in his significa- tion of God's redeeming and honouring love.[219]

There is another slightly odd expression at James 2.1, which could be translated as 'our glorious Lord Jesus Christ',[220] or possibly 'our Lord Jesus Christ the glorious one'.[221] Again the thought is probably eschato- logical, referring to the state and status of the Risen Lord.

The author of 2. Peter has an interesting phrasing at 1.3, 'the know- ledge of him who called us by his own glory and goodness'. There is discussion as to whether the 'him' here is God or Christ; I share Melick's view that God is the reference here.[222] What we can know of God, God's outward manifestation, and God's *aretē* (perhaps more 'excellence' than mere 'goodness', and a parallel expression of what is manifest to us of God) draws from 'us' ('those who have received a faith as precious as ours', 1.1) a response. At 1.17 God's glory is *megaloprepos*, majestic, a 'grandiose' term, according to Melick, that aims to convey 'the splendour and brilliance of God himself'.[223] This then would be placed towards the 'essence' end of our spectrum of senses of divine glory.

From God Jesus received honour and glory at the Transfiguration. As J. H. Neyrey shows, the emphasis on this in 2. Peter is different from that of the Synoptics – there the vision on the mountain (as we saw earlier in this chapter) 'authorizes [Jesus'] way to Jerusalem, his cross and vindication' whereas in the epistle this event 'is perceived as a prophecy of his parousia'.[224] The final reference in 2. Peter, 3.18, is

[219] Achtemeier, *1 Peter*, 111; J. B. Green, *1. Peter* (Grand Rapids, MI: Eerdmans, 2007), 29. Ferreira sees here a contrast to the Fourth Gospel, in that 'For the author of 1 Peter, Jesus suffered first and then entered into his glory'. *Ecclesiology*, 155.

[220] M. Dibelius, *James: A Commentary on the Epistle of James*, transl. M. A. Williams (Philadelphia: Fortress Press, 1975), 128.

[221] S. McKnight, *The Letter of James: The New International Commentary on the New Testament* (Grand Rapids, MI: Eerdmans, 2011), 178. *Tēs doxēs* as a title would be very attractive to our thesis here, having the connotation that Jesus was the very Shekinah of God, all that could be known of the Godness of God. But this cannot be a confident reading; it requires a higher Christology than can be found in the Jewish Christianity of the period (D. C. Allison, Jr., *James* (London: Bloomsbury, 2013), 383.)

[222] Melick, 'Glory', 101.   [223] Ibid., 103.

[224] J. H. Neyrey, *2 Peter, Jude* (New York: Doubleday, 1993), 173.

doxological, an expression of the writer's praise of Christ, as are the two references in Jude (24, 25).

Finally, we need to consider briefly the references to the glory of God and of Christ in Revelation. Overwhelmingly the thought is doxological – praise and blessing is offered (1.6, 4.9, 4.11, 5.12, 5.13, 7.12, 11.13, 19.1) or should be offered (14.7, 15.4, 16.9). This is in keeping with the eschatological thrust of the great vision of Patmos; at the final conflict it is vital to stress what is and is not to be worshipped. At 15.8 there is what appears to be an echo of Isaiah 6.1f., or possibly 1 Kings 8.10–11 – 'the temple was filled with smoke from the glory of God and his power'. David Aune is wary of making too strong a connection with Isaiah 6, preferring to invoke a combination of the theophanic cloud and smoke in the Sinai tradition with the smoke filling the holy place when incense was burned, as in Leviticus 16.2.[225] However, Aune's point that the manifestation of the power of God is negative and associated with judgment and destruction, in contrast to other passages where no human can approach the cloud (Ex 40; 1 Kgs 8; 2 Chr 5–7),[226] perhaps draws us back to the associations with Isaiah 6. At Revelation 18.1 the *doxa* is of an angel. At 21.11, 23 the holy city is said to have the glory of God, another way of speaking of the Godness of God coming to be with human beings (21.3).

In this brief survey of the non-Pauline New Testament writers' use of *doxa* for the glory of God and of Christ (and related uses of forms of the cognate verb *doxazō*) we have found much doxology – the authors express their worship, and/or they affirm the worship-worthiness of God, and sometimes Christ. We have seen much affirmation of the glory of God, either glimpsed as sign, or affirmed as a way of expressing the essential Godness of God. We have also seen much mention of God's eschatological glorification of the Risen Jesus, and some sense that the Spirit-filled believer's life is a prolepsis of humans' participation in that consummation.

FURTHER REFLECTIONS

To return to the options discussed in the Introduction, it seems to me that a semiotic approach does most justice to divine glory as having physical expression but not being confined to the physical. This also accords with

---

[225] D. Aune, *Revelation 6–16* (Nashville, TN: Thomas Nelson Pubs, 1998), 880.
[226] Ibid., 881.

the unanimous reluctance of Hebrew Bible commentators to reduce *kavōd* to an attribute of God (such as honour) and their insistence that it connotes what can be apprehended of the Godness of God, Godness that is always both revealed and concealed.

Absolutely central though Christological reflection must be for Christian theology, I agree with Terrien when he claims that theology is too often reduced to Christology.[227] Within that frame there tends to be a focus on the extraordinary witness of the love that Jesus showed, especially at his Passion, and his atoning death for the sins of the world. Terrien's book helps to remind us that the Christian confession is also of the God of the thick darkness of Sinai, and of the terrifying visions of Isaiah and Ezekiel. A God of awe and mystery, whose primary characteristic is an absolutely free exercise of sovereignty. And even the Christic prophecies of the eschaton are not uniform expressions of love. As many Gospel passages stress, it will be a time of judgment.[228] Kaiser's thesis that the early confession 'Jesus is Lord' is also 'the Lord is Jesus'[229] is a reminder of the awesome nature of the glorified Christ.

Nevertheless, the world two thousand years after the Resurrection seems replete with suffering, which does not seem to diminish as the post–Resurrection era unfolds. I gave in *The Groaning of Creation* the outline of a compound theodicy, which seemed to me the least-worst answer to why God would create and sustain a world to which the disvalues of suffering and extinction seem so intrinsic. I continue to think of that compound formulation as the least-worst answer. But I am more and more struck by the untheodicies of Scripture itself (especially Job 38–41, Lk 13.1–5, and Jn 9.1–5). So I am confirmed in my sense of the need to explore the glory of God as honestly as possible, at the expense of attempting any formal theodicy. Humans cannot set limits on the power, the knowledge, or the love of God, nor should they imagine limits to the divine freedom. But also, our exploration of the New Testament suggests to me that we cannot be sure in every case what constitutes a disvalue. The Cross itself shows that wisdom, power and love can shine within an event of apparent folly, powerlessness and the exposure of innocence to hatred.

---

[227] Terrien, *Elusive Presence*. In some parts of the Church, theology is instead reduced to pneumatology, an equal impoverishment.

[228] Especially in Matthew – Mt 10.15, 11.22–24; 12.36–42. Cf. also John 15.6: 'Whoever does not abide in me is thrown away like a branch and withers; such branches are gathered, thrown into the fire and burned.'

[229] Kaiser, *Seeing*, chapter 5.

CONCLUSION

That concludes our brief survey of the way the biblical writers handle the theme of glory, including the way in which the Gospel of John transforms the Hebrew Bible's understandings of the theme in order to depict Christ as the central locus of apprehensible glory. I have also explored how it might be that even the bleakest moments of Christ's life might be indicative of glory.

As we began this chapter by noting, it is of the essence of seeing through lenses that it brings some aspects of objects into focus, while leaving other aspects blurred. Other lenses would give a different interpretative picture. My choice of threefold hermeneutical lens – *Gloria mundi, Gloria crucis, Gloria in excelsis* – may be evaluated both by the consistency of its results with the Scriptures, and by the generativity of the images produced by applying its use to other contexts. In Chapter 3, the lenses are applied to the natural world, but in a sense they will be used there in the reverse direction. Rather than looking at texts of glory, and considering the generativity of reading them as signs of God's reality, we shall look for signs of God's activity, and consider the potential of those signs to function as manifestations of glory.

3

Glory in the Natural World

The previous chapters explored the roots of the concept of divine glory and proposed a spectrum of ways that concept might be understood, from the semiotic to the ontological. At the ontological end of the spectrum, glory is a term referring to something very close to the essence of the reality of God, that for a sight of which Moses longs in Exodus 33. At the semiotic end of the spectrum, we located the theophanic disclosure of something of God through an encounter with a remarkable physical phenomenon, as in the covering of smoke on Sinai in Exodus 19, or that great sign of God we find in the life of Jesus, culminating in his Passion.

The purpose of this chapter is to explore whether contemplation of the natural world reveals signs of God's reality and hence discloses God's glory. While not at all ruling out the possibility of God giving great revelatory signs within the created order – the Resurrection is the greatest such example – we shall be concerned here with signs of God that have to be worked for, signs that can only be understood by deep engagement with phenomena that might otherwise appear ordinary. We might, like Isaiah, find ourselves caught up in a manifestation of extraordinary holiness, which causes us to confess that 'the whole earth is full of His glory' (Is 6.3). But I want here to wonder whether, under the guidance of the Holy Spirit, it might be possible to look at aspects of the created world in its ordinary operation in such a way as to reach the same conclusion.[1]

---

[1] Echoed at Sir. 42.16 ... as part of ben Sira's beautiful hymn to the Creator at Sir. 42.15–43.33. The NRSV translates this: 'The work of the Lord is full of his glory', which is helpfully consonant with a reading of glory as signification. John G. Snaith renders it 'the glory of the Lord fills his creation' (*Ecclesiasticus or The Wisdom of Jesus*

To cite my favourite Psalm: 'the heavens are telling the glory of God' (Ps 19.1),[2] not only in occasional theophany, but, as the Psalmist continues, 'day to day' and 'night to night'.[3]

Gerard Manley Hopkins writes, 'The world is charged with the grandeur of God/It will flame out, like shining from shook foil.'[4] Not, note, that God is continually 'shaking' the 'foil' to show off God's grandeur. Some of the biblical writers clearly assert that God communicates God's nature by causing mighty (and sometimes very destructive) phenomena in nature (of the very numerous examples of this, see, for instance, Ex 7–10, Job 38.35, Ps 144.5). But there is also a sense within Scripture of the natural rhythms of creation (famously at Eccl 3, but also see Ps 104, Job 38–41, and a number of places in the Gospels, e.g., Mt 16.2–3, Mk 11.13). As modern, scientifically informed readers of the creation, we think more or less instinctively of God putting in place systems and processes (which lie behind the rhythms of nature we observe) rather than acting directly and specially in every instance. Our question here is whether (and how) the results of these systems and processes may disclose to the discerning interpreter something of the nature of their creator.

What I want to suggest in this chapter is that our every encounter with the created world is an encounter that can be eloquent of the divine reality. Honest and reverent contemplation of God's creation should reveal these signs, and hence, the creation can speak of God's glory. Therefore, part of our task as creatures is to learn to contemplate the created world more attentively so as better to able to respond to such signs.

A remarkable recent example of such contemplation can be found in the playwright Dennis Potter's last interview with Melvyn Bragg, at a time when Potter's terminal cancer was very advanced. Here he is talking of the plum blossom outside his study window:

Son of Sirach (Cambridge: Cambridge University Press, 1974), 208. The creation as a whole may be thought of as one huge sign of the reality of God as creator.

[2] A thought perhaps echoed at Romans 1.20, '[God's] eternal power and divine nature, invisible though they are, have been understood and seen through the things he has made'. So A. M. Ramsey, *The Glory of God and the Transfiguration of Christ* (London: Longmans, Green, 1949), 46.

[3] A certain (Spirit-given) openness of heart is necessary to see and hear this ubiquitous glory. As A. M. Allchin puts it: 'By the transformation of the heart, through the realisation of God's presence there at the centre of man's being, it becomes possible to see that "heaven and earth are full of God's glory"'. *The World Is a Wedding: Explorations in Christian Spirituality* (London: Darton, Longman and Todd, 1978), 40.

[4] G. M. Hopkins, *Poems and Prose: Selected with an Introduction and Notes by W. H. Gardner* (Harmondsworth: Penguin, 1953), 27.

Instead of saying 'Oh, that's nice blossom'... I *see* it is the whitest, frothiest, blossomest blossom that there ever could be, and I can see it ... the newness of everything is absolutely wondrous ... There's no way of telling you, you have to experience it, but the glory of it ... The fact is, if you see the present tense, boy do you see it![5]

This is the intense seeing that can disclose to the Christian contemplative the 'flaming out' of the *kavōd* of God even in the most apparently ordinary aspects of the natural world. As Thomas Traherne claimed, 'The world is a mirror of infinite beauty, yet no man sees it.'[6] McGrath glosses this: 'the human eye all too often skims the surface of reality, failing to penetrate deeper, lacking commitment and discernment'.[7] It is that committed discernment that we attempt here.[8]

In a sense what we are doing here is turning round the hermeneutical lens with which we approached Scripture in the previous chapter. Instead of looking at glory-texts through a (threefold) interpretative lens based on an understanding of glory as typically semiotic, seeking the new insights about God and the world that might emerge from such looking, we now examine the ordinary operation of the world through this same lens, hoping to see signs of God in that world, and hence glory.

How can we justify this use of this threefold lens? First, it takes with utmost seriousness the relation of creatures to creator. In an age that is philosophically sceptical of inferences in natural theology, and psychologically suspicious of claims to visionary experience, it reiterates Hopkins's sense that the world is charged with God's grandeur. Second,

---

[5] D. Potter, 'An Interview with Melvyn Bragg' in *Seeing the Blossom: Two Interviews, a Lecture and a Story* (London: Faber and Faber, 1994), 5, emphasis in original. Potter, not any sort of conventional Christian, goes on fascinatingly to say 'religion to me has always been the wound, not the bandage'; ibid.

[6] T. Traherne, *Centuries* (London: Faith Press, 1960), 1.31.

[7] A. McGrath, *Re-Imagining Nature: The Promise of a Christian Natural Theology* (Chichester: Wiley-Blackwell, 2017), 69. Stephen Mulhall (writing of Heidegger and Wittgenstein) speaks of their sense of the need to maintain 'a continuous perception of the perplexing extraordinariness of the ordinary, a continually recovered sense of amazement at the sublimity of the world': 'Wonder, Perplexity, Sublimity' in *Practices of Wonder: Cross-Disciplinary Perspectives*, ed. S. Vasalou (Cambridge: James Clarke, 2012), 121–43, at 122. Sometimes a revived sense of wonder at the ordinary can be engendered by a technological advance; Claude-Olivier Doron gives the example of the microscope producing 'wonder in response to the ordinary, the despised and the minute': 'The Microscopic Glance' in *Practices of Wonder*, 179–200, at 180.

[8] With all humility, given T. S. Eliot's perception that acute discernment of reality 'is an occupation for the saint': *Complete Poems and Plays* (London: Faber and Faber, 1969), 190.

it does not reduce that creature-creator relation to a single image, such as that of God as designer, but allows the contemplation of creation to open up possibilities of gazing on hints of the depths of the divine reality. Importantly, it does not suppose that the 'God-element' in any given created entity or event is simple, or necessarily without ambiguity. Our understanding of glory as including the shocking and the ugly, gleaned from our reading of the Fourth Gospel in Chapter 2, stretches the range of what within the natural world might disclose for us the divine reality.

Note also that Christian contemplation of the natural world, in search of glory, is that attentive, vivid 'seeing the present tense' of which Potter speaks, but it is yet more, because all three of our lenses can be brought to bear: the lens of *Gloria mundi*, the wonder of the processes and particularities that result from the Creator's ingenuity and love; the lens of *Gloria crucis*, in respect of beauty lost, torn apart, or trodden under, which yet may serve a redemptive purpose; the lens of *Gloria in excelsis*, which promises us a future from which destruction has been eliminated. Scientific, poetic and prophetic seeing can thus be combined.

THE RELATION OF GLORY IN THE NATURAL WORLD TO THE ENTERPRISE OF NATURAL THEOLOGY

I mentioned earlier the widespread scepticism in recent theology at the use of natural-theological inferences from the character of the natural world to the character of God. I accept the telling criticisms offered by David Hume against versions of natural theology that seek to argue simply from the character of the natural world to the existence and character of God the Creator. Hume was right to point to the difficulty in arguing conclusively from nature, with all its apparent imperfection and suffering, to a single benevolent and omnipotent creator.[9] The combination of Hume's philosophical attack on the Enlightenment's deist forms of natural theology with Barth's theological attack on twentieth century liberal forms has been, until recently, devastating for the Christian enterprise of reading the things of God for the natural world.[10]

---

[9] For a summary and evaluation of Hume's arguments in this area, see J. F. Sennett and D. Groothuis (eds.), *In Defense of Natural Theology: A Post-Humean Assessment* (Downers Grove, IL: Inter-Varsity Press, 2005).

[10] For a brief summary of the difficulties of natural theology see J. Macquarrie, *Principles of Christian Theology* (London: SCM Press, 1977), 46–54.

There has however been an important revival of interest in the enterprise of natural theology, arguably initiated by the revival of the debate between theology and the natural sciences, in, for example, the work of John Polkinghorne,[11] and taken forward in the United Kingdom especially by Alister McGrath.[12] McGrath rejects definitions of natural theology that either presume a neutral starting point involving no religious beliefs or find no place for revealed truths.[13] Rather he wants to see natural theology as 'the re-imagination of nature' with 'a principled attentiveness'.[14] Two of the most helpful elements of McGrath's book are his emphases on (1) the importance of semiotics for a full account of how we 'read' nature and (2) the contribution of the imagination, and hence the value to natural theology of poetry and the other arts. Both are very much in accord with the approach taken here.[15]

The form of natural theology I pursue begins with a conviction as to the existence and character of the God revealed in the Christian Scriptures and understood within the Christian tradition, and then asks what further might be understood of the ways of that God with the world on the basis of the contemplation of creatures, and the systems within which they live.[16]

My approach closely resembles what is described by John Wisdom, when he writes:

---

[11] J. Polkinghorne, *Faith, Science and Understanding* (London: SPCK, 2000).

[12] McGrath, *Re-Imagining*, drawing on his *Darwinism and the Divine: Evolutionary Thought and Natural Theology* (Oxford: Wiley-Blackwell, 2011) and *A Fine-Tuned Universe: The Quest for God in Science and Theology: The 2009 Gifford Lectures* (Louisville, KY: Westminster John Knox Press, 2009). See also D. Fergusson, *Faith and Its Critics: A Conversation* (Oxford: Oxford University Press, 2009) and more generally, R. ReManning (ed.), *The Oxford Handbook of Natural Theology* (Oxford: Oxford University Press, 2013).

[13] McGrath, *Re-Imagining*, 181.   [14] Ibid., 8.

[15] McGrath's recent book is also important for his contextualization of Barth's attack on natural theology (ibid., 144–9).

[16] This is in keeping with the patristic approach as reported by H. U. von Balthasar, who notes that the Fathers 'possessed a theology of creation which ... attributed creation's aesthetic values *eminenter* to the creating principle itself': *The Glory of the Lord: A Theological Aesthetics*, Vol. 1, Seeing the Form, transl. E. Leiva-Merikakis, ed. J. Fessio, S.J., and J. Riches (Edinburgh: T&T Clark, 1982), 38. Post-Darwinian theology has been attracted to the move of distancing God from the details of creation by interposing scientific principles and processes. While fully committed to the explanatory value of these principles and processes, I consider that God cannot be distanced from involvement with creation, as immanent within it and as its 'depth dimension' (cf. J. Haught, *Deeper than Darwin: The Prospect of Religion in the Age of Evolution* (Oxford: Westview, 2004).

The theist goes over the details of his world, tracing and emphasizing patterns and connections that support his conviction, and presumably also trying to explain the gaps and recalcitrant facts that count against his belief. The very conviction from which he begins perhaps causes him to notice connections that would not otherwise have been noted, or to be painfully aware at other points of a seeming lack of connections. In the long run, the picture must be acknowledged to be ambiguous, in the sense that no finally conclusive proof in support of his conviction can be offered by the theist, or, for that matter, by the atheist who has been calling attention to other elements in the picture. Yet it has been important that the theist has exposed his conviction to a confrontation with the observable facts of our world, and has shown that is at least not incompatible with them.[17]

So what are the 'details' of the theist's world? Darwin himself was aware of two types of natural theology that could be done from the 'picture' that was emerging from his studies of the natural world. He wrote both:

1. 'what a book a devil's chaplain might write on the clumsy, wasteful, blundering, low and horridly cruel works of nature'[18]

and also, in concluding the 'tangled bank' paragraph that ends *The Origin of Species*

2. 'Thus, from the war of nature, from famine and death, the most exalted object which we are capable of conceiving, namely, the production of the higher animals, directly follows. There is grandeur in this view of life, with its several powers, having been originally breathed into a few forms or into one; and that, whilst this planet has gone cycling on according to the fixed law of gravity, from so simple a beginning endless forms most beautiful and most wonderful have been, and are being, evolved.'[19]

There are, then, grave problems in simply making inferences of Darwin's type (2) – that the biosphere reflects the work of a God of a grand design,

---

[17] J. Wisdom, *Philosophy and Psychoanalysis* (Oxford: Blackwell, 1953), 149. I note, however, that aspects of the Christian confession are not compatible with 'the observable facts of the world' at least as they are normally observed. It takes the kind of deep prayerful looking I discuss in this chapter to see the consonance between what is confessed – about the Resurrection, and the consummation of all things – and what is observed.

[18] C. Darwin, 'Letter to J. D. Hooker, dated July 13, 1856', Letter No. 1924, www. darwin project.ac.uk.

[19] C. Darwin, *On the Origin of Species by Means of Natural Selection, Or, the Preservation of Favoured Races in the Struggle for Life* (London: John Murray, 1859), 490.

which through the operation of laws gives rise to 'endless forms most beautiful', in the light of data of type (1).

As I noted previously, Hume was already very well aware of the apparent imperfection of creation. Darwin's work allows us to go beyond Hume by understanding:

1. the intrinsic connection between the competition between creatures and the refinement of their characteristics.[20] *The same process* – evolution by natural selection – engenders both. It is *through* 'war' and 'famine and death' that the 'grandeur' emerges.[21] Therefore, inferences to the ingenuity of a creator God cannot ignore God's involvement in creaturely suffering.

2. that cooperation in nature can be, indeed would be expected to be, self-interested. Indeed what might at first appear altruistic can often be explained in terms of evolutionary advantage to that individual or lineage. So very intricate networks of cooperative behaviour are perfectly compatible with a strongly Darwinian reading of the world. Therefore, observation of the extent of cooperation in the biosphere cannot be attributed to the loving design of the Creator without reference to competition between creatures.[22]

So the sort of natural-theological exploration pursued here is that described in the previous quote from Wisdom: provisional, looking with the eyes of faith, but very aware of ambiguity and difficulty, not attempting to *prove* anything, but hoping to bring to light connections not previously explored in sufficient detail. Crucially, I want to connect the observation of signs of God's working in the natural world with the concept of divine glory that we are exploring. Whatever in creation speaks of the work of the creator is a sign of the deep reality of God. Hence any such sign, however disturbing, or yet however apparently mundane, is a manifestation of glory.

It will be seen that I am arguing for a realist epistemology – our investigations can disclose, albeit fallibly and provisionally, something of what is really the case. But, crucially, I am arguing for an understanding of reality that requires both naturalistic, scientific investigation and

[20] Cf. H. Rolston, III, 'Disvalues in Nature', *The Monist* 75 (1992), 250–78.

[21] More generally, as Frances Young notes, 'What we perceive as good or bad is so closely intertwined as to belong to a single geotapestry': *God's Presence: A Contemporary Recapitulation of Early Christianity* (Cambridge: Cambridge University Press, 2013), 67.

[22] C. Southgate, 'God's Creation Wild and Violent, and Our Care for Other Animals', *Perspectives on Science & Christian Faith* 67 (2015), 245–53.

the imaginative resources of the religious poet.[23] So descriptions of nature are complemented and fed by descriptions of nature as creation, and vice versa. This is akin to the 'transcendent realism' for which Rowan Williams argues in his Clark Lectures.[24]

When Christians turn from their preoccupation with their own state with God, and God's mission in human affairs, to consider the non-human creation, two tendencies set in. One, very properly, is to lament the ways humans have damaged the natural world – a vital theme though not the one that occupies us here. The other is to dwell on the beauties of creation, on verdant meadows and coruscating sunsets. All too often when I have lectured or preached on the ambiguity of creation, my words have been preceded by hymns or powerpoints that stress only the beauty.[25]

That, in turn, is one of the driving forces behind this book. We know very well that the world is not in any simple sense a palace of beauty – it is full of beauty, but also of harshness and pain. It is rather, as Arthur Peacocke has it, reworking a line from Thomas Traherne,[26] a palace of *glory* in the sense being explored here, a place where the reality of God's nature as creator is reflected (and also a place where God's purposes in redemption are being effected).

THE RELATION OF GLORY IN THE NATURAL WORLD TO SACRAMENTAL THEOLOGY

The particular form of natural theology being attempted here, searching for the glory of the Lord in creation, clearly also has significant over-lap with sacramental theology, especially with theologies that stress the

---

[23] This emphasis on the importance of the contribution of the imagination is also found in McGrath, *Re-Imagining*.

[24] R. Williams, *Grace and Necessity: Reflections on Art and Love* (London: Continuum, 2005), 21.

[25] David Bentley Hart puts it well when he writes 'now that we exercise so comprehensive a technological mastery over whole regions of nature at whose mercy our ancestors lived out their lives, we enjoy the unprecedented luxury of being able to render the "natural" both remote and benign. It is we who summon it, rather than the reverse, and we do so at our pleasure; it dwells with us, not we with it. We are free to sentimentalize it or romanticize it, or even weave a veil of empty and unthreatening sanctity around it – until the moment when disease, age, infirmity, or random violence suddenly defeats us, or fire, flood, tempest, volcanic eruption, or earthquake surprises us by vaulting past our defenses. Then nature astonishes and horrifies us with its power, immensity, and sublime indifference': *The Doors of the Sea: Where Was God in the Tsunami?* (Grand Rapids, MI: Eerdmans, 2005), 47.

[26] A. R. Peacocke, *The Palace of Glory: God's World and Science* (Hindmarsh, South Australia: ATF Press, 2005).

sacramentality of the world.[27] It would not be right to attempt to make a hard and fast distinction between these areas of exploration. There is much in common between the sort of contemplation of the natural world advocated here, searching for glory, and contemplation of 'sacramentality'. Which Anglican thinker would want to say of the classic list of the Church's sacraments that they were not signs of the depths of the divine reality, gracious communications from God inviting a response? But I do want as far as possible to bracket off the Church's own sacraments from this discussion. As Oliver Quick insisted long ago, Christians cannot be satisfied with an account of the Church's sacraments that they are *merely* signs, not effective unless understood.[28]

A sacrament *effects* something that it also signifies. It effects it on a human scale, as a result of God's action combining with that of humans. It has an effect independent of an explicit response. The classic sacraments are moreover enacted by humans. Patrick Sherry identifies three components of such human-enacted sacraments – sign, word, and effectiveness. He shows how that classic combination is diluted as we speak more widely of the sacramentality of the world.[29] It is harder, when sacramentality is pointed to on a broader canvas, to see that by–definition effectiveness at work, or yet the role of the word, of performative utterance.[30] So I prefer to restrict sacramental language to those performed rituals that the Church believes to effect what they symbolise, and to explore not so much the sacramentality of the world as what might be termed its 'doxasticism' (ugly word), its capacity to manifest divine glory.[31]

The sort of manifestation of glory that concerns this book is, paradoxically, at once something much grander and wilder and at the same time more open and uncertain than the operation of a sacrament as usually

---

[27] For example, R. Thompson, *Holy Ground: The Spirituality of Matter* (London: SPCK, 1990); A. R. Peacocke, *Paths from Science towards God: The End of All Our Exploring* (Oxford: Oneview, 2001).

[28] O. C. Quick, *The Christian Sacraments* (London: Collins, 1964[1927]), 9–15.

[29] P. Sherry, 'The Sacramentality of Things', *New Blackfriars* 89 (2008) 575–90.

[30] Sherry, 'Sacramentality'.

[31] By which I do not mean the world's *doxology*, in the sense of the response of praise that all creatures return to their Creator. On human praise, see D. F. Ford and D. Hardy, *Living in Praise: Worshipping and Knowing God* (London: Darton, Longman and Todd, 2005); on the praise returned to God by the wider creation, see R. Bauckham, 'Joining Creation's Praise of God', *Ecotheology* 7 (2002), 45–59; C. Southgate, *The Groaning of Creation: God, Evolution and the Problem of Evil* (Louisville, KY: Westminster John Knox Press, 2008), chapter 6. But as we saw in Chapter 1, praise is not glory but creaturely response to it, which cannot add to the Godness of God.

conceived. What concern us here are signs of the unspeakable depths of God, and yet which are at the same time open ended, inviting of human response rather than effective *ex opere operato*. Such signs, once rightly contemplated, give a profound sense (though necessarily, given human limitations, very provisionally and incompletely) of the nature of those divine depths. But the human response is not on the same scale as the sign given, whereas the classic dominical sacraments are given in grace to be re-enacted and have their effect within the grain of human life. The characteristic response to those sacraments is thanksgiving and renewal whereas the characteristic response to glory, as we have already seen, is wonder.

So, our concern here is with signs of God in the ordinary operation of the world. Wendy Farley shows us that longing is the complement of glory; even as God communicates Godself through the creation, humans' longing for God can and should be expressed in the attention we give that creation. 'Desire', she writes, delights in [the goods of the world] as they are: lovely, perishable, temporary, replete with faults.'[32] I explore this theme of longing further in Chapter 5.

Lovely and replete with faults. This book began by calling attention to the ambiguity of the natural world. Talk of the sacramentality of the world, and of the contemplation of nature more generally, leads all too often to an overselective and oversentimental view of the world.[33] It is important and salutary for Christians to listen to the two verdicts on the natural world quoted earlier from Darwin, and the contemporary equivalent in Holmes Rolston describing the natural world, as 'random, contingent, blind, disastrous, wasteful, indifferent, selfish, cruel, clumsy, ugly, full of suffering, and, ultimately, death' but also 'orderly, prolific, efficient, selecting for adaptive fit, exuberant, complex, diverse, regenerating life generation after generation'.[34]

Awareness of this ambiguity in creation is essential if we are to conduct our exploration of signs of the reality of God in creation with honesty and clear-sightedness. As I have noted, this contemplation requires 'three-lensed seeing'. Such a multiple contemplative lens opens up a view of glory in which what we see of the struggles in the natural world – profoundly rich and important though the picture is – can be seen in counterpoint

---

[32] W. Farley, *The Wounding and Healing of Desire: Weaving Heaven and Earth* (Louisville, KY: Westminster John Knox Press, 2005), 15.

[33] A charge tellingly levelled at some feminist ecotheologians by Lisa Sideris in her *Environmental Ethics, Ecological Theology, and Natural Selection* (New York: Columbia University Press, 2003).

[34] H. Rolston, III, 'Does Nature Need to Be Redeemed?' *Zygon* 29 (1994), 205–29, at 213.

with a sense of God's depth of engagement with all creaturely suffering.[35] *Gloria mundi*, what the not-yet-completely redeemed world discloses of its creator, must be appropriated and understood in the context of *Gloria crucis*, of the gift of the Incarnate Christ and his self-surrender on the Cross, and God's identification through that Cross with every creature that suffers. But these two views in counterpoint must be combined in an overlapping triptych with an eschatological perspective, the creation as it will be in its transformed state, the song of the new creation, in which creaturely flourishing will be attained without creaturely struggle. As Michael Ramsey puts it, 'There is no escaping from the facts of this world. Rather does membership in the world-to-come enable Christians to see the facts of this world with the Cross and resurrection upon them.'[36] So also Stephen Garrett:

> By looking *protologically* back through Christ's redemptive suffering and glorious resurrection, we see the fittingness of the created order such that it declares the glory of God (Ps 19). Yet, it is precisely because of our need of Christ's redemption that we must look forward *eschatologically* towards the hope of glory.[37]

Later in his book Garrett helpfully locates the Eucharist as, in effect, the great training ground for three-lensed seeing. He writes:

> *our performance of the eucharist serves to triangulate our actions in the present as we live in the presence of the risen Christ in the Spirit with reference to redemptive history yet in light of his eschatological glory.* A robust imagination is necessary to integrate our remembering and envisaging – what *was* with what *is* and *is to come*, bringing a sense of meaning and understanding to the present so we can participate fittingly and creatively in the dramatic movements of God's triune life.[38]

It may fairly be asked: are there more lenses than three? In a sense there must be – indeed there must be any number of micro-lenses that arise when Christians perform the Scriptures[39] and view the world from the

---

[35] This engagement is emphasised in A. R. Peacocke, 'The Cost of New Life' in *The Work of Love: Kenosis as Creation*, ed. J. Polkinghorne (London: SPCK, 2001), 21–42; cf. also D. Edwards, 'Every Sparrow That Falls to the Ground: The Cost of Evolution and the Christ-Event', *Ecotheology* 11 (2006), 103–23; J. McDaniel, *Of God and Pelicans: A Theology of Reverence for Life* (Louisville, KY: Westminster John Knox Press, 1989).

[36] A. M. Ramsey, *The Resurrection of Christ: A Study of the Event and Its Meaning for the Christian Faith* (London: Fontana, 1961 [1945]), 33.

[37] S. L. Garrett, *God's Beauty-in-Act: Participation in God's Suffering Glory* (Eugene, OR: Pickwick Books, 2013), 130, emphasis in original.

[38] Ibid., 192, emphasis in original.

[39] Cf. F. Young, *The Art of Performance: Towards a Theology of Holy Scripture* (London: Darton, Longman and Todd, 1990).

perspective of particular texts. Nevertheless our three lenses of glory seem to me to frame the Christian narrative of God's ways with the world in an all-encompassing way, without the need to complicate the hermeneutical approach further.[40]

The Pauline literature seems to identify our place in the story as being firmly in the eschatological phase, though how 'realised' a transition to the eschaton is envisaged varies between those key texts on the non-human creation – Romans 8.19–23 and Colossians 1.15–20.[41] Somehow or other the liberty of the creation depends on humans coming into the liberty of their glory (Rom 8.21). So the creation still manifests its proto-logical glory with which it is 'charged', a glory full of 'groaning', a glory which we confess to be only the beginning of the story. McGrath quotes C. S. Lewis as calling nature 'only the first sketch of a greater glory'[42] and McGrath goes on 'A Christian natural theology helps us discern and appreciate the veiled beauty and wisdom of that "first sketch" while engendering hope and longing for which it signifies and promises'[43]: a pleasing restatement of two of the lenses of 'three-lensed seeing', *Gloria mundi* and *Gloria in excelsis*. So also Sarah Coakley, insisting that con-templation extends to the intuiting of '"the groaning of all creation" straining towards its final goal.'[44]

I am inviting consideration of creation with scientific and poetic eyes, but the contemplative approach I am outlining here, that of three-lensed seeing, stretches our discernment of glory still further. Three-lensed seeing brings to every entity and event in the drama of creation the perspective that God became incarnate and suffered for the transformation of the world, and thus identifies with all creaturely suffering, and that there will be a transformed state of that world in which those creatures that appear victims in the first story know flourishing in the third.[45] This last is a move to be made only with the utmost caution. It is disastrous, in my view, to suggest that simply to view an event of suffering within creation

[40] The three lenses are already found, in compressed and poetic form, in Colossians 1.15–20.

[41] D. G. Horrell, C. Hunt, and C. Southgate, *Greening Paul: Rereading the Apostle in a Time of Ecological Crisis* (Waco, TX: Baylor University Press, 2010).

[42] C. S. Lewis, *The Weight of Glory and Other Addresses* (Grand Rapids, MI: Eerdmans, 1949), 13.

[43] McGrath, *Re-Imagining*, 183.

[44] S. Coakley, *God, Sexuality and the Self: An Essay 'On the Trinity'* (Cambridge: Cambridge University Press, 2013), 84.

[45] Southgate, *Groaning*, chapter 5; Edwards, 'Every Sparrow'; McDaniel, *Pelicans*.

within this larger perspective of redemption and eschatological consummation somehow dissolves out the suffering of the creature, or prevents that suffering from troubling us. Apart from anything else, that would seem to me to make light of the depth of the travail of the Cross. There are no easy fixes or short circuits in theodicy.[46]

A different pair of the three lenses of seeing is powerfully caught in Gerard Manley Hopkins's famous sonnet 'The Windhover'.

> To Christ our Lord
>
> I caught this morning morning's minion king-
>   dom of daylight's dauphin, dapple-dawn-drawn Falcon, in his riding
>   Of the rolling level underneath him steady air, and striding
> High there, how he rung upon the rein of a wimpling wing
> In his ecstasy! then off, off forth on swing,
>   As a skate's heel sweeps smooth on a bow-bend: the hurl and gliding
>   Rebuffed the big wind. My heart in hiding
> Stirred for a bird, – the achieve of, the mastery of the thing!
>
> Brute beauty and valour and act, oh, air, pride, plume, here
>   Buckle! AND the fire that breaks from thee then, a billion
> Times told lovelier, more dangerous, O my chevalier!
>
>   No wonder of it: sheer plod makes plough down sillion
> Shine, and blue-bleak embers, ah, my dear,
>   Fall, gall themselves, and gash gold-vermilion.[47]

The first stanza is an exquisite description of a sign of God's ingenuity in creation, in the masterful flight of a raptor seen against the dawn sky.[48] The poet's 'heart in hiding/stirred for a bird, – the achieve of, the mastery of the thing!' As Gardner points out in his study of the Fourth Gospel, 'The poem works so powerfully on the reader because, like the Gospel, it first fills us with a conventional notion of glory and then shatters it, slinging us forward into something that our eyes can barely take in. It trains us to see.' He continues, 'This is what glory looks like: the falcon "striding" across the sky.'[49]

The second stanza 'slings' us into following the kestrel as its wings flash into the stoop, as mastery 'buckles'. The Christic reference is only in the

---

[46] As McGrath comments, a *theologia crucis* challenges the meaningfulness of (all) explanations of suffering: *Re-imagining*, 65.

[47] Hopkins, *Poems and Prose*, 30.

[48] T. Gardner, *John in the Company of Poets: The Gospel in Literary Imagination* (Waco, TX: Baylor University Press, 2014), 119.

[49] Ibid.

epitaph 'To Christ our Lord', but the 'lovelier, more dangerous' image of the 'buckled' flight speaks, as Gardner recognises, of what we encountered in the last chapter, the 'redefined' glory John sees in Christ's self-sacrifice.

At first sight 'The Windhover' is an appeal to beauty, to the colour of the falcon, and its rapport with the air.[50]

At second sight it is an appeal to ingenuity, 'the mastery of the thing'.

Looking more deeply, the poem appeals to beauty and ingenuity in a killer, a bird that sinks talons into mice and carries them off, often still alive.

Hopkins wants us to have fourth and fifth sight – the dedication 'To Christ our Lord' invites us to see Christ in the beauty, 'the achieve' of the bird – and armed with this theological connection, to see Christic signs in bleakness, and toil, and dying life.

Hopkins will be our guide into our more intensive investigations of the natural world in the second half of the chapter. I am committed to the notion that signs of God can be seen in that world, that in Augustine's words 'I saw [God's] invisible things understood through the things which are made',[51] or to offer a more contemporary quotation 'All finite things in one way or another reveal something about God.'[52] Andrew Louth talks of 'the way in which we may overcome our cultivated deafness and hear the 'whisper of His ways, becoming aware of the signs of creation that point to God and do not simply reflect our own expectations.'[53]

In this chapter I pick up on Hopkins's assertion that 'We see the glories of the earth/But not the hand that wrought them all',[54] that creatures can manifest something that is a sign of the depth of the reality of their creator, while that creator's essential nature remains hidden. As I have sought to emphasise, we must not however be selective and suppose that beautiful sunsets teach us of God, but we can ignore ugliness in nature. Diogenes Allen reminds us that, 'We are not to take the pleasantness of

[50] Also, incidentally, an appeal to the power of human interpretation, what Hopkins called 'instressing' – 'I *caught*'. See later in the chapter for more on instress and inscape.
[51] Quoted in A. Garcia-Rivera, *The Community of the Beautiful: A Theological Aesthetics* (Collegeville, MN: The Liturgical Press, 1999), 30.
[52] Ibid., 82.
[53] A. Louth, *The Wilderness of God* (London: Darton, Longman and Todd, 2003), vii–viii.
[54] Hopkins, 'Nondum', quoted in H. U. von Balthasar, *The Glory of the Lord: A Theological Aesthetics*, Vol. 3, Studies in Theological Style: Lay Styles, transl. A. Louth, J. Saward, M. Simon, and R. Williams; ed. J. Riches (Edinburgh: T&T Clark, 1986), 367. Hopkins here cites Isaiah 45.15.

nature as evidence of [God's] care and ignore the fact that the very same laws of nature also bring us storms, earthquakes and drought.'[55]

How then can the ugliness, and the ubiquitous suffering, within creation, be associated with glory? How can God be seen in them? This is the problem I wrestled with in *The Groaning of Creation*, and I offered some rather brief suggestions there as to how the triune God might interact with creatures. I talked about God, Father, Son, and Spirit giving to creatures existence, form and particularity, *and* also delighting in their flourishing and suffering and lamenting with them in their pain.[56]

God's *kavōd* is reflected in this universe in all sorts of ways – in the sheer extent of the divine work, containing even within this space-time continuum over a hundred billion galaxies each containing perhaps a hundred billion stars, and around these, we are increasingly coming to realise, millions of planets that may well be capable of supporting life; in the vast timescales over which the divine purposes have been in operation, including on Earth the seven hundred million years or so before life even existed even in its most primitive form, and possibly twice that length of time again before the first eukaryotic cell evolved; in the tectonic processes that move continents, with a strength far beyond anything a human civilisation could ever contrive (even the 'minor' slippage between plates that caused the tsunami of December 2004 had the energy of ten thousand hydrogen bombs); in the myriad ingenious ways that creatures find to live and reproduce; and in the human animal (we shall return in Chapter 4 to Irenaeus' famous saying that the glory of God is a human being fully alive).

For Peacocke, creation is both symbol and instrument of God's purposes.[57] It must therefore symbolise God's nature. This, I would say, is not only in the great beauty we see there, but also in the unimaginable spatial and temporal scale of the cosmos, and the enormous power of the forces that shaped, and continue to shape it. Creation has also effected God's purposes in making possible the emergence of the human, the creature in the image of God, and ultimately the emergence of the possibility of incarnation. But what of the cost? What of the ugliness of so much natural process, of creatures torn apart while still living, or eaten out from the inside by parasites?

---

[55] D. Allen, *Temptation* (Princeton, NJ: Caroline Press, 1986), 49.
[56] Southgate, *Groaning*, chapter 4.   [57] Peacocke, *Paths from Science to God*, chapter 9.

I begin to explore this via a quotation from Traherne, who writes:

The WORLD is unknown till the Value and Glory of it is seen, till the Beauty and Serviceableness of all its parts is considered. When you enter into it, it is an Unlimited field of Variety and Beauty where you may lose yourself in the multitude of Wonder and Delights. But it is a happy loss to lose oneself in admiration of one's own Felicity: and to find God in exchange for oneself, Which we then do when we see him in his Gifts and adore his Glory.[58]

This short passage has several themes that cohere with the exploration of this book. First, the importance of contemplation. The value and glory of the world must be seen, not just on its surface but in its parts and their interconnection (their 'serviceableness'). To see truly in this way is to be caught up, in von Balthasar's sense,[59] to lose one's own self, in a measure, for only in that self-giving, that movement of deep trust, does the contemplative become sufficiently open to receive what can be received of God.[60] But even to be thus caught up is not to see God wholly, but to 'see him in his Gifts and adore his Glory'. The glory of God is usually best thought of as only a sign of God's nature, but because it is utterly true signification, it provokes the response of awe and adoration.

'Serviceableness' in that passage from Traherne is a fascinating word. He will have had a sense (who in an agrarian society would not?) of the redness in tooth and claw of natural processes. He cannot have had a sense of how those processes drive evolution – that had to wait two hundred years for the insights of Darwin. But messy as the biological world clearly was, Traherne was confident that it was serviceable in effecting God's purposes. The creation is able to be an instrument of the

---

[58] Quoted in Peacocke, *Palace*, 75.

[59] H. U. von Balthasar, *The Glory of the Lord: A Theological Aesthetics*, Vol. 7, Theology: The New Covenant, transl. B. McNeil C.R.V., ed. J. Riches (Edinburgh: T&T Clark, 1989), 24.

[60] Paul S. Fiddes puts it thus: The human interpreter of signs empties herself in the direction of others; this human self-emptying ... is held within the love of the triune God. Just as God does not lose God's self in self-emptying, but becomes more truly God, so the human self becomes itself even as it gives itself away. Here we can bring together the perception of semiotics that signs are always vanishing into something else (an object, another sign) and the theological affirmation that the signs of the world are bursting with divine presence and glory. Both can be true, because they share in the trinitarian movement of a vanishing for the sake of another. Not only the interpreter, but created signs themselves exist in the self-giving movement of God. Thus they witness to the glory of God, not by denoting God as an object or describing God literally. They signify God by drawing the interpreter to participate in a God who is communicating and giving God's own self: *Seeing the World and Knowing God: Hebrew Wisdom and Christian Doctrine in a Late-Modern Context* (Oxford: Oxford University Press, 2013), 289–90.

divine purpose. Not as being the medium of the caprices of a divine being who is forever suspending natural laws, but in that the very created processes themselves are 'serviceable'. Through them God has given rise to astonishing creaturely beauty, diversity and creativity, so that indeed to attend to them is to be caught up into an awareness of the Creator's glory.

But those who try and think their way through this must still stub their theological toes on the cost, the imperfection, the suffering, the apparent waste within biological processes. This is a problem that has preoccupied me in the last few years. It needs further analysis here both because of the understanding of glory being explored here, which does not allow glory to be reduced to mere beauty, and because in order to see the world aright, we must dispense with the notion that God's activity can be separated from the ugliness and suffering we see in nature. I therefore make clear in the next section why assigning disvalues in nature to forces other than the activity of God will not work.

EXCURSUS: FALL-EVENT-BASED EXPLANATIONS OF DISVALUE IN NATURE

As I noted in the Introduction, it is essential to dispense with the traditional view that God's perfect – not just serviceable but perfectly beautiful and good – world was disrupted by the rebellion of the first humans in Eden (Gen 3). This is so much at variance with the chronology offered by evolutionary science that alternative ways of reading that Genesis text must be found.[61]

A type of fall-story with potentially more theological traction is some form of primordial fall. The possibilities are explored by Michael Lloyd,[62] whose preference is for an angelic fall, but who has to concede that there

---

[61] The only scholars to make a recent attempt to 'park' evolutionary suffering on human sin are William Dembski, *The End of Christianity: Finding a Good God in an Evil World* (Milton Keynes: Paternoster, 2009) and (in a different way), Stephen Webb, *The Dome of Eden: A New Solution to the Problem of Creation and Evolution* (Eugene, OR: Wipf and Stock, 2010). See C. Southgate, 'Does God's Care Make Any Difference? Theological Reflection on the Suffering of God's Creatures' in *Christian Faith and the Earth: Current Paths and Emerging Horizons in Ecotheology*, ed. E. M. Conradie, S. Bergmann, C. Deane-Drummond, and D. Edwards (London: Bloomsbury, 2014), 97–114, at 104–5 for comment on these eccentric solutions.

[62] M. Lloyd, 'Are Animals Fallen?' in *Animals on the Agenda: Questions about Animals for Theology and Ethics*, ed. Andrew Linzey and Dorothy Yamamoto (London: SCM Press, 1998), 147–60; 'The Humanity of Fallenness' in *Grace and Truth in a Secular Age*, ed. Timothy Bradshaw (Grand Rapids, MI: Eerdmans, 1998), 66–82.

is no strong evidence for the existence of these 'revolting' angels, and that this element of his argument has to be 'carried' by the rest. A more sophisticated option is offered by Neil Messer in his effort to recruit Karl Barth to the dialogue between theology and evolution.[63] Barth's language of *Das Nichtige*, a factor that is not willed by God but arises in tandem with creation and affects it negatively, is used by Messer to suggest that there are factors within evolution that are not divinely willed. This might be called a 'mysterious fallenness' strategy in evolutionary theodicy.

I have endeavoured to show, however, that such a move is:

1. not necessarily in keeping with Barth's own thought;
2. scientifically incoherent, since it dissects out the theory of natural selection into desirables and undesirables, neglecting the fact that the two are integrally bound together in Darwinian understanding;
3. theologically problematic. A huge price is paid when a Christian theologian seeks to assert that the sovereign Lord of the universe sought to create a good and suffering-free world, and was unable to do so.[64]

When I write of glory as a sign of what is most deeply real, and posit that that deep reality is reflected in a creation that is ambiguous – full of suffering as well as of beauty – I do not mean to imply that all suffering is a function of the character of the creation. Much of the creaturely suffering that has afflicted the world in the last few thousand years is directly the result of human sin, and indirectly of the evil forces that aid and abet that sin. I address the problem of moral evils in Chapter 4. However, my point here is that I do not consider that either human agency, or some underlying evil force, was able to alter the character of the creation as a whole, or that all disvalue can be ascribed to such activity. Much suffering in the history of the world is a product of the

---

[63] N. Messer, 'Natural Evil after Darwin' in *Theology after Darwin*, ed. M. S. Northcott and R. J. Berry (Milton Keynes: Paternoster, 2009), 139–54.

[64] See C. Southgate, 'Re-Reading Genesis, John and Job: A Christian's Response to Darwinism', *Zygon* 46 (2011), 370–95. It is important to clarify that I am not supposing that evil forces do not affect the world as it is. It seems impossible to do justice either to the New Testament, or to the experience of the Christian tradition, and the Church's continued need to retain a ministry of exorcism, or to contemplate our contemporary experience – that even something as generative as the Internet has become a vehicle for computer viruses, confidence tricksters, pornography and the grooming of minors – without a conviction as to the addictiveness and multiplicativeness of sin. What I am questioning is whether evil has the power to frustrate God's will for the underlying physical processes of the universe.

processes by which the Earth was made, and by which life evolved and became the marvellously diverse and beautiful phenomenon that we observe it to be.

FALL-EVENT-FREE ACCOUNTS OF DISVALUES IN NATURE

A theological narrative lacking a chronological fall is not without its problems. First, ways must be found to read not only Gen. 3 but also the repeated affirmation in Gen. 1 that what was created was *tôv* – good, even *tôv meōd*, very good (1.31).[65] Second, a necessary implication of supposing that evolution by natural selection was God's will in creation, and not a mixture of divine creativity and some primordial negativity (Messer) or 'wheat' interfused with 'tares' sown by an 'enemy',[66] is that such a creation was the only way, or the best way, in which to give rise to the sorts of values that we observe in an evolved and evolving creation. In other words, this was *the* way God could give rise to a 'serviceable' creation, despite all the individual struggle and suffering this involved for myriad creatures, many of whom lived and died without any fulfilment as creatures.[67] That in turn poses the question, why *could* God not have given rise to a pain-free creation – a question sharpened by the eschatological hope that indeed such a pain-free state will be the final consummation of the creation.

Faced with such difficulties, it is natural to consider the theological strategy of Wesley Wildman, who poses very sharply the question of natural evil, and the associated question – why did God not just create heaven? Wildman concludes that the logical way forward is to embrace a form of 'ground-of-being' theism. He writes that suffering in nature is 'neither evil nor a by-product of the good. It is part of the wellspring of divine creativity in nature, flowing up and out of the abysmal divine depths like molten rock from the yawning mouth of a volcano'.[68] God here is the ground of being, but neither loving, nor indeed malevolent,

---

[65] The Hebrew word *tôv* means not so much 'perfect' as 'fit for purpose'. See Southgate, *Groaning*, 14–15.

[66] N. Hoggard Creegan, *Animal Suffering and the Problem of Evil* (New York: Oxford University Press, 2013).

[67] Southgate, *Groaning*, 47–8.

[68] W. J. Wildman, 'Incongruous Goodness, Perilous Beauty, Disconcerting Truth: Ultimate Reality and Suffering in Nature' in *Physics and Cosmology: Scientific Perspectives on the Problem of Natural Evil*, ed. N. Murphy, R. J. Russell, and W. R. Stoeger, S. J. (Berkeley, CA: CTNS and Vatican City: Vatican Observatory, 2007), 267–94, at 294.

rather the author of 'weal and woe alike' (Is 45.7). Wildman's God is not a benevolent force in the cosmos, but merely a creative force, a source of energy rather like a waterfall. But not a personal, loving being.

One could indeed adapt the sort of theology of glory being explored here to such a strategy. If the deep reality of God, signified by the *kavōd* of God, were indeed this morally indifferent creativity, then that *kavōd* would be recognised most truly in events such as stellar supernovae, and on Earth in volcanic eruptions and tectonic shifts, rather than in the tender actions of creaturely motherhood, or indeed the delicate beauty of a flower. Such a *theologia gloriae* could be articulated in a very persuasive way. It does indeed have a certain amount in common with the depiction of *Gloria mundi* I am developing here (and illustrate later in this chapter using case studies). But I continue to hold to the notion that the doctrine of God emerging from the Scriptures is overwhelmingly personal, suffers with the suffering, and redeems the world through the Cross of Christ. The theological task is therefore to give some account of that divine personhood, care for creatures, and costly atoning redemption, rather than to abandon it because it makes theodicy hard (which it does).[69] In other words, the lenses of *Gloria crucis* and *Gloria in excelsis* necessarily change the way we see through the lens of *Gloria mundi*, and return us to an understanding of God as taking personal, and infinitely costly, responsibility for the disvalues in creation.[70]

Having rejected, then, moves that assign the cause of the disvalues in evolution to some sort of fall-event, and moves based on parting company altogether with the benevolence of God, I note McGrath's proposal that the natural world is 'more than morally and aesthetically *ambiguous*; it is theologically *opaque*'.[71] This seems to be first because of the need to view the world eschatologically in order to have a clear picture – in this McGrath goes some way towards my model of three-lensed seeing. But it is also, I suspect, because, like so many Christian thinkers, he finds it difficult to associate ambiguity with God.

In order to see into the apparent opacity of the world, I claim we have to be bolder, to recall that description in Isaiah 45 of God as the God of

---

[69] Ultimately theodicy – carried out not as a reductive philosophical defence but as real exploration within the life of faith – must rest on trust (cf. von Balthasar on the theodicy of the Psalms and Job: *GL1*, 131–3). It must be carried out within the second naïvete that apprehends the force of all critical questions, but does not allow them to disable spiritual and theological search.

[70] Southgate, *Groaning*, chapter 4; Young, *God's Presence*, 247, on God taking responsibility.

[71] McGrath, *Re-Imagining*, 98, emphasis in original.

'weal and woe alike',[72] to accept, at least in part, the logic of Wildman that the character of the creation does not speak straightforwardly of the personal omnibenevolence of God, and to recognise that God is the author – whether through logical constraint or not – of an ambiguous world full of value and disvalue alike. But we also need, so this book contends, to adopt that three-lensed seeing that looks honestly at the creation as it is, *and* sees, albeit through a glass darkly, the eschatological hope for a suffering-free world, *and* recognises the cruciform character of so many situations in creation, and the intimate connection between the suffering Christ and the sufferings of all sentient creatures. McGrath has a similar perception,

A natural theology engages nature as it is presently known and experienced; yet this must be set against the eschatological hope of a renewed world, which will displace the broken and damaged reality that we now know, experience and inhabit. A theology of the cross thus invites us to recognize the penultimacy of the present natural order and our attempts to develop a natural theology based on it.[73]

We are now in the territory of a further option in the area of the theodicy of evolution, which may be termed the 'passion play' option, language much promoted by Holmes Rolston, III. This idea of the 'cruciformity' of the creation proposes that threaded through the creation – not because of a Fall but because of the will of the Creator – are suffering and lives sacrificed for others. The narrative of evolving life is tough and full of casualties, for whatever reason or reasons. It is like a drama in which sacrifices are continually asked of the weak, the vulnerable, the blameless. Rolston himself would say that it was a drama that also contains, intrinsic to it, processes of redemption – a point of view that I have challenged.[74] A related approach to Rolston's seems to be at work in Celia Deane-Drummond's invocation of 'theodrama' as the most appropriate genre into which to cast the interaction of theology with evolutionary biology.[75]

---

[72] For a similar thought, see Job 1.21; Sir 33.15.

[73] McGrath, *Re-Imagining*, 98. Very much the approach adopted here, although I would myself prefer the verb 'transform' to 'displace'. The new creation is a transformation, not a replacement, of the old.

[74] Southgate, *Groaning*, 45.

[75] C. Deane-Drummond, *Christ and Evolution: Wonder and Wisdom* (Minneapolis, MN: Fortress Press, 2009). I find Deane-Drummond's emphasis on theodrama profoundly helpful. I am not wholly clear what her terminology of 'Shadow Sophia' (185–91) is intended to connote, but it seems to me that her evolutionary theodicy falls most naturally into a passion play category (though it could also be understood in terms of mysterious fallenness).

A poet on whom we shall rely extensively in Chapter 4 is R. S. Thomas, and a version of this view of creation as profoundly ambiguous can be found in Thomas's work. M. Wynn Thomas says that in his early collection *The Stones of the Field,* R. S. T. 'pictured the world not as reliably ordained and managed by a humanity-orientated God, but as provocatively neutral – glorious and harsh in equal measure, and expressing something of divinity in both its aspects.'[76] Many elements of the created world are not in any sense beautiful, and yet they are God's creation and in their own way eloquent of the work of God. Even after reflecting on his extraordinary encounter with a flock of goldcrests in a thicket in Lleyn, one of the few experiences of divine disclosure on which R. S. Thomas meditates directly, autobiographically, as opposed to in poetry, he goes on 'What talons and beaks were not in waiting for [them] on the way south'.[77] He reflects that

Life has to die in the cause of life. If there is any other way on this earth, God has not seen fit to follow it . . . As far as this world is concerned, Isaiah's vision of the wolf dwelling with the lamb, and the leopard lying down with the kid, is a myth. The economy doesn't work like that.[78]

It is easier, then, to accept the 'groaning' state of creation, and to insist that it 'can be, simultaneously, reflective of a divine fullness and glory'.[79] In the poem 'Rough', the system is accepted as 'Perfect/a self-regulating machine of blood and faeces.'[80] Insofar as the 'economy' testifies to the system God has 'seen fit' to create, that economy testifies thereby to the divine nature; the 'talons and beaks' manifest divine glory.

Thomas makes no effort to resolve this paradox into a theological system. Rather he is at work 'preserving and balancing its existence and, ultimately, moving toward a deeper acceptance of what he seems to view as the fundamentally paradoxical nature of existence itself'.[81] In his poem 'January', R. S. Thomas paints a picture of a wounded fox. D. Z. Phillips comments that 'the poet is faced with building a bridge between two irreconcilables, grace on the one hand and various types of affliction on

[76] M. W. Thomas, *R. S. Thomas: Serial Obsessive* (Cardiff: University of Wales Press, 2013), 32.

[77] Quoted in C. Morgan, *R. S. Thomas: Identity, Environment and Deity* (Manchester: Manchester University Press, 2003), 70.

[78] R. S. Thomas, *Autobiographies* (London: Orion Books, 1998), 95–6.

[79] Morgan, *R. S. Thomas,* 72.

[80] R. S. Thomas, *Collected Poems 1945–1990* (London: J.M. Dent, 1993), 286.

[81] Morgan, *R. S. Thomas,* 73.

the other'. Phillips continues perceptively, 'Perhaps the idea of God must itself incorporate, from the outset, those elements which we confusedly suppose are incompatible with it.'[82]

In a sense, that category of creation as passion play is the one in which I also, necessarily, find myself. I cannot give an account of why it was metaphysically impossible for an utterly transcendent, utterly sovereign God, the God to whose *kavōd* the wondrous scale of the universe bears witness, to give rise to a suffering-free world. That constraint on the possibilities open to the creator of the cosmos *ex nihilo* does remain a mystery in my scheme. I can only say that, *scientifically,* the notion that this is the only sort of universe where values of beauty, ingenuity and diversity could *evolve* (as opposed to being beamed down by divine *fiat*) is highly plausible.

Note that this constraint on God must be presumed to be a logical constraint. It is generally accepted that God's omnipotence does not extend to being able to make 2 + 2 = 5, or the mathematical number e greater than pi. What I am inferring scientifically and theologically, without being able to demonstrate it in logical terms,[83] is that there is a logical constraint on God being able to give rise to this sort of world except by a long and (in terms of creaturely suffering) costly process of evolution by natural selection.

Such an assertion is properly the subject of much debate, and indeed is rejected by many as an unsatisfactory constraint on the power of God. Typically, such thinking leads people back into some version of a fall-account, and I hope I have shown in this brief survey that the theological costs of such a move are in fact higher.

Two other moves are important in trying to understand how indeed God can still be thought of as loving when that God is the creator of processes leading to so much suffering.

First, I return to von Balthasar's ur-kenosis or deep intratrinitarian kenosis, which we encountered in Chapter 1.[84] In this view – 'The Father gives himself into the otherness of the Son, which is then returned in

[82] D. Z. Phillips, *Poet of the Hidden God: Meaning and Mediation in the Poetry of R. S. Thomas* (London: Macmillan, 1986), 20.

[83] We should not be afraid to admit an ignorance of the logical undergirdings of how universes come to be, any more than we should allow our ignorance to restrain our enquiry into whether different sorts of universe are possible.

[84] H. U. von Balthasar, *Theo-Drama, Theological Dramatic Theory,* Vol. 4: The Action, transl. G. Harrison (San Francisco: Ignatius Press, 1994), 323–4; Southgate, *Groaning,* chapter 4.

obedient love, with the Trinity in effect seen as "a community constituted by differences which desire the other"'[85] – self-giving is of the very nature of the triune persons, and creation is the overflow of that outpouring of love. This ur-kenosis ties the *theologia gloriae* to the *theologia crucis*; it asserts that the wild, mysterious holiness of the God of the Hebrew Bible theophanies *is* from all eternity that holiness that hands itself over in the Incarnate Son for the life of the world. And conversely, the glory of that Son at his Passion speaks of the divine reality as it has always been (not of some impulse rescue mission responding to the failures of human beings).

Paul Fiddes also lists Hopkins with Balthasar and Bulgakov as those who propose this sort of kenosis. Fiddes writes:

In the doctrine of the Trinity the source of all signs lies in a different kind of movement, in a rhythm of mission ('sending') which makes room for the world. This movement also, however, involves a self-emptying (*kenōsis*) of God. With Sergius Bulgakov, Balthasar, and the poet Gerard Manley Hopkins we may discern three moments of *kenōsis* or self-sacrifice in God: in eternal generation, creation, and the cross of Jesus.[86]

This is of a piece with my conviction that the Incarnation is not a response to the Fall but rather that – as in the thought of Hopkins, and behind him Bonaventure – 'the sacrifice of the Son is God's first thought of the world'[87] – it is 'the primary way in which the self-emptying, the pure being for another of God's personal, trinitarian being can be manifest externally'[88] Hopkins yet more radically suggested in a sermon that 'It is as if the blissful agony or stress of selving in God had forced out drops of sweat or blood, which drops were the world.'[89] This God of costly creation, I hold, is also intimately involved in the 'passion play' of creaturely suffering. God is an actor in the passion play, intimately present to all creatures in their suffering, so that none suffers or dies alone.[90]

The second move I would make is to hold that God offers new and fulfilled life to all those creatures that have known no fulfilment in their

---

[85] D. Brown, *Divine Humanity: Kenosis and the Construction of a Christian Theology* (Waco, TX: Baylor University Press, 2011), 239–40. The inner quotation is from Graham Ward.

[86] Fiddes, *Seeing*, 289.

[87] Von Balthasar, *GL3*, 380. The New Testament hints at this at 1. Peter 1.19–20; Revelation 13.8.

[88] Von Balthasar, *GL3*, 381.

[89] G. M. Hopkins, *The Sermons and Devotional Writings of Gerard Manley Hopkins*, ed. C. Devlin (London: Oxford University Press, 1959), 197.

[90] Southgate, *Groaning*, 50–3; 56–7.

first creaturely existence. Those lives devoid of flourishing can be viewed also through the lens of *Gloria in excelsis*.[91]

We have arrived, then, at a position that recognises that God has responsibility both for the evidently beautiful elements in the natural world, and for those processes that give rise to suffering and extinction. It also hypothesises that this creative activity of God speaks of some constraints on the possibilities available to God, as well as of the extraordinary fecundity and generosity of that activity. My position also suggests that the divine love is present to every creature in whatever state of *extremis* it finds itself. Therefore, signs of God's activity and love may be glimpsed in all sorts of situations, and may be read as manifestations of glory.

MODES OF CONTEMPLATION: VON BALTHASAR'S 'SEEING THE FORM'

That returns us to the focus of this present study, which is not theodicy but doxology – examination of glory. We shall consider two ways of expressing modes of contemplation: von Balthasar's language of 'seeing the form' and Hopkins's language of inscape and instress.

Von Balthasar used the enigmatic language of 'form' to express how the visible relates to the depths of reality. He writes:

Visible form not only 'points' to an invisible, unfathomable mystery; form is the apparition of this mystery, and reveals it while, naturally, at the same time protecting and veiling it. Both natural and artistic form has an exterior, which appears, and an interior depth, both of which, however, are not separable in the form itself. The content (*Gehalt*) does not lie behind the form (*Gestalt*) but within it. Whoever is not capable of seeing and 'reading' the form will ... fail to perceive the content. Whoever is not illumined by the form will see no light in the content either.[92]

His sense that 'eyes are needed that are able to perceive the spiritual form',[93] and 'Only that which has form can snatch one up into a state of rapture. Only through form can the lightning-bolt of eternal beauty flash'[94] sums up much of what I am attempting to convey in this present book about signs of the divine reality.

[91] For a justification of this position see Southgate, *Groaning*, chapter 5.
[92] Von Balthasar, *GL1*, 151. See also Garcia-Rivera, *Community*, especially chapter 3 for helpful insights into what von Balthasar might have meant.
[93] Von Balthasar, *GL1*, 24.   [94] Ibid., 32.

Interestingly too, von Balthasar equates the contemplation of 'what is really said' in Scripture with 'the aesthetic contemplation that steadily and patiently beholds those forms which either nature or art offers to its view'.[95] There is much to ponder on in this comment because it seems to me that Scripture offers a level of ambiguity of value analogous to that which I have been describing in the natural world. Scripture contains hard texts interwoven with ones more evidently beautiful and 'God-breathed', and the two types of text cannot be satisfactorily dissected out from each other. So 'steady and patient' faithful reading of Scripture and nature alike must endure and make sense of beauty and ugliness interwoven.

I share, moreover, von Balthasar's antireductionist instincts, as when he writes that all human evolutionary history and psychological make-up is subsumed in the 'form of man', but 'It would not be worthwhile being human if man [*sic*] were but the amalgamation of such "material."'[96] And again 'we can never again recapture the totality of form once it has been dissected and sawed into pieces'.[97] When von Balthasar says of form that

[it] would not be beautiful unless it were fundamentally a sign and appearing of a depth and a fullness that, in themselves and in an abstract sense, remain both beyond our reach and our vision ... The form as it appears to us is beautiful only because the delight that it arouses in us is founded upon the fact that, in it, the truth and goodness of the depths of reality are manifested and bestowed ... The appearance of the form, as revelation of the depths, is an indissoluble union of two things. It is a real presence of the depths, of the whole of reality, and it is a real pointing beyond itself to these depths.[98]

he says exactly what I mean about glory when I associate glory with depth of reality, but yet insist that ultimately it is only a sign of that depth.

Note, however, the constraint that his language of 'form' faces. It takes real discernment to apprehend 'form': the true creaturely reflection of the divine glory is not on the surface, but reveals itself only to the persistent and faithful contemplative, one moreover who is prepared to be 'caught up', to be changed by his or her perceptions. As von Balthasar goes on,

We 'behold' the form; but if we really behold it, it is not as a detached form, rather in its unity with the depths that make their appearance in it. We see form as the splendour, as the glory of Being. We are 'enraptured' by our contemplation of those depths and are 'transported' to them.[99]

---

[95] Ibid.   [96] Ibid., 26.   [97] Ibid., 31.   [98] Ibid., 118.   [99] Ibid., 119.

MODES OF CONTEMPLATION: THE NATURE METAPHYSICS
OF HOPKINS – INSCAPE AND INSTRESS

The intensely disciplined contemplation we find in Gerard Manley Hopkins also offers a helpful way to express perceptions of God's world, fragmentary and sometimes opaque as his writing is. Hopkins used the science of the day to aid his seeing, and brought religiously informed poetic observation of the natural world to a pitch that, arguably, has never been equalled. He developed an approach to creation based on his concepts of 'inscape' and 'instress'. These terms are very complex, and Hopkins's use of them not necessarily consistent.[100] For the purposes of this exercise, they can be understood as follows:

the inscape of an entity [or scene or event] may be considered to contain what sort of thing it is scientifically – what patterns and regularities govern its existence – but also its particularity, its 'thisness' ... every creature has both its pattern of life and membership of its species, and also its particularity as an individual creature. The scientific account of an organism is based on trends, regularities, patterns, over a range of individuals – the perception of the particularity of a specific creature, its 'thisness', is more the preserve of the poet and contemplative.[101]

Bernadette Waterman Ward is right to point to the epistemological dimension of inscape. It needs the perceiver.[102] Hence the importance of Hopkins's other, related term, 'instress' – which is still more difficult to pin down than 'inscape'.

The poet seems to use 'instress' for: i) the cohesive energy that binds individual entities into the Whole, ii) the impact the inscape of entities makes on the observer,

---

[100] For an exhaustive analysis, see the work of D. Sobolev, *The Split World of Gerard Manley Hopkins: An Essay in Semiotic Phenomenology* (Washington, DC: Catholic University of America Press, 2011), chapter 1. Sobolev helpfully points out that the term can be used for groups of entities, for transient phenomena, or for underlying unity in music or artworks. However, his own preferred definition 'embodied organized form' seems to me to do too little justice either to the particularity of entities (remembering that Hopkins made strong connections between Scotus and inscape; see his journal for 18.7.1872, *Poems and Prose*, 128), or yet to entities' theological status as created. By contrast, Bernadette Waterman Ward, while pointing helpfully to the link between Hopkins' thought and Scotus' *formalitates*, seems to me to underrate the unity of inscape as Hopkins expresses it: *World as Word: Philosophical Theology in Gerard Manley Hopkins* (Washington, DC: Catholic University of America Press, 2002), chapter 7.
[101] Southgate, *Groaning*, 97. Also Sobolev, *Split World*, 49: Hopkins' poetics is characterised by 'the dialectics of particularity and unity'.
[102] Ward, *World*, 186. Cf. those telling lines in 'Hurrahing in Harvest': 'These things, these things were here and but the beholder/Wanting. Hopkins, *Poems and Prose*, 31.

and iii) the observer's will to receive that impact … The value of this odd terminology is that it gives full value to descriptions of entities in scientific terms, as being examples of whatever class of entities they belong to, but also acknowledges their particularity and createdness.[103]

'Instress', then, is used 'for both the object and the subject: things express their instress, their deep, unique act, which establishes them, holds them together and holds them in tension, and there is required in the subject an answering stress'.[104] Since instress can be, as a noun, either subject or object, and can also be a verb; it is a complex term indeed. In this account I try and use the term as simply and consistently as possible, concentrating on the verbal sense of instressing as what a contemplating human does in receiving the impact of another creature or event.

Hopkins was keenly interested in the sort of description of the world we now call science. But W. H. Gardner says of him that he would have parted company with the (scientific) rationalists in saying that 'the human spirit must be nourished by the spurting fountains of supra-rational instress, by that "deep poetry" which is nothing less than intuitive ontology – the knowledge of the essence and being of all things'.[105] Ultimately, instress and inscape depend on the radical immanence of God in creaturely selves.[106] Von Balthasar, in his essay on Hopkins, writes, 'The free word of a free self can only … radiate [God's] solitary glory, and therefore the whole world must speak of God.'[107] Those not willing to hear God speaking in this way will not recognise inscape, for 'the true inscape of all things is

---

[103] Southgate, *Groaning*, 97–8. See also P. S. Fiddes, *Freedom and Limit: A Dialogue between Literature and Christian Doctrine* (Macon, GA: Mercer University Press, 1992), chapter 6.

[104] Von Balthasar, *GL3*, 365.

[105] W. H. Gardner, *Gerard Manley Hopkins: A Study in Poetic Idiosyncrasy in Relation to Poetic Tradition*, Vol. 2 (Oxford: Oxford University Press, 1958), 350. In a related way, Shelley distanced himself from the rationality of Hume, asserting according to McGrath that 'Hume's account of causality reduced the level of human engagement with nature to that of "habitual noticing", devoid of any sense of wonder or amazement': McGrath, *Re-Imagining*, 114, referring to the work of Ross Wilson.

[106] Though Hopkins is clear that this radical immanence is always protected by divine transcendence. He writes: 'a being so intimately present as God to other things would be identified with them were it not for his infinity': *Sermons*, 128. For a reaffirmation that inscape speaks of the creature's relation to God, see Thomas Merton: '[Creatures'] inscape is their sanctity. It is the imprint of [God's] wisdom and His reality in them': *New Seeds of Contemplation* (New York: New Directions, 1961), 30.

[107] Von Balthasar, *GL3*, 376.

Christ; God's grace is the stress within them.'[108] So right instressing gives insight into the signs of divine immanence present in all things. And this is the particular gift and calling of human beings.[109]

Sobolev offers a dense analysis of Hopkins's method, concluding that he has an 'understanding of the world as a system of spiritual signs'.[110] That raises the question of how this can be reconciled with Scotism. Sobolev distinguishes between the inscape of created entities and events (in which can be found a concentrated and reduced application of Scotus's sense of the univocity of being) from this semiotic application of natural world to the mysteries of the life with God. Sobolev is right that that the poems often move from one to the other. For instance, the first, observational six and a half lines of 'The Windhover' lead to the poet's own existential reaction and on from there into a series of allegorical uses of physical phenomena. Observation leads to 'sermonic' reflection (as again in 'As Kingfishers Catch Fire').

I consider that Sobolev underestimates the extent to which Hopkins himself would have seen these as a unity. 'The Windhover' begins 'I caught', and the whole instressing – of observation and iconography – of intense seeing and sophisticated interpretation – unfolds from the moment of seeing. But I altogether agree with Sobolev's eventual conclusion that Hopkins believes he is *discovering* aspects of God's Book of Nature:

On the one hand, the material world in its wholeness is a vehicle of divine presence ... At the same time, singular objects and their groups are created in order to signify and reenact spiritual messages; they are 'uttering the spiritual reason' of their being.[111]

The poet is not writing his own 'book', but seeing and reading deeply into God's.

Inscape, like 'form', depends on a holistic vision of the entity contemplated, and both depend on the integration of that vision with a Christian metanarrative. Where there would be a difference in emphasis between Hopkins and von Balthasar is in the importance attached to particularity.

---

[108] Ibid., 387. Richard Rohr reaches for a yet more interesting point when he writes: 'Anything can convert you once you surround it with this reverent silence that gives it significance, identity, singularity, importance, value, or what Duns Scotus called the "thisness" of everything': *Silent Compassion: Finding God in Contemplation* (Cincinnati, OH: Franciscan Media, 2014), 24. So perhaps divine silence is the ground of inscape, what enables us to discern entities and events in their 'thisness'.

[109] As Hopkins expresses in 'Ribblesdale', 'And what is Earth's eye, tongue or heart else, where/Else, but in dear and dogged man': *Poems and Prose*, 51–2.

[110] Sobolev, *Split World*, 95–112, quotation on 95.   [111] Ibid., 108–9.

For Hopkins, after he came under the influence of Duns Scotus and his concept of *haecceitas*, the 'thisness' of the individual creature, its particularity, assumes great significance. Von Balthasar writes, 'In the unique, the irreducible, there shines forth for Hopkins the glory of God, the majesty of his oneness.'[112] Unifying laws must not be allowed to drown this distinctiveness.[113]

Now it is possible so to stress the individuality of an entity as to lose a sense of what kind of creature it is, and that is surely unhelpful.[114] But what we are struggling with here is the issue of the creation of an ambiguous world, and that world's capacity to evince some reflection of the divine glory despite being full of suffering. And suffering is always particular – it is what happens to individuals and has its meaning and significance in the experience of individuals. Indeed, the more individuality of experience a creature has, the more it has a sense of itself, the greater the trauma attached to that self being threatened, trapped, wounded or in intractable pain. Particularity, thisness, is therefore vital to our exploration. We are not considering any concept of perfection in general. Since Hopkins's terminology gives more scope to emphasising particularity, and moreover does not depend on rendering hard-to-translate concepts from German, I therefore work mainly with Hopkins's language of inscape and instress rather than von Balthasar's language of 'form'.

Von Balthasar, writing on Hopkins, notes that 'The objective instress is taken up by the subject *that is open to it*, that is moved in its depths by the depth of its power of being.'[115] True instressing of the inscape of an entity is built up of the understanding that comes from the natural sciences, the poetic appreciation of the entity in its particularity, and the theological and spiritual appreciation of its createdness. It involves an openness to being moved by the act of contemplation. But what that last quotation from von Balthasar suggests is that those who are not willing to see the

---

[112] Von Balthasar, *GL3*, 357.

[113] Ibid., 374. See also A. Rumsey, 'Through Poetry and the Call to Attention' in *Beholding the Glory: Incarnation through the Arts*, ed. J. Begbie (London: Darton, Longman and Todd, 2000), 47–63, on the importance of particularity (quoting Hopkins' 'Pied Beauty' on 54).

[114] That would be to lose a sense of its form in the sense that Maximus proposes (drawing on Plato) that created entities have *logoi*; cf. Southgate, *Groaning*, chapter 4. Indeed, Hopkins for all his stress on *haecceitas* saw the Platonic idea 'as thoroughly incarnated in nature'. Von Balthasar, *GL3*, 364.

[115] Von Balthasar, *GL3*, 365, emphasis mine.

entity in that complex, holistic way not only cannot see the glory that lies behind it, but in a sense cannot 'see' it at all.[116]

Von Balthasar is preoccupied (very properly) with the form of the Incarnate One, the One whose glory 'unites splendour and radiance with solid reality',[117] as our best clue to the glory of Being, and moreover the One into whose crucified and glorified body it is our hope and destiny to be caught up. He says, 'If we seek Christ's beauty in a glory which is not that of the Crucified, we are doomed to seek in vain.'[118]

In other words, the lens of *Gloria crucis* is indispensable to Christian contemplation.

HOPKINS, CONTEMPLATION, AND PEIRCE'S SIGN-TYPES

The language of inscape and instress can be profitably combined with the insights of semiotics that I introduced in Chapter 1. There I noted that a sign-process is irreducibly triadic, always containing sign, and a reality of which the sign is sign, the object, and an interpreting entity. In terms of this study, the human contemplative is the interpretant, and 'instressing' is the process of interpretation.

The easiest category of sign-relation to assign in Peircean terms is that of any creature to its Creator. The relationship between sign (creature) and object (Creator) is a lawlike relation, informed by the laws by which God set up the universe, with all the constraints that implies. The sign-object relation is thus that of a legisign. The presumption of this whole chapter is that contemplation of creatures tells us something about God as Creator; hence, creatures in general, as their creatureliness points to God their creator, will be indexical legisigns.

This is where Hopkins's Scotist instinct towards particularity comes in. The sort of creature a creature is counts indeed as an indexical legisign, but the individual creature in its *haecceitas* is a once-off, it is very particularly itself, even though it 'deals out that being indoors each one dwells'[119] very much like another entity of the same type. It therefore functions as an indexical sinsign. The entity's 'inscape' contains both this pattern and

---

[116] 'Only the apprehension of an expressive form in the thing can give it that depth-dimension between its ground and its manifestation ... [that] frees the striver, allowing him to achieve the spiritual distance that makes a beauty rich in form desirable in its being-in-itself ... and only thus worth striving after.' *GL1*, 152.
[117] Ibid., 124.   [118] Ibid., 55–6.
[119] Hopkins, 'As Kingfishers Catch Fire', *Poems and Prose*, 51.

this particularity. In both cases, what is signified is the creator-creature relation. This is most evidently a relation of divine transcendence. The 'legisignness' of the creature includes the constraint that creatures cannot be God, that God's nature as Creator always transcends any such creaturely sign. More elusive is a sense of divine immanence within creatures.

One of Hopkins's most remarkable observations in his Journals – themselves an outstanding training ground for any poet of nature – goes as follows: 'I do not think I have seen anything more beautiful than the bluebell I have been looking at. I know the beauty of our Lord by it. It[s inscape] is [mixed of] strength and grace, like an ash [tree].'[120]

There is a sense in which to see an entity truly, to instress it, is to give oneself to it, to give one's whole sympathy and attention, as we see Hopkins doing with the bluebell. 'There is no seeing without being caught up.'[121] True seeing, then, the seeing that gives the self away in sympathy, allows that self to be caught up in the reality of the creature that is seen. And because that creature *is* created by God, participation in its inscape means participation in the life of the Creator who made it.

Von Balthasar writes this in relation to portraiture:

if God appears in the signs of his creation, he can do so only within the tension that ... marks the appearance of the ground in the image ... this appearance can look like the uttermost manifestation of the ground in the image ... The image, then, is filled to the brim with the whole significance of the ground – so much that the vessel appears almost to overflow, better, that what the vessel contains seems greater than the vessel itself. By the same token, worldly truth, by God's gift, often appears to contain ... an immediate gleam of God's eternity and infinity.[122]

He might have been writing of that 'overflowing' experience Hopkins had of his bluebell.

Natural theology pursued along these lines is very far from the effort to inspect the natural world from a neutral standpoint to find evidence for God. It is dynamic, participative, existential, it recognises knowing as involving the whole self. It both relies on faith and informs faith. The quotation from Hopkins's response to the bluebell makes clear just how far beyond ordinary seeing this 'foolish' instressing, at its most intense, can take us. The bluebell took Hopkins to *knowledge* of the beauty of

---

[120] Hopkins, *Poems and Prose*, 122. The extraordinary detail with which Hopkins follows this insight shows the concentration that lay behind it.

[121] Von Balthasar, GL7, 24.

[122] Von Balthasar, *Theo-Logic: Theological Logical Theory*, Vol. 1: Truth of the World, transl. A. J. Walker (San Francisco: Ignatius Press, 2000), 235.

God in Christ – it might therefore be said to be natural theology at its purest and most direct.

I noted earlier in this chapter that most created entities function as indexical signs – as creatures they point to a creator.[123] Interpretation of these indexes requires a commitment to look for createdness, and it will be richer instressing if it includes an understanding of the character of the entity in scientific terms. It will be still richer if a poetic imagination, an eye for particularity, is at work. Beyond that too comes to some the sort of mystical moment Hopkins describes with his bluebell, when he apprehends quality, as well as particularity, as well as scientific description, and thereby receives the glory of the moment in an especially intense way. He sees with his mystical poet's eye the iconicity of the sign, the way the beauty of the flower is like the beauty of Christ.

But very few of us have that sort of depth of capability of instress. We might be able to see iconicity – signs-by-likeness to God – in a great theophanic encounter. We may see a rainbow and be reminded of the symbolic legisign God gave in the Noachic covenant. But most of the time we see only indexes. And what this chapter will have made clear is the importance of not ignoring the ambiguous character of the range of indexes that we see in the natural world, and simply selecting out beauty as signification, seizing upon the sunset and the peacock's feather as signs-by-likeness of the beauty of God.

Moreover, it is possible for contemplation of the natural world to penetrate beyond mere following of indexical signs to a closer sense of the creator, immanent as well as transcendent, to which they point. Hopkins's bluebell shows the power and depth to which this signification can go. So intensely does he contemplate the flower that the window onto God that it opens is especially transparent.[124] Its particularity, its sinsignness, acquires a character that is not just indexical but iconic – 'I know the beauty of our Lord by it.' At its most profound, this contemplation can lead into an instressing of the inscape of creatures so complete that the contemplative is seeing in them Christ, agent of creation and Incarnate

---

[123] As indexes they point towards the reality of the divine creator. So A. Robinson, 'the character that makes the index a sign would be lost if the object were removed': *God and the World of Signs: Trinity, Evolution, and the Metaphysical Semiotics of C.S. Peirce* (Leiden: Brill, 2010), 119.

[124] Cf. also Sobolev, *Split World*, 43: 'If inscape is related to the material world itself, the intensity of instress makes objects transparent, and the mind becomes capable of experiencing the invisible depths of creation'.

One (*Gloria mundi*), Crucified One (*Gloria crucis*) and Lord Risen in Glory *(Gloria in excelsis)*.

But note what lay behind these apprehensions of Hopkins – a deep schooling in Christian philosophical theology, an intense appreciation of the developments of the science of the time and an extraordinary openness to the natural world. The same intensity of holy contemplation is advocated by Bonaventure when he writes of 'the second way of seeing' that:

> The supreme power, wisdom and goodness of the Creator shine forth in created things in so far as the bodily senses inform the interior senses … In the first way of seeing, the observer considers things in themselves … the observer can rise, as from a vestige, to the knowledge of the immense power, wisdom and goodness of the Creator. In the second way of seeing, the way of faith … we understand that the world was fashioned by the Word of God.[125]

Deane-Drummond quotes a further passage from Bonaventure indicating that to be able to develop this way of seeing, the contemplative must:

> bring the natural powers of the soul under the influence of grace, which reforms them, and this he does through prayer; he must submit them to the purifying influence of justice, and this in his daily acts; he must subject them to the influence of enlightening knowledge, and this, in meditation; and finally he must hand them over to the influence of the perfecting power of wisdom, and this in contemplation. For just as no one arrives at wisdom except through grace, justice and knowledge, so it is that no one arrives at contemplation except through penetrating meditation, holy living and devout prayer.[126]

One of the great problems of natural theology is to wrestle with the problem of sin, and its possibly distorting effects on our ability to learn truly from the creation. So it is significant that Bonaventure so strongly stresses the importance of prayer to contemplation – what T. S. Eliot called 'the purification of the motive in the ground of our beseeching'.[127] Moreover, the emphasis in the second quotation from Bonaventure not just on prayer but on right living as a necessity for right contemplation is very striking. To quote Hopkins once again, 'The just man justices'[128]

---

[125] Quoted in C. Deane-Drummond, *Wonder and Wisdom: Conversations in Science, Spirituality and Theology* (West Conshohocken, PA: Templeton Foundation Press, 2006), 57.

[126] Quoted in Deane-Drummond, *Wonder*, 57. Cf. also McGrath, quoting (a) the Catalan natural theologian Raymonde de Sebonde: 'No one can see this wisdom, or read this said open Book [of Nature and Creatures] by themselves, unless they are enlightened by God' (*Re-Imagining*, 15) and (b) the Cambridge Platonist John Smith, 'though the whole of this visible universe be whispering out the notions of a Deity [we] cannot understand it without some interpreter within' (*Re-Imagining*, 29).

[127] Eliot, *Poems and Plays*, 196.   [128] Hopkins, *Poems and Prose*, 51.

and in doing so becomes able not just to tell out what lies deep within his being, but to draw in truly the way the created world speaks of God.

CONTEMPLATION OF GLORY IN CREATION

For the rest of this chapter, I want to explore in particular *Gloria mundi*, to ask where glory can be seen in this first creation, into which redemption is only gradually working its way. An evolving creation makes possible intricacy of cooperation, loveliness of form, ingenuity of life-strategy. Both individual life and overall scheme testify to the divine glory as creator. But this witness is not the simple one of beauty, but something much more complex.

My approach involves fusing, as much as possible, scientific insights with those of poets and other contemplatives. Macquarrie writes that 'this descriptive type of philosophical or natural theology does not *prove* anything, but it *lets us see*, for it brings out into the light the basic situation in which faith is rooted, so that we can then see what its claims are'.[129] The natural sciences help to bring out into the light in very powerful ways the basic situation in which Christian faith is rooted. Biology and ecology show us the extraordinary beauty and intricacy of that world. They tell us (albeit provisionally, since their depictions are always moving on) things beyond all ordinary seeing – how the light-utilising properties of certain photosynthetic pigments maintain an oxygen atmosphere on Earth unlike that of any other known planet, how the salt-avoiding strategies of certain marine organisms cause the recycling of sulphur, which land-based organisms vitally require, how in Rolston's memorable phrase 'the cougar's fang has carved the limbs of the fleet-footed deer, and vice versa'.[130] Biology and ecology also prevent us from escaping the ambiguity of that world – they make us confront the conclusion that that same process of 'carving' is founded on the inevitability of suffering. The fawn that is too slow to learn to run is cougar meat; the lamed cougar starves. Also the biosphere we have now in a sense rests on a vast history of extinction – as many as 99 per cent of all species that have ever existed are now lost.

However, as has often been claimed in recent years, science by itself tends to 'disenchant' the world, to give rise to reductive ways of seeing that do not do full justice to the human imagination or necessarily

---

[129] Macquarrie, *Principles*, 56, emphasis in original.
[130] H. Rolston, III, *Science and Religion: A Critical Survey* (Philadelphia: Templeton Foundation Press, 2006 [1987]), 134.

promote human cherishing of the non-human world.[131] To put it baldly, science may give us facts, it may even promote wonder (on this McGrath and Dawkins are agreed),[132] but it cannot by itself make us see glory.

What we are exploring is deep instressing of the realities of the creation. This means drawing fully on the scientific understanding of creatures. We need to take seriously the sometimes paradoxical conclusions that 'the unnatural nature of science'[133] offers us. We are not, then, concerned only with the feelings evoked by entities under contemplation, but with a feeling-aided elucidation of what is objectively present in their natures.[134] But this sort of contemplation goes beyond that to instress the 'thisness' of the object investigated – the particular bluebell in the particular moment.

Even beyond that, such contemplation rests on discerning how God loves the creature concerned, knowing the long history by which it has come to be, knowing how it and its ancestors have striven for selfhood, delighting in its flourishing, entering into the passion play of its frustrations and suffering, and imagining how God longs for the creature to transcend its narrow self-interest.[135]

CREATION'S PRAISE OF GOD

Thus, intense instressing of everything about the creature reveals (if the observer's instrumentation is appropriate and her heart is true) something of the inscape of the creature and of the way that inscape speaks of the depth of the reality of the God who made it, of the glory manifested in and through it. But it will be remembered that divine glory glimpsed in a creature is itself only ever a sign.

It follows further that this process of instressing the deep reality of the creature, what it most truly is and does, must be a process of listening to the music of its creaturely praise of which there are many hints in the Psalms (especially at Pss 19.1–4, 148), though also a sense, at least in some translations of Ps 19.3–4, that this is a music we can never

---

[131] Cf. A. McGrath, *The Reenchantment of Nature: Science, Religion and the Human Sense of Wonder* (London: Hodder and Stoughton, 2002).

[132] Ibid., 171–8; R. Dawkins, *Unweaving the Rainbow: Science, Delusion and the Appetite for Wonder* (London: Penguin, 1998).

[133] L. Wolpert, *The Unnatural Nature of Science* (London: Faber and Faber, 1992).

[134] Cf. von Balthasar, *GL3*, 362–3, talking of this search for objectivity being already present in Ruskin.

[135] Southgate, *Groaning*, chapter 4.

properly hear.[136] But I suggest that deep contemplation, faithful instressing, can recover something of this language, and hence something of the depths of the way creatures are signs of their creator.

It may be objected that talk of creaturely praise is mere poetic whim on the part of the Psalmist, but I suggest that to say this is to lose a dimension of the creature-creator relation that is both rich and fundamental. It may be further objected that praise is an attribute only of conscious entities that have the power of self-expression. I accept that that is true of thanksgiving. Indeed, part of the distinctive vocation of the human creature must be to give thanks to God on behalf of all creation, an action most characteristically expressed in the Eucharist. But like many other authors, I take very seriously the hints in the Psalms that praise is a much more general attribute of creatures.

We have seen that whatever is a sign of the reality that underpins all of existence is a manifestation of the divine glory. I suggest that the truest reality of any creature is that it *is* a creature, owing its existence from moment to moment to God. The creaturely response that is a sign of this dependence is praise. The total inscape of a creature therefore includes not just what may be known of it scientifically and poetically, but also what it means to God. The creature's own return of praise to its Creator is a vital element of this.

Richard Bauckham among others has sought to analyse the character of this creaturely praise and to suggest that creatures praise God in their most characteristically being themselves.[137] All creaturely entities, then, reflect the divine glory by returning praise for their existence, and they do so by acting in their most characteristic way. That returns me to the point I noted in Chapter 1 – glory is not necessarily to be equated with beauty. The hyena pack that seize a newborn impala calf and tear it apart before extracting with great skill every last bit of nutrition from the bones is not in any conventional sense acting beautifully, but is acting characteristically, praising God in its action, manifesting its creatureliness in a way that is a sign of the work of its Creator. Even a more magnificent creature like an orca acts in a way most would call ugly when two orca toss a sea lion between them, apparently just for fun, before killing it. But that too is characteristic action, orca being themselves, and so part of creaturely praise, part of the manifestation of *Gloria mundi*.

---

[136] On this theme of creaturely praise see Bauckham, 'Joining'; Southgate, *Groaning*, chapter 6.

[137] Bauckham, 'Joining', 47.

It may be that creaturely praise actually reaches its fullest extent when creatures are in distress, when they most know their need of their Creator. Bauckham's proposal about creatures praising by being themselves may need augmenting in respect of this dimension, that the music of creaturely praise is intensified in lament. I derive this thought from Karl Barth in whose writing the theme of creaturely praise is (perhaps surprisingly) strong. In his study of glory in *Church Dogmatics 2/1*, Barth notes that creaturely response to God is:

their secret that will one day come out and be revealed. And it is to this that we are always required and will always find it worth our while to attend and look ... [Creatures echoing and reflecting the glory of the Lord] do it along with us or without us. They do it also against us to shame us and instruct us.[138]

So Barth, for all his profound suspicions of natural theology, does recognise that we need to attend to the silent music of other creatures' praise, and that that praise may be a source of instruction. Humanity, as we slowly accept our destiny in Christ,

is only like a late-comer slipping shamefacedly into creation's choir in heaven and earth, which has never ceased its praise, but merely suffered and sighed, as it still does, that in inconceivable folly and ingratitude its living centre man does not hear its voice, its response, its echoing of the divine glory, or rather hears it in a completely perverted way, and refuses to co-operate in the jubilation that surrounds him.[139]

In a remarkable passage, Barth suggests that perhaps creation praises God most intensely in what he called its 'shadowy side'. He writes:

creation and creature are good even in the fact that all that is exists in this contrast and antithesis. In all this, far from being null, it praises its Creator even on its shadowy side, even in the negative aspect in which it is so near to nothingness ... For all we can tell, may not His creatures praise Him more mightily in humiliation than in exaltation, in need than in plenty, in fear than in joy, on the frontier of nothingness than when wholly orientated on God.[140]

---

[138] K. Barth, *Church Dogmatics*, Vol. 2, Part 1: The Doctrine of God, transl. T. H. L. Parker, W. B. Johnston, H. Knight, J. L. M. Haire, ed. G. W. Bromiley and T. F. Torrance (Edinburgh: T&T Clark, 1957), 648.

[139] Ibid.

[140] K. Barth, *Church Dogmatics*, Vol. 3, Part 3: The Doctrine of Creation, transl. G. W. Bromiley and R. J. Ehrlich, ed. G. W. Bromiley and T. F. Torrance (Edinburgh: T&T Clark, 1961), 296–7. Interestingly, that ancient hymn the 'Benedicite', drawn from the 'Song of the Three Holy Children' in the *Apocrypha*, which calls on all creation to praise the Lord, includes components of it that are profoundly destructive of various living things, components such as winds, frosts and cold, lightning and floods. (See also Bauckham, 'Joining', 46–7.)

That returns us in a very fascinating way to the image of the passion play. Not only may we postulate that God is a participant in the play, a companion in the creature's suffering, but that the creator-creature relationship is actually intensified in suffering. The creature's dependence on, pre-conscious awareness of, the source of its life, and the response of praise, is if Barth is right at its most intense in times of suffering. And God's commitment to being present to the creature, which is always there, may perhaps develop a new intensity in these times.

This creator-creature relationship can be expressed in terms of praise and compassion, as earlier in this chapter, or in terms of blessing – or indeed in terms of gift-exchange – the creator's gift of life, a value in itself even in times of great distress, the creature's offering of praise, met with the gift of companionship and compassionate love, the creator's offering of presence even in moments of dying, and ultimately of redeemed life in the eschaton.

DARWINIAN CONTEMPLATION

It should by now be apparent just how much more complex it is to read the signs of glory in the created order than merely to register beauty, and order, which have been the preoccupation of most Christian natural theology.

Hopkins has been our metaphysical and poetic guide through some very difficult territory. It is a frustration to me that he did not live long enough to engage more fully with the picture of the natural world emerging from the Christian appropriation of Darwinism. Only in two poems do I see hints of his wrestling with the ambiguity of nature as a post-Darwinian thinker might wrestle. The first is his remarkable curtal sonnet 'Pied Beauty':

> GLORY be to God for dappled things –
>   For skies of couple-colour as a brinded cow;
>   For rose-moles all in stipple upon trout that swim;
> Fresh-firecoal chestnut-falls; finches' wings;
>   Landscape plotted and pieced – fold, fallow, and plough;
>   And áll trádes, their gear and tackle and trim.
>
> All things counter, original, spare, strange;
>   Whatever is fickle, freckled (who knows how?)
>   With swift, slow; sweet, sour; adazzle, dim;
> He fathers-forth whose beauty is past change:
>   Praise him.

Hopkins might well have written, in my view, that the glory of God is especially to be searched for, and delighted in, when the world of creatures is dappled, complex, and particularly where those creatures exhibit behaviour that is 'counter, original, spare, strange'.

With extraordinary density of thought, this poem roams across Hopkins's landscape of praise, his response to contrast, his facility and originality of connection – a sky, bizarrely but so accurately, like the hide of a cow. But it is the very dense line 'All things counter, original, spare, strange' that intrigues me. Hopkins draws near to the thought I am pursuing here, that it is the unexpected in nature (the 'counter', and 'strange'), those life-strategies that are not seen in any other form (the 'original'), and those that express their nature (inscape) in a particularly direct and uncluttered way (the 'spare'), that draw the nature-contemplative particularly to praise. And that response of praise is, I hold, a response to glory, to signs of the creative nature of the creating God, who as Father, Son and Spirit gives to creatures their existence, form and particularity.[141]

Even to tease out this line of Hopkins is to reduce the force of what it seeks to convey. In a sense the poem is its own 'counter, original, spare, strange' song of praise, and no exegesis can enhance it. But I draw strength from the line all the same, and its underlying sense that glory is to be looked for, and responded to, in surprising places.

A determined Darwinian contemplative can perhaps elicit some encouragement from that 'counter' line.[142] But the only real encouragement I get that Hopkins was thinking evolution-informed thoughts is in his late irregular sonnet 'That Nature Is a Heraclitean Fire and of the Comfort of the Resurrection'.[143]

Cloud-puffball, torn tufts, tossed pillows | flaunt forth, then chevy on an air-
built thoroughfare: heaven-roysterers, in gay-gangs | they throng; they glitter in
    marches.
Down roughcast, down dazzling whitewash, | wherever an elm arches,
Shivelights and shadowtackle ín long | lashes lace, lance, and pair.
Delightfully the bright wind boisterous | ropes, wrestles, beats earth bare
Of yestertempest's creases; | in pool and rut peel parches
Squandering ooze to squeezed | dough, crust, dust; stanches, starches
Squadroned masks and manmarks | treadmire toil there
Footfretted in it. Million-fuelèd, | nature's bonfire burns on.
But quench her bonniest, dearest | to her, her clearest-selvèd spark

---

[141] Southgate, *Groaning*, chapter 4.

[142] And possibly from the phrase 'Brute beauty' in 'The Windhover', Hopkins, *Poems and Prose*, 30. Note also that the cold of the shipwreck in 'The Wreck of the Deutschland' is God's cold, 18.

[143] Hopkins, *Poems and Prose*, 65–6. He does call Nature 'bad, base and blind' in the little-known poem 'Brothers', 48–9.

Man, how fast his firedint, | his mark on mind, is gone!
Both are in an unfathomable, all is in an enormous dark
Drowned. O pity and indig | nation! Manshape, that shone
Sheer off, disseveral, a star, | death blots black out; nor mark
        Is any of him at all so stark
But vastness blurs and time | beats level. Enough! the Resurrection,
A heart's-clarion! Away grief's gasping, | joyless days, dejection.
        Across my foundering deck shone
A beacon, an eternal beam. | Flesh fade, and mortal trash
Fall to the residuary worm; | world's wildfire, leave but ash:
        In a flash, at a trumpet crash,
I am all at once what Christ is, | since he was what I am, and
This Jack, joke, poor potsherd, | patch, matchwood, immortal diamond,
        Is immortal diamond.

Down to 'time beats level', this seems to tune to the concerns that a Darwinian contemplative might have. In a letter to Coventry Patmore written five years before that poem, Hopkins wrestles with struggle in nature but very much in Aristotelian terms. The limitations of material causes can sometimes prevent formal causes from generating the health and beauty that would be their full outworking. 'This explains why [in nature] "ugly good" is found.' Hopkins goes on to distinguish this from 'beautiful evil', which 'comes from wicked will'.[144] What this pre-Darwinian view grasps is the possibility of constraints in nature as to what is possible; what it misses is Darwin's great insight that, in effect, the good stems from the ugly and is inseparable from it. Natural selection drives refinement of characteristics, and that necessarily involves strategies that seem to us ugly.

But Hopkins is driven in this very late sonnet not to insist on creation's beauty, or even its ugly good, but to an admission of its bleakness, and then to a complete break, and a coda on the Resurrection, glory of a very different sort. Janet Morley writes of this poem:

The final two and a half lines are a statement of classic belief, but *I don't think they function as any kind of rejection of the delicious, exhilarating, destructive and creative natural world* of the poem so far. That world has simply, as in this poem, been broken into by the act of God in taking human flesh.[145]

---

144 G. M. Hopkins, *Correspondence, Vol. II, 1882–1889*, ed. R. K. R. Thornton and
    C. Phillips (Oxford: Oxford University Press, 2013), 605. I explore harms arising from
    moral wickedness and neglect further in Chapter 4.
145 J. Morley, *Our Last Awakening: Poems for Living in the Face of Death* (London: SPCK,
    2016), 165, emphasis mine.

This is very important. *Gloria mundi* is not rejected in the contemplation of Incarnation and Resurrection. It retains its importance within glory contemplated until such time as it is completely gathered up and God is 'all in all'.

Paul Fiddes in a fine essay on Hopkins suggests that the poet 'has a theology in which knowledge of God can be gained from nature, but at his best he understands this not as a matter of observation and deduction by the unaided use of human reason, but as encounter with a self-revealing God'.[146] This is very much the position I have been articulating, whereby signs graciously given by God in creation can be instressed by right contemplation. But Fiddes questions whether the poet may not have been guilty in his early period of overstating the way creation's beauties speak sacramentally of Christ. This is balanced however by those late sonnets in which Hopkins articulates his desolation and the apparent hiddenness of God. In his last period we 'find descriptions of a natural world in which the glory of God is veiled and more ambiguous,'[147] and 'a movement away from a sense of total withdrawal of God to a recognition of his hidden presence'.[148] Fiddes' theological analysis, seeing fallenness as 'a line of tension' between creaturely freedom and finitude, rather than a plunge from primordial perfection,[149] has much in common with my own more scientifically informed proposal. Certainly I concur with his conclusion, reflecting on Hopkins last poem 'To R. B.'[150] that 'the world, or rather the Creator, is responsible [both for the suffering of Hopkins's 'winter world' and for divine hiddenness] and must join with Hopkins in offering an ... explanation. Theology must grapple with this protest.'[151]

This appeal for intense contemplation and right understanding of the natural world, complex mixture as it is of beauty and ugliness, may sound all very well. To call its created character glory might seem to be at risk of baptizing all this creaturely ambiguity, to fail to protest against ugliness, to lack direction towards a future harmony. But note that this book's subtitle is *Glory and Longing*. The category of creaturely glory does go beyond beauty and is only apprehended by the right instressing of entities and processes that include what we find profoundly ugly. But a complete, three-lensed perception of God's ways with the world, including both creation and redemption, must include not just the way creatures are, in which they praise God by being themselves, but also their ultimate state at

[146] Fiddes, *Freedom*, 144.   [147] Ibid., 141.   [148] Ibid., 143.   [149] Ibid., chapter 3.
[150] Hopkins, *Poems and Prose*, 68.   [151] Fiddes, *Freedom*, 145.

the eschaton. I illustrate this type of analysis in the next section. First I begin the sort of grappling for which Fiddes calls.

Part of the mysterious dynamic of creation is that, first, God created creaturely selves via an evolutionary process that involved and continues to involve great struggle, and in which cooperation, though very widespread in ecosystems, is always accompanied by 'selving', entities exerting themselves to promote their self-interest at the expense of other selves. This prompts many evolutionary theodicists to suppose that this must have been the only way in which such an array of creaturely values could have come into existence (an assertion that seems to me necessary, though not sufficient, for evolutionary theodicy, but which continues to attract criticism[152]). Second, God seems to be awaiting human fulfilment before consummating the creation as a whole (Rom 8.19–22). Creation groans in labour pains, and God longs to relieve those pains, but the project of creation has to go full term, and that seems to involve humans coming into the 'freedom of their glory', a resonant phrase – very central to the theme of this book – which I explore further in Chapter 5.

We saw earlier in this chapter that true instressing involved the hearing of the music of creaturely praise, so as to discern truly the inscape of creatures and hence the way they testify to the divine glory. What is emerging now is something more: that true hearing of the creaturely situation would include also a sensitivity to the divine longing. Perhaps this divine longing is for creatures to enter into self-transcending patterns of cooperation with other creaturely selves.[153] More confidently, we can assert that human beings are called to relate to each other, and other creatures, in the freedom that is the true human nature, the true glory of being a human fully alive.

I have built up here a picture of the inscape of an entity or event as a complex matrix. It involves the nature of entities as they can be described scientifically. It involves the existential impact of their particularity on the observer (instressor). It involves an understanding, to the limited extent of which humans are capable, of the place of the entity or event in the story of God's ways with the world. That in turn involves the three phases of that story – God's activity as the giver of existence, form and particularity, and God's longing to see creaturely self-transcendence, but also God's engagement with the world in the Incarnation and Passion, and also

---

[152] For example, N. W. O'Halloran, S. J., 'Cosmic Alienation and the Origin of Evil: Rejecting the "Only Way" Option', *Theology and Science* 13 (2015), 43–63.

[153] Southgate, *Groaning*, chapter 4.

God's promise of eventual consummation, of a state of being of which the Resurrection of Christ is the foretaste.

Such an aesthetic of contemplation is difficult to arrive at and maintain. Faced with the ugliness of the Darwinian world, as good an observer as Annie Dillard wants to 'shake her fist' at creation; Rolston responds that he would rather 'raise both hands and cheer'.[154] At times this formulation of the manifestations of God's *kavōd* in the world could come very close to Wildman's ground-of-being theism. The deep reality of creaturely life, reflecting its creator, is one of ceaseless creativity accompanied by ubiquitous suffering. Hence, Wildman abandons his belief in the benevolence of God. Where I differ from Wildman is in insisting that this theodrama is a passion play in which God is an actor, in co-suffering compassion, not merely the animateur, or yet the stage. An actor, moreover, who will ultimately transform the drama.

I had the opportunity a few years ago to experience very forcibly the dark and ambiguous character of the natural world I am seeking to describe. My favourite mountain in Scotland is that extraordinary peak in the far North-West Highlands called Suilven. It is not very high, nor is any great technical skill required to reach the main summit. But many will testify to its fascination, born of its strange shape, seen so differently from different angles, and its isolation in a wilderness of rock and water. In 2010 I reached the ridge to find a high wind blowing straight down the mountain from east to west. A small amount of shelter came from the narrow eastern peak. But as I climbed towards the summit, the wind shifted to blow hard from the south, straight across the ridge, and torrential rain set in. I just managed to find a crevice in which to shelter. Up on that ridge, completely alone, and in extreme weather, I had a strong sense of the extraordinary power of the natural world – both of the processes that had formed this magnificent mountain, which seemed in that moment to be my whole world, and a very hostile one at that, all rain-blackened rock and sheer drops on either side, and of the wind and the rain blasting and soaking me.

My point is that Suilven is *both* the mountain beloved of nature photographers, a lyrical shape at sunset, or under snow, and also the barely habitable ridge in a gale-force rainstorm. At the time, it was impossible not to think of the theophany to Elijah on Horeb in 1 Kgs 19. So this was a sign to me not only of that power in the creation that dwarfs the

---

[154] H. Rolston, III, 'Naturalizing and Systematizing Evil' in *Is Nature Ever Evil?* ed. W. B. Drees (London: Routledge, 2003), 67–86, at 82.

ordinary powers of human beings, but also of the way surprising shelter can be found, as though as a gift. In that shelter, in the Elijah story, God's voice can be heard in the sound of sheer silence. I too felt sheltered and held, even in the danger of my physical situation. The deep reality of nature is of processes of unbelievable power that have shaped and continue to shape the world. Very many human lives are lived in a technological cocoon that keeps these forces – usually – at one remove. But to look for glory in the world is to bear, to the greatest extent possible, the way things really are, in all their ambiguity and hazard, and look for and listen for God within them.[155]

It might be thought that I am simply baptizing every feature of the creation, lovely or cruel, beautiful or destructive, as, arguably, Wildman's theology does, or as, in a different way, Holmes Rolston may be charged with doing. And I do want to say with Ruskin that we must gaze 'without shrinking into the darkness'.[156] Indeed, I want to say, deeply challenging though this is, that every inscape, correctly instressed under the guidance of the Spirit, is a reflection of God's glory in creation (which is in turn a sign of God's inner nature).

One very significant objection to this approach to theology – one which is not afraid to acknowledge that processes involving violence, and to which suffering is intrinsic, ultimately derive from God's creative activity – is that God is made the metaphysical ground of violence, even 'the metaphysical ground of Auschwitz'. This charge is levelled with characteristic energy by David Bentley Hart.[157] I am not entirely clear that any theology of creation *ex nihilo* can escape this charge. If God is the ground of all existence, God is the ground of what creaturely existence can do. The charge is certainly not escaped by refuge in mysterious counter-forces that God is not able to resist.[158]

CASE STUDIES OF DIVINE GLORY IN TROUBLING ASPECTS OF CREATION

The more difficult issue arises where God seems to have *used* processes that necessarily involve violence as part of God's creative plan – not only

---

[155] I take up this theme of bearing reality in Chapter 4.

[156] Quoted in McGrath, *Re-Imagining*, 75. McGrath continues, rightly, 'In practice, many observers of nature are highly selective, filtering out what they do not wish to see.'

[157] D. Bentley Hart, *The Beauty of the Infinite: The Aesthetics of Christian Truth* (Grand Rapids, MI: Eerdmans, 2003), 160.

[158] Southgate, 'Re-Reading'; also J. Friesenhahn, *Trinity and Theodicy: The Trinitarian Theology of von Balthasar and the Problem of Evil* (Aldershot: Ashgate, 2011), 149.

the processes of competition in evolution, but also those tectonic and volcanic processes that made the earth fruitful and continue to keep it habitable. But it is deeply unsatisfactory to write, as Bentley Hart does *in re* the Indian Ocean tsunami of 2004, of God 'who sealed up the doors of the sea [permitting] them to be opened again by another, more reckless hand ... that that [God's] will can be resisted by a real and ... autonomous force of defiance'.[159] That dualistic model forces apart the unity of our scientific understanding in as awkward a way as we noted earlier with Neil Messer.

Rather, considerations of the unity of the science and the absolute sovereignty of God force us to the inexorable conclusion that God honours the regularities of the processes God has made (the Resurrection being the striking exception) that the tsunami – difficult as it is even to begin to articulate this thought – also speaks of the way God created, and continues to create, the world. Its colossal force is testament, in a deeply difficult way, to the glory of God in creation. It is a very terrible sign of that creative power, causing as it did, directly or indirectly, the deaths of some 230,000 human beings.

A very sophisticated level of discernment, of instressing, is necessary to see the glory of God in the tsunami. One would hardly want to say that God communicated God's nature by such a sign. Rather, reflection on such phenomena shows how in relation to the natural world it seems better to speak of God, through the Holy Spirit, enabling human beings to instress the inscape of created entities, rather than to think of those entities as always constituting signs of specific divine self-communication.[160]

My position is that the whole divine element in the inscapes of every created entity or event constitutes glory – utterly reliable (though often hard to interpret) signification of the divine nature. Not, then, that the tsunami was glorious, but that it manifested elements of glory in God's bringing into existence massive forces that have made this planet fruitful for life; in the capacities of animals to sense the tsunami coming (*Gloria mundi*); in God's huge compassion for every victim, a suffering-with that is an echo of the self-giving of Christ on the Cross (*Gloria crucis*), God's presence to the puzzled, angry and needy worshipper in Word and

---

[159] Bentley Hart, *Doors*, 63.

[160] As well as the considerations already named, this may include the sort of analysis of the constraints on God's action that Philip Clayton and Steven Knapp have recently offered, using this same example of terrible human suffering. They conclude that, morally, God could not intervene even once in the flux of events around the tsunami. P. Clayton and S. Knapp, *The Predicament of Belief* (New York: Oxford University Press, 2011), chapter 3.

Eucharist, and God's promise of redeemed and fulfilled life from which every tear has been wiped away (*Gloria in excelsis*).

When we rightly instress the tsunami, we see, then, a complex array of signs pointing to the deep reality behind the event. These signs, taken together, constitute glory. And they call, as the definition insists, for a response, or set of responses, which in the case of the tsunami will include – properly – the following:

1. anger, that for all God's power God did not do more to prevent suffering, combined with
2. compassionate action to help and support all those affected, and
3. worship, entering more deeply into the mystery of our relationship with this God who seems so powerful and powerless,
4. repentance, for the folly of draining so many mangrove swamps that protected shorelines, for the war in Banda-Ace that drained communities' strength to respond to the catastrophe, for the false economy of refusing to install the early warning system that already existed in the Pacific, and
5. longing, for flourishing life with God that has no end or element of tragedy.[161]

I do not suppose that this type of analysis could be offered to someone in a state of profound suffering. Thus, for some thinkers[162] it is simply inadmissible. But it seems to me that to pursue these questions with the maximum honesty, however awkward and easily misunderstood they might be, is the task of the theologian taking, as Barth said, 'rational trouble over the mystery'.[163]

The tsunami resulted from a physical process not generated by life forms. For the actions of living creatures, we need a somewhat different analysis based on the one in *The Groaning of Creation*. I wrote there about how every living creature 'selves', defining itself over against its environment. Also about God's longing to see creatures transcend those selves – through novel and more ingenious behaviours, and through cooperation with others. So it is possible to speak of the creaturely 'no' to

---

[161] Note that each of these responses carries the danger of defaulting to self-indulgence, to sentimentality. Cf. J. S. Begbie, 'Beauty, Sentimentality and the Arts' in *The Beauty of God: Theology and the Arts*, ed. D. J. Treier, M. Husbands and R. Lundin (Downers Grove, IL: IVP Academic, 2007), 45–69.

[162] Such as Kenneth Surin, *Theology and the Problem of Evil* (Oxford: Blackwell, 1988).

[163] Quoted in Southgate, *Groaning*, 17.

the divine invitation.[164] And some strategies of creaturely selving are distinctly troubling – as in the life of the 'insurance' pelican chick, whose life is usually short and seems to contain nothing but suffering.[165]

Consider the case of a golden eagle quartering the moorland in the Scottish Highlands, hunting down a mountain hare. Here the inscape of the event includes long evolutionary histories of predator and prey (as well incidentally as the notorious nineteenth-century 'clearances' of those Highlands, which have opened up additional habitat for both). It includes the power and expertise of the flight of the eagle, its extraordinary visual acuity that picks out its prey at a vast distance, the hunger of the predator, the quickness and agility of the hare, the twists and turns of the hunt, and the fear and pain of the victim. It includes (I venture to suggest) God's delight in all those creaturely skills, and God's closeness to the suffering hare, in a particular and peculiar relationship of love and praise *in extremis*, a relationship made rich by Christ's own extremity of suffering. All these creaturely strategies for living are signs of the fruitfulness and generosity of God's creative activity. So the search for those signs of the divine that constitute glory again involves a complex discernment, with elements of the counter-intuitive. It is emphatically not a way of saying that everything is lovely when seen in a big enough perspective. The world is complex and troubling, and yet charged with the grandeur of God.

My last example is perhaps the most troubling of the three. On the lower slopes of a mountain in Africa, a young child has her blood sucked by a female anopheles mosquito. The protozoan *Plasmodium falciparens* is transmitted to her blood, through which it travels to her liver to multiply. Sexual reproduction of *falciparens* becomes possible when the now malarial child is bitten again by another plasmodium-carrying mosquito. Malaria has recently spread up the mountain because of climate change – the family had neither familiarity with the disease nor with precautions against it. As with my first example, the tsunami, a complex mixture of human casualness and neglect is associated with this suffering. Again as with the tsunami, divine compassion and eventual redemption is a component of the inscape of this event. But another element is the intricacy and efficacy of the complex life cycle of the parasite. There is a sort of evolved ingenuity even within this form of 'cheating' on cooperation[166] that expresses something of the fecundity and generativity of creation.

---

[164] Ibid., chapter 4.   [165] Southgate, *Groaning*, 46.
[166] Cf. Southgate, 'Does God's Care?'

As such it too, hard and troubling though it is to say, is an aspect of the divine glory.[167]

I borrow here from what is perhaps my least favourite hymn, Cecil Frances Alexander's "All things bright and beautiful'. What I have been at pains to try and convey is that much of nature is not 'bright and beautiful', but (to stretch Alexander's thought further, I am sure, than she meant to take it[168]) even what strikes us as ugly may meet the description 'wise and wonderful'. Even the ingenious strategies of parasites might be regarded in this light.

This is one of the most difficult areas of our exploration. The God of weal and woe is yet the God of Calvary, and of the Emmaus Road, and of Pentecost. In acknowledging this, in the way I see as vitally necessary to honest speaking about God, there is a danger of defaulting into a kind of Marcionism that attributes all the woe to the God of creation, and all the love to the God of salvation. Vital to the Christian confession is the affirmation that the God viewed through each lens is one and the same God – 'For it is the God who said, 'Let light shine out of darkness', who has shone in our hearts to give the light of the knowledge of the glory of God in the face of Jesus Christ' (2 Cor 4.6).

From all eternity the Son points beyond himself to the Father; as the Incarnate One, the Crucified, and the Risen One, he becomes the perfect sign to the world of the Godness of God, of the Godness-glory shared between Father and Son from all eternity (Jn 17.5).[169] However atonement is understood, Cross and Resurrection inaugurate a process by which the world is drawn into consummation, in which its labour pains give birth to a new creation. In the power of the Spirit, God's self-offering for the world does not return to God empty, but gathers the creation to Godself in a way of which we can only catch glimpses, but glimpses that act as signs of the state in which God will be all in all. So, the overflow of Godself in self-giving can – must – be seen through the lenses we have been calling *Gloria mundi, Gloria crucis, Gloria in excelsis*. We cannot therefore explore signs of God in creation without relating these signs to what is knowable about Godness from the Cross and Resurrection.

---

[167] Young too calls for 'a perspective humbled by the wondrous ways in which we ourselves are integrated into the natural order, with DNA sequences similar to the malarial parasite!' *God's Presence*, 68.

[168] The hymn was written in 1848 before the publication of Darwin's theory of evolution by natural selection. Indeed, its sentiments smack more of the natural theology of Paley.

[169] For more on John 17, see Chapter 5.

The language of glory, then, allows us to admit God's deep involvement in situations in which the creation harms the creatures, and to interpret, scientifically and poetically, the array of signs to be found in these events, but also to acknowledge the element of mystery to which these events give rise. The God of *glory* is never reducible to a neat set of philosophical attributes, or to a set of data obtainable by the natural theologian – the reality of such a God is always more, and more mysterious than we can imagine. I have been asked, when presenting this three-lensed seeing of the natural world, what set of propositions connects the lenses. Again, I think we should be reluctant to connect them too neatly. That tends in the direction of a systematic theodicy – concern over the adequacy of which was precisely what led me into this study.

What has been the merit of turning our threefold hermeneutical lens round and searching the natural world for signs of glory? First, it takes very seriously that world *as* creation, perfused with signs of its creator. Second, it stresses that it is not enough to view creatures through the single lens of *Gloria mundi*. The ambiguity of the world, and its not-yet-completely redeemed character, requires three lenses of seeing to do justice to its contemplation.

I have deliberately chosen difficult areas of exploration, staying away from those moments, with which every reader will be familiar, when the sheer beauty or magnificence of an element of the natural world evokes a profound sense of wonder. I have tried to show that even very disturbing events in nature, rightly contemplated, can evoke the response of the seraphim in Isaiah 6: 'Holy, holy, holy is the Lord of Hosts. Heaven and earth are full of His glory.' It is worth noting that the prophet's response to this vision contains within it aspects other than pure worship or praise of the divine glory. It contains (or so we may well imagine) an element of dread, a deep sense of repentance, and a longing to respond to the Lord – to respond to the divine longing for a human emissary with a longing to be the one sent, to be caught up (so a post hoc Trinitarian reading might have it) into the great divine mission by which the Father sends the Son, and all his emissaries, to search out the lost.

It will be clear that this exploration of mine, into loci of pain and tragedy, is not theodicy, or at least not in any apologetic sense. Nor is it a way of thinking that could offered in any simple way to a victim of the tsunami, or of malaria (or yet to a farmer who was losing lambs to an eagle). As Surin insists, the practical theologian must allow her story of reality to be interrupted – indeed silenced – by the sheer distress of the sufferer.[170] But the stories, ultimately, fuse in a search for a deeper understanding of the God who made the world and saves it.

It seems to me that an orthodox Christianity that insists on the unity of creation and redemption must suppose two constraints on God. The first is the one I, controversially, outlined in *The Groaning of Creation*: that indeed a world evolving by natural selection, and therefore necessarily involving the suffering of sentient creatures once sentience evolved, is the only sort of world in which the values represented by complex and diverse life could arise. As I noted earlier in this chapter, that this is a logical necessity is something that cannot be demonstrated, but it must be a logical necessity if it is to be a constraint on the power of the sovereign Lord who created existence out of nothing. The second constraint on God, amply familiar from Christian teaching, though still not clearly or univocally understood, is the necessity, oft-repeated through the Gospels, that the Incarnate Son should have to endure degrading execution to release, finally and fully, the redemptive purposes of God into the world.

The first of these constraints is unfamiliar to most Christians; the second is routinely confessed in various ways throughout the Church. But I would submit that they are comparable mysteries – indeed, if anything, the first is easier to understand than the second, since the first has the intuitions of physical science to commend it, whereas the intuitions of the culture that articulated the precursors to theologies of atonement, a culture based on a sacrificial system, are remote from us. In responding to glory, then, we respond to the mystery of God of staggering power, and yet a God who can only effect certain things in certain ways – ways that, in both creation and redemption, involve taking creaturely pain into the heart of the Godhead.

So to contemplate God in relation to the natural world is to contemplate both immense, staggering, unimaginable power, and at the same time a powerlessness we cannot quite fathom either – the creation we so delight in and wonder at cannot arise de novo but only by an immensely long birthing, full of 'futility' (Rom 8.20). Just as to contemplate God's response to the freely chosen harms committed by humans is to engage both with the enigma of the Passion of Jesus, and the triumph of his Resurrection. (I take up the question of freely chosen harms, so-called moral evil, further in Chapter 4.)

---

[170] Surin, *Theology*.

The doxology often attached to the Lord's Prayer (based on manu-script additions to Mt 6.13) might seem at first sight to join three parallel terms 'thine is the kingdom, the power and the glory'. But I wonder if this need be read so simply. There is sufficient paradox in Jesus' teachings of the Kingdom to suggest that it is a place of power reversal, a place where things are not as 'among the Gentiles' (Mk 10.42–45), a place where self-giving love proves transformative for many. So the doxology could be read as saying God's is the servanthood and the sacrifice, and the power and the sovereignty, and the glory that speaks of all of these together.

This is a different way to approach natural theology from the more familiar appeals to order, design and beauty in the natural world. It is a shift that may take a bit of adjustment. I am reminded of the shift in aesthetic required to appreciate Stravinsky's *Rite of Spring* in Nijinsky's revolutionary choreography, after being schooled in the appreciation of classical ballet. The dancers had to be taught to dance on their heels instead of their points. To ground our contemplation of the natural world on a real appreciation of the ambiguous character of that world is to be forced back on our heels by the weight of the reality of that world, but therefore to dance in a more grounded way.

CONCLUSION

This chapter has explored whether our hermeneutical lens can be turned round, so that signs of the Creator in the natural world could be read in terms of glory. That in turn led to the application of the notion of three-lensed seeing as vital to do justice to glory in the whole Christian narrative. It was necessary to engage both with the literature on natural theology, and with the descriptions of contemplation in terms of 'form' and 'inscape'.

Finally, we applied our understandings of glory to three very troubling events in nature, events to which suffering was intrinsic, and sought to infer what could be said about glory in these instances, as limit cases of the effectiveness of the model. In teasing out how disturbing events can nevertheless contain signification of divine glory, I stressed also the divine solidarity with every creature in its suffering and pain, and the utter commitment of God to this passion play, enacted millions of times a day as creatures with significant sentience kill and are killed, struggle with disease, fail in their efforts to flourish. Another necessary element in the contemplation of creaturely glory is the eventual consummation of crea-tion in a state in which there is no more suffering.

Having started to learn to 'dance on our heels' in the contemplation of nature, we turn now to the dance of the human world, and ask how this approach to glory might work itself out in limit cases in that world, in art and poetry, and in the work of a mystic writing under conditions of terrible oppression.

4

Glory in the Arts and in Mysticism

INTRODUCTION

In the last chapter we explored the difficult notion that divine glory might
be seen even in those aspects of the natural world that seem to us ugly, or
disturb us by their violence. I also developed the idea that in order to
apprehend to the full that glory, Christians need to cultivate 'three-lensed
seeing': a willingness to explore with great honesty the character of the
creation, a preparedness, having been willing to perceive the divine reality even within Christ's 'hour' of what the world saw only as dishonour
and death, to relate all creaturely suffering to God's self-disclosure in the
Passion, and also a faith that the present age must be seen in the context of
God eventually becoming 'all in all', and creating an age in which there
will 'be no more crying'.

I showed that the skills needed to contemplate the natural world
involved those of the poet, and Hopkins was our great ally. But I also
laid great stress on the contributions of the sciences. In this chapter
I develop the notion of three-lensed seeing in relation to the human
world. Again poets will be important to us, especially T. S. Eliot and
R. S. Thomas. I also draw on other artforms, including painting and
music. But to enter the very difficult territory of how glory may be
perceived even within situations of suffering or oppression, I also seek
to learn from writing of the sort that is usually called mystical. The effort
of the chapter will be to continue to reflect on what it is to see divine
glory, shifting now to what it is to catch sight of that glory within the
human world.

THE PROBLEM OF MORAL EVIL

The problem will at once be posed: what is the relation between the reading that has been offered of the non-human world in relation to divine glory, and the world of human activity? This question concerns in particular so-called moral evil. To put that question at its sharpest: if the ingenuity of the *plasmodium* that gives rise to malaria is a sign of the ingenuity of God as creator, can the same not be said of a human instrument of torture? Is not harm infliction by humans also part of the God-given order of the world?

I need to make it clear why I answer that question in the negative, why I place freely chosen human actions in a different category from the actions of creatures without any self-conscious freedom of choice. At once I have to qualify these terms – I am not suggesting that any given human action is completely free. I acknowledge how much of our activity results from our neurological wiring and our familial and cultural conditioning. I also acknowledge that our self-consciousness is likewise limited and conditioned. I nevertheless hold that human experience suggests compellingly that within those constraints is a real if partial freedom, and that the scientific evidence does not rule that out.[1]

I write this as the coroner's verdict on the disaster at the Hillsborough football stadium in Sheffield in 1989 is finally announced. The ninety-six who died, and the many injured, and all those whose lives were devastated by the disaster, are acknowledged to have suffered from the incompetence and neglect of the police responsible, aggravated by an attempt to cover up this culpability. (The structure of the stadium itself was also inadequate.) When we contemplate such harm-infliction and negligence by humans, I hold that we cannot expect to see signs of God *in those causes* (in the way that we were able to do with the underlying physical cause of the tsunami). God gave the humans concerned freedom, and the causes of the tragedy were to be found in the misuse of that freedom.

As I shall develop further in Chapter 5, the full expression of the image of God involves human beings becoming 'self-given selves',[2] and fulfilling their destiny by living in a Christlike way, truly returning love to God with

---

[1] For a painstaking analysis giving the scientific account the utmost purchase, see P. Clayton, *In Quest of Freedom: The Emergence of Spirit in the Natural World: Frankfurt Templeton Lectures 2006*, ed. M. G. Parker and T. M. Schmidt (Göttingen: Vandenhoeck and Ruprecht, 2009).

[2] C. Southgate, *The Groaning of Creation: God, Evolution and the Problem of Evil* (Louisville, KY: Westminster John Knox Press, 2008), 71–3.

heart, mind, soul, and strength, and seeking the good of the neighbour with a truly generous heart. This contrasts with other creatures, which fulfil their natures just by being the creaturely selves they are, be they the crocodiles that tear the flesh of zebra as they flounder across an African river, or the orca that rip away at a whale until it dies, or yet the anopheles mosquito. I wrote in *The Groaning of Creation* of God's continual invitation to creatures to explore more and more cooperative strategies of being, but no moral censure attaches to the creaturely 'no' to that invitation, where that 'no' is not a conscious choice.[3] In contrast, freely chosen human harming and violence, committed for selfish ends, is a sin against the God who invites humans into responses of self-giving love.

At the root of all moral evil is a failure first of recognition, of the otherness of God and of neighbour, and second of responding to that recognition in self-giving love. Hopkins formulates this in an interesting way, drawing on the myth of the archangel Lucifer and his fall. He says that Lucifer's sin was 'an exclusive "instressing of his own inscape" ... an excessive dwelling on his own likeness to God'.[4] This prevents both a contemplation of God as God in God's utter otherness, and an acceptance of other beings as equally loved by God and deserving of love.

A parallel analysis can be deployed to the one offered in respect of natural evil.[5] Human beings are, ultimately, part of God's creation, and we may respond to their sinful acts with a mixture of worship of the true God, protest, lament, and practical assistance, just as was suggested in respect of the tsunami. Three-lensed seeing is still required. Such seeing will involve attending carefully to the experience of the sufferers, and relating that experience, if only tacitly, to God's suffering in the Cross of Christ. It will involve protest, and a search for justice, such as so strikingly animated the families and supporters of the Hillsborough victims. It will involve seeing the extraordinary gift in creation that is human life, holding to the astonishing conviction that Christ confronted all sin in his Passion, and therefore pursuing the effort to see with him that

---

[3] Ibid., chapter 4.

[4] G. M. Hopkins, *The Sermons and Devotional Writings of Gerard Manley Hopkins*, ed. C. Devlin (London: Oxford University Press, 1959), 115 (Devlin quoting Hopkins).

[5] And is offered in the radical scheme of Simone Weil, in which evil, including moral evil, is all an aspect of the providence of God. See L. McCullough, *The Religious Philosophy of Simone Weil: An Introduction* (London: I. B. Tauris, 2014). But I draw back from Weil's scheme, holding human beings responsible for their freely chosen evil acts, and therefore regarding moral evil in a different category from natural evil, not as a particular case of its operation as in Weil.

perpetrators of wicked acts 'know not what they do' (Lk 23.34). Even the enemy is to be loved as fellow-creature, in imitation of God's love that never lets the creature go.

But the balance of the response must be different in the case of moral evil. The *dominant* dimension of response must be protest against all injustice and rejection of all gratuitous harming, followed when possible by the exploration of the possibility of reconciliation. A commitment to the latter is part of seeing with the third lens, believing that God's redemptive love will ultimately break down every barrier between persons.

THREE-LENSED SEEING FURTHER EXPLORED

The concept of three-lensed seeing is related to the famous insight of George Steiner in *Real Presences* that we live as though in the time of Holy Saturday, '[b]etween suffering, aloneness, unutterable waste on the one hand and the dream of liberation, of rebirth on the other'.[6] Steiner however omits the dimension that we have called *Gloria mundi*, which as it were sets the 'ground-rules' that lie behind Good Friday, Holy Saturday, and Easter Sunday. Ground rules characterised – as we saw in the last chapter – by a world governed by physical laws and the constraint of limited resources, and also by the emerging of freedom of choices within the unfolding of the biosphere. These hugely generative constraints on life established the conditions that ultimately made possible the Incarnation, just as the human drive to escape those constraints, by seizing at more than can equitably be attained, set up the conditions for the rejection of the Incarnate sign of God's glory, and hence for all those things by which Steiner characterises the 'Friday' of his narrative. The 'Sunday' is the vision of *Gloria in excelsis*, which is glimpsed by Christians already in the Resurrection. But believers also want to insist on the glory of the Friday, where, to quote Gregory of Nyssa, God's power 'is in no way fettered in the midst of conditions contrary to its nature'. Gregory goes on: 'The greatness is glimpsed in the lowliness.'[7] Christ's abasement begins his 'hour' of ultimate glory.

This has potent implications for 'Saturday' living. It means that no abyss of suffering, no extent of impotence before the wicked and torturing

---

[6] G. Steiner, *Real Presences* (Chicago: University of Chicago Press, 1991), 232.

[7] Gregory of Nyssa, quoted in Hans Urs von Balthasar, *Mysterium Paschale: The Mystery of Easter*, transl. A. Nichols (San Francisco, CA: Ignatius Press, 1990), 34.

powers of the world, is a place absent of the presence of Christ. He remains, through his Passion, the ultimate sign of God's involvement even in conditions contrary to the divine nature, an involvement borne out of supreme love for His creatures. But the Christian confession goes further and wants to claim that this involvement is not only compassion at its purest, but is also transformative. That it is associated with the power of the Resurrection in a way that no other powers, however evil, however cynically brutal, can subvert. To see situations in that way is the three-lensed seeing of the Christian Gospel. But it is the difficult delay in seeing the liberating effects of the victory of the Cross that makes this core confession of the divine glory so problematic. While we see so little sign of the transformation of the world we remain Steiner's 'Saturday-dwellers'. We need, in his terms, 'The apprehensions and figurations in the play of metaphysical imagining, in the poem and the music, which tell of pain and of hope, of the flesh that is said to taste of ash and of the spirit which is said to have the savour of fire.'[8]

Shelly Rambo in a very different analysis also writes of 'Saturday living' and of the importance of 'remaining' in the face of traumas, and 'witnessing' to their reality.[9] That thought leads me to a further insight essential for our exploration.

THE BEARING OF REALITY

In the last chapter I wrote about how honest contemplation of the natural world could reveal manifestations of glory, signs of the deep reality of God as creator, and that those signs had to be read with three-lensed seeing. As in that analysis, I want to insist that it is by facing up, as much as possible, to the way things really are, that signs of the divine reality can be seen.

In his play about the martyrdom of Thomas Becket, *Murder in the Cathedral*, T. S. Eliot gave Becket the resonant line 'Human kind cannot bear very much reality.'[10] It is a sign of Eliot's own recognition of the importance of this insight that in the poem 'Burnt Norton', which began

---

[8] Steiner, *Real Presences*, 232.
[9] S. Rambo, *Spirit and Trauma: A Theology of Remaining* (Louisville, KY: Westminster John Knox Press, 2010).
[10] T. S. Eliot, *The Complete Poems and Plays of T. S. Eliot* (London: Faber and Faber, 1969), 271.

as 'off-cuts' from *Murder* and became ultimately the first poem of *Four Quartets,* he deploys the sentence again.[11]

This sense of the importance of facing up to 'necessity' is strong in Simone Weil. Weil came to place great emphasis on breaking through ersatz realities to make contact with the authentically real.[12] She wrote that she herself 'must move towards an abiding conception of the divine mercy, a conception which does not change whatever event destiny may send'.[13] All reality must be borne, and a true vision of God must survive such bearing. A further quotation from her Notebooks illustrates the radical character of her insistence on reality-bearing: 'Not to accept some event taking place in the world is to desire that the world should not exist.'[14] As Harries summarises, 'It is fundamental to [Weil's] thought that we have to accept and come to love the world in its totality.'[15]

Eliot's line can be read in a variety of ways. In its initial context in *Murder*, it means that humans cannot bear, in the sense of face up to, very much of the way things really are 'unless and until we see it fulfilled as the figure of God's purpose'.[16] In 'Burnt Norton' the line floats freer of the context of impending tragedy, and may perhaps connote humans' limited ability to comprehend the complex interplay of time and history, Word and silence, that occupies Eliot in the *Quartets*, and indeed our inability, in the terms of the previous chapter, to instress much of the huge complexity of creation. There is in the line in 'Burnt Norton' an implicit yearning for enlightenment, in moments that connect past, present, and future with particular directness. But not much of such reality can be borne.

There is a third sense of the saying, that of 'bearing' not just in terms of 'facing up to' – 'bearing with', but actually bearing in the sense of taking up, as Christ's followers are exhorted to take up their cross (Mk 8.34). Now the saying might mean that humans are not able to carry our role in, to play our full part in, the flux of reality.

---

[11] Ibid., 172, now with a line break after 'Human kind'. The thought may derive originally from Eliot's study of F. H. Bradley (I thank Dr Daniel Pedersen for this suggestion).

[12] See McCullough, *Religious Philosophy*, chapter 1.

[13] Quoted in R. Harries, *The Beauty and the Horror: Searching for God in a Suffering World* (London: SPCK, 2016), 204.

[14] Quoted in Harries, *Beauty and the Horror*, 176.   [15] Ibid.

[16] So D. Donoghue, *Words Alone: The Poet T. S. Eliot* (New Haven, CT: Yale University Press, 2000), 256. Cf. also Thomas Merton, 'To work out our own identity in God ... demands close attention to reality at every moment': *New Seeds of Contemplation* (New York: New Directions, 1961), 32.

All of these senses relate to our theme of glory. If that term at its fullest and richest is most about signs of the deep reality of God, the way things most truly are, in all their complexity and indeed mystery, then the study of glory is indeed a learning to bear reality more fully. I heard a fine sermon once by the late Bishop Jim Thompson to the effect that it is always difficult to define health, but one definition could be in terms of bearing the maximum amount of reality. In terms of this study, that would mean being as fully receptive as possible to the signs of God within the ambiguities of life. So the path to health is the path to glory, but not in any obvious, or simple, or yet world-denying way.[17]

This phrase of Eliot's about bearing reality may also help Christians with what can be a difficult phrase in Paul's hymn to love in 1 Corinthians 13. Where the Apostle writes that love 'bears all things' (v. 7), this can be misunderstood in terms of the necessity of submission even to injustice and abuse. But if the text is read rather in terms of love bearing the maximum possible extent of reality, perceiving with three-lensed seeing, and responding with lament and protest as well as acceptance, that becomes a springboard for growth and transformation, the very reverse of oppression and degradation.

A remarkably powerful example from Judaism of this courageous facing up to the way things really are, without losing a sense of hope, can be found at the end of David R. Blumenthal's *Facing the Abusing God*. His reflections on God in the light of the Shoah culminate in his closing address to God, which ends, very remarkably:

I do not deny You or Your Torah. You denied us, for we were innocent. You crushed us, yet we were guiltless. You were the Abuser; our sins were not commensurate with Your actions. The responsibility is Yours, not ours ... In spite of all this, we will gather our strength and support one another. We will build our world. We will love one another. We will defend our people and our land. We will believe in You, we will place our hope in You. We will yearn for You, we will wait for You, and we will anticipate the time when we will see Your Face again.[18]

Parables of the bearing of reality can be found in the music of J. S. Bach and Beethoven. Music is of course much associated with glory as often understood in terms of extraordinary beauty. But another of music's great

---

[17] The Eucharist, with its profound recollection of the past and complete openness to God's future, must for Christians be the great training ground in the healthy bearing of reality.

[18] D. R. Blumenthal, *Facing the Abusing God: A Theology of Protest* (Louisville, KY: Westminster John Knox Press, 1993), 299. It will be evident that Blumenthal does not distance his God from the fact of moral evil as I sought to do earlier.

strengths is its ability to evoke struggle and pain. Arguably, it is one of the most eloquent ways humans express the way things really are.[19] In his two great Passion oratorios, Bach creates an astonishing array of signs that focus the human attention on the great sign that is the Passion itself. The same could be said of Handel's *Messiah* as a sign of Christ – Nativity, Passion, Resurrection. But instrumental music can also function as this profound array of signs. This effect is much harder to write about – indeed, all verbal description is reductive of the effects of music on the hearer. Perhaps the closest any words come to describing the effects of great music come in Eliot's *Four Quartets* when he writes of 'music so deeply heard/ that you are the music/ while the music lasts'.[20] Eliot, significantly, wrote to Spender that he hoped to do in verse something of what Beethoven does in music in the late A Minor Quartet.[21] Indeed, those string quartets are – for those with a taste for such interpretation – remarkably concentrated disclosures of the way things really are. At one point in this strange musical journey, Beethoven, out of his deep deafness, and the agony of his many lost hopes, so much passionate longing dispersed or subverted, writes over the score at the beginning of the last movement of the Op. 135 Quartet the heart-rending question '*Müss es sein?*'.[22]

That question, though often interpreted in a comic vein, can be thought of as indicative, in this last phase of Beethoven's quartet writing, of a profound struggle to bear reality. One of the great moments in the expression of the human struggle, one of the great signs of reality borne by a consummate artist, comes when Beethoven can write over the score at the main section of the movement the three further words '*Es müss sein*'.[23] This is not the hope-free acceptance of the writer of Ecclesiastes. Nor is it any blithe conclusion, but one fought for, struggled for, through the medium of the music Beethoven himself never heard. It has the sense that what 'must be' is deeply underpinned by God's own being and love. What 'must be' is not arbitrary or random, but reaches down into a meaning beyond any words.

[19] For a reflection on Bach in the context of divine and created beauty, see J. S. Begbie, 'Created Beauty: The Witness of J. S. Bach' in *The Beauty of God: Theology and the Arts*, ed. D. J. Treier, M. Husbands and R. Lundon (Downers Grove, IL: IVP Academic, 2007), 19–44.

[20] Eliot, *Poems and Plays*, 190.

[21] T. S. Eliot, 'To Stephen Spender, 28 March 1931' in *The Letters of T. S. Eliot*, Vol. 5: 1930–31, ed. V. Eliot and J. Haffenden (London: Faber and Faber, 2014), 529.

[22] 'Must it be?'   [23] 'It must be.'

This is one of the most famous examples in the arts of the bearing of reality, facing up to the way things really are. Beethoven finds this in his struggle. He hears, in his deafness, in the depths of his spirit, glory. He makes us hear it, those who have ears to hear. Myriad listeners have found in these sound-worlds the material for courage, determination, and exhilaration, but obtained out of, through, facing things as they really are. Certainly late Beethoven was a great inspiration to Eliot, and one wonders if those words '*es müss sein*' were in his mind as he composed the character of Becket, going steadfastly to his martyrdom at Canterbury.

In turn this reflection enables us to draw out more of what God's gift to us is in Jesus. We saw in the Introduction that Jesus is the quintessential sign of the deep reality of God, Christ's is glory as of the only-begotten son of the Father, full of grace and truth (Jn 1.14 KJV). We also identified manifestations of the divine reality as calling for a human response.

One of the greatest sayings of the early Church Fathers is Irenaeus of Lyons's pronouncement that '*Gloria enim Dei vivens homo*' usually translated 'The glory of God is a human being fully alive.' This is a magnificent statement of what human life can be. It seems to me a directly Christological statement – the true *vivens homo* is Christ, the authentic 'image of the invisible God' (Col 1.15). We can associate Jesus' full bearing of the divine image with his full response to the glory of the Father in the power of the Spirit. He is completely open to the Father in prayer, even in times of great agony (such as Gethsemane, and the cry of dereliction on the Cross), and this makes him both *the* great sign of God in the world, *and* the great paradigm of human response to divine self-disclosure.

One way to understand the completeness of Jesus' response is that he bears reality to the full. We do not see him evading either his vocation, or the vast spectrum of human need that faced him in his ministry. (Where we do see him apparently limiting his vocation, at the story of the Syro-Phoenician woman in Mark 7.24–9,[24] he allows himself to address the woman's complaint, allows his eyes to be opened to face up to her faith and her need.) So much of modern Western life seems to me to consist of an expedient limiting of what can be asked of us by whom. We strive to create comfort zones, from which are excluded the awkward challenge of the stranger, the beggar, the demented person and the migrant, let alone those who starve in far-off places out of sight, and, largely, mind.

---

[24] And the Matthean parallel of the Canaanite woman at Matthew 15.21–8.

We cannot bear all of this reality and so we make compromises that cut us off from most of it. The Gospel accounts of Christ's itinerant ministry of teaching and healing are a salutary reminder of how inadequately Christians follow his example.

Most profoundly, of course, that ministry of Jesus culminated in his 'being handed over'[25] to the powers of evil. Jesus at his hour bears the whole reality of human sin and the power of evil, with all the God-forsakenness that that involves. I have long pondered the Christian claim that Jesus' suffering was the most extreme a human being has borne. Many of the Good Friday addresses I have heard focus on the extremity of the torture of the crucifixion, the length of the nails, the physical symptoms of asphyxiation as the strength fails. I do not for a moment doubt these details, or the brutality of the punishment, or the degradation it constituted for a Jew. But many of the stories of suffering that the modern world has made us aware of, from the experiments in the concentration camps, to the regime on the Burma Railway, to some of the ways we know women have been and are treated, again often as a matter of military policy, seem to me to throw this claim about the absolute extremity and distinctiveness of Jesus' physical suffering into serious doubt.

So I hold that it is the spiritual suffering of the Cross that is its unparalleled extremity. Throughout the Passion Jesus shows us the God-ness of God in the extremity of dignity, humility, and forgiving love in the Incarnate One. In doing so he has to face, to bear the unbearable reality of, human cruelty, cynicism, and callousness, be it in the vested interests of religion and empire, or the fickleness of crowds, or the casual inhumanity of guards. But beyond that he had to face what Richard Harries calls 'the most fundamental darkness ... our alienation from God ... it is this he entered and overcame'.[26] Jesus had to face the spiritual reality Paul calls Sin,[27] a power that emerges out of the accumulated human rejection of God, and which both seduces and enslaves. Jesus, we are told, had to bear the reality so intimately that Paul can say 'For our sake [God] made him to be sin who knew no sin' (2 Cor 5.21).

Unthinking cruelty abounds in human life. But it is those instances where extreme suffering is inflicted as a deliberate and explicit part of a *system* that, to me at least, are the most disturbing and toxic manifestations of the human capacity for evil. So the claim about Jesus and the

---

[25] W. H. Vanstone, *The Stature of Waiting* (London: Darton, Longman and Todd, 1982), discussed in Chapter 2.

[26] Harries, *Beauty and the Horror*, 135.   [27] For example, at Romans 3.9.

extremity of his suffering must be a claim about his encountering the range of evil, from casual cruelty to religious cynicism, and torture and agonizing and degrading execution used as an instrument of state. Behind that, the reality he bore was that of the apparent victory of the powers of evil, the reviling and destruction of all he had sought to be and do in the years of his ministry, the demoralizing and scattering of his group. All of this, it seems to me, is contained within the cry of dereliction at Mark 15.34 (see Chapter 2).

We saw in the last chapter that facing up to the ways things really are – bearing reality as I now term it – involves desentimentalising the natural world, and recognising how ambiguous and disturbing that world is. What Jesus does in Passion Week is to face to the full the reality of the moral world, what God's gift of human free will means for the creation.

THE BEARING OF REALITY IN THE HEBREW BIBLE

Before the coming of Jesus, the Bible already contained three remarkable essays on the bearing of reality, the determination to face up to the way things really are and pursue their exploration in search of the divine reality, the glory within the flux of creaturely reality. These are the Psalter, the Book of Ecclesiastes, and most famously the Book of Job. Job (a man of uncertain nationality and religious tradition) represents all human searching for signs of the divine in the face of misfortune. The Book is a deeply troubling document for all those who would tidy up the story of human suffering, or yet the story of God. It serves to link the concept of divine glory that is being developed here with the challenge of facing up to the way things really are – bearing reality to the greatest possible extent.

The first troubling element in Job is that God allows the Satan to test Job's uprightness to destruction. Job 1–2 and 42 form a neat little folk-tale of the Satan's failure. But Chapters 3–41 deepen and stretch the folk tale into the masterpiece that has come down to us. They make, powerfully, the point that everyone who has worked in the field of mental health knows so well, that when humans' comfort zones are not just transgressed but torn apart, the capacity of most sufferers to bear the new reality is severely compromised. The sufferer shifts to a new place, which *may*, as Diogenes Allen suggests, be one of reflection on the evil, and the transcendence of her previous state precisely in the acceptance of her limitations. A new possibility *may* open up of knowing the gracious presence of God which 'gives a felicity that is beyond the calculations of the pluses and minuses of the pleasant and unpleasant things of life.'[28] All too often, however, and all too understandably, the response is one of dissociation from reality, the mind escaping into a place where less, rather than more, reality is faced, and egocentricity, far from being transcended as Allen hopes, becomes all consuming.

It might be said that Job fights throughout the Book for a level playing field with God, for some forensic process that will judge the divine righteousness. Instead he gets something very different, which could be represented as a divine rebuff, a rejection of the possibility of that level playing field, but seems to me to be something much more profound. Job is drawn into a far deeper understanding of the inscape of things – into the glory of creation as it reflects its creator.

This is where the Book of Job offers us such an extraordinary third way, beyond easy blessing, or destruction of the personality. Serial catastrophes leave the protagonist cursing the day of his birth, and repeatedly rejecting all the reasonable solutions offered by his friends. He is determined to be given an answer by God, such as would be given in a law court. And what is so striking, when the answer at last comes in Job 38–41, is that it is no answer but a magical mystery tour round God's glory in creation. In fact, Job gets what amounts to a lecture on divine glory, including attention to the appetites of young lions, and prey for the ravens (Job 38.39–41). This literally amazing array of signs of the divine work evokes in Job a response, translated in the NRSV as 'therefore I despise myself, and repent in dust and ashes' (42.6), but perhaps better rendered 'therefore I will be quiet, comforted that I am dust'.[29] Job does *not* accept his limitations through a Stoic reflection on his fragility, as Allen seems at times to advocate. Job persists, he batters away at the reality of his situation until *God shows him his littleness face-to-face, until he sees glory*, and in that encounter his healing begins.[30] Furthermore, he

---

[28] D. Allen, *Theology for a Troubled Believer: An Introduction to the Christian Faith* (Louisville, KY: Westminster John Knox Press, 2010), 79.

[29] S. Mitchell, *The Book of Job* (London: Kyle Cathie, 1989).

[30] I am reminded of M. Wynn Thomas's verdict on R. S. Thomas's theology, that R. S. T. 'shows that an understanding of the divine starts at the point at which man is brutally thwarted in his attempt to hold God simply accountable to human standards of reason, decency and justice': *R. S. Thomas: Serial Obsessive* (Cardiff: University of Wales Press, 2013), 178. So also Frances Young, 'made to respect nature for nature's sake, [Job's] ashamed of his narrow, self-pitying attitude to God's miraculous gift of existence. Face-to-face with the Creator, Job's questions melted away': *God's Presence: A Contemporary Recapitulation of Early Christianity* (Cambridge: Cambridge University Press, 2013), 84.

is then not offered an answer but a deepened relationship, and a new life that is not restoration of his former state but a 'new creation'.[31]

The quest to bear the maximum amount of reality is not necessarily one of acceptance.[32] Passionate protest in prayer may indeed be the most blessed element in the quest, which may also, as we saw in the previous chapter, involve lament, and remedial action. I do not suggest that any given path would suit every situation. But Job, like some of the Psalms, teaches us that protest can be an important way to draw nearer to the mysterious ways of God with the world, though for others, acceptance may be the path to a deeper contact with glory. I return to examples of acceptance later.

The Book of Ecclesiastes catches that mode of reality-bearing from which protest has departed. It is a book that shows us that when our will to protest for a higher vision is weak the answer does not lie in escapism, but in the seeking out of 'acceptable words' (Eccl 12.10 KJV). It reminds us that the unfolding of the rhythms of the cosmos is on a scale larger than human life – all we can glimpse is the fittingness of certain times for certain purposes (Eccl 3.1–8). As such it had a deep influence on Eliot, the author of our lines on reality-bearing.[33]

Ecclesiastes as noted previously is a very interesting text for our purposes because it functions as an anti-doxology, which throws into relief the claims made in other texts. If we are understanding glory as an apprehensible sign of the depths of the divine reality, then Ecclesiastes rejects the possibility of such signs, such glory. All human endeavour and discernment must ultimately fail. God is unknowable, and provides no hope beyond the familiar rhythms of life, after which, in the KJV translation, 'desire shall fail, and man goeth to his long home' (Eccl 12.5). The human experience of *hebel/mataiotēs*, of which the traditional English translation is 'vanity', is that signs of the transcendent, of the presence of

---

[31] Some of this thinking about Job was aided by a reading of J. Friesenhahn, *Trinity and Theodicy: The Trinitarian Theology of von Balthasar and the Problem of Evil* (Aldershot: Ashgate, 2011), 88–97.

[32] Serene Jones quotes movingly from Maya Angelou: 'History, despite its wrenching pain, cannot be unlived; but if faced with courage, it need not be lived again': *Trauma and Grace: Theology in a Ruptured World* (Louisville, KY: Westminster John Knox Press, 2009), 33. Note, however, the importance in cases of possible traumatisation of acknowledging the fact of what has happened.

[33] See the references to Eliot in E. S. Christianson, *Ecclesiastes through the Centuries* (Oxford: Blackwell, 2007).

God in human life, with its disclosure of divine depth and invitation to response, are absent.

But Ecclesiastes is, in the end, a flattened form of contemplation. When it is read in the Christian canon, it reminds believers to grind their first lens of seeing, *Gloria mundi*, as truly and realistically as possible. It has its force on the Christian reader precisely because the other two lenses – through which we see God's redemptive purposes in this violence-filled and sometimes pointless-seeming world, *Gloria crucis* and *Gloria in excelsis* – are veiled.

The Psalms, in their rich and baffling diversity, fall between the poles marked out by Job and Ecclesiastes. The Psalms explore to the full the world of violence and apparent pointlessness as it was understood at their time of writing. But, typically, they do not let go either hope or protest. They affirm the meaningfulness of lament. They are for the ordinary Christian the primer in reality-bearing, exploring as they do such a range of contexts and emotions in which situations must be confronted as they really are.

That these three texts are in the Hebrew Bible reflects the extent to which the Jewish people, both in the journey recounted in the Scriptures and in their later journeys, teach the world about the bearing of reality. But why, for the ordinary Christian, is this motif of bearing reality so important?

The most obvious reason must be ethical. Only if Christians recognise the reality of the predicament of so many human beings, and so much of the non-human creation, can they hope to be of appropriate help. But in the terms we have been exploring here, there is a more profound theological reason. This relates to my proposal of the importance of three-lensed seeing – of seeing events both in the human and the non-human world in terms of creation, Cross, and that eschatological realm that begins with the Resurrection. As Christians bear reality to the fullest extent possible, they also endure 'all things' (1 Cor 13.7), for the sake of what Christ endured in manifesting his glory, and believe and hope all things about the salvation that comes through him.

THREE-LENSED SEEING IN VISUAL ARTS AND ARCHITECTURE

I established in the previous section that three-lensed seeing of the world must be pursued with the maximum honesty, bearing to the full the reality of this not-yet-fully-redeemed world. That means Christians feeding off the Scriptures, the array of signs of the story of God that allows the lenses of glory to be constructed. But believers also need the vision of artists and architects, to sharpen their seeing through each of the lenses. And they need mystics who have glimpsed what remains hidden from most of us. We explored the Scriptural basis of glory in Chapter 2, and I return to it in Chapter 5 when we consider what it might be to be 'transformed from one degree of glory to another' (2 Cor 3.18). For von Balthasar, although God's light 'centrally illumines the incarnate Son ... [i]t could be the case (God alone can distinguish here) that God's true light also falls on figures of the human imagination ... and ... can lead ... through their partial truth to the God of revelation'.[34] He is interested there in myths, but I want to explore here whether figures of the human imagination such as visual and literary art can also help to illumine the divine glory.

I am helped here by Rowan Williams's comments on art in his Clark Lectures of 2005, in which he explores the influence of Jacques Maritain on twentieth-century artists, especially David Jones and Flannery O'Connor. Williams writes:

art seeks to reshape the data of the world so as to make their fundamental structure and relation visible. Thus the artist *does* set out to change the world, but – if we can manage the paradox – to change it into itself.[35]

This clearly has links to the understanding of glory being explored here, that it consists of signs of the way things really are in a world created, companioned, loved, and redeemed by God. Artists, on Williams' terms, are capable of generating just such signs of the fundamental data of the world[36] – central to which data is that the world *is* created, loved, and redeemed. This generation of signs, this discovery of glory, does not require the artist to be a Christian, or yet a morally good person; that is one of the enigmas of artistic making.

Felix Ó Murchadha's fascinating but dense study of *A Phenomenology of Christian Life*[37] is intriguingly subtitled 'Glory and Night', and he makes considerable play in the middle of the book of themes of night

[34] H. U. von Balthasar, *The Glory of the Lord: A Theological Aesthetics*, Vol. 1, Seeing the Form, transl. E. Leivà-Merikakis, ed. J. Fessio, S. J. and J. Riches (Edinburgh: T&T Clark, 1982), 156.

[35] R. Williams, *Grace and Necessity: Reflections on Art and Love* (London: Continuum, 2005), 17–18, emphasis in original.

[36] Under the prompting of the Spirit, as I would say, or reflecting 'God's formative mental activity within our own,' as Williams puts it (ibid., 23).

[37] F. Ó Murchadha, *A Phenomenology of the Christian Life: Glory and Night* (Bloomington, IN: Indiana University Press, 2013).

and darkness. These themes seem to stem from his perception that Christ, the light coming into the world, was not known by the world. This was a light that shone in darkness, and was seen only by the eye of faith.[38] Therefore, there is a sense in which true seeing means going beyond what is obvious by the light of day. It also means going beyond temporal limitation to be able to see eschatologically, therefore with hope as well as faith, bound together by love.

Lovers of English poetry will immediately be reminded of Henry Vaughan's phrase in his poem 'Night', 'a deep but dazzling darkness'. Vaughan evokes Nicodemus' journey to meet Jesus by night (Jn 3.1–21). In a recent reading of the poem, Thomas Gardner concludes:

> Like the Nicodemus of our reading, Vaughan's speaker acknowledges that he is blind and does not know. He admits that it is not more of the world's light he needs. What he desires is what the Nicodemus he imagined coming by night had – the care-silencing night of God's presence itself ... God's darkness is 'deep', because it overwhelms every attempt to know and control, but is also 'dazzling', since it contains the sun of God's glory.[39]

Ó Murchadha goes on to say very similar sorts of things about being open to the singular being of created entities to the ones I outlined in the previous chapter. True seeing involves seeing an other in his or her (or its) particularity, and also in the context of the whole Christian narrative of creation and redemption. It is a form of seeing in the night, being open to the radiance of the things contemplated, and thus being able to give praise for them as gifts of God.[40] Never, then, being satisfied by their beauty, but allowing desire to go beyond creatures to their creator. Extending that thought in the light of the last chapter, I suggest that the contemplation of nature is beset by risks of idolatry, of partial instressing that ends up turning back to the perceiver. If the creature perceived is controlled, if the one seeing it refuses to look through and beyond it to its creator, then in the end what is being contemplated is the controlling self.

There are definitely points of intersection between Ó Murchadha's book and the present study, though his approach to glory and night draws on this mystical approach to authentic seeing, rather than on a sense of the ambiguity of the natural world. But his sense that 'glory is dark' and seeing

---

[38] More generally, he claims that 'Concealment, secrecy, disguise is constitutive of all revelation; being revealed is being concealed' (ibid., 128).

[39] T. Gardner, *John in the Company of Poets: The Gospel in Literary Imagination* (Waco, TX: Baylor University Press, 2014), 55–6.

[40] Ó Murchadha, *Phenomenology*, 126.

glory means 'developing a way of seeing in the dark'[41] forms a very interesting introduction to my next section in which I look at the way in which
some artists and mystical see-ers have discerned glory in situations of
doubt or darkness.

Here I consider specific examples from the arts and architecture that
illustrate this strange, darkened aspect of glory. New York City provides
my architectural examples of glory in the sense being explored here – signs
of a reality beyond our comprehension. The first is seemingly accidental –
it is the dark, windowless dome of the unfinished Cathedral of Saint John
the Divine. Above the crossing, where the eye is naturally drawn to the
highest, most 'Godward' point of the church, is only darkness. After the
very tall Gothic nave, this sudden mystery arrives as an extraordinarily
effective sign that our search for more transparent signs of the Godness of
God is doomed to failure. The eye is lifted away into darkness. It is enough.
Ironically, the dome is 'temporary', though I hope it long survives.

In Chapter 2 the Cenotaph in London was used as a visual aid to illustrate the Hebrew word *kavōd*. The very blockiness of the monument
conveys the weight of the costs of war. As I remarked there, the only
theological element of the monument is the way the blocky sides point
upwards to a place beyond themselves. They hint, ever so subtly, at *Gloria
in excelsis*. I now consider my second New York artefact, the 9/11
Memorial.

Constructed to a design by Michael Arad, this consists of two massive
granite-lined square hollows, each within the footprint of one of the
destroyed towers of the World Trade Center. Within each of the hollowed-
out areas, a deeper hollow sits, its base below the level to which the eye
can travel. Water falls vertically down the outside walls, streams inwards,
and falls down the inner well. The outer waterfalls flow fast, catch light,
drift a little in the breeze. The sun evokes rainbows in the bouncing spray,
and they find reflections in the dark walls. That same water then slips,
slides, undramatically, relentlessly down the inner well, into darkness.
Occasional white roses are stuck into the names incised around the rim
of the monument; these are telling reminders of the particularity of grief.
The seemingly endless downward path of the falling water suggests that
this grief goes as deep as grief can go. For the believer, naturally, this is
into the heart of God, and into divine depths beyond all human understanding. A very profound metaphor for an aspect of divine reality can be

---

[41] Ibid., 128.

glimpsed in this nominally secular monument.[42] It must be so, when a truth so profound finds articulation uncontaminated by signs of worldly power or celebrity. The memorial's downward draw on the eye is a remarkable contrast to the new towers arising around the perimeter.

When I visited the Memorial the flow down the outer walls of the North Pool had been switched off. The friend I was with remarked how much more beautiful it was with the water going. But considered only from the standpoint of glory, only of the depths of the divine grief symbolised in the water still tumbling into the central well, the fountainless North Pool was the purer study. There was nothing to draw the eye but the deep inexorable falling of the last of the fallen water into that dark, apparently bottomless inner well.

Contemplating the memorial leads to the extraordinary thought that perhaps one reason why humans cannot look on the divine glory is that we cannot be exposed to the profundity of the divine sorrow at creaturely suffering.

The Memorial to 9/11 should remind us not just of *Gloria crucis*, the immeasurable pathos within the heart of God, to which the Cross points us, but also of an important aspect of our third lens, that of *Gloria in excelsis*. Eschatological consummation brings all sins into the light of divine justice. To see through this lens is deeply consoling and life giving to the sufferer, but it is not a comfortable seeing for those (most human beings living in the West) caught in collusive structures that denigrate the value of human life and neglect the environment today's children will inherit. Still less for those who have set their hearts on paths of violence.

My next example is a painting, one that illustrates the tension between beauty and glory that I began to explore in the Introduction. Piero della Francesca's extraordinary study of the Resurrection, which hangs in his home town of Borgo San Sepolcro, was called by Aldous Huxley 'the greatest picture in the world'.[43] Huxley marvelled that it could be found in such an utterly unremarkable little town. And indeed San Sepolcro is a very ordinary Tuscan town, which I visited on a quiet Sunday morning in spring. The fresco has been moved from the *Residenza* where it was painted to the civic museum for ease of preservation and access. A short

---

[42] It functions therefore as a kind of 'built theodicy' in the phrase of Avril Alba: *The Holocaust Memorial Museum: Sacred Secular Place* (Basingstoke: Palgrave Macmillan, 2015).

[43] A. Huxley, 'The Best Picture' in *Along the Road: Notes and Essays of a Tourist* (London: Triad/Paladin Books, 1985 [1925]) 106–12, at 107.

sunlit walk through quiet squares took me to the museum, and after unremarkable rooms comes the main salon with the Resurrection high on a wall. As soon as you are in this room the piercing gaze of the Risen Christ addresses you, searches you, anatomises your inner longings. This painting is a sign indeed, of the certainty of the divine triumph, of the inevitability of the divine judgment which the Father has placed in the Son's hands (cf. Rom 2.16, 2 Cor 5.10). But also and very especially, it is a sign of the searching of the hearts of human beings that is part of God's ways with the world. The gaze of Piero's Risen Lord calls unquestionably, indeed immediately, for a response, for repentance, amendment of life.

So the face, the gaze of the Christ is glorious, in the terms in which we have been working. It is a sign of the deep reality of the God who is with the world, and of those saving divine purposes that necessarily involve judgment. But it is not to my eye aesthetically pleasing. It is as disturbing a face as I have seen from the Italy of the period. And appropriately so – Piero shows us a face that has seen death. The face is perfectly featured, but has this devouring searchingness that prevents the response of delight, insists on the response of contrition.

The contemplation of this painting offers an interesting example of three-lensed seeing. The background is of steep Italian hill country, pines, and mountains behind. It is a (stylised) depiction of the area where Piero grew up, and which he loved. God's creation honoured, *Gloria mundi*. The tomb on which the Risen Christ puts his foot, the pose of sovereignty holding a banner aloft, and the sense of confusion in the sleeping soldiers, are all signs of Christ the first fruits of the new age, the beginning of the conquest of death that leads to God being all in all. God's new creation, proclaimed – *Gloria in excelsis*. But the face of the Christ is a face with death in it. It witnesses to the reality of death faced by the Incarnate One, *Gloria crucis* – hell encountered – and harrowed.

This is a painting, as Huxley says, of 'natural, spontaneous and unpretentious grandeur'[44] (that word again, which is so close to 'glory'). It is a superb visual parable of glory as the Godness of God, apprehensible to the full only through three-lensed seeing that recognises the complexity, and the drama, of God's ways with the world.

Salisbury Cathedral, where I gave the lectures from which this book arises, provides two further remarkable visual parables of my understanding of glory. The cruciform font in patinated bronze on a stone plinth,

---

[44] Ibid., 108.

designed by William Pye, is eloquent of so much of what one would want to say about the Godness of God. The font is full to the brim with water, which gives a beautiful still reflection of the space and light and strength of the Cathedral nave and vault. But there is also a darkness in the depths of the font, which the reflection hides. That hidden darkness speaks of the death that baptism involves (Rom 6. 3–4), which in turn is given power and reality by the death of Christ. And the extraordinary Prisoners of Conscience east window (Gabriel Loire) is an eloquent sign of the profundity and sadness of the journey of those who give up out-ward freedom for inner conviction. It is a spectacular sign of *Gloria crucis*, the deep reality of that struggle, and of the prisoners' encounter with Christ crucified.

So we see in visual artists and architects, in Piero, in Arad, in the artists of Salisbury Cathedral, the human ability to make signs of the deep reality of God.

GLORY IN THE WORK OF AN IMPORTANT TWENTIETH-CENTURY POET

I now move to considering our understanding of glory in the work of an important modern religious poet. I choose as my poet of glory the Welsh priest-poet R. S. Thomas (1913–2000), whose perceptions of nature helped us also in Chapter 3. This choice may seem surprising at first. A more obvious one would have been William Blake, a visionary who could, famously, see eternity in a grain of sand, heaven in a wildflower, and, on gazing at the sun, not 'a round Disk of fire somewhat like a Guinea?' but rather 'an Innumerable company of the Heavenly host crying "Holy Holy Holy is the Lord God Almighty!"'.[45] Blake, these passages suggest, was an expert in interpreting signs of transcendent reality. But the ethos of this book is to look for glory in the most difficult, paradoxical places, places where it might not ordinarily be looked for. As we shall see, the work of R. S. Thomas offers us new insights into such glory, at the edge of our understanding.

Thomas is proverbially a poet of the reality of religious doubt, of a sense of God's silence, even God's absence. Tony Brown writes,

---

[45] W. Blake, 'A Vision of the Last Judgment' in *Poetry and Prose of William Blake*, ed. G. Keynes (New York: Random House, 1946), 652.

His is a religious poetry for our time not because of his faith – though the expression of that faith can be deeply moving – but because of his anguish and uncertainty, because of the strenuousness of his questioning and the persistence of his search for something eternal.[46]

So it is interesting to read in an interview Thomas gave in 1969 that he saw the role of the poet as 'to show the true glory of life ... to elevate man [*sic*] also, and life, and the earth'.[47]

Thomas, then, is famous for his explorations of his own hesitations in faith, as well as for his sometimes acerbic assessments of the Welsh hill farmers among whom he ministered. That makes the more remarkable the experiences of theophany that his work contains.

What will more easily be conceded than that Thomas is a poet of glory is that he is a poet of the bearing of reality. In 'Priest and Peasant' he speaks of God

Who sees you suffer and me pray/And touches you with the sun's ray,/That heals not, yet blinds my eyes/And seals my lips as Job's were sealed/Imperiously in the old days.[48]

The same honest record of his sadness at human illness can be found in the poem 'Evans': 'It was not the dark filling my eyes/And mouth appalled me ... It was the dark/Silting the veins of that sick man/I left stranded upon the vast/And lonely shore of his bleak bed.'[49]

This is uncomfortable truth-telling about God and human life, but it is real, true to the most profound experience of the ways of God with human beings. Thomas's work, as D. Z. Phillips has said,

so far from wanting solutions to pain and suffering which consist in attempts to explain them away in terms of higher aims, attempts to mediate a sense of 'the higher' in religion by accepting the pain and suffering on their own terms. God becomes involved in the suffering and is no longer the external justification of it.[50]

Phillips continues that Thomas 'shows us a religious faith which actually depends on embracing the mixed character of human life in a way which

---

[46] T. Brown, *R. S. Thomas* (Cardiff: University of Wales Press, 2013), 117.
[47] T. Brown, '"On the Screen of Eternity": Some Aspects of R. S. Thomas's Prose' in *Critical Writings on R. S. Thomas*, ed. S. Anstey (Bridgend: Seren Books, 1992), 182–201, at 189.
[48] R. S. Thomas, *Collected Poems 1945–1990* (London: J. M. Dent, 1993), 62.
[49] Ibid., 74.
[50] D. Z. Phillips, *Poet of the Hidden God: Meaning and Mediation in the Poetry of R. S. Thomas* (London: Macmillan, 1986), 43.

does not deny its character ... No larger system emerges in which suffering is the means to a higher good'. It is true that there is no redemptive *system* in Thomas's poetry, but there is hope, as in the remarkable ending to his bleak poem 'Geriatric':

> ... I come away
> comforting myself, as I can,
>   that there is another
> garden, all dew and fragrance,
>   and that these are the brambles
> about it we are caught in,
>   a sacrifice prepared
> by a torn god to a love fiercer
>   than we can understand.[51]

Here in the coda we see Thomas, in response to his grim experience of the geriatric ward, resorting to a hope of *Gloria in excelsis*.

Thomas is continually searching in his work for signs of the divine reality, so he is very much, in my terms, a poet of divine glory. But so much of his work, particularly in his later phase, is about the elusiveness of such signs. Arguably, he comes to believe that the elusiveness *is* the most typical sign of the divine reality. In what follows I explore both his theophanies and his exploration of divine elusiveness, or absence.

It is Thomas's surprise at divine disclosure that gives his epiphanies such power and resonates so strongly with contemporary spiritual searches that go on hoping, but expect little, certainly in the way of glory. His poem 'The Bright Field', from his 1975 collection *Laboratories of the Spirit*, is indicative of his approach:

> I have seen the sun break through
> to illuminate a small field
> for a while, and gone my way
> and forgotten it. But that was the pearl
> of great price, the one field that had
> the treasure in it. I realize now
> that I must give all that I have
> to possess it. Life is not hurrying
>
> on to a receding future, nor hankering after
> an imagined past. It is the turning
> aside like Moses to the miracle

---

[51] R. S. Thomas, *Collected Later Poems 1988–2000* (Newcastle upon Tyne: Bloodaxe Books, 2004), 213.

> of the lit bush, to a brightness
> that seemed as transitory as your youth
> once, but is the eternity that awaits you.[52]

The word 'glory' is not mentioned, though the image of brightness is profoundly suggestive. It is the invocation of the burning bush that marks this out as a poem of theophany. The 'lit bush' is the quintessential Old Testament disclosure of the deep reality of God (see Chapter 2). Exodus 3.1–4.17 speaks of God's overpowering holiness, accompanied by an invitation (in Moses' case very strong) to transformation. Thomas marks out the 'turning aside ... to a brightness' – if only we could remain sufficiently focused and courageous to contrive it – as the deep reality of human life lived in response to God. The outer eye goes on its way, but as Christopher Morgan puts it, the Kingdom (indicated by the two parables from Mt 13) 'waits to be glimpsed, experienced, albeit momentarily, in and through the natural world, but also it is easily overlooked'.[53] 'Turning aside' is of the essence, just as the Lord's perception in Exodus 3 that Moses turned aside to the burning bush leads to the auditory theophany.[54] The coda of the poem is the conclusion that that current of relationship, that radiance responded to, can never fail. Put in the terms of three-lensed seeing, Thomas comes to realise the reality of *Gloria in excelsis*, for which the sunlit field serves as a wistful metaphor.[55]

In a 1974 radio talk, republished in his *Selected Prose*, Thomas ponders the possibility that 'alongside us, made invisible by the thinnest of veils, is the heaven we seek ... To a countryman it is the small field suddenly lit up by a ray of sunlight ...[Indeed] It is even closer ... It is within us, as Jesus said'.[56] So theophanic signs can be glimpsed in the exterior world, but they can also be found within. Nature mysticism, as Morgan points out, gives way in Thomas to 'the experience of pure mysticism'.[57]

---

[52] Thomas, *Collected Poems*, 302.

[53] C. Morgan, *R. S. Thomas: Identity, Environment and Deity* (Manchester: Manchester University Press, 2003), 65.

[54] G. W. Savran, *Theophany in Biblical Narrative* (Edinburgh: T&T Clark, 2005), chapter 1.

[55] As A. M. Allchin says, 'We step out from the insistent horizontal line which hurries us from past to future, and begin to be aware of the present moment as a moment which is touched by eternity and thus full of the riches of eternity': 'Emerging: A Look at Some of R. S. Thomas' More Recent Poems' in *Critical Writings on R. S. Thomas*, ed. S. Anstey (Bridgend: Seren Books, 1992), 100–11, quotation on 106.

[56] R. S. Thomas, *Selected Prose*, ed. S. Anstey (Bridgend: Poetry Wales Press, 1983), 152.

[57] Morgan, *R. S. Thomas*, 69.

In the late poem 'The Indians and the Elephant', Thomas seems to combine the two, writing:

> . . . I, though I am
> not blind, feel my way
> about God, exploring him
> in darkness. Sometimes he is
> a wind, carrying me off;
> sometimes a fire devouring
> me. Rarely, too rarely
> he is as the scent
> at the heart of a great flower
> I lean over and fall
> into. But always he surrounds
> me, mostly as a cloud
> lowering, but one through which
> suddenly light will strike,
> burnishing the cross
> waiting on me with spread wings.
> like the fiercest of raptors.[58]

The divine encounters are essentially interior, but can only be expressed in terms of natural forces.

Another fine R. S. Thomas poem of 'glory', as this book understands it, is 'In a Country Church', from his 1955 collection *Song at the Year's Turning*. This also warrants reproducing in full.

> To one kneeling down no word came.
> Only the wind's song, saddening the lips
> Of the grave saints, rigid in glass;
> Or the dry whisper of unseen wings,
> Bats not angels, in the high roof.
>
> Was he balked by silence? He kneeled long,
> And saw love in a dark crown
> Of thorns blazing, and a winter tree
> Golden with fruit of a man's body.[59]

Here in nine lines are many of the themes that engage us here. The unknown protagonist is denied a 'word' in the conventional sense of a heard encounter with God – such as he might have been seeking. What he hears is 'the wind's song', and we may catch with that an echo of the first section of Psalm 19 – creaturely praise goes out from them in their 'song' but without 'words' humans can discern. William V. Davis seems to catch

---

[58] R. S. Thomas, *Collected Later Poems*, 252.   [59] Thomas, *Collected Poems*, 67.

the same allusion when he calls this 'a kind of cosmic speech perhaps, but still not a fully interpretable "word"'.[60] And the bats too have their part in the song of praise, though they are not the bright, spectacular winged messengers of God for whom, again, the pilgrim pray-er might have begun by longing.

The poem may be read as saying that its final epiphany came after persistence in prayer overcame the disappointment of God's apparent silence. But I invite the reader to consider whether the wordless songs of the first stanza do not in a way prepare for the epiphany of the second, in which the Passion of Christ and the appearance to Moses are coevoked, and a new vision of praise found in a tree that can bear the fruit of salvation. The 'songs' of the bats and the wind, on this reading, prepare for the vision – they are not discarded when it comes. *Gloria mundi* – perceived through the realities of the created world, not some trite or sentimental version – paves the way for a vision of *Gloria crucis*.

The task of the contemplative is to kneel long, 'striking my prayers on a stone/heart' as Thomas says in 'The Empty Church'.[61] It is to yearn for that directness of vision that came to Isaiah in the year King Uzziah died (Is 6.1f.), through which the prophet came to understand that the whole earth is full of the signs of God's reality. But the way to such a vision is not merely through persistence, refusal to be 'balked' in the poem's word; it is also through those lesser encounters, those subtler songs, that come through the natural world to those with ears to hear. Though the songs sing of ambiguity, and of pain, as we noted in the previous chapter, they can prepare us to see what cannot be named other than as 'love'. And note that the love itself recognises and faces the ambiguity. The crown is a dark one.

In 'The Bright Field', the sign of eternity, *Gloria in excelsis*, is what the poet wants to show is often missed; in 'In a Country Church', the *Gloria crucis* is perceived only after long kneeling. But in these poems Thomas establishes himself as a contemplative open to theophany. And as Carys Walsh notes, 'the moment of epiphany requires a response: perhaps it fulfils its sacramental potential only in the surrender, turning aside, resting or stopping which is evoked'.[62]

[60] W. V. Davis, *R. S. Thomas: Poetry and Theology* (Waco, TX: Baylor University Press, 2007), 45.

[61] Thomas, *Collected Poems*, 349.

[62] C. Walsh, 'The Sacramental Vision of R. S. Thomas' (Ph.D. thesis, Heythrop College, University of London, 2010), 194.

However, the theme of positive epiphany becomes less explicit as Thomas's work develops, and the hiding of overt expressions of glory a more and more important theme. Morgan notes that there is a transition around the time Thomas moves to Aberdaron (1967), with a more sustained 'inward and downward metaphysical probing of the nature of deity and of the individual self'.[63] By the collection *Frequencies* (1978), there is a strong sense of the search for God within, rather than 'out there'. Signs of God are to be found in the long mystical process of meditating on God's immanent, but often profoundly elusive, self, rather than being glimpsed in the sunlit field.[64]

In a way, the poem 'Sea-Watching'[65] acts as a complement to 'The Bright Field'. Both poems, fascinatingly, come from the same 1975 collection. This time the poet-contemplative is determined not to go on his way forgetting. Rather he is prepared to wait and watch,[66] recognising that the 'rare bird' of spiritual epiphany *is* rare. 'It is when one is not looking,/at times when one is not there/ that it comes.' And he comes to realise that there is a beauty in the watched scene from which brightness is absent, a beauty of singleness of mind longing for God. This is a related thought to that very powerful coda to the poem 'Kneeling', 'The meaning is in the waiting'.[67]

Davis comments interestingly on 'The Empty Church', as follows:

> this prayer is a petition to God not for his presence, not for his return in some sort of new incarnation, but ... that God assert himself in the speaker's heart, imprint himself on 'its' walls, illuminating them with even the 'shadow' of a faith in the reality of a source beyond it, no matter how vague and incomprehensible it might be, no matter how much it might elude the head, the intellect, and the rational understanding, still it would be there, if not as a present reality, at least as a real presence, both mysterious and meaningful simultaneously.[68]

In other words, the purest form of prayer is just for contact, by whatever sign, even, as Walsh has it, through 'felt absence but understood presence'[69] with the Godness of God. It *is* Moses' prayer, show me your glory

---

[63] Morgan, *R. S. Thomas*, 13.

[64] So in the later collection *Counterpoint*, Thomas remarks that we 'draw a little nearer to/ such ubiquity by remaining still': Thomas, *Collected Later Poems*, 118.

[65] Thomas, *Collected Poems*, 306.

[66] To learn to look, as Allchin puts it, and 'to look beyond our own desires and illusions to what is actually there': 'Emerging', 103.

[67] Thomas, *Collected Poems*, 199.   [68] Davis, *Poetry*, 50–1.

[69] Walsh, 'Sacramental Vision', 141.

(Ex 33.18), which we began to explore in Chapter 2. And the response, at most, is mysterious. Charged with meaning, but sometimes the meaning remains in the waiting, the longing, however plaintive, for the *Gloria in excelsis*. Often in Thomas the longing for theophany is met by an absence, though also with a sense, nevertheless, of the value of the search, the prayer, the waiting.[70]

In a radio interview in 1981, Thomas used the remarkable image of the 'form' a hare makes when it settles itself in grassland. Thomas had found one of these 'resting nests' still warm, 'and this is my feeling for God – that we don't actually find him, but we find where he has been, we find the place still warm with his presence'.[71] So the suggestive absence turns out to be a sign of the divine reality, but what is principally signified is that God's *elusiveness*. That of course is an aspect of the *kavōd Yahweh* as we explored it in Chapter 2, that it cannot be adequately described or pinned down. Waterman's sense is that 'Thomas's focus is on an all-powerful, elusive, unpredictable and amorphous God to whom it is very hard to relate';[72] this is more uncomfortably close to the God of most of the Bible than many Christians would be willing to admit. So 'one should feel a sense of human belonging with God in any case, but should be in awe, in fear, in love with the ineffable'.[73] God is not domesticable or describable or summonable in human ways (and we should be very glad of that, for whom would we trust to do the summoning?). 'God's presence can be

---

[70] Walsh's thesis is very valuable on the theme of absence in Thomas, and I thank her for directing me to it as well as for valuable feedback on this chapter. She writes of Thomas's later poetry: 'the absence to be found in empty space becomes redolent with presence … Thomas's vision of world as sacrament deepens. Absence, void and space become sources for God's revelation in the world': 'Sacramental Vision', 158–9. Cf. also Alastair Heys' comment that Thomas's negative theology involves 'the discovery of what is present through an absence that is suggestively too complete': *R. S. Thomas and Romanticism* (Plovdiv: Pygmalion Press, 2004), 136. I note also Richard Rohr's point that God's silence can be very powerful, as in the brooding over the formless void in Genesis 1.2, or Jesus' eloquent silence before Pilate (Mk 15.5, Jn. 19.9) – a powerful sign that earthly power has no coercive hold on divine love. R. Rohr, *Silent Compassion: Finding God in Contemplation* (Cincinnati, OH: Franciscan Media, 2014), 2–6.

[71] Quoted in R. Waterman, *Belonging and Estrangement in the Poetry of Philip Larkin, R. S. Thomas and Charles Causley* (Aldershot: Ashgate, 2014), 176. Perhaps surprisingly, we find C. S. Lewis, a much more overt apologist than R. S. Thomas, writing that '[i]f one cannot "practice the presence of God", it is something to practice the absence of God, to become increasingly aware of our own unawareness': *The Four Loves* (London: Geoffrey Bles, 1960), 160.

[72] Waterman, *Belonging*, 177.   [73] Ibid., 177.

experienced only on his own terms.'[74] We saw in 'Sea-Watching' 'the importance of divine absence that somehow connotes presence. That might be seen as the late twentieth-century equivalent of the much more physical and anthropomorphic language of Yahweh's response to Moses at Exodus 33.18f., in which the human seeker is hidden in a cleft of the rock, while the Lord passes by.

Can we get any closer to how an experience of divine absence might be connected with glory? In two senses, it seems to me. First, in the sense on which Brueggemann reflects in *Ichabod toward Home*. The Christian life means, very often, *waiting* – for the 'Sunday' joy of being part of the journey of all things toward eternal life, which is the Christian reading of the Psalmist's joy that 'comes in the morning'. Facing up to the way things really are in their not-yetness, being prepared to wait, within the divine economy, for transformation 'yields all the unimaginable thickness of humanness given as gift, task, burden by the God who calls all things into existence'.[75] That Christians wait, that they long for what we occasionally glimpse but do not have as a 'continuing city' is part of the drama of God's glory, *mundi, crucis, in excelsis*. Prayerful waiting, like that of Thomas in 'Kneeling', is within a frame, symbolised spatially in the poem by a church building but in reality temporal, theo-dramatic, to use von Balthasar's concept, the frame of the 'now but not yet' of Christian soteriology.

The second sense is the more elusive, but nevertheless has a very important place in Christian spirituality. From Pseudo-Dionysius the Areopagite in the fifth/sixth century CE onwards, the tradition has recognised a theology and spirituality built around a *via negativa* which takes various forms. For an important introduction to this tradition, see Denys Turner's *The Darkness of God*.[76] Turner brings out well the very paradoxical nature of attempts to express the *via negativa*. Both because the absence of an experience is still a form of experience, and also because all

---

[74] Ibid., 179. In discussing the poem 'Shadows', Walsh writes: 'We are left ... in a world which both points to God and guards against the intensity of God's presence in absence': 'Sacramental Vision', 218–9.

[75] W. Brueggemann, *Ichabod toward Home: The Journey of God's Glory* (Grand Rapids, MI: Eerdmans, 2002), 140.

[76] D. Turner, *The Darkness of God: Negativity in Christian Mysticism* (Cambridge: Cambridge University Press, 1995). David Brown traces a yet more radical theology of darkness and unknowing back to Gregory of Nyssa: *Divine Generosity and Human Creativity: Theology through Symbol, Painting and Architecture* (London: Routledge, 2017), 84–5.

our God-statements are metaphorical, and therefore not negated in the way that propositions may be negated, but rather through the holding together of contradictories.[77] R. S. Thomas seems to adopt this 'dazzling darkness' strategy when he writes of absence like presence.

The *via negativa* can mean a withdrawal from positive, 'cataphatic' propositions about the deity; it can mean an ascetic withdrawal from the world of the senses; it can mean a cultivation of an extreme sense of the unworthiness of the human to approach God directly, accompanied by a sense that not having to look into the face of God is a form of protection.[78] John of the Cross identified a phase in the spiritual journey as 'the dark night of the soul'. This is not the depression or discouragement so often experienced by Christians as they begin to try to make sense of the Gospel in the world (to search for signs of glory within so much disappointment). It is rather a recognisable stage in the experience of the 'advanced' mystic, 'a love story, full of the painful joy of seeking the most elusive lover of all'.[79] It is a sign of the *Deus absconditus*, the elusiveness of God (and of the very emptiness of the notion of the 'advanced mystic', before the infinitely mysterious character of God). Rowan Williams in a very helpful introduction to John of the Cross[80] explains that in the 'dark night', from which all divine consolation has been withdrawn, the believer is in solidarity with Christ on his Cross, experiencing the utter abandonment of the Father. But I do not see this connection with the *Gloria crucis* in R. S. Thomas, whose Christ suffers 'beautifully' ('The Musician'[81]), whose Cross is often 'untenanted'.[82]

Thomas seems closer to the thought of Simone Weil when she writes: 'God can only be present in creation in the form of absence.'[83] Harries, writing of Weil in a way very reminiscent of R. S. Thomas's formulations, talks of 'the point, which she termed the void, reaching out with nothing for nothing, at which we find God, for that absence is also a presence'.[84] Or again Weil talks of:

the hidden God, the inconceivable and ineffable God, the God of sudden unanticipated gift and revelation. The hidden God is the one actually encountered through the void, in the midst of the dark night of faith. God is most truly known through

[77] Cf. Turner, *Darkness*, chapter 2.   [78] Morgan, *R. S. Thomas*, 173–5.
[79] B. B. Taylor, *Learning to Walk in the Dark* (New York: HarperCollins, 2014), 137.
[80] R. Williams, *The Wound of Knowledge: Christian Spirituality from the New Testament to St. John of the Cross* (London: Darton, Longman and Todd, 1979), chapter 8.
[81] Thomas, *Collected Poems*, 104.   [82] For example, in the poem 'In Church', ibid., 180.
[83] Quoted in Harries, *Beauty and the Horror*, 34.   [84] Ibid., 178.

void, for when illusion is burned away there is nothing in the void but nothingness, and within that nothingness emerges the 'nothingness' of God, who is the 'fullest possible fullness'.[85]

Thomas in his poem 'Pilgrimages' describes God as 'a fast/God, always before us and/leaving as we arrive' and concludes that God will always be 'dark rather and/inexplicable'.[86] All the searcher can do is persist, like the watcher in 'Sea-Watching', finding even in the emptiness presence, even in the apparent absence a form of affirmation. This is very much Thomas's approach to the *via negativa*, reflection on the existential experience of absence, rather than the practice of asceticism.[87] In 'The Absence' he sets out

> It is this great absence
> that is like a presence, that compels
> me to address it without hope
> of a reply.

ending

> What resource have I
> other than the emptiness without him of my whole
> being, a vacuum he may not abhor?[88]

You must speak without hope of reply; you must long for your emptiness to be acceptable to God; you must wear your eyes out as others their knees, or like Elijah endure in hiding the massive forces of nature, awaiting the sound of sheer silence that calls you forth.[89]

Turner makes an important distinction within apophaticism between 'the cataphatic employment of conflicting negative-and-affirmative images at the first-order level [within a basically cataphatic schema] and the apophatic negation of the negation between those first-order descriptions at the second-order level'.[90] In other words, although negative imagery is used at both levels, only at the second level do we find the true apophaticism of, for instance, Meister Eckhart, or the author of *The Cloud of*

---

[85] Quoted in McCullough, *Religious Philosophy*, 48.
[86] Thomas, *Collected Poems*, 364.   [87] Cf. Morgan, *R. S. Thomas*, 177.
[88] Thomas, *Collected Poems*, 361.
[89] Elijah in 1 Kings 19 endures in patient waiting the drama and violence of the mountain, a place where natural forces are evidently and powerfully present. What draws him forth to the front of the cave is 'the sound of sheer silence' (NRSV) or 'a fine-grained silence'. It is an absence of sound that is like a presence, and Elijah realises that this is the sign that he must be ready to learn from the Lord.
[90] Turner, *Darkness*, 252.

Unknowing. After careful consideration, I conclude that the poetry of R. S. Thomas always operates at the first level.

But the paradox remains – that absence and elusiveness can be signs of the divine reality, signs calling for a human response. But that it seems to me is the spiritual world that R. S. Thomas evokes in these poems that are easy to read at one level but inexhaustibly challenging at another.

In what sense does this encounter/non-encounter with the God who hides Godself, hides even the consolation of the assurance of presence, and exposes the searcher (in John of the Cross) to solidarity with all Christ's alienation on the Cross, correspond to the understandings of glory we have been exploring in this book? I make two suggestions.

First, the God of the dark night, of the absence/presence, confronts the searcher with something akin to a photographic negative – a chill grey-black light that nevertheless has the capacity to expose the not-Godness of so much on which religious observances dote. The purity and unique-ness of the divine reality with which the believer can come eventually into union is perceived by the determined contemplative even within this negative image. This is the glory of God encountered in the *via negativa*, bleak, and fraught with the possibility of misinterpretation, of setback and abandonment of the search, and yet ready, if the believer's soul is ready, in John of the Cross's framework, when her knees are worn out with kneeling, in R. S. Thomas's, to be 'developed' into a positive image of unforgettable brightness.

Second, strands of the tradition of the *via negativa* reject all experience, even that of waiting in the presence of a divine absence, in favour of an acceptance of the condition of unknowing, within which, according to the author of *The Cloud of Unknowing*, we may send 'a secret thrust of love' at the unknowable God.[91] This is not the search of a sign of the divine reality, but an apophatic longing for contact with that reality in and of itself. It relates therefore to the opposite end of our spectrum of senses of divine glory. Moses, after he has seen many signs of God's reality, prays at Exodus 33.18 to see the divine *kavōd* at the other end of its spectrum of meaning, to see the essential Godness of God. To do so is a kind of death, because 'no-one may see God and live'. Turner quotes from a sermon of Eckhart:

[91] *The Cloud of Unknowing and Other Works*, ed. A. C. Spearing (London: Penguin, 2001), 33.

Then how should I love God ... You should love him as he is nonGod, a nonspirit, a nonperson, a nonimage, but as he is pure, unmixed, bright 'One', separated from all duality, and in that One we should eternally sink down, out of 'something' into 'nothing'.[92]

To return to R. S. Thomas: at times he seems to come very close to the fatalistic acceptance of the preacher in Ecclesiastes, but he never quite arrives there because the very inaccessibility of God exerts such an influence on him. Unlike Qoheleth, Thomas always retains the longing of one who has glimpsed theophany. In another poem from *Frequencies* (1978), 'The Answer', he can confess that

> There have been times
> when, after long on my knees
> in a cold chancel, a stone has rolled
> from my mind, and I have looked
> in and seen the old questions lie
> folded and in a place
> by themselves, like the piled
> graveclothes of love's risen body.[93]

A magnificent coda to the poem, and a reminder that poems can do things that prose will always struggle either to express or to exegete. Here in the Thomas poem, the end of long contemplation is the (transient) setting aside of questions, which is like indirect evidence of resurrection. Here the divine semiosis is attenuated to an absence that resembles a presence. The paradox for this sort of mystic is that the signs of the divine reality are so elusive, in their experience, that most of the burden falls on the human interpreter, and yet the task of that interpreter, as is well understood in John of the Cross and T. S. Eliot, is to be still, in attentive humility, to 'wait without hope/For hope would be hope for the wrong thing'.[94]

As Williams notes, R. S. Thomas moved in the 1970s through a phase of the rhetoric of the violent and the guilty God, as we see in many of the poems in *Laboratories of the Spirit*.[95] M. Wynn Thomas also notes this phase in R. S. Thomas, describing poems in *H'm* as 'that Gnostic version of the monstrous god of creation'.[96] The R. S. Thomas of the 1980s is

---

[92] Quoted in Turner, *Darkness*, 185.   [93] Thomas, *Collected Poems*, 359.

[94] Eliot, *Poems and Plays*, 180. Even, in Thomas, to see 'the meaning' *in* 'the waiting', for the divine speech: 'Kneeling', *Collected Poems*, 199.

[95] R. Williams, 'Dangerous Thoughts in R. S. Thomas' in *The Page's Drift: R. S. Thomas at Eighty*, ed. M. Wynn Thomas (Bridgend: Seren, 1993), 82–98.

[96] M. Wynn Thomas, *Serial Obsessive*, 243. The poem 'Rough' from *Laboratories of the Spirit* is a savage example. In *H'm*, M. W. T. cites 'Soliloquy', 'Echoes', 'Making', 'The Island', 'Repeat', and 'The Other'. Tony Brown (*R. S. Thomas*, 75) says that 'The God of

more concerned to find in a language of divine absence a presence that leaves questions folded and lying at peace (as I noted earlier in this chapter in exploring 'The Answer'). There is a possibility that 'there might be a legitimate word or thought, an utterance beyond suspicion, if it held to a point of pure tension, articulated in a way that *showed*, rather than imposing, the co-presence of God and the world'.[97]

We get a hint of this in the earlier poem 'The Moor', which reads:

> It was like a church to me.
> I entered it on soft foot,
> Breath held like a cap in the hand.
> It was quiet.
> What God there was made his presence felt,
> Not listened to, in clean colours
> That brought a moistening of the eye,
> In a movement of the wind over grass.
>
> There were no prayers said. But stillness
> Of the heart's passions – that was praise
> Enough: and the mind's cession
> Of its kingdom. I walked on
> Simple and poor, while the air crumbled
> And broke on me as generously as bread.[98]

This extends our analysis in fascinating ways. There is a voiceless presence, to which the human response is only a stilling (a reminder that the 'interpretation' of a sign does not have to be an act of cognition). The response, the unspoken, hardly even thought 'Be it unto me', the existential 'turning aside to a brightness', in turn makes possible a richer disclosure of the divine grace.

There is a related thought in a later poem, 'The Flower', where Thomas writes, 'I gave my eyes/and my ears, and dwelt/in a soundless darkness/in the shadow/of your regard.'[99] Brown comments that 'The presence of that regard manifests itself not in speech or even sign but by a shift in the speaker's consciousness, a new awareness that can be described only metaphorically.'[100]

H'm is essentially a parody of the god that humankind has created in its own image, the anthropomorphized god who can be addressed directly as 'Lord', 'King', 'Father', a being to whom supplication can be made and yet who can in response to the world's suffering and pain seem, in the human terms in which he has been constructed, illogical and cruelly indifferent.'

[97] Williams, 'Dangerous Thoughts', 93, emphasis in original.
[98] Thomas, *Collected Poems*, 166. [99] Ibid., 280. [100] Brown, *R. S. Thomas*, 112.

So Thomas offers us surprised epiphany, the honest bearing of reality, the idea that the very elusiveness of God can be a sign of the divine reality, and the response of stillness to a wordless divine generosity. Thomas also enables us to see that the reality we bear is not a comfortable one. He writes in 'Hebrews 12.29'

> Who was it said: Fear
> not, when fear is an ingredient
> of our knowledge of you? The mistake
> we make, looking deep into the fire,
> is to confer features upon a presence
> that is not human; to expect love
> from a kiss whose only property is to consume.[101]

This is the sort of important corrective that discourse about glory can contribute to Christian theological conversation – resisting the dilution of the Godness of God. It is all too easy to resort to phrases and ways of thinking that are ready to distil out of the divine mystery an essence that can simply be approached (indeed recruited to the ministry team) without a sufficient sense of the sovereignty and mystery of that God. The image in the last line is particularly striking. It is a reminder that infinite as is God's redeeming love, it is nevertheless 'the fire that refines' as Dante has it in the *Purgatorio*,[102] or indeed consumes.

GLORY IN THE EXPERIENCE OF AN IMPORTANT TWENTIETH-CENTURY MYSTIC

I now consider the witness of a modern mystic who can also disclose something of divine glory seen in the most surprising of places. The whole journey of mystical exploration is a journey towards a reality that lies beyond the world of everyday sensing. So we might explore what it is to bear reality more fully via, for instance, the great seventeenth-century Spanish mystics – via Teresa's interior castle or the dark night in John of the Cross – or yet more contemporary spiritual searchers such as Thomas Merton or Henri Nouwen. But I want instead to reflect on the experience of a young woman writing during the Second World War. My choice of mystic is Etty Hillesum (1914–43), the young Jewish woman whose

---

[101] Thomas, *Collected Poems*, 484.
[102] Dante, *Purgatorio XXVI* in *The Divine Comedy*, transl. C. H. Sisson (Oxford: Oxford University Press, 1993), 148.

diaries and letters of the last two years of her life, before her deportation to Auschwitz and death there at the age of twenty-nine, make such
extraordinary reading.

I make this choice with due care and circumspection. It is very difficult
to speak appropriately about the horrendous violence and cruelty of the
Holocaust; this must be done with great caution. And it is a fraught
exercise to do Christian theology around the experience and suffering
of a Jewish person. I venture to do this only because of Hillesum's own
fascination with the Christian Gospel, especially the Gospel of Matthew.
In what follows I need to make clear that I am fully aware of the risk of
oversimplifying the life of a very complex person, and the complexity as
well as the horror of all that Jewish people had to bear. Also that I recognise that the responses of Jewish thinkers to the Shoah has been very
various. My colleague David Tollerton has written of the range of reading
strategies applied to the Book of Job after the Holocaust.[103] Important
and radical work has been done on the post-Holocaust doctrine of God
by thinkers such as David Blumenthal, Emil Fackenheim, and Hans Jonas
(as well as such Christian thinkers as Jürgen Moltmann).

I also need to make it clear that I do not regard Hillesum's sometimes
extraordinary pronouncements about her life under the daily threat of
deportation and death as in any way ameliorating the brutal inhumanity
of what was done. The systemic cruelty stands as what it was: a blas-
phemy of the most radical kind against the understanding – deeply
embedded in biblical thinking and also that of the Enlightenment – of
the common humanity of all persons.[104] So: Etty's writings in no way
make the Holocaust any less evil. Nor should they be taken as normative,
in such a way that other responses are diminished. But they are none-
theless very illuminating. Her writings do not offer a philosophical, or
yet a theological, system. Yet for Tzvetan Todorov, 'she offers us the rare
example of someone who achieves a moral understanding at the very
moment the world is collapsing around her. In the midst of the deepest
despair, her life glitters like a jewel'.[105]

---

[103] D. C. Tollerton, *The Book of Job in Post-Holocaust Thought* (Sheffield: Sheffield
Phoenix Press, 2012).

[104] As does the often overlooked parallel in Japanese treatment of prisoners of war –
unforgettably evoked in Richard Flanagan's novel *The Narrow Road to the Deep
North* (London: Vintage, 2015).

[105] T. Todorov, *Facing the Darkness: Moral Life in the Camps*, transl. A. Denner and
A. Pollak (New York: Henry Holt, 1996), 198.

I approach Hillesum's story through her own writings[106] and the very helpful distillation provided by Patrick Woodhouse in his *Etty Hillesum: A Life Transformed*. This (in Woodhouse's words) 'emotionally confused, sexually adventurous and intellectual young woman from a dysfunctional family'[107] makes an odd candidate for sainthood. Ria van den Brandt notes the equivocal reception of Hillesum's writings when they were first published,[108] some seeing her as an 'overgrown selfish schoolgirl',[109] and yet the witness of her response to the Nazi persecution, her care for and delight in others, and her refusal to hate her persecutors, has about it a tang of holiness, wild and strange.

This passage from a late letter of Etty's, written from the transit camp of Westerbork, from which the only onward destination was Auschwitz, shows precisely how her experience ties into our theme:

> The misery here is quite terrible; and yet, late at night when the day has slunk away into the depths behind me, I often walk with a spring in my step along the barbed wire. And then, time and again, it soars straight from my heart – I can't help it, that's just the way it is, like some elementary force – the feeling that life is glorious and magnificent, and that one day we shall be building a whole new world.[110]

This shows, more clearly and convincingly than any theologian in the comfort of his study could express, what it is to bear an external reality of extraordinary harshness – not to deny it or seek to escape it (for Etty refused several opportunities to go into hiding) – but to face up to it, and despite it, within it, even because of it, to find glory and magnificence. Beyond that, too, to know a very profound hope, grounded entirely in faith, since no external factors in the Holland of the time provided evidence by which to hope.

So using Woodhouse's account as my guide, I now explore some of what Etty concluded in her diaries and letters, how she bore the reality

---

[106] E. Hillesum, *Etty: The Letters and Diaries of Etty Hillesum 1941–1943*, ed. K. A. D. Smelik, transl. A. J. Pomerans (Grand Rapids, MI: Eerdmans, 2002).

[107] P. Woodhouse, *Etty Hillesum: A Life Transformed* (London: Bloomsbury, 2009), 134.

[108] R. van den Brandt, *Etty Hillesum: An Introduction to Her Thought*, transl. H. Monkel (Zürich: LiT Verlag, 2014). Cf. also M. G. Coetsier, *Etty Hillesum and the Flow of Presence: A Voegelinian Analysis* (Columbia, MO.: University of Missouri Press, 2008), 26.

[109] Van den Brandt, *Etty Hillesum*, 17. Van den Brandt also notes that the major English translation of Etty's writings smooths over some difficult passages, such as her references to her attempts at self-abortion in 1941, 9–10.

[110] Hillesum, *Etty*, 616.

that confronted her, and came to experience – 'instress', in the terminology of Chapter 3 – the world as 'glorious and magnificent'. Etty's
experience is particularly important to this study because it is the reverse
of the tendency noted in the last chapter to approach God only through
the positive elements in creation and in life. She went full face into the
horror and cruelty of life under the Nazi regime, and was still able to
experience a sense of glory. A fellow-detainee, Friedrich Weinreb, wrote
of Etty that:

> What I found most striking was her religious sense of things, a quality which she
> had recently discovered in herself. There was something about her that spoke of
> an ancient, primeval struggle, the weight of thousands of years – and at the same
> time something light and joyful.[111]

There are two very interesting words in this account, which tap deep in
the project being explored here, the words 'quality' and 'weight'. I wrote
in Chapter 1 of Andrew Robinson's work on Jesus' life as a qualisign of
God, and I return to that insight in Chapter 5. There was a quality in
Hillesum that spoke eloquently to others. And that life also spoke of
weight, of reality more substantial than just the present moment.[112] Its
quality and weight, we may suppose, conveyed something of the glory of
God, understood by Irenaeus as 'a human being fully alive', a quality at
once sublimely weighty, and light with joy.[113]

In terms of the Eliot quotation we are exploring here, Hillesum was
bearing reality, lacking what she called the 'armor of position, esteem and
property',[114] and immersed in 'the ways things really are',[115] in terms
both of the violence with which humans can treat each other,[116] and our
common inheritance of the image of God.[117] Despite its bleakness and
threat of death, she can conclude in a late letter that her life 'is one long

---

[111] Quoted in Woodhouse, *Hillesum*, 109.

[112] She wrote, 'we carry everything within us, God and Heaven and Hell and Earth and Life
and Death and all of history' (Hillesum, *Etty*, 463).

[113] Even as the ghettoisation of Amsterdam proceeded, she could write, 'above the one
narrow path still left to us stretches the sky, intact ... I find life beautiful, and I feel free.
The sky within me is as wide as the one stretching above my head.' Ibid., 434.

[114] Ibid., 590.

[115] She wrote, 'Mysticism must rest on crystal-clear honesty, can only come after things
have been stripped down to their naked reality' (ibid., 426), and again 'at unguarded
moments when left to myself, I suddenly lie against the naked breast of life' (ibid., 386).

[116] In September 1943, Etty and her family were finally deported in crowded cattle trucks
the three days' journey to Auschwitz. Etty threw postcards out of the train, one of which
included the words 'We left the camp singing' (ibid., 659).

[117] As noted by Woodhouse in his thoughtful conclusion, *Hillesum*, 143.

sequence of inner miracles'.[118] That is another interesting word, since a miracle is not merely an internal thing within a life, but always also revelatory. A life of miracles develops the quality of a sign. (I return to this in Chapter 5.)

Etty writes 'to me the greatest reality is still the sun on the hyacinths, the rabbit, the chocolate pudding, Beethoven, the grey hair at his [Spier's] temple'.[119] This is strange glory indeed, but that is what she is writing about. These were, for that mystic in that context, 'living heaven in hell',[120] the signs of the reality that lies beyond our ordinary seeing, and which she learned to call God. And Etty's own 'glory'[121] was that she persisted in being able to see these signs. She wrote once,

> My life has become an uninterrupted dialogue with You, oh God, one great dialogue. Sometimes when I stand in some corner of the camp, my feet planted on Your earth, my eyes raised towards Your heaven, tears sometimes run down my face, tears of deep emotion and gratitude ... Things come and go in a deeper rhythm, and people must be taught to listen; it is the most important thing we have to learn in this life.[122]

Under the influence of Julius Spier, Etty began in the last phase of her life to speak of God, and to God.[123] Coetsier writes that 'when she went into herself, she found within herself the presence of a transcendent Other. That which she found within her was "transcendent" in the sense that it was not "present" in the same way that things and people in the world are present to one another. *Cor in cor loquitur*: heart speaks within heart'.[124] Rachel Feldhay Brenner sees a movement in Hillesum's God-language, from 'the "compelling" God, a God who can draw her to himself in love and help her to maintain her dignity and self-respect' to a role-reversed God, whose 'existence is predicated on the faith of those whom he cannot save'.[125] Brenner notes that 'Finding God ... is therefore predicated on the ability to dissociate oneself from total absorption in the suffering,

---

[118] Hillesum, *Etty*, 640.
[119] Ibid., 252. Etty had ongoing intimate relationships with two much older men, her landlord Han Wegerif and her therapist Julius Spier.
[120] Coetsier, *Etty Hillesum*, 4.
[121] See Chapter 5 for exploration of the believer herself being able to participate in glory.
[122] Hillesum, *Etty*, 640.
[123] On the day Spier died, she wrote that 'You taught me to speak the name of God without embarrassment' (ibid., 516).
[124] Coetsier, *Etty Hillesum*, 197.
[125] R. F. Brenner, *Writing as Resistance: Four Women Confronting the Holocaust* (University Park, PA.: The Pennsylvania State University Press, 1997), 112.

tormented self ... The presence of God emerges in self-transcendence that liberates from fear and despair.'[126] For Etty Hillesum (as for Anne Frank), writing was an essential part of the self-transcendence.[127]

There are some strange echoes in Etty Hillesum of the contemplative who was our guide in much of the last chapter, Gerard Manley Hopkins, for whom also writing was a huge part of his personhood. At first sight they seem poles apart, from different eras and cultures and faith traditions as well as genders. Yet when Etty writes of herself searching to 'sound my own depths' and find 'a basic tune, a steady undercurrent',[128] she is articulating in quite similar terms some of what Hopkins writes about 'pitch', and what he crystallises in that astonishing poem 'As Kingfishers Catch Fire'. Hopkins writes of created beings 'selving', as follows:

> Each mortal thing does one thing and the same:
> Deals out that being indoors each one dwells;
> Selves — goes itself; *myself* it speaks and spells,
> Crying *Whát I dó is me: for that I came.*

Etty seems to capture the same movement of thought in writing of finding her 'basic tune'. And Hopkins goes on:

> I say móre: the just man justices;
> Keeps grace: thát keeps all his goings graces;
> Acts in God's eye what in God's eye he is –
> Christ – for Christ plays in ten thousand places,
> Lovely in limbs, and lovely in eyes not his
> To the Father through the features of men's faces.[129]

When one reads witnesses to Etty's presence in the transit camp (and allowing of course for Hopkins's gendered language and Christian lens), there seem clear echoes. Her strange unsubduable delight, her selved 'tune', kept all her goings graces. And her refusal to hate must have allowed her features to express the play of love in an extraordinary way. She had learned 'how spacious the heart can be'.[130]

The other strong bond between Hopkins and Hillesum is their ability to draw strength from contemplation of the natural world, especially

[126] Ibid., 115.
[127] 'One always has the feeling here of being the ears and eyes of a piece of Jewish history, but there is also the need sometimes to be a still, small voice': E. Hillesum, *Letters from Westerbork*, transl. A. J. Pomerans (New York: Pantheon Books, 1986), 124.
[128] Hillesum, *Etty*, 72.
[129] G. M. Hopkins, *Poems and Prose: Selected with an Introduction and Notes by W. H. Gardner* (Harmondsworth: Penguin, 1953), 51.
[130] Hillesum, *Etty*, 240.

flowers. Woodhouse notes that '*As the world around her grew uglier, her eye and need for beauty grew keener.*'[131] Her 'small narcissi light up a portrait on the wall above "like radiant stars" ... the colour of an open yellow tea rose "makes one believe in God"'.[132]

It is tragic that Etty's life, so full of faith and living, was cut so short, and that she spent most of its last sixteen months in an environment so full of ugliness and cruelty, so devoid of natural beauty (Westerbork and then Auschwitz). Yet in a way her 'ministry' flowered at Westerbork; or to change the image, it 'caught fire' as kingfishers do in the sunlight.

Hopkins's last years were spent in obedient service to his Church but in what must have seemed more or less exile in Ireland, immersed in academic drudgery. In his 'terrible sonnets' he bears reality in a profound way, without taking his eyes off his God. Hopkins's poem 'Thou art indeed just' expresses much of this reality-bearing sorrow of Hopkins.[133] He looks hard into reality, and sees its paradoxes, especially in the thriving of the lustful, greater than that of the poet who spends his life in God's cause. He sees the loveliness and intricacy of natural processes, but not in a sentimental way. Rather Hopkins's concluding prayer is one of longing purified by struggle: 'send my roots rain'.

There is a significant difference in theology between Hopkins and Hillesum, which cannot be glossed over. Hopkins's God remains the transcendent master of the flux of events, the one to whom the author of the terrible sonnets cries out in longing for rain. Strikingly, Etty comes to conclude that God will not, cannot, help those in the camp. All they can do is 'safeguard that little piece of You, God, in ourselves'.[134] Her God has handed Godself over to the world, entering the human heart, and being 'guarded' by those with the least worldly power. She writes: 'there must be someone to live through it all and bear witness to the fact that God lived, even in these times'.[135] Her concern is 'that God is in safe hands with us despite everything'.[136]

There is a fascinating echo here of the German Jewish philosopher-theologian Hans Jonas. Jonas' God empties Godself of mind and power in giving the creation its existence, and then allows the interplay of chance and natural law to take its course. God's only further involvement is that God holds a memory of the experience of the creation – God receives God's

---

[131] Woodhouse, *Hillesum*, 48, emphasis in original.   [132] Quoted in ibid., 70.
[133] Hopkins, *Poems and Prose*, 67.   [134] Hillesum, *Etty*, 488.   [135] Ibid., 506.
[136] Ibid., 657.

being back 'transfigured or possibly disfigured by the chance harvest of unforeseeable temporal experience'.[137]

Woodhouse notes in Hillesum some theological echoes of Dietrich Bonhoeffer, who was also responding to the same tyranny, and concluded that God was 'weak and powerless in the world'.[138] This motif seems a very far cry from glory, and yet if it is an authentic discernment of the divine, then it would be a response to signs manifested of the divine nature, albeit very far from those signs in Exodus and Isaiah that we explored in Chapter 2. (Closer indeed to the glory seen in Jesus at his 'hour', after he has been handed over to the powers of evil.)

Both Hillesum and Hopkins, then, find signs of the reality of God amid the bearing of profound struggle. That they interpret the signs differently is not to be wondered at, where the signs are not overpowering theophanies but hints within inscapes. As I explored in my ecohermeneutical work with David Horrell and Cherryl Hunt,[139] interpretations of particular texts and events will tend to be governed by a larger narrative, and such narratives will tend to fall into one of four characteristic genres.[140] As we indicated in respect of ecotheologies, metanarratives in all four of Frye's genres can be justified by using different biblical texts as lenses through which to view the data of text and world.[141] Etty's faith, as she discovers it – interestingly without benefit of worshipping community, strong family background, or formal discipline of practice – seems to me to correspond to Frye's category of the ironic, which Hopewell frames theologically as the 'empiric'.[142]

Etty is sure that her God will not, perhaps cannot, help her. The biblical book from which such a genre of narrative takes most encouragement is Ecclesiastes. Her 'pitch', the tone she found for her life, and the quality

---

[137] H. Jonas, *Mortality and Morality: A Search for Good after Auschwitz*, ed. L. Vogel (Evanston, IL: Northwestern University Press, 1996), 125.

[138] Quoted in Woodhouse, *Hillesum*, 50.

[139] D. G. Horrell, C. Hunt, and C. Southgate, *Greening Paul: Rereading the Apostle in a Time of Ecological Crisis* (Waco, TX: Baylor University Press, 2010).

[140] See J. Hopewell, *Congregation: Stories and Structures*, ed. B.G. Wheeler (Philadelphia: Fortress Press, 1987), working from the critical studies of Northrop Frye.

[141] Horrell et al., *Greening Paul*, Chapter 7.

[142] Characterised, Hopewell claims, by 'Reliance upon data objectively verifiable through one's own five senses. The integrity of one's own person requires realism about the way things demonstrably work and the rejection of the supernatural.' *Congregation*, 69. Hillesum does not exactly reject the supernatural, but she does, crucially, reject the possibility that its powers would come to her aid.

she evinced, is one of acceptance, lacking 'lamentation or complaint'.[143] Unquestionably however, she also lived in and with the Psalms. And on her final postcard, flung out of the train taking her and her family to Auschwitz, she found her God, whom she identified with 'what was deepest and best in her'[144] to be indeed a 'high tower'[145] for her spirit, even though she was convinced that that God would not rescue her. But there is also a hint of the comic (in the technical literary sense) in that passage from Etty with which we began, 'time and again, it soars straight from my heart – I can't help it, that's just the way it is, like some elementary force – the feeling that life is glorious and magnificent, and that one day we shall be building a whole new world'.[146] An unreasonable hope persists.

We have seen that Etty Hillesum was able to find beauty, and signs of love and meaning, while facing up to her situation to the full, bearing to the greatest possible extent the reality of it. As Todorov shows, she was not by any means alone in responding to beauty even in the depths of misery. He quotes Louis Micheels' recollection of Bach being played on the guitar in Auschwitz: 'The contrast between the purity of his music and our misery seemed to imbue every phrase with special depth. The horror of our situation made the beauty of life so much more poignant and precious.' Todorov continues, 'Laks and Coudy, musicians themselves, recall how "during the short time the music lasted we became normal human beings once more as we listened with religious awe"'.[147] The phrasing here is interesting. The prisoners became 'normal', or perhaps more than normal, in bearing their reality yet responding with 'religious awe', discerning in that moment glory. Where Hillesum is so striking is both in her explicit use of the language of glory, and also in the way she seems to have sought out passionately these moments of disclosure. They did not just happen to her. She could write that life was 'glorious and magnificent'[148] not by ignoring its ugliness and cruelty but by facing it, bearing it, to the greatest possible extent.

Todorov offers an analysis[149] of Hillesum's response to suffering, in three 'registers' (again a reminder that we should not look for *system* in

---

[143] Woodhouse, *Hillesum*, 119.   [144] Hillesum, *Etty*, 83.

[145] Quoting Psalm 94.22, or possibly 18.2, or 61.3, or Proverbs 18.10? Denise de Costa notes that Etty on this postcard used the Dutch word *vertrek*, which can connote 'departure', or yet 'retreat', an interesting ambiguity indeed. D. de Costa, *Anne Frank and Etty Hillesum: Inscribing Spirituality and Sexuality*, transl. M. F. C. Hoyinck and R. E. Chesal (New Brunswick, NJ: Rutgers University Press, 1998), 237.

[146] Hillesum, *Etty*, 616.   [147] Todorov, *Facing*, 95.   [148] Hillesum, *Etty*, 616.

[149] Todorov, *Facing*, 204–9.

her writings). He detects the response of *indifference*: 'If you have a rich inner life … there probably isn't all that much difference between the inside and outside of a camp.'[150] He also sees a stoic *acceptance*: 'I accept everything from your hands, oh God, as it comes.'[151] Sometimes this takes on an Eastern quality, perhaps reflecting her interest in Taoism, 'We have to become as simple and as wordless as the growing corn or the falling rain. We must just be.'[152] Etty concludes that 'you must be able to bear your own sorrow … [it] must become an integral part of yourself … Give your sorrow all the space and shelter in yourself that is its due'.[153] Suffering then is contained, detoxified, and prevented from spreading by being given its own space in the ecology of the spirit. Even despair can be robbed of its power.[154] (She even came to a related conclusion about her own death – 'He has a place in [her life] now, and I know that he is part of it.'[155]

But Todorov also sees a *preference* for suffering in Hillesum which he finds much more difficult. She grows to love the transit camp, with a joy that disturbs him. For Todorov 'she was, without question, an extraordinary human being … [yet in] her most exalted moments there is something superhuman – and, therefore, inhuman – about her'.[156] I do not think that quite does justice to Etty, because she writes of that suffering that she seems almost to welcome: 'If all the suffering does not help us to broaden our horizons, to attain a greater humanity by shedding all trifling and irrelevant issues, then it will all have been for nothing'.[157] Or again, 'if we fail to draw new meaning from the deep wells of our distress and despair, then it will not be enough'.[158] In other words, the suffering can, must, have a transformative effect on human nature. She also writes, 'And I also believe, childishly perhaps but stubbornly, that the world will become more habitable again only through the love that the Jew Paul described to the citizens of Corinth in the thirteenth chapter of his

---

[150] Hillesum, *Etty*, 279.   [151] Ibid., 515.   [152] Ibid., 483.   [153] Ibid., 308.

[154] Woodhouse makes here an interesting link with the theology of Paul Tillich. Both Tillich and Hillesum independently used the phrase 'the courage of despair'. Woodhouse writes of this phrase, 'You do not pretend that despair is not there. You acknowledge it: it is part of you. *But, by living courageously in the face of it, you rob it of its power*': *Hillesum*, 150 (emphasis in original). He notes Tillich's resonant conclusion that 'Love is stronger [than death]. It creates something new out of the destruction caused by death; it bears everything and overcomes everything.' P. Tillich, *The Boundaries of Our Being: A Collection of His Sermons with His Autobiographical Sketch* (London: Fontana Library, 1973), 280–1.

[155] Hillesum, *Etty*, 464.   [156] Todorov, *Facing*, 208.   [157] Hillesum, *Etty*, 502.

[158] Hillesum, *Letters*, 31.

first letter'.[159] In other words, the love that 'bears all things' will be transformative. Indeed, the three categories of indifference, acceptance, and preference describe three modes of 'bearing reality' in love, and Christian tradition has always found a place for the third, the willing bearing of suffering for the sake of its capacity to form part of blessing (e.g., Col 1.24, 1 Pet 3.9). This too is part of the lens of seeing *Gloria crucis*.[160]

For the purposes of this present study, Etty Hillesum enables us to take yet a further step, analogous to the one we were exploring in the previous chapter when we considered the tsunami, the very difficult and controversial step of looking into the *cause* of the suffering itself and finding signs there of the deep reality of God.

This is where Etty's extraordinary ability to see the humanity of her persecutors is so telling. For Woodhouse this is rooted in her ability to see every human being as created in the image and likeness of God.[161] She writes in her journal: 'All the appalling things that happen are no mysterious threats from afar, but arise from fellow beings very close to us.'[162] Or again, 'We have so much work to do on ourselves that we shouldn't even be thinking of hating our so-called enemies.'[163] Todorov notes that it was not until forty years after his imprisonment that Primo Levi could write, 'They were made of the same cloth as we, they were average human beings, averagely intelligent, averagely wicked: save the exceptions, they were not monsters, they had our faces.'[164] For Todorov, 'Hillesum, one of Eichmann's victims, would never, in any circumstance, have acted as he did, but she is able to understand Eichmann as those like him by looking

---

[159] Ibid., 36. Lawrence Langer criticises her for this very stance, importing Christian attitudes into the understanding of Jewish suffering. L. L. Langer, *Admitting the Holocaust: Collected Essays* (New York: Oxford University Press, 1995), 69–73, at 70. In a searingly critical passage, Langer mocks Hillesum for 'breathtaking naïveté' (70), and for 'a certain arrogance of tone and style' (72), above all for still embracing 'the legacy of a Romantic era ... that no grief is ultimate, that the human capacity for suffering is equal to any anguish' (71). I would only note Etty's own perception that she strove to work from 'crystal clear honesty' and to 'lie on the naked breast of life', and that she wrote from 'the courage of despair' (Woodhouse, *Hillesum*, 150).

[160] Which is not to deny that the desire to cultivate, and indeed to impose, suffering for its purifying effects has at times been a deeply toxic element in the tradition.

[161] Woodhouse, *Hillesum*, 142-3.That this is a key doctrine for her is shown by such writing as this: 'I sank to my knees with the words that preside over human life: And God made man after His likeness. That passage spent a difficult morning with me,' (Hillesum, *Etty*, 644). Cf. also Alexandra Pleshoyano, 'She had room for everyone and everything within herself, no matter how soiled the likeness of God might appear': 'Etty Hillesum: For God and with God', *The Way*, 44 (January 2005), 7–20, at 11.

[162] Hillesum, *Etty*, 259.   [163] Ibid., 529.   [164] Quoted in Todorov, *Facing*, 136.

at herself.'[165] When summoned before the Gestapo, she can write 'And that was the real import of this morning: not that a disgruntled young Gestapo officer yelled at me, but that I felt no indignation, rather a real compassion.'[166] She makes clear: 'The absence of hatred in no way implies the absence of moral indignation. I know that those who hate have good reason to do so. But ... it has been brought home forcibly to me here how every atom of hatred added to this world makes it an even more inhospitable place.'[167]

When this teaching is pushed to its logical conclusion, to look at another human, even one in *feldgrau* with a gun pointing at you, even one with a list transporting your family to certain death, even someone who makes members of your community draw up the list, is itself to look upon someone created in the divine likeness, to see a sign of God's activity as creator. Hugely controversial ground. What element of the divine reality is signified to this sort of seeing? First the freedom of God, that God creates according to God's own freely chosen will, and not as the reproduction, or yet emanation, of some philosophical ideal. Second, that God's will is to give freedom to humans, radical, extravagant freedom. Third, that God loves the little child within each human, however brutal, the child who in its turn is longing for love.

We are extrapolating now from Etty Hillesum's inspiration, but all this seems entirely consonant with what she wrote, and how she is recorded as having behaved. And just as with the tsunami, the instressing of situations requires attention to the larger narrative in order to understand the contours of glory, so also with this situation of human brutality. In a remarkable essay J. R. Jones writes of love for the other being evoked by the other's sheer existence:

It is seeing the love of a thing with the whole of existence as background to it. It is seeing the miracle of the existence of the thing. And this means it is the same as seeing things *sub specie aeternitatis*; it is seeing things as God sees them. And you cannot see living things in this way, without blessing them, without gratitude for their existence, without profoundly thanking God for the miracle which made them, for the miracle of their existence.[168]

A fine statement of the perception of *Gloria mundi*.

---

[165] Ibid, 138.   [166] Hillesum, *Etty*, 259.

[167] Hillesum, *Letters*, 36. Todorov notes that this was not by any means a unique position – Eugenia Ginzburg and Irina Ratushinskaya, in their own ways, make similar responses, and Primo Levi's later reflections come to related conclusions. Todorov, *Facing*, 201.

[168] J. R. Jones 'Love as Perception of Meaning' in *Religion and Understanding*, ed. D. Z. Phillips (Oxford: Blackwell, 1967), 141–53, at 149, italics in original.

Within the Christian confession we can extrapolate further. To look upon a human being is to look upon someone for whose sins Christ died, therefore in a sense to look upon Christ. To look, therefore, on the infinitely costly love with which God responds to human freedom, to look upon them within *Gloria crucis*. This is, if you like, the scandal of the Incarnation at its most intense – the oppressor, who 'knows not what' he does, is weak even in his apparent power, he is thus Christ in his need to be ministered to, picking up in an admittedly rather unusual way on the teaching of Matthew 25.[169] His victim is likewise Christ. This incarnational dynamic is an extraordinary sign of the reality of the God who gives Godself to the world, 'being found in human form' (Phil 2.7).

I am emphatically not trying to convey that Hillesum's was *the* appropriate response to the Holocaust (or yet that her situation was in some way exemplary of that colossal suffering).[170] We know, for instance, nothing of her story in Auschwitz, the last and most brutal chapter of that short life. Nor I am trying to suggest that there were not courageous Jewish responses that knew nothing of the Gospel of Matthew, or would have seen it as an enemy book. But in Hillesum, as in Bonhoeffer, the reality of a situation was being borne, and yet those caught up in the infliction of violence were still seen as God's creatures. Just as with the tsunami discussed in Chapter 3, the contemplative has to look at the larger narrative to instress the contours of glory. So also with Etty and her guards. Signs of God's work in creation and redemption are still there to be interpreted as glory even in the bleakest contexts.

Before bringing this chapter to a conclusion, I want to explore whether we can find any links between the glory-search of Hillesum and R. S. Thomas. De Costa says that Hillesum's God was 'an immanent God, a God deep within herself, who is consistent with her dreams and thoughts'.[171] Etty was massively constrained by the oppressiveness of her situation (though in other ways hugely freed by the generosity of her spirit, the breadth of her reading, and the inspiration of her lovers and friends). She is drawn both by her own loss of external freedom, and by her psychotherapeutic journey, to a God to be found deep within the self. This God is the ground of her freedom; she comes to realise that she can

---

[169] To alter the ancient Latin saying about the guarding of the guards themselves, we might here pose the question, *Quis custodes ipsos liberabit?* (Who shall free the guards themselves?)

[170] For a range of theological responses, see, for example, D. Garner (ed.), *Antitheodicy, Atheodicy and Jewish Mysticism in Holocaust Theology* (Piscataway, NJ: Gorgias Press, 2012).

[171] De Costa, *Anne Frank*, 228.

also name God as the source of her zest for finding glory even within darkness. But strikingly her God-consciousness takes her towards, not away from, other people. She writes:

> Sometimes people seem to me like houses with open doors. I walk in and roam through hallways and rooms. Every house is furnished a little differently, and yet they are all the same, and each one of them must be turned into a dwelling dedicated to you, God. And I promise you, yes, I promise that I shall try to find room and refuge for you in as many houses as possible ... I walk up to the front door and seek shelter for you.[172]

She moves from seeing signs of God in the outside world, such as in flowers, or music, deep into herself, and emerges from the journey determined both to see the divine likeness in others and to help others become God-bearers. (We shall explore further how humans can become truer signs of God in Chapter 5.)

R. S. Thomas is also profoundly constrained in his God-search, though in different ways. By temperament a solitary and a nature mystic, he is constrained from too easy a reading of God from the beauty of the natural world because he recognises the ambiguity of that world. He is also persuaded, perhaps by the bleakness of his temperament, perhaps by the stuckness and suffering he sees in parishioners, that God is not a providentially active God, not a God liberal with signs of God's existence. Those signs are hard won, by journeys of stubborn kneeling that take him deep into himself and enable him finally to perceive absence that is like presence. So his God too is the ground of his being 'who sees you suffer and me pray/And touches you with the sun's ray,/That heals not, yet blinds my eyes'.[173] Yet in the coda of the poem 'Pilgrimages', allowing for his very different temperament and spirituality, Thomas comes close to a thought Hillesum might have had. He writes:

> Was the pilgrimage
> I made to come to my own
> self, to learn that in times
> like these and for one like me
> God will never be plain and
> out there, but dark rather and
> inexplicable, as though he were in here?[174]

---

[172] Quoted and adapted by de Costa, *Anne Frank*, 238.

[173] Thomas, *Collected Poems*, 62.

[174] Ibid., 364. As has often been remarked of Thomas (for example, by Daniel Westover in his fine study, *R. S. Thomas: A Stylistic Biography* (Cardiff: University of Wales Press, 2011)) the line breaks here are disconcertingly powerful, reinforcing the sense of search and unknowing.

It is hard to see how Etty Hillesum and the author of Job can both be right. Either God is transcendently powerful, or God is powerless to save, and instead entrusts Godself to the world. And yet who can doubt the authenticity of both interpretations of the Godness of God? As we have seen in the last two chapters, the Creator's relationship to processes involving violence, and the interplay of ugliness and beauty, is a complex one. Hence the 'compound theodicy' attempted in *The Groaning of Creation*,[175] and the call for three-lensed seeing in the present work.

Job's story sits within *Gloria mundi*, as we see from God's 'lecture' to Job in Chapters 38–41. *Gloria crucis*, as W. H. Vanstone so clearly perceived in his study *The Stature of Waiting*, involves the utterly willing being-handed-over of Godness to the world. Godness bears the full reality of human selfishness, fear, lust for power, and all other idolatries. This passion of God for the world is salvific only 'soul by soul and silently',[176] not in the ostentatious forms of human glory. Looking through the lens of *Gloria crucis*, interpreting the signs of the Godness of God that the Passion reveals, requires a very particular sort of seeing. It is important for Christians to see with that lens into the harshnesses of the world, into the trauma that affects the lives of so many. The liturgy of Good Friday cannot be short-circuited by lust for Easter. Equally, Christians cannot allow their vision to be stuck in that place, in *Gloria crucis*, any more than simply bearing the reality of the world as revealed by the lens of the creation, *Gloria mundi*, can do justice to a resurrection faith.

Those who would look with the lens of *Gloria in excelsis*, however, must bear the reality that we hope for things not seen (Rom 8.25). That the divine project is a long way from resolution, that human experiments with their freedom continue to fragment faith, and fill the world with the abuse of power. That the freedom that is able to put away all idols and respond gladly and lovingly to the other seems rare enough indeed. (Perhaps we are able to glimpse it in Etty Hillesum precisely because all the comfort and security of her life, all the things that might have kept her in a zone of selfishness and complacency, were stripped away by irresistible external forces.)

We see then all too little of the 'freedom of the glory of the children of God' (Rom 8.19–21). Seeing in our third lens, *Gloria in excelsis*, must

---

[175] Southgate, *Groaning*, 16.
[176] From the poem 'Urbs Dei' by Cecil Spring Rice, sung as the hymn 'I vow to thee my country'.

concede that the project of the transformation of the world seems to be in its infancy, and that believers' hope is, like Etty's, for an outcome for which there is all too little evidence.

In drafting this chapter I did not expect to find connections between my chosen poet of glory glimpsed at the edge of doubting contemplation, and my mystic, stubbornly seeing glory even in conditions of terrible cruelty. But there is a striking common theme, which is that both thinkers look deep inside themselves, though they approach mystical encounter from opposite directions.

Hillesum, out of her therapeutic engagement with Julius Spier, became committed to deep inner work on herself. Spier also enabled her to use God-language. Discovering (or interpreting) God in the deepest flow of her life proved to be her deepest and most intense and abiding adventure. Out of that work she is enabled to see God's work in others. Her lifelong conviction that all others are in the divine likeness (and by inference can be read as signs of the divine reality, such that [in the terms of this book] to encounter another human being is to encounter the glory of God[177]) allows her to be steadfast in her refusal to hate any other individual.

Thomas's journey is very different. He never arrives at that place of acceptance of others that came early to Etty. He develops instead into a nature mystic, which seems to have come readily to him despite being brought up in a town. He sees signs of the divine reality – sometimes disturbing ones as we noted in Chapter 3[178] – and at some very moving moments he is able to encounter God through intense being with nature.[179] The practice of contemplation, of lying in wait for moments of disclosure in nature, leads him into his own depths. It leads him into a spirituality which is so much about search that God's very elusiveness comes to be a sign of God's presence. Both hint at contact with the very being of God: Thomas in intuiting the divine as the ground of being; Hillesum in finding God to be her greatest adventure.

In Chapter 2 I sought to show how an understanding of divine glory on a spectrum from sign to essence, and the cultivation of a three-lensed

---

[177] Pursuing the thought of Irenaeus, the encounter is at its fullest and truest when both parties are 'fully alive'.

[178] 'Anyone who has seen a peregrine falcon falling like lightning on its prey is sure to experience a certain thrill that makes him feel quite humble ... One of the unfailing rules of that world is that life has to die in the cause of life.' R. S. Thomas, *Autobiographies*, transl. J. W. Davies (London: Orion Books, 1998), 93.

[179] As recounted for instance in Thomas, 'A Thicket in Lleyn', *Collected Poems*, 511.

seeing, enabled us to understand glory in both the dramatic theophanies of Exodus, Isaiah, and Ezekiel, and also the 'great sign' of God that is the life and death of Christ. In Chapter 3 I sought to show how every detail of the natural world, even those that contain violence and lead to great suffering, can be explored as a sign of the Creator and hence as a manifestation of glory. In this present chapter I have reiterated this theme of the often disturbing character of disclosures of divine reality, and therefore the need for the contemplative to face up to the character of those disclosures, as part of bearing the maximum possible amount of reality. I have tried to show how artists and mystics also show us glory even in difficult places – in the severity of Piero's *Resurrection*, in the dissonance of late Beethoven, in the *via negativa* searchings of R. S. Thomas, and in the extraordinary, heaven-in-hell world of Etty Hillesum's last years. In Hillesum we discovered someone for whom misery and oppression seemed to release a sense of glory; she therefore serves as a paradigm case of bearing reality. She finds glory despite the processes she knows will lead to her death, and in her refusal to hate I suggest she finds vestiges of glory even within those systems (in the human beings caught up in them, not in their inhumanity). Such signs of the divine reality reach down into, or are found in, the depths of the human spirit, created as it is in the likeness of God.

This is glory at its most difficult and attenuated – glory glimpsed behind the helmet of a Nazi guard, in God's reckless creation of freedom and God's longing for response – glory glimpsed in the presencelike absence that 'rewards' the deep searcher – glory found in the deepest part of the self, honestly explored. There is a sense at the extremes of this type of glory that the human searcher appears to be doing almost all the 'work', in stubbornly and honestly seeking to bear with authenticity the fleeting and paradoxical character of this 'absent' God, yet ultimately it is still God who makes Godself known.

This journey of contemplation serves to exhort the reader to search fearlessly for disclosures of divine reality, and to search for them even within discouragement, silence, apparent absence experienced kneeling long, even – rare as this response may be – within totalitarian oppression and a system of transit camps to Auschwitz. We have seen R. S. Thomas (in his poetic persona) learn to turn aside to the miracle, to persist in prayer and spiritual search. In Hillesum we see how her perception of the gloriousness of life fuelled that joy that made others in turn respond (as we saw for example in the quotation from Weinreb).

So in their very different ways a poet and a mystic have helped us see glory, and to see it, once again, in bright glimpses, but also in paradoxical absences, and even manifest in the context of brutality and oppression. In the next chapter I return from these depths, to consider how my understanding of glory might play itself out in the life of the ordinary Christian believer, and how that might relate to the theme of divine longing.

5

Glory in the Christian Journey

In the last chapter we looked at the example of Etty Hillesum and her remarkable capacity to perceive glory within a life full of misery, oppression, and threat. We established the importance of bearing to the greatest possible extent the reality of situations in life. We also extended the sense of the importance of 'three-lensed seeing' for authentic contemplation among Christians.

It may have seemed from the preceding two chapters that I see contemplation of divine glory as a rarefied gift. That seeing glory through nature might depend on advanced poetic and scientific insights, and that only exceptional individuals can see glory in apparent divine absence, or in conditions of great harshness or oppression.[1]

Rather I claim that the discernment of divine glory is an ordinary human capacity, which is capable of being enhanced in the lives of ordinary believers, even though under the challenge of extreme suffering this perception will often fail. The analysis of this book is not offered for pastoral reasons, except insofar as the bearing of reality must ultimately tend to be health giving. But neither is it offered as a rarefied or elitist model of contemplation. In Hillesum's language, all human beings are, at

---

[1] A view that would have parallels in the thought of Simone Weil; see L. McCullough, *The Religious Philosophy of Simone Weil: An Introduction* (London: I. B. Tauris, 2014), especially chapter 6.

least potentially, 'houses with open doors ... and each one of them must be turned into a dwelling dedicated to you, God.'[2]

So I shall try to indicate in this last chapter how the contemplation of divine glory is part of every human vocation. I shall explore, moreover, how in both Paul and John believers come to share in the divine glory.[3]

This chapter, then, concerns less extreme examples than that of Etty Hillesum, and it does not rely on the extraordinary insights of prominent poets. It aims to consider what significance glory might have in the life of the ordinary Christian seeking to grow on the journey of faith. If divine glory is best understood as whatever functions as a sign of the deep reality of God, and if, therefore, the life, death, and resurrection of Jesus functions as the archetypal case of such a sign, the most direct manifestation of glory to which Christians have access, we can ask further whether the lives of Christians, as they respond to Christ in the power of the Holy Spirit, can in turn function as signs of the sign that is Jesus. This chapter tests that proposal against evidence from the New Testament, especially the writings of Paul.

My colleague Andrew Robinson has written very persuasively of Jesus' life as an iconic qualisign, in Peircean terms, of the life of God. As we noted in Chapter 1, a qualisign is a sign that is able to function as a sign because of its sheer quality of being. The more I think about that idea of Robinson, the more powerful it seems to me to be. In Jesus' case, his actions functioned as various types of sign of the nature of God,[4] but it was the overall 'colour' of his life, its quality, that functioned most

---

[2] Quoted and adapted by D. de Costa, *Anne Frank and Etty Hillesum: Inscribing Spirituality and Sexuality*, transl. M. F. C. Hoyinck and R. E. Chesal (New Brunswick, NJ: Rutgers University Press, 1998), 238.

[3] *Theosis*, partaking of the divine nature, is sometimes thought to be confined in the New Testament to 2 Peter 1.3–4, but participation in divine glory is strongly alluded to at 2 Corinthians 3.18 and Romans 8.30; cf. 1 Thessalonians 2.12, 2 Thessalonians 2.14, and 2 Timothy 2.10. Carey Newman adds 2 Thessalonians 1.10, claiming that in Paul's 'electric' use of the verb *sundoxazō* 'believer's transformation into Glory' is found coordinated with future divine self-manifestation: *Paul's Glory-Christology: Tradition and Rhetoric* (Leiden: Brill, 1992), 159. The theme of theosis in Paul is developed by Michael Gorman in his trilogy *Cruciformity: Paul's Narrative Theology of the Cross* (Grand Rapids, MI: Eerdmans, 2001); *Inhabiting the Cruciform God: Kenosis, Justification and Theosis in Paul's Narrative Soteriology* (Grand Rapids, MI: Eerdmans, 2009); and *Becoming the Gospel: Paul, Participation and Mission* (Grand Rapids, MI: Eerdmans, 2015). See also the closing section of this chapter for a related proposal in relation to John 17.

[4] A. Robinson, *God and the World of Signs: Trinity, Evolution, and the Metaphysical Semiotics of C. S. Peirce* (Leiden: Brill, 2010), 120–5.

eloquently as a sign of the divine life.[5] Whereas we saw the great theophanies of the Hebrew Bible as iconic sinsigns, and as signs especially of
the awesome transcendence of God, Christ's life as qualisign is eloquent
of the possibility that the colour of a human life could signify the divine
immanence. Our analysis opens up the further possibility that the lives of
believers might become iconic qualisigns of the life of Christ,[6] that their
lives might take on, at least partially and fitfully, that overall 'colour' that
is Christlikeness, and hence reflect the divine life itself.[7]

That is the way in which I have come to understand that strange and
wonderful verse 2 Corinthians 3.18, which the NRSV renders:

And all of us, with unveiled faces, seeing the glory of the Lord as though reflected
in a mirror, are being transformed into the same image from one degree of glory to
another; for this comes from the Lord, the Spirit.[8]

Earlier in 2 Corinthians there is already language suggestive of believers functioning as signs. At 2.14, Paul writes of God in Christ putting
believers on display like captives;[9] at 3.2–3, he first calls the Corinthians
his 'letter' and then 'a letter of Christ'. There is a strong sense here that the
Christian community is functioning as some sort of sign of Christ.

I treat 3.18 in much more detail later in this chapter. But I begin
by exploring the juxtaposition in that verse of *tēn autēn eikona meta-
morphoumetha* 'we are being transformed into the same image' with

---

[5] So also S. Terrien, *The Elusive Presence, toward a New Biblical Theology* (Eugene, OR:
Wipf and Stock, 2000 [1978]). Christians saw the final epiphany not just in Jesus'
ministry, 'but also in the totality of his person, dying and alive' (471).

[6] J. M. F. Heath writes that the apostles are turned into 'the same image' in the sense that
they too become Christian icons (*eikones*) who can be gazed at in a way that transforms
their beholders unto life (2. Cor. 4.12 with 3.18)': *Paul's Visual Piety: The Metamorphosis
of the Beholder* (Oxford: Oxford University Press, 2013), 227.

[7] A. Robinson, *Traces of the Trinity: Signs, Sacraments and Sharing God's Life* (Cambridge:
James Clarke, 2014), 67–82. The New Testament writers express a related thought, albeit
with a very different metaphor, when they write of the 'sonship' of Christ and hence of
believers (e.g., at Jn 1.14, Gal 4.5, etc.).

[8] Of this astonishing verse Paul Ricoeur writes: 'Is an icon that is not an idol possible? ... It
is to this reinterpretation of the glory of God figured through the person of Christ that Paul
grafted the extraordinary theme of the transformation of the Christian into this same
image': *Figuring the Sacred: Religion, Narrative and Imagination*, transl. D. Pellaurer, ed.
M. Wallace, (Minneapolis, MN: Fortress Press, 1995), 267–8.

[9] Cf. T. B. Savage, *Power through Weakness: Paul's Understanding of the Christian
Ministry in 2. Corinthians* (Cambridge: Cambridge University Press, 1996), 103–4. The
verb used here, *thriambeuō*, is a very interesting one in this context. Believers are presented as a sign of triumph and at the same time a sign of their own abasement. On this
word, see also D. J. Williams, *Paul's Metaphors: Their Context and Character* (Peabody,
MA: Hendrickson, 1999), 275, n. 9.

apo doxēs eis doxan (literally 'from glory to glory'). Note the combination of the terms *doxa* (glory) and *eikōn* (image). That Paul associated these terms suggests that, in respect of divine glory expressed in human form, he was definitely thinking in terms of image, and hence of a kind of sign of the divine 'original'.

My attention to this link between *doxa* and *eikōn* arises from Timothy Savage's book *Power through Weakness*.[10] The clearest link between the words seems to me to be that difficult passage beginning 1 Corinthians 11.7:

> For a man ought not to have his head covered because he is the *eikōn* and *doxa* of God; but woman is the *doxa* of man.

Paul claims that the man is *doxa theou*, the woman *doxa andros*. The man, for Paul, is a sign of the divine reality, specifically through Christ who is his 'Head' (v. 3); the wife (regrettably) is thought of as being only indirectly such a sign, through the husband who is her 'head'.[11] But what engages us here is that *eikōn* and *doxa* are used in parallel.[12] Both, I suggest, are ways of expressing that the human being can be a sign of the divine.

The terms are used in an 'anti-parallel' sense at Romans 1.23, where humans are accused of exchanging the glory of the immortal God for the image of a mortal human being. In other words, they contemplate a statue of an idol as sign of reality rather than looking to a sign of the divine reality. Another very important example of the juxtaposition of *eikōn* and *doxa* is at Romans 8.29–30, in which Paul claims that God 'predestined [those called and foreknown] to be conformed (*summorphous*) to the image of [God's] son' and goes on to claim that those whom God justified he also glorified.[13] In the hermeneutical approach being proposed here, the process of being conformed to the great sign of God that is Christ is also the process of being raised to the state of being a sign of that sign.

---

[10] Savage, *Power*, 149–50.

[11] See N. A. Meyer, *Adam's Dust and Adam's Glory in the Hodayot and the Letters of Paul: Rethinking Anthropogony and Theology* (Leiden: Brill, 2016) for a helpful reading of this passage in terms of the original creation, the hierarchy being set aside in the eschatological state described at Galatians 3.28.

[12] In a sense, the great vision of divine glory in Ezekiel 1 already prepares for this thinking in Paul. The *kavōd* is already associated with a human form, that form which Genesis 1 expresses to be in the image and likeness of God.

[13] See H. Goranson Jacob and N. T. Wright, *Conformed to the Image of His Son: Rethinking Paul's Theology of Glory in Romans* (Downers Grove, IL: IVP Academic, 2018), for detailed treatment of this passage.

Haley Goranson Jacob insists that *doxa* in Paul should be detached from its familiar association with splendour[14] and emphasizes the importance of Romans 8.17–30 for understanding the Apostle's use of *doxa*, in Romans and elsewhere.[15] It will be clear from the analysis offered thus far that I do not equate divine glory necessarily with splendour but typically with whatever functions as a sign of the Godness of God. I do not, therefore, seek out 2 Corinthians 3–4 for its light imagery. And I acknowledge the vital importance of Romans 8 for our understanding of the great plan of God, both for humans and the non-human creation.[16] But the driving force of Paul's rhetoric in Romans is just that – the great plan of *God*. What concerns us in this chapter is to learn how human *response* to God can be about glory, understood in terms of divine sign. For this purpose the 2 Corinthians passage, and especially 3.18, with that depiction of the Christian removing the veil from her face[17] to contemplate glory,[18] and that extraordinary and compelling phrase *apo doxēs eis doxan* as a description of the trajectory of the believer, is necessarily an important focus.

2 Corinthians 3–4 will therefore be our guide in this chapter as we seek to explore the full ramifications of believers becoming signs of the sign of God that is Jesus. Whereas in Chapter 2 we looked at the way the Fourth Evangelist transforms our understanding of divine glory, here we shall focus particularly on the Apostle Paul's transformation of the concept of divine glory, and what Carey Newman terms his 'glory-Christology'.[19] I shall conclude that looking on Christ 'with unveiled face' leads to a Spirit-given freedom, which is also a process of being transformed into the one, true image of God that is Christ.

However, a problem for Christian ethics for the whole of its life has been what to do with this freedom, how it should be directed in this

---

[14] So also George Caird, 'To [Paul] the *essence* of doxa is the dynamic grace and saving activity of God, even when it manifests itself in radiant light': 'The New Testament Conception of Doxa' (D. Phil. Thesis, Oxford University, 1944), 225, emphasis mine.

[15] H. Goranson Jacob, personal communication.

[16] I also note the importance of Romans 3.23 – 'all have sinned and fallen short of the glory of God'. Here, I suggest, glory is best understood at the other end of the spectrum of meaning we have been exploring – in terms of a restatement of the holiness, righteousness, and Godness of God.

[17] Or allowing the Spirit to remove it.

[18] See C. B. Kaiser, contrasting this bold contemplation with Rabbinic Jewish spirituality: *Seeing the Lord's Glory: Kyriocentric Visions and the Dilemma of Early Christology* (Minneapolis, MN: Fortress Press, 2014), 142, n. 25.

[19] Newman, *Paul's Glory-Christology*, especially chapter 9.

now-but-not-yet time while we glimpse but do not see clearly the coming Kingdom of God. So a major section of the chapter explores the theme of longing – our longing for God, yes, but also, as an extension of that, our longing for what God longs for. Our exploration of longing will end, like so many Christian journeys, back at the deceptively simple-sounding longings in the prayer Jesus taught his disciples – 'Thy kingdom come, thy will be done'.

First, however, I consider other resources in the New Testament for understanding the response of the believer to signs of the divine reality.

THE BELIEVER'S RESPONSE TO GOD'S GLORY

Most of our discussion up to now has concerned the discernment of the signs of the divine reality that I have ventured – deeply controversially at times – to term glory. But those signs, according to my understanding, always call for a response.

Our work in Chapters 3 and 4 will have shown in what vast diversity of situations manifestations of divine glory may be discerned. Can we then generalize at all about responses to glory? George Savran, writing of the theophany of Jeremiah 1, interprets the Lord's affirmation 'you have seen well' (Jer 1.12) as referring 'not to the emergence of the divine in the theophanic moment, but to the prophet's ability to discern the traces of divine intention in everyday reality.'[20] In insisting (Chapter 3) that signs of the divine reality can be found in every part of the natural world, and even (Chapter 4) in the bleakest and most painful aspects of human life, I am affirming that possibility of 'seeing well'. But how is that well-seeing to be translated into an actual response?

The classic locus in the New Testament at which we see human response to glory is the story of the Annunciation. Luke tells us that, through the medium of an angel, God signifies to Mary the role she is to play in the salvation of the world. Mary's response is to offer herself to be, in von Balthasar's words, 'simply a life that lets God dispose of it as he will'. Von Balthasar continues, 'Mary's life possesses no detached form of its own ... her form is inundated in a light radiating from [Christ].'[21] To anticipate our discussion of 2 Corinthians 3.18 later in this chapter,

[20] G. W. Savran, *Theophany in Biblical Narrative* (Edinburgh: T&T Clark, 2005), 83.
[21] H. U. von Balthasar, *The Glory of the Lord: A Theological Aesthetics*, Vol. 1, Seeing the Form, transl. E. Leivà-Merikakis, ed. J. Fessio, S. J., and J. Riches (Edinburgh: T&T Clark, 1982), 564.

Mary both receives and reflects the glory of the Lord. Some readers will be glad to think of Mary as the one human to have this receiving–reflecting role before the Resurrection (or the second, if Moses is thought of as the first). Others will think this is too much of an extrapolation from a very few verses. But the core of Mary's response, for which she is so rightly venerated, is her willingness to receive, however immense and alarming the divine gift, and to be a medium by which the gift can transform the lives of others.

At the same time, Jason Fout is right to challenge von Balthasar here. Fout points out that Mary's first response to the angel is a question, indeed a protest – 'How can this be …' (Lk 1.34). Fout uses this to strengthen his overall thesis that God's glory does not take all human agency out of our response. 'Faithful questioning' is an appropriate part of human engagement with divine glory.[22] We saw in our exploration of the tsunami in Chapter 3 that as well as the classic elements of awe and fear, protest and lament may also be components of the response to glory. These responses are validated by the presence in the canon of the Book of Job, and the Psalms of lament. However, even Job is ultimately transformed by his contact with the divine. We are concerned here with God's offer of healing transformation, and what might be the most authentic human response.

That the divine self-communication calls for response is central. The Transfiguration is a classic example: the revelation is accompanied by the command 'listen to him' (Mk 9.7). So Garrett notes that 'God's beauty is not fit for disinterested contemplation … [it] draws … perceiving subjects out of themselves and into God's drama of redemption'.[23]

Another enormously significant range of responses to the manifestation of the reality of God is found in the various depictions of the Resurrection. There is the response of joy, explored in different ways in the different Gospels. But there are also other types of reaction. Of the biblical accounts, perhaps the most important for the present study is that found in the shorter ending of Mark. The response of the women who witness the empty tomb is described thus: 'So they went out and fled from the tomb, for terror and amazement had seized them; and they said

[22] J. Fout, *Fully Alive: The Glory of God and the Human Creature in Karl Barth, Hans Urs von Balthasar and the Theological Exegesis of Scripture* (London: Bloomsbury T&T Clark, 2015), 140–2.

[23] S. M. Garrett, *God's Beauty-in-Act: Participation in God's Suffering Glory* (Eugene, OR: Pickwick Books, 2013), 145–6.

nothing to anyone, for they were afraid' (Mk 16.8). The recognition that God's reality penetrates and transforms even the darkest depths of hopelessness, and even the utmost constraint of life, biological destruction, and death, leads the women to an amazed and fearful silence. This is an utterly convincing reaction, which perhaps should attract more attention within current Christian reflection on Easter.[24] Another interesting exploration of responses to resurrection, and the uncertainty and liminality of that experience, can be found in Shelly Rambo's *Spirit and Trauma*, reflecting on Magdalene and the beloved disciple in the Fourth Gospel, and urging Christians, in effect, not to take short cuts through the narrative to a story only of triumph.[25]

Fout offers an additional dimension to human response that is also important to this book. He points to the importance of *discernment* in the response to manifestations of divine glory.[26] This is essential to a semiotic understanding because in Peirce's triadic scheme an interpretant is necessary to the realization of a sign. Discernment is an important element in this. Biblically, it enabled the apostles to distinguish the moving of the Spirit from, for example, the magical performances of Simon Magus (Acts 8). In contemporary contemplation, it involves, as we saw in Chapter 3, a judicious use of the resources of both science and poetry when instressing the manifestations of glory in the natural world.

However, I want to acknowledge how prone to error human response to God can be. Some of these errors are so familiar in Christian thought as to need little discussion. The first is idolatry, the failure to discern the divine glory accurately and the consequent response of making one's own idol. The classic case is of course the incident of the golden calf in Exodus 32, a reaction, it might be argued, to the apparent over-transcendence, and excessive divine reserve, experienced by the people when Moses mediated most of their encounters with Yahweh. But the first biblical case of idolatrous misinterpretation of the divine self-communication is found in Genesis 3, where humans misconstrue their own autonomy as implying the need to transgress God-given limits.

Arguably, the sort of idolatry to which the contemporary West is most prone is a mixture of these two traits. We idolize our own freedom

---

[24] Austin Farrer defended the importance of the shorter ending of Mark in, e.g., *The Glass of Vision* (Westminster: Dacre Press, 1948), 136–45.

[25] S. Rambo, *Spirit and Trauma: A Theology of Remaining* (Louisville, KY: Westminster John Knox Press, 2010).

[26] Fout, *Fully Alive*, 141–2.

without seeing that it might be helpfully shaped and constrained by consideration of the Kingdom of God,[27] and we construct our own images of God. Most commonly, in my experience, postmodern Western people react against the apparent overcommunication of God in Scripture, and the apparent partiality of God for the particular as a path to salvation, by constructing a vague panimmanent wisdom as our golden calf – all the more insidious for being unseen. We worship the autonomous and self-authenticating character of our own spiritual experience. In addition, of course, to worshipping what humans have always tended to worship – power, wealth, and forms of physical (including sexual) experience guaranteed by power and wealth. Interestingly, one of the classic human idols, religion as all-consuming practice, practice that first veils and then blots out the vision of divine grace, seems to be declining in power in the West. That makes it harder for Western people to understand not only the lives of ardent Muslim sects, but also Jesus' own critiques of the religion of his day.

THE PAULINE WITNESS TO DIVINE GLORY, AND ITS IMPLICATIONS FOR THE BELIEVER

The Pauline letters are a central locus for considering human response to divine glory. I now give them sustained consideration (returning at the end of the chapter to the Fourth Gospel).

I am sure von Balthasar is right to point to the centrality for Paul of his visionary experience of Christ. Some very distinguished scholars have downplayed its importance to Paul.[28] However, both Alan Segal and Carey Newman make an eloquent case that Paul's 'Christophany' (placed by Luke on the Damascus Road) is the determinative event shaping Paul's Gospel.[29] It is not just that Paul, the Pharisaic intellectual, experiences

---

[27] Cf. J. K. A. Smith, *Desiring the Kingdom: Worship, World-View and Cultural Formation* (Grand Rapids, MI: Baker Academic, 2009).

[28] Newman gives Albert Schweitzer, W. D. Davies, and E. P. Sanders among his examples: *Paul's Glory-Christology*, 166. He cites Davies as an example of someone who sees Paul's understanding of glory as deriving from Rabbinic tradition, rather than personal revelation. Newman, *Paul's Glory-Christology*, 168–9; see W. D. Davies, *Paul and Rabbinic Judaism: Some Rabbinic Elements in Pauline Theology* (Philadelphia: Fortress Press, 1980).

[29] Segal is clear that Paul expresses at 2 Corinthians 4.6 the result of his own conversion: *Paul the Convert: The Apostolate and Apostasy of Saul the Pharisee* (New Haven, CT: Yale University Press, 1990), 61.

through that event a transfer of his allegiance and receives his call to be a Christian prophet[30] and apostle. It is that, as Newman rightly insists, Paul experiences glory and comes to see Christ as the eschatological sign of God's glory, the true image of the invisible God.[31] Moreover, I think Newman is right, as against Segal, to suppose that Paul felt he had received the content of his gospel, his kerygma, as well as his call, from that experience (Gal 1.12), rather than through the community into which he came as a result of the experience.[32] The particular contribution Segal makes is to connect the Damascus Road vision with the theophany in Ezekiel 1.[33]

Where I differ from von Balthasar is in not supposing that what Paul saw was necessarily beauty, in any ordinary sense. It is, as many scholars have pointed out, very hard to know what Paul saw, and in terms of any extended description we have only Luke's accounts (Acts 9; 22; 26) to go on.[34] But we may reconstruct it theologically from Paul's 'gospel'. The Apostle saw *Herrlichkeit*, he saw the lordliness of Christ as a sign of God the eschatological redeemer. He saw that all that was vital to know about God as saviour was known in Jesus, the crucified one, whom he had now to confess 'the Lord of glory' (1 Cor 2.8).[35] What he saw must have been as awe inspiring as the vision of Isaiah in the Temple, and even more life wrenching. But whether to see the lordliness of the Crucified One was to see beauty in any ordinary sense of that word is beyond our reach to know.

---

[30] See Newman, *Paul's Glory-Christology*, 246.

[31] 1 Corinthians 2.8, 2 Corinthians 4.4, Col 1.15, cf. Newman, *Paul's Glory-Christology*, chapter 11. So also Stephen Finlan, 'Forever after he retained the idea of the resurrection body as glorious, neither an ordinary earthly body, nor a disembodied spirit': 'Can We Speak of *Theosis* in Paul?' in *Partakers of the Divine Nature: The History and Development of Deification in the Christian Traditions*, ed. M. J. Christensen and J. A. Wittung (Grand Rapids, MI: Baker Academic, 2007), 68–80, at 73.

[32] Newman, *Paul's Glory-Christology*, 180–2, citing Segal, *Paul*, 320, n. 64.

[33] Segal, *Paul*, 9.

[34] Though Newman lists a whole range of places in Paul that he considers to refer to the 'Christophany' – for example 1 Corinthians 9.1, 15.3–11; Gal 1.11–17; Philippians 3.2–15; 2 Corinthians 5.16: *Paul's Glory-Christology*, 165–6. He makes a specific link between *ōphthē kamoi* 'he appeared also to me' in 1 Corinthians 15 and the wilderness theophanies (ibid., 187–91). He also claims – perhaps more speculatively – that 'References to the Christophany permeate 2 Corinthians 3.4–4.6: the comparison of the old and new covenants – with their representative administrators, Moses and Paul.' Ibid., 165.

[35] A phrase that Newman traces back to the throne visions of 1 Enoch, ibid., 237.

James Dunn, writing on Colossians 1.11, which speaks of believers 'being empowered with all power according to the strength of His glory to all patience [*hupomonē*] and endurance [*makrothumia*]' notes that 'divine glory as a manifestation of power ... a thought ... rooted in the folk memory of the fearful numinous power (*mysterium tremendum*) of such theophanies (Ex 19.16–26, Num 16.19–35, Is 6.4–5) [is] in Paul ... understood as beneficial power, transforming for the better'.[36] Or to put this in the terms of the present study, the awesome signs God gives of Godness culminate in an empowering Incarnate sign, and that great sign empowers believers, in the present age, not to self-glorification in a worldly sense, but to *hupomonē* and *makrothumia*.

Paul tells us that 'the mind that was in Christ Jesus' was not to seek to grasp, or to retain, status, but to take the form of a servant (Phil 2.5–7). The Apostle tells us that Christ was 'in the form of God', *en morphē theou*, which may itself be a statement about his (pre-existent) glory.[37] Yet he took on the form of a servant. For Savage, Christ in so doing 'did not empty himself of the divine likeness. He perfectly expressed it'.[38] Again we find that the glory of the Incarnate One is expressed in paradoxical humility, and that signifies something very important about God. The Christian calling is to have this 'mind', and become servants in turn (2 Cor 4.5), servants who are willing to suffer in serving.

The other key aspect of Christification is that Jesus' followers come to be authentically one community, which Paul calls the body of Christ. These two aspects of the Christian vocation, the individual and the corporate, come together in 2 Corinthians 3.18 – '*beholding* the glory of the Lord we are metamorphosed into *the same image*'.[39] This verse is very important for all studies of glory since it is the one that most explicitly draws the human being into the divine glory – it is as Finlan puts it, 'the most frankly theotic passage in Paul'.[40] We shall explore those italicized words in much more detail later in this chapter. For now it is enough to note that the response to the sign of God that is Christ, in his

---

[36] J. D. G. Dunn, *The Epistles to the Colossians and Philemon: A Commentary on the Greek Text* (Grand Rapids, MI: Eerdmans, 1996), 74.

[37] D. Steenburg, 'The Case against the Synonymity of *Morphē* and *Eikōn*', *Journal for the Study of the New Testament* 34 (1988), 77–86, calls *morphē theou* 'the visible aspect of appearance of God'. Meyer links the phrase with the theophanies of Exodus and Ezekiel (*Adam's Dust*, 151, n. 194).

[38] Savage, *Power*, 151.   [39] Translation mine.

[40] Finlan, 'Can We Speak', 75. Cf. Newman, 'Paul teaches a process of human deification based on mystical vision' (citing 2 Cor 3.18): *Paul's Glory-Christology*, 168.

crucified and resurrected lordship, is to be transformed into one, as an image, and that is the image of Christ, who is the true image of God (Col 1.15, 2 Cor 4.4).[41]

Such beholding *must* transform us – as von Balthasar puts it so memorably, 'there is no seeing without being caught up'.[42] 'To be transported, moreover, belongs to the very origin of Christianity.'[43] Equally, it must be insisted, there is no being caught up without seeing – there must be a willingness to be exposed to the sign of God that is Jesus, if there is to be the beholding that transforms. There must be, to return to the imagery of 2 Corinthians 3.18, a willingness to unveil the face. Von Balthasar notes that, at least in some of the Fathers, this contemplation can eventually ascend to become 'the flashing anticipation of eschatological illumination, the presaging vision of transparent glory in the form of the Servant'.[44] In other words, such is the grace of Christ that contemplation of his form can render our third seeing lens, the *Gloria in excelsis*, brilliantly plain and radiantly vivid. Yet Christ remains the Servant, the Crucified One. We cannot dispense with the lens of *Gloria crucis*.

We noted in Chapter 2 that the writer of the Fourth Gospel revises the concept of divine glory through associating Jesus' glorification with the Passion.[45] I suggest that Paul the Apostle revises the concept in two related ways. First, his direct experience of the risen Jesus in his vision or visions convinced him that the Nazarene was none other than the special representative of God in a visionary tradition including First Enoch and the Book of Daniel, but reaching behind them to the vision in Ezekiel 1. Paul sees Christ as a being 'in the form of God' (Phil 2.6), infinitely rich yet becoming poor for our sake (2 Cor 8.9), a sign of the extraordinary mercy and costly love of God for all people, a visible manifestation of the imminent redemption of the whole cosmos. Second, Paul perceives that believers can be caught up into the divine life, and this because in

---

[41] It is the close association with 2 Corinthians 4.4 that persuades me that what is beheld in 3.18 is *Christ*, not *God*. So Heath, *Paul's Visual Piety*, 217–8. See later in this chapter on N. T. Wright's proposal that 'the Lord' in 3.18 should be read as 'the Spirit'.

[42] H. U. von Balthasar, *The Glory of the Lord: A Theological Aesthetics*, Vol. 7, Theology: The New Covenant, transl. B. McNeil C.R.V., ed. J. Riches (Edinburgh: T&T Clark, 1989), 24.

[43] H. U. von Balthasar, *The Glory of the Lord: A Theological Aesthetics,* Vol. 1, Seeing the Form, transl. E. Leiva-Merikakis, ed. J. Fessio, S.J. and J. Riches (Edinburgh: T&T Clark, 1982), 33.

[44] Ibid., 39.

[45] At the end of this chapter, I discuss John 17, and the Fourth Gospel's version of the possibility of Christian disciples being drawn up into the divine glory.

contemplating the face of Christ they are in the sort of intimacy with
God that Moses knew on the mountain, an intimacy that does not fade
but rather is progressively deepened and transformed. I now explore this
latter conclusion derived from 2 Corinthians 3.1–4.6.

This passage poses us a sharp question – how *can* human beings be
transformed from one degree of glory to another, or to put it in the terms
of this study, how can they become progressively truer signs of the sign of
God that is Christ?[46] I begin by acknowledging the complexity of the
passage[47] and that no non-specialist can hope to do the secondary literature justice. I note with von Balthasar that some older exegetes think
of *apo doxēs eis doxan* as moving from the glory of one Testament to
another.[48] Fout, as we have noted, insists that the believer becoming conformed to the image of Christ is not a creature without its own agency.[49]
Indeed, part of the significance of the Incarnation is that creaturely agency
can be itself and at the same time perfectly in accord with the will of God
the Father. And just as Jesus could be himself, and still a qualisign of the
divine life, so believers too can be agents exploring, learning through,
growing within, their own lives, and still know those lives being transformed into the quality of Christ's life. As Fout points out, Moses' identity
was not effaced by the shining that he experienced on his face.[50]

Fout distances himself from von Balthasar's emphasis on glory as
splendour, as opposed to Fout's own stress on 'God's honour and praiseworthiness, filled out by the shape of God's acts'.[51] My own emphasis
here very much accords with God's glory being given shape by God's
acts – since God's acts are direct reflections of the Godness of God,
ultimately mysterious though that Godness is.

I have posited throughout this study that the theme of glory is larger,
and subtler, than the familiar image of radiance that the word so often
evokes. Images of light and vision are by no means excluded from my

---

[46] Cf. Paul Ricoeur's formulation, 'it is to this reinterpretation of the glory of God figured
through the person of Christ that Paul grafted the extraordinary theme of the transformation of the Christian into this same image. In this way he forged the central metaphor
of the Christian self as christomorphic, that is, the image of the image par excellence.'
Quoted in Fout, *Fully Alive*, 162.

[47] Newman's adjective for 2 Corinthians 3.18 is 'vexing': *Paul's Glory-Christology*, 227.
For important analyses of the argument of 2 Corinthians 3 outside the standard com-
mentaries, see F. Watson, *Paul and the Hermeneutics of Faith* (London: T&T Clark/
Continuum, 2004), chapter 6; R. B. Hays, *Echoes of Scripture in the Letters of Paul*
(New Haven, CT: Yale University Press, 1989), chapter 4.

[48] Von Balthasar, *GL1*, 210.   [49] Fout, *Fully Alive*, 164–5.   [50] Ibid., 165.

[51] Ibid.

understanding of glory as primarily about sign. The phrase *apaugasma tēs doxēs*[52] in Hebrews 1.3 illustrates this well – Jesus, as the divine Son sent as the climax of God's loving self-expression, is the perfect manifestation of God's love in creation and redemption. Jesus is as eloquent of the divine nature as the sun's rays are of the sun.[53]

As Giorgio Agamben notes, in this dense argument in 2 Corinthians 3, Paul builds up his 'theory of glory' exclusively 'through optical images'.[54] The passage, with its sustained light imagery, is therefore perhaps the most awkward text for my effort to detach glory from its customary association with radiance. In it Paul is explicitly using the theme of greater and lesser radiance to contrast the old covenant with Spirit-filled faith. Indeed, in a major commentary on 2 Corinthians, Victor Furnish translates *doxa* by 'splendor' throughout this passage.[55]

So I have to accept that in the overall meaning of *kavōd* in the Hebrew Bible, and *doxa* in the New Testament, a subsection of references to signs of the divine reality do use light imagery as Paul does in 2 Corinthians 3. That leads however to the question, how should we read the glory imagery in the verse at the climax of that chapter, 3.18? I shall seek to show that what at first might seem to conflict with my general scepticism about glory as radiance, namely the pervasive light imagery of 2 Corinthians 3, proves on closer investigation to help and extend my proposal about glory as sign.

What Paul's somewhat tortuous midrashic treatment of Exodus 34 in 2 Corinthians 3[56] implies is the sense that something can be a sign of the divine, and yet have the possibility of passing away, or indeed of being transformed into a yet more faithful sign. The giving of the Law (which for Paul comes to be 'the ministry of death' [3.7]) was accompanied by glory in the sense that what could be seen on Moses' face was a sign of the holiness of God, hard even to look upon. But (later) this same sign comes

---

[52] 'Reflection of [God's] glory'.

[53] See J. D. G. Dunn for the likely origin of this imagery in Philo: *Christology in the Making: An Inquiry into the Origins of the Doctrine of the Incarnation* (London: SCM Press, 1980), 226f.

[54] G. Agamben, *The Kingdom and the Glory: For a Theological Genealogy of Economy and Government (Homo Sacer II, 2)*, transl. L. Chiesa (with M. Mandarini) (Stanford, CA: Stanford University Press, 2011), 203.

[55] V. Furnish, *II Corinthians* (Garden City, NY: Doubleday & Co., 1984).

[56] Paul picks one of the very few passages in the Hebrew Bible in which divine glory, or at least a sign of it, seems to pass to a human (contrast Is 42.8, 'my glory I give to no other').

to be seen as hardly a sign at all compared with the all-surpassing clarity of the new sign, Christ (3.10). We saw in Chapter 2 that the perceived iconity of the theophanies of Yahweh was largely replaced after the Exile by the indexical sign that was the Law (though theophany reappears in apocalyptic visions such as those of Daniel and Enoch). Here, Paul says, the all-surpassing icon of God becomes available to all believers.

The glory that passes away (3.7) still arose in association with a sign of the divine holiness; how much more will that which is of eternal value be marked by signs of wonderful clarity and abiding truth. Indeed, the opposition forces (4.4a) prevent signs of God from being interpreted by the people of the old covenant – the veiling has now transferred itself from Moses' face to the hearts of those who would otherwise be able to discern holiness behind the Law when it is read in the synagogue (3.15). But the Gospel removes this veil, and enables us to see glory. The Spirit forms a new community in Christ which can live directly from the contemplation of Christ, rather than from the 'letter' of the Law. In Peircean terms, an iconic qualisign of God is now available which has a directness transcending (so Paul alleges) that of the indexical legisign of the Law on which synagogue worship was based.[57]

One of the most beautiful and telling verses in the whole New Testament is what follows at 3.17, identifying the presence of God with the presence of the Holy Spirit, such a strong experience of those earliest churches, and going on to assert that where the Spirit is, there is freedom.

Stephen Finlan traces three phases to the believer's transformation:

first there is an earthly conformation to the Christlike pattern of dying to sin; then there is reception of godly righteousness and light, and finally there is physical death and resurrection, which entails receiving a transformed body modeled on Christ's body.[58]

The understanding of glory as sign, in association with this key motif of freedom made possible by the Spirit, provides a way to approach the key verse 3.18, which seems to depict a *process* in the believer,[59] being transformed from one degree of glory to another. It seems plausible to

---

[57] See Chapter 1 for a discussion of these categories of sign.

[58] Finlan, 'Can We Speak?', 73.

[59] Terrien makes the important point that *katoptrizomenoi* is participial, implying an ongoing process – this is no passing theophany: *Elusive Presence*, 458.

associate this with the second of Finlan's phases, the 'reception of godly righteousness and light'.[60]

2 Corinthians 3.18 poses three key exegetical questions:

1. *Katoptrizomenoi tēn doxan kuriou* – does that verb mean 'beholding' or 'reflecting' the glory of the Lord?
2. What is that clause *tēn autēn eikona*, 'the same image' doing?
3. Lastly and crucially, what does it mean to be transformed *apo doxēs eis doxan*, from one degree of glory to another?

First – *katoptrizomenoi*. The commentators have argued for centuries about this word. Its more normal meaning of reflecting, as in a mirror, is usually now rejected in favour of beholding in a mirror.[61] Mark Seifrid analyses this issue.[62] He notes that N. T. Wright and L. L. Belleville prefer the translation 'reflect'.[63] However, Seifrid stresses that the context is Moses going up to behold God with unveiled face. He is also much influenced by a passage in Philo, who writes this petition (in Moses' voice): 'May you not appear to me through heaven or earth or water or air or in any other way through the creation; may I not see you as in a mirror (*katoptrisaimēn*) in anything other than you who are God'.[64]

This connects with some of the motifs we explored in Chapters 2 and 3. In Chapter 3 we sought to behold signs of the divine reality precisely through the created world. Philo has Moses long for more direct vision, a related 'more' to the possibility Paul explores here – that of beholding with unveiled face the glory of the Lord. But note that both Philo and Paul still use this rare verb for beholding *as in a mirror* – the human beholder is

---

[60] N. T. Wright – the focus here is not Paul's own ministry but 'the state of heart of his hearers': 'Reflected Glory: 2 Corinthians 3.18' in *The Glory of Christ in the New Testament: Studies in Christology: In Memory of George Bradford Caird*, ed. L. D. Hurst and N. T. Wright (Oxford: Clarendon Press, 1987), 139–50, at 144.

[61] So F. Young and D. F. Ford, *Meaning and Truth in 2 Corinthians* (London: SPCK, 1987), 90. Examples of commentators taking this view include Furnish, *II Corinthians*, 239–40; M. E. Thrall, *The Second Epistle to the Corinthians: A Critical and Exegetical Commentary*, Vol. 1 (Edinburgh: T&T Clark, 1994), 290–5; P. Barnett, *The Second Epistle to the Corinthians* (Grand Rapids, MI: Eerdmans, 1997), 204–6.

[62] M. A. Seifrid, *The Second Letter to the Corinthians* (Grand Rapids, MI: Eerdmans, 2014), 180–4.

[63] Ibid., 180, n. 293, citing N. T. Wright, *The Climax of the Covenant: Christ and the Law in Pauline Theology* (Minneapolis, MN: Fortress Press, 1992), 188–9; L. L. Belleville, *Reflections of Glory: Paul's Polemical Use of the Moses-Doxa Tradition in 2. Corinthians 3.1–18* (Sheffield: JSOT Press, 1991), 279–82.

[64] Seifrid, *Second Letter*, 181, n. 294, quoting Philo, *Legum Allegoria* 3.101, translation mine.

still seeing an image, a sign of the ultimate reality, not looking upon it directly. The image is a true one, an utterly faithful sign, but to look on God directly 'face to face' is reserved for the eschaton. We only glimpse indirectly *Gloria in excelsis*, a thought that echoes Paul's related formulation (though in other language) at 1 Corinthians 13.12. To see 'in a glass darkly' (KJV) is not to see a deceiving image, but simply not to see face-to-face.[65]

Importantly Seifrid goes on to note that the glory of the Lord is revealed '*sub contrario*, hidden under its opposite'.[66] I would express this thought rather differently, drawing on our analysis of the Gospel of John in Chapter 2. It is not, in my view, that glory is 'hidden under its opposite' in the Passion of Christ or the persecution of believers. Again I draw on that quotation from Gregory of Nyssa: 'The greatness is glimpsed *in* the lowliness.'[67] Christ's abasement begins his 'hour' of ultimate glory. The power of love that is at the depths of divine reality is seen in a new way when it is exposed to oppression and persecution.

The line of interpretation I want to suggest allows us to hold both the alternative meanings of *katoptrizomenoi* together – believers *both* behold Christ, the perfect reflection of the perfect love of God, the perfect mirror, if you like, *and also* reflect that love.[68] After coming to this conclusion, that *katoptrizomenoi* must be allowed to carry both meanings, I was

[65] Lambrecht also notes that this enigmatic verb of Paul conveys the indirectness of the vision, and makes the same connection with 1 Corinthians 13.12 – seeing 'in a mirror of enigmas'. J. Lambrecht, 'Transformation in 2 Corinthians' in *Studies on 2 Corinthians*, ed. R. Bieringer and J. Lambrecht, (Leuven: Peeters, 1994), 295–307; cf. also A. E. Harvey, *Renewal through Suffering: A Study in 2 Corinthians* (Edinburgh: T&T Clark 1996), 51–2, on the language of glory as providing an indirect way to speak of the divine reality.

[66] Seifrid, *Second Letter*, 183. He cites those wonderful, resonant passages, 2 Corinthians 4.7–15, 6.3–10, describing the predicament of the believers, 'afflicted in every way, but not crushed', etc.

[67] Quoted in Hans Urs von Balthasar, *Mysterium Paschale: The Mystery of Easter*, transl. A. Nichols (San Francisco, CA: Ignatius Press, 1990), 34, emphasis mine. Or as C. F. D. Moule puts it, 'Glory follows humility' – that is a way of affirming faith in the glory; but 'the humility is the glory' represents a deeper insight': 'Reflections on Triumphalism' in *The Glory of Christ in the New Testament: Studies in Christology: In Memory of George Bradford Caird*, ed. L. D. Hurst and N. T Wright (Oxford: Clarendon Press, 1987), 219–27, at 225.

[68] It is the redemptive work of the Holy Spirit that has made this possible, for 'all have sinned and fallen short of the glory of God' (Rom 3.23) and therefore 'forfeited the privilege of reflecting [God's] glory'. R. B. Gaffin, Jr., 'Glory, Glorification' in *The Dictionary of Paul and His Letters*, ed. G. F. Hawthorne and R. P. Martin (Downers Grove, IL: Inter-Varsity Press, 1993), 348–50, at 348.

delighted to find that Frances Young and David Ford come to the same conclusion.[69] C. K. Barrett's commentary even suggests that such a double reading goes back to Chrysostom.[70]

This two-way movement, differently derived, is also found in the work of N. T. Wright. Wright puts it thus:

> Where and how, after all, do 'all of us ... gaze at the glory of the lord as in a mirror'? Clearly, I believe, when 'we' are looking at one another: the Corinthians at the apostle, *and the apostle at the Corinthians*, and indeed *the Corinthians at one another*. The lord, the spirit, is at work in their midst, and they are being transformed, whether they know it or not, whether they like its effects or not, whether it is culturally offensive or not, into 'the same image', since each is 'reflecting' in his or her own way the same lord, who is himself 'the image of God' as Paul will say a few verses later.[71]

This formulation allows Wright to retain the most obvious meaning of *katoptrizomenoi* as 'beholding', while still maintaining that the glory beheld is reflected glory. I think Wright is correct to emphasise that being transformed into the same image involves the internal dynamic of the fellowship of believers, but I see that dynamic as Spirit-catalyzed, yet focused on Christ, rather than Spirit-focused. Paul after all goes on to stress the importance of the contemplation of *Christ*, at 4.4 and 4.6.

It is moreover hard to agree with Wright's very bold suggestion in *The Climax of the Covenant* that 'the Lord' in the phrase 'the glory of the Lord' 'need not be identified as either 'God' or 'Christ' but may, perfectly

---

[69] Young and Ford, *Meaning and Truth*, 90–4. So also Fout, 'for "all of us" behold God's glory in such a fashion that God's glory is reflected on "our" faces', *Fully Alive* 161; also Finlan, 'The Christ believer can fearlessly approach that which frightened Aaron and the Israelites. Moreover, believers go on to embody and to reflect the glory that they have beheld': 'Can We Speak', 76. Savage in effect comes to the same conclusion, by choosing 'behold' and then concluding that believers 'ought also to radiate His glory': *Power*, 146, and quotation on 152. Heath also opts for 'behold' but can then write, as I noted earlier in this chapter, of believers as 'Christian icons ... who can be gazed at in a way that transforms their beholders unto life:' *Paul's Visual Piety*, 227.

[70] C. K. Barrett, *A Commentary on the Second Epistle to the Corinthians* (London: A&C Black, 1973), 125; see also Belleville, *Reflections*, 280. There is a hint of a precedent for this double meaning in Isaiah 60.1–5 with the prophecy which begins 'Arise, shine; for your light has come, and the glory of the Lord has risen upon you. For darkness shall cover the earth, and thick darkness the peoples; but the Lord will arise upon you, and his glory will appear over you', and culminates in verse 5 with '*Then you shall see and be radiant*' (italics mine).

[71] N. T. Wright, *Paul and the Faithfulness of God: Christian Origins and the Question of God* (London: SPCK, 2013), 726, italics in original. See also 'Reflected Glory', 145, and *Climax*, chapter 9.

consistently within the thought of the chapter as a whole, refer to the Spirit.'[72] He holds, then, that what is being beheld with unveiled face is not the contemplated Christ, but the 'peculiar glory of the Spirit that is seen when one looks at one's fellow Christians'.[73] This does have resonances with the mentions of the Spirit in verses 17–18, but seems out of keeping with the stress placed by Paul on the contemplation of the face of Christ at 4.6. Wright's reading also seems to me altogether too far from the theophanic context in which Paul sets the passage.[74]

However, if Wright's reading of 3.18 were adopted, this would not jeopardise my proposal of believers becoming signs of the great sign of God that is Christ. Wright's understanding places 3.18 in the middle of the process of the believers being transformed from one degree of glory to another – the community for Wright *already* reflects the glory of the Lord, who is the Spirit, whereas my reading imagines this 'optical' process starting from the beginning of believers' contemplating the face of Christ.[75]

I concede, however, that Wright's interpretation would function as a secondary effect within my scheme. Recognising other believers (and the Apostle himself) as signs of the sign of God that is Christ would contribute to our contemplation of the primary sign. Wright does also make an important point when he reminds us that 'the glory which is seen, as in a mirror, in Paul's ministry is the glory that shines through suffering'.[76] The community's reflecting and beholding of glory is not of some perfect idealised state based on some vaunted spirituality (such as Paul encounters later in the Letter in the 'super-apostles'). Rather it is a reflection and beholding of that condition of believers so memorably expressed later in 2 Corinthians 4.7–11 and 6.4–10.

Michael Gorman has characterised theosis in Paul as 'transformative participation in the kenotic cruciform character of God through Spirit-enabled conformity to the incarnate, crucified and resurrected/glorified Christ'.[77] The Lord who is contemplated is the Crucified One; believers

---

[72] Wright, *Climax*, 186.   [73] Wright, 'Reflected Glory', 145.

[74] Remembering that the unveiling of the face parallels Moses' looking upon God on the mountain. So Segal, 'Paul's phrase the Glory of the Lord must be taken both as a reference to Christ and as a technical term for the *Kavod*, the human form of God appearing in biblical visions': *Paul*, 60.

[75] With a special type of seeing, to which the role of the Spirit is intrinsic. See Heath (citing the work of Frances Back), 'a particular kind of seeing, namely a spirit-powered, visionary prophetic reception of revelation': *Paul's Visual Piety*, 185.

[76] Wright, 'Reflected', 149.   [77] Gorman, *Becoming*, 14.

carry around in the body the death of Jesus (2 Cor 4.10).[78] This is of central importance. Believers put on not only *Gloria in excelsis*, but *Gloria crucis*. The sign that they are becoming has death in it.[79] Affliction is preparing them for an eternal weight of glory (4.17) – for the time when signs of God give way to God's wholly manifest reality. In the meantime it is the *cruciform* community, characterised by its endurance in self-sacrificial love after the example of its Lord, that reflects glory. The great sign of God is Christ. The community seeking to be conformed to his image functions as a sign of that great sign, a sign with death in it, as well as the conquest of death, *Gloria crucis* as well as *Gloria in excelsis*.[80] This is what it is to be conformed to the body of Christ's glory (Phil 3.21).

Believers do not simply receive of God's love and then give it out. They have the boldness to look directly at the sign of the divine reality that is the glory of the Lord, seen in the face of Jesus Christ (cf. 2 Cor 4.6) and they respond to that sign by mirroring it.[81] Paul's thought can be redescribed as follows: not only that the people of the Gospel are able to look into the perfect sign of God's holiness and love, as by the power of the Spirit they contemplate their Crucified and Risen Lord, but also that those people become signs themselves.[82] Their freedom, their knowing only their Lord, and serving him alone, is their glory – their faces shine with his love.

What of *tēn autēn eikona*, 'the same image'? *Eikōn* has not been mentioned until then, but we saw earlier in this chapter that this word in this context is very close to *doxa*. It seems most likely that what is being spoken of is that the effect of contemplating Christ forms believers

---

[78] So Gorman, 'Paul reminds his readers that the glory and image of God ... into which all believers are being transformed, is the paradoxical glory of power in weakness, of life in death': *Inhabiting*, 120–1.

[79] See Heath, *Paul's Visual Piety*, chapter 8 for a range of links between 2 Corinthians 3–5 and the Servant Songs of Deutero-Isaiah, especially Isaiah 52.13–53.12.

[80] Wright again, 'the glory of God, at which Christians look with unveiled face ... is seen precisely in the paradoxical pattern of Christ, that is, the pattern of suffering and vindication': 'Reflected', 149.

[81] Garrett, 'properly perceiving subjects look outward away from themselves toward others in order to perform fittingly and flourish within the dramatic theatre of God's glory': *God's Beauty-in-Act*, 164. David F. Ford, calling Christ's a 'self-effacing glory', writes, 'To look in faith towards it is to have one's gaze directed towards others in the way that [Christ] gazed at them': *Self and Salvation: Being Transformed* (Cambridge: Cambridge University Press, 1999), 129.

[82] Or as Segal has it, they become 'a message from Christ ([2 Cor] 3:2), who is equated with the Glory of God': *Paul*, 60. Or again Heath: believers become vessels, bearing 'Jesus' name, life and death before others': *Paul's Visual Piety*, 236.

into his image, which is in turn the true, perfect, image of God (4.4).[83] Christians through their beholding/reflecting of the glory of the Lord are becoming more and more one – they are being transformed into the body of Christ. Presumably, noting the use of *metamorphousthai* in Romans 12.2, this is by the renewal of their minds.[84] I explore this theme of the forming of believers into the image of Christ further later in this chapter.

That brings us to *apo doxēs eis doxan*, rendered in the NRSV 'from one degree of glory to another'. It is a most resonant but also a most mysterious phrase. On my thesis that divine glory is a sign of ultimate reality, and Jesus is the ultimate such sign, it seems to me that the natural reading of *apo doxēs eis doxan* is that the believer is being transformed into a progressively more faithful, more reliable sign of Christ, who is in turn the *eikōn tou theou*, the utterly reliable sign of God's unfathomable nature. So the two phrases *tēn autēn eikona* and *apo doxēs eis doxan* are to be understood in parallel.[85] *Apo doxēs eis doxan* is to be read as an amplification, a clarification, an extension of *tēn autēn eikona*. Believers become signs of the one perfect sign, they reflect the way the Lord Jesus acts as a sign of the ultimately loving character of the divine.

To be a truer and truer sign is also to become a more authentic interpreter. In a remarkable poem of Bonhoeffer's, '*Christen und Heiden*', he writes that 'Christians and others' pray to God in their distress, and receive God's redemptive grace, but Christians alone 'stand by God in His agony'.[86] Or, to put it in the terms we have been exploring, Christians' particular call is to be not only beneficiaries of the saving work of Christ, but witnesses to and interpreters of the profoundly paradoxical sign of God that is the Passion of Christ. Christians are bearers of the interpretation that glimpses something of the deep reality of God that is seen when God undergoes degradation and abandonment, not only so that we might be free, but that we might understand and imitate the character of love freely given. Christians then are the witnesses at Golgotha, but also the

---

[83] Heath says we should take *eikona* 'closely with the metaphor embedded in *katoptrizomenoi*'. The image is the one beheld in the mirror, 'the glorious face of Christ, the image of God' (*Paul's Visual Piety*, 221).

[84] Note that this is always a corporate process. So Gorman, 'we should interpret [the] experience of contemplation and transformation, not as something private or internal, but as something that that occurs in community *and in witness to the world*', *Inhabiting*, 170, n. 9, emphasis mine. It will be noted that Gorman therefore includes reflecting as well as beholding.

[85] Savage even claims that the reader might have expected *tēn autēn doxan*: *Power*, 147.

[86] D. Bonhoeffer, *Voices in the Night: The Prison Poems of Dietrich Bonhoeffer: A New Translation with Commentary by Edwin Robertson* (Trowbridge: Eagle Pub., 2003), 46.

overhearers and beneficiaries of the High Priestly Prayer of John 17, which I discuss further later in this chapter.

In Chapter 4 I made mention of the famous saying of Irenaeus of Lyons that the glory (true sign of deep reality) of God is a human being become fully alive, as an authentic sign of the divine life within him or her, and (Irenaeus continues) the [authentic] human life is the contemplation of God.[87] A human being approaching fullness of life will continually long to look upon the face of God, and so to be yet further refined towards, and reflect, the likeness of Christ, the perfect sign.

This semiotic formulation has connections to Gorman's concept of 'missional participation' in the crucified and risen Christ.[88] The 'missional' element in Gorman's scheme tallies with what is being proposed here in terms of the believing community acting as a sign of Christ. Gorman in turn cites N. T. Wright's formulation that Christian communities:

> were ... the advance signs of that time when the whole world would be filled with the divine glory. Each lamp that was lit [each Christian community] ... was a point of light, of divine presence, as a sign of the dawn that would come when the whole world would be so illuminated.[89]

In other words, a sign of the redeeming divine reality bringing the whole groaning world to consummation.

QUALISIGNS OF GOD AND CHRIST

I return here to Robinson's idea of Jesus' life as a qualisign of the life of God. In Jesus' case, his actions functioned as various types of sign of the nature of God, but it was the overall quality of his life, its 'colour', that functioned most eloquently as a sign of the divine life.[90] This is very helpful as we try to see how the believer can become progressively a truer

---

[87] Irenaeus' saying, then, picks up the two-way seeing that is our interpretation of *katoptrizomenoi*.

[88] Gorman, *Becoming*. Garrett also wants to speak of theosis as 'missional participation': *God's Beauty-in-Act*, 170–4.

[89] Wright, *Faithfulness*, 437.

[90] As Roy A. Harrisville notes, commenting on the Gospel of John, 'the entire life of Jesus is described as a theophany': *Fracture: The Cross as Irreconcilable in the Language and Thought of the Biblical Writers* (Grand Rapids, MI: Eerdmans, 2006), 216. Von Balthasar: 'Jesus bears witness to God as a man, by using the whole expressional apparatus of human existence from birth to death', *GL1*, 29.

sign of Christ, the qualisign of God, when most humans' individual actions are so full of muddle and mixtures of motives. The overall quality of human lives can still start to take on the colour of Christ's life. In a local community a single action may be very influential, it may serve as an indexical sinsign, a once-off pointing to the importance of God in that community, but over time it is the overall quality, the overall character of a life that speaks of God's life to that community. It is as qualisigns that we are being transformed *apo doxēs eis doxan*. Paul's imagery is consistent with believers acting as a 'colour-sample' of Christ. He writes, 'For while we live, we are always being given up to death for Jesus' sake, so that the life of Jesus may be made visible in our mortal flesh' (2 Corinthians 4.11).

There is related thinking in the Hopkins sonnet I quoted in Chapters 3 and 4, 'As Kingfishers Catch Fire'. In the sestet we read, 'The just man justices;/Keeps grace: that keeps all his goings graces;/Acts in God's eye what in God's eye he is/Christ'.[91] So if a person can be called just, it is because that person's life acts that out, acts out a state of grace that is a sacrament of Christ. Bernadette Waterman Ward puts it thus: 'the just man is a *res et sacramentum*, inimitably himself, but also a symbol and a vehicle for the relationship of Christ to the world.'[92]

In this study we have been able to discern a spectrum of sign-types within the divine self-communication. We saw in contemplation of the natural world the ubiquity of indexical signs – created entities pointing to their Creator's transcendent giving of existence, pattern and particularity to every aspect of the biosphere. We saw icons of that transcendence in Hebrew Bible theophanies. We saw in the case of Hopkins's bluebell (Chapter 3) that particularly intense contemplation could lead to the discernment of iconicity in a creature – not just as icon of transcendence but of the immanent signification of creation, Cross and eschaton. Then we saw in considering Jesus Christ that a human life could be the 'cloth' of an iconic qualisign, in which the divine life could be immanent through and through. We glimpsed too the possibility that believers could take on, albeit incompletely and often transiently, that immanent colour, and reflect it in turn to others.

[91] G. M. Hopkins, *Poems and Prose: Selected with an Introduction and Notes by W. H. Gardner* (Harmondsworth: Penguin, 1953), 51.

[92] B. W. Ward, *World as Word: Philosophical Theology in Gerard Manley Hopkins* (Washington, DC: Catholic University of America, 2002), 222.

What is this 'colour' of life that Jesus evinced and is the goal and destiny of believers' (corporate) transformation? From all the Gospels, we know that it will be infused by a continual turn to prayer. That key moment when Jesus is recognised at Emmaus suggests that the blessing of God's gifts will be absolutely characteristic, so much so as to give rise to instant recognition (Lk 24.30, cf. also Mk 8.6, 14.23). From John we know that the 'colour' is 'full of grace and truth' (Jn 1.14), and so close to God in prayer as to be in the very 'bosom of the Father' (1.18). From Paul we know that it is a quality of life both cruciform and 'anastiform' – that is to say, it bears, indissolubly, the colours of Cross and Resurrection.[93]

As Gorman puts it,

a life of faith, hope, and love; of Christlike self-giving ... above all is something [believers] do, something indeed they *are*. And people actually *are* something – something that stands in some sense in contrast to normal living – they will provoke reactions: sometimes quite positive, sometimes more negative.[94]

This is a timely reminder to the human response to signs of the redeeming divine reality may well be rejection. 'He came to his own and his own knew him not' (Jn 1.11 KJV).

But just as our explorations of the Hebrew Bible revealed hiddenness and paradox in God's ways with the world – one has only to think of God's treatment of Job, or indeed God's attack on Moses at Exodus 4 – or God's response to Elijah at 1 Kings 19 – so Jesus as qualisign is not always a comfortable sign. As depicted in the Gospels, he is often stern, teaches puzzlingly and sometimes seemingly impossibly, and even in the great story of his risen appearance on the road to Emmaus he upbraids the traumatised disciples for their foolishness. In the encounters with a Gentile woman related in Mark 7 and Matthew 15, he shows a derogatory partiality for his own people. In contemplating Christ as the great sign of God, it seems to me important to face the difficulty and mystery of

---

[93] Finlan, 'Can We Speak', 78. In her very moving reflections on her life with her profoundly disabled son Arthur, Frances Young makes clear that Arthur's life can also be such a sign. She writes, 'Surely persons with even the most profound limitations have a vocation; they are 'sign' in the biblical sense, pointing beyond themselves': *God's Presence: A Contemporary Recapitulation of Early Christianity* (Cambridge: Cambridge University Press, 2013), 285. She goes on to conclude that she has made 'the move from struggling with theodicy to seeing that, through Arthur, I have privileged access to the deepest truths of Christianity' (404).

[94] Gorman, *Becoming*, 48, emphasis in original. This emphasis on self-giving is also important for A. Michael Ramsey, *The Gospel and the Catholic Church* (London: Longmans, Green, 1956), 92.

the New Testament accounts. The wildness, mystery, and paradox of 'God-colouredness' cannot be neglected in an interpretation that involves three-lensed seeing, though the disclosures of the Cross and Resurrection establish a very strong 'leading' colour, which shapes our account of freedom, image, and longing given later in this chapter.

Interestingly, Paul (also a stern and paradoxical figure) urges the Philippians to imitate *him* (Phil 3.17), to become then signs of Paul, a sign of Christ the great sign of God.[95] The quality of life in the image of the great sign that is Christ seems to me to have three key aspects needing further exploration. Two stem directly from our work on 2 Corinthians 3.17–18. The first is *the freedom of the believer*, made possible by the Lord, who is the Spirit (3.17). The second is how we are to understand *the image of Christ, the true image of God* (4.4), into which Christians are being transformed (3.18). The third aspect is *longing*. The believer is on a journey of transformation and can only long to 'see face to face' (1 Cor 13.12), to come through all her creaturely groanings into the liberty of her glory (Rom 8.21–3). We do not yet see all things brought into subjection to Christ. We do not yet see the signs of God we are calling glory fully identified with the divine essence because God has not yet become 'all in all' (1 Cor 15.28). Believers' seeing remains three-lensed – rooted in the world as created with all its struggle and ambiguity, knowing themselves caught up in Christ's Passion, his exemplary and atoning love by which his hour of glory can be fully known, and glimpsing and longing for the glory of the eschaton. That glory is called believers' destination (1 Thes 2.12, Col 3.4). It is Christians' confident hope (Rom 5.2, Col 1.27), transcending all their sufferings (Rom 8.18, 2 Cor 4.17).[96]

I propose that believers' longing, at its truest, is in sympathy with God's own longing for that final reconciliation. So after considering 'freedom' and 'image' I explore in some detail how longing functions in the Christian

---

[95] A semiotic reading of Christ, and of the lives of believers, may help to make sense of that notoriously difficult verse Colossians 1.24, in which Paul (if he be the author) writes: 'I am now rejoicing in my sufferings for your sake, and in my flesh I am completing what is lacking in Christ's afflictions for the sake of his body, that is, the church.' This can hardly mean that something is lacking in what Christ effected through his suffering for the sins of the world. That would be out of keeping with the tenor of every other text on atonement in the New Testament. But insofar as Christ, as well as effecting atonement through his Passion, serves as a sign of the depths of vulnerable love in the Godhead, then it is possible to imagine Paul serving as a sign of that now vanished sign in a way that would be visible to the churches, and efficacious in building up their common life.

[96] See Newman, *Paul's Glory-Christology*, 5–6.

tradition and how human longing might be most appropriately oriented in this 'Holy Saturday' time of waiting for that consummation.

THE FREEDOM OF THE BELIEVER IN CHRIST

Freedom in Christ is, arguably, the heart of Paul's Gospel. Of course the concept of freedom itself needs to be very carefully parsed (and runs the risk of getting lost in the process). But its huge importance is emphasised by its appearance in the coda to the theological analysis in Romans, when Paul concludes at Romans 8.21 that the liberation of creation awaits 'the freedom of the glory of the children of God'. This human freedom, then, has cosmic importance.

That rather strange and much argued-over phrase in Romans. 8.21 – in Greek *tēn eleutherian tēs doxēs tōn teknōn tou theou* – may be understood as a hendiadys. The freedom of the children of God is their glory, is a sign of the divine reality. The glory of the children of God, what makes them truly themselves, is their freedom. Paul goes on to put this a different way in Romans 8.29–30, when he sees God's predestining activity as involving both conforming believers to the image of the Son – making them reflect the great sign of God – and glorifying them, making them – in terms of the analysis presented here – signs of the great sign of God and participants in the divine life.[97]

Freedom, perfected, as Cranmer so beautifully put it in the Anglican Book of Common Prayer,[98] in the service of God, makes of each human being in Christ a sign of the divine reality. Freedom therefore has as many faces as there are human beings, and yet it has only one face, that of Christ.[99] Every believer's face that knows authentic freedom shines with Christlikeness, and is therefore a sign of the divine reality.

---

[97] I therefore set aside the reading of N. T. Wright, in which he specifically rejects hendiadys, regarding the glory of the children of God in Romans 8.21 as their return to right dominion over creation (as stewards): *Faithfulness*, 488–9. Not only does this cast the new creation as a return to the condition in Genesis 2, a contentious notion in itself, but it ignores the problems with dominion and stewardship that have so troubled contemporary interpreters. For comment on Wright and an alternative eco-eschatological reading, see D. G. Horrell, C. Hunt and C. Southgate, *Greening Paul: Rereading the Apostle in a Time of Ecological Crisis* (Waco, TX: Baylor University Press, 2010), 140, 176–8.

[98] 'The Second Collect, for Peace', The Order for Morning Prayer in *The Book of Common Prayer*, www.churchofengland.org.

[99] Cf. Hopkins – 'Christ plays in ten thousand places': *Poems and Prose*, 51.

The importance of freedom to 2 Corinthians 3.18 has, I think, been somewhat overlooked. And yet it is the last word of the preceding verse. It is therefore the punch-line of that extraordinary verse *ho de kurios to pneuma estin; hou de to pneuma kuriou, eleutheria.*[100] There is a risk of being so puzzled by the first half of that verse, 'the Lord is the Spirit', that we give insufficient attention to Paul's conclusion that the central, the definitive gift of the Spirit, the definitive sign of the Spirit's presence, is freedom. It seems to me important to apply that in the next verse (as Paul himself does at its end): to reflect the glory of the Lord is to show what a free creature looks like.

I have always found this a particularly inspiring element of Paul's Gospel, the emphasis on freedom from the idolatries that enslave. So I invite the reader to consider that that might be a very important element in humanity coming into the image of Christ. What then is the character of freedom, as it applies to a creature in the image and likeness of God? Post-Enlightenment human beings have been preoccupied with freedom as autonomy, and indeed this is a tempting way to construe freedom in the image of God, who is pure freedom of action. The extent to which freedom of action genuinely exists in an embodied neurophysiological creature has been well analysed by Philip Clayton in his book *In Quest of Freedom.*[101] Clayton concludes that freedom of choice exists at the very least (though possibly only) in the deep existential choice to side with ultimate reality. This is very interesting in the light of the understanding of glory being advanced here. That movement of freedom to which Clayton refers can be thought of as the movement of each human being responding positively to whatever signs of the divine reality are available to that individual – responding, then, to glory – all the while recognizing that that divine reality is always more, and more unknowable, than can ever be comprehended.

The centrality of freedom, as the characteristic of transformed human existence, is also emphasized by Adam Neder in his study of Karl Barth. Neder writes, 'What humanity needs, according to Barth, is not deification but freedom.'[102] However, I also draw on the work of Gorman, who is more convinced by the theme, indeed the centrality, of deification/theosis

---

[100] NRSV: 'Now the Lord is the Spirit, and where the Spirit of the Lord is, there is freedom.'

[101] P. Clayton, *In Quest of Freedom: The Emergence of Spirit in the Natural World: Frankfurt Templeton Lectures 2006*, ed. M. G. Parker and T. M. Schmidt (Göttingen: Vandenhoeck and Ruprecht, 2009).

[102] A. Neder, *Participation in Christ: An Entry into Karl Barth's* Church Dogmatics (Louisville, KY: Westminster John Knox Press, 2009), 69.

in Paul.[103] This question depends a great deal on what understanding of theosis is adopted. If this is 'only' being transformed into Christlikeness, then many of the Barthian objections disappear. As Finlan says, 'Becoming Christified does not mean becoming Christ, but rather Christlike in substance and character.'[104]

Crucially, however, that free response, of believing in, trusting in, the ultimately unknowable God, which for the Christian is the response to Christ through the Holy Spirit, is also the response of putting one's self at the service of that God. This is central to my understanding of humans in the image of God, the theme to which I now turn. As I have tried to indicate in other writing,[105] the response to the freely given love of the Lord is also the response of the authentic surrender of the self to the purposes of love. That is what it is for the human creature to be in the *imago Trinitatis*. To be transformed (by the renewing of the mind) into the 'same image' is to be transformed into that freed image of God that is able to respond to God in perfect service, as we see Christ doing. For believers to be transformed *apo doxēs eis doxan* is to be purified and perfected as signs of that freedom. This is the only surrender of the self that is not destruction, for if the self is surrendered to an idol, it cannot flourish, and must disintegrate, and if the self is not surrendered in community with others being transformed into the same image, then freedom itself becomes the idol.

THE TRANSFORMATION OF BELIEVERS INTO THE IMAGE OF CHRIST, WHO IS THE TRUE IMAGE OF GOD

How does this thinking connect with the Genesis teaching that humans are created in the image and likeness of God (1.26–7), supplemented for Christians by the Pauline conviction that Jesus is 'the image of God', as we have just noted in 2 Corinthians 4, or 'the image of the invisible God' (Col 1.15)? This Pauline teaching suggests that the image is incomplete in all other human beings.

A helpful classification of approaches to the *imago Dei* was provided by Noreen Herzfeld in 2002, and subsequently developed by Wentzel

---

[103] Gorman, *Cruciformity, Inhabiting,* and *Becoming.*   [104] Finlan, 'Can We Speak', 79.
[105] C. Southgate, 'Re-Reading Genesis, John and Job: A Christian's Response to Darwinism', *Zygon* 46 (2011), 365–90, at 373–87.

van Huyssteen in his Gifford Lectures.[106] The four possibilities for inter-preting the image of God in humans can be summarised as follows: substantive, based on some property distinctively possessed by human beings; functional, based on some role or vocation allotted by God to humans; relational, based on both capacity and call, to enter into loving relations with God and neighbour; and eschatological, based on the idea that humans' true nature lies ahead of them – it is a goal rather than a present reality. This last is obviously a tempting interpretation in the light of the New Testament texts.

However, all of these possible formulations of the doctrine of the *imago* are problematic. The substantive one has been particularly heavily criticised on the grounds that it was used in the tradition to over-privilege rationality, and to demean the body, the emotions, the female intellect, and the humanness of those with what we now call learning difficulties. The functional one can be critiqued on the grounds that it can collude with inappropriate relationships between humans and the non-human creation, encouraged by the language of dominion and subjugation in Genesis. The relational one has been accused of playing into a crypto-tritheistic model of the Trinity. Like the functional formulation, the rela-tional one contains hidden substantival elements – what properties are required of humans to carry out the divinely appointed function, or yet to enter into loving relationships? Lastly, the eschatological interpretation of the *imago Dei* seems to wrench the tenses of the Genesis text, which does not have any explicit eschatological connotation.

I have proposed that the image of God in human beings should be thought of in terms of humans' response to the self-giving love found in, and received from, God the Holy Trinity.[107] I point out that this view is substantival, in terms of a presupposed capacity for love, functional, in terms of being a fundamental human vocation, relational, by its very nature, and eschatological, in that it is only as humans grow into the example of that self-giving response that we find in the Incarnate Christ that we start fully to manifest the divine image that is perfectly instanti-ated in Jesus.

I now develop this understanding of the *imago Dei*, both in relation to love for God and for neighbour. God's love for each person has a

---

[106] N. Herzfeld, *In Our Image? Artificial Intelligence and the Human Spirit* (Minneapolis, MN: Fortress Press, 2002); J. W. van Huyssteen, *Alone in the World: Human Unique-ness in Science and Theology* (Göttingen: Vandenhoeck and Ruprecht, 2006).

[107] Southgate, 'Re-reading'.

unreserved quality, it makes no calculations, holds nothing back (not even the life of the Incarnate Son). It seeks an unreserved response. It reduces that natural element of calculation by which humans commute their love for others. It also – vitally – refocuses that love, away from the idols that always crowd in on the human imagination, and back towards the one Lord of creation and salvation. Purification and sanctification are two stuffy-sounding words, overused in pious homilies, but they are among the effects of an authentic response to the love that pours moment by moment from the Trinity, a love that creates as well as forgives.

Crucial questions for my position are first, whether all humans are capable of making that loving and self-giving response to the divine love, and second, whether my suggestion does sufficient justice to the blanket status that the Genesis text seems to give humans. It is not only when humans are doing a specific thing – responding in love to the divine love – but all the time that humans are created in the image and likeness of God. This leads me to reconsider the foundational text in Genesis. Why, I wonder, need we read it in terms of once-for-all creation of any given human being? Might we not read it in terms of continuous creation? To imagine God saying in the heavenly court, 'Let us, *continually*, be creating humans in our image.'[108]

That has advantages in terms of an evolutionary understanding of human being. There is always a problem in reconciling the picture that science gives, of the gradual emergence of what we think of as humanness, with the seeming once-off creation of humans in Genesis 1, and indeed Genesis 2. But the Christian tradition has rightly emphasized the import-ance of God's creation as not only initial but continual.[109] So is it not reasonable to postulate that God's image-making creativity acted conti-nually on the emerging human and has acted on each human being ever since, not once-for-all, but *continually, from moment to moment, in the offer of love that invites a response of love?*

---

[108] Young makes a related move, helpfully emphasising the corporate dimension, when she claims that: 'Together, through communion in community, the gift of God's image and likeness is being received and developed' (*God's Presence*, 181). She continues, 'this account acknowledges human failings and distortions while celebrating for the contemporary world the high dignity of God's gift' (183).

[109] For example, Kristine A. Culp, 'God is always forming and re-forming the mundane, vulnerable stuff of creaturely existence, breathing life and glory into it': *Vulnerability and Glory: A Theological Account* (Louisville, KY: Westminster John Knox Press, 2010), 94.

This view is very different from Richard Middleton's important study, which represents an appreciable weight of exegetical opinion on Genesis 1.26–27.[110] Middleton concludes on exegetical grounds that the *imago* as understood by the writer must be seen in functional terms, and in terms of humans doing as God's representatives what humans can distinctively do, of all the creatures – namely, bringing social and cultural organisation to the earth. God, for Middleton, steps back on the seventh day to allow humans to exercise that role throughout history. I propose the reverse, that God's creative activity must be seen as continuous, creating humans from moment to moment into themselves.

But there is a congruence between Middleton's account and my own. I also see humans as being empowered to do what humans can distinctively do, but from a twenty-first-century standpoint I regard the distinctive emergent as being self-giving love, rather than cultural organisation. That also seems to me much more in tune with the Christ being seen as the image of God. I freely admit that this view could not simply be read off from Genesis 1.26–27. My proposal requires those texts to be read through a Christological lens – much as James Kilner does in his book *Dignity and Destiny*.[111] Like Kilner, though with a different conclusion, my focus is Jesus as the quintessential image of God (in the Pauline understanding). Jesus' vocation was more about disclosing divine love than organizing the world. I hold that it is perfectly plausible, in a twenty-first-century context, to hold that indeed image is about what humans can distinctively bring to creation, as Middleton would hold, but to regard that distinctive contribution, that vocation, as being (individually and corporately) Christlikeness. And therefore the perfectly free return of the divine gift of self-giving love. Authentic altruism, in other words, can be seen as the most distinctive emergent in the history of humanity, and therefore constituting the ultimate fulfilment of the creative process (as indeed the Genesis 1 writer has it).

What of the effects of this moment-by-moment love, this image-forming, response-inviting love, on the human love of neighbour? First and foremost, God's love evokes a real desire, a hunger, for the good of the other. In offering a view of the good going beyond the obvious, it also engenders

---

[110] J. R. Middleton, *The Liberating Image: The Imago Dei in Genesis 1* (Grand Rapids, MI: Brazos Press, 2005).

[111] J. F. Kilner, *Dignity and Destiny: Humanity in the Image of God* (Grand Rapids, MI: Eerdmans, 2015). See also D. H. Kelsey, *Eccentric Existence: A Theological Anthropology*, Vol. 2 (Louisville, KY; Westminster John Knox Press, 2009), 938, 1002. Young makes it clear that this hermeneutical approach goes back to the patristic era (*God's Presence*, 179).

wisdom. Conversely, this love is a moment-by-moment critique of selfishness, of violence, of cruelty.

To return to the semiotic analysis I gave earlier in this chapter, being conformed to the overall quality of Christ's life allows the lives of human beings to show forth that quality, but only the moment-by-moment offer of Christ's example can allow that moment-by-moment receiving of the quality of life of which humans are capable. A common example given of a qualisign is of a colour that might be found in a piece of dyed cloth. Pursuing that analogy, it is as though in the life of Christ the 'God-colour' is colour fast, proof against even the most extreme temptation, but the lives of believers are like fading watercolour and need to be renewed moment-by-moment if they are to hold their 'colour', their God-offered quality.

How then is this to work in the life of a contemporary human, and how is it to resist the various objections that have very properly been levelled at models of the *imago*? My suggestion is that God continually, in every moment, offers that love that makes life what it is, with all its possibilities. And that offered love also creates the opportunity for the love to be returned, and spread to the neighbour, however understood. So the divine love creates the self in its freedom, and the opportunity for the self to be given away in unselfish love. God's love, then, God's faithfulness and mercy, are imagined then as not just new every morning (Lam 3.23) but new every moment.

As with my previous position on the *imago Dei*, this is a view which is about substance, in proposing that humans have evolved an attribute – that of being capable of responding, however patchily and incompletely, to the continual invitation of the divine love, by transcending our selfish impulses – and it is clearly relational, and it is functional – this response is the human vocation, to be worked out in our relationships with other human beings and the whole creation. It is also eschatological – the image is only now being perfected by the transforming work of salvation in Christ.

My view has resonances with thinkers from very different elements of the Christian tradition. Vladimir Lossky, writing from within Orthodoxy, holds that 'Man created "in the image" is the person capable of manifesting God to the extent to which his nature allows itself to be penetrated by deifying grace'.[112] Note that that is a continuous process, being penetrated

---

[112] V. Lossky, *In the Image and Likeness of God*, ed. J. H. Erickson and T. E. Bird (Oxford: Mowbray, 1975).

by deifying grace, not a once-off. F. LeRon Shults, in a fine early book, also understands the *imago* in terms of theosis. He writes, 'the *imago Dei* is not a static likeness between two substances but a dynamic longing that constitutes creaturely personhood, a longing for participation in the peaceful life of the eternal Trinitarian God'.[113]

One of the advantages of this model is that it does describe a process of imaging, a human response that reflects the divine initiative. Even in its most theotic formulations it does not equate the human property with the divine, but rather imagines the human being responding to God's moment-by-moment initiative by reflecting the love that it has received. It therefore seems to pick up that language of mirroring in the 2 Corinthians 3 passage that has preoccupied us here, and which leads on to Paul's affirmation of Christ as the image of God. In moments the wholeheartedness of some humans' response to God will approach that of Jesus Christ, whose whole life consisted of this quality of response. That is what makes Christ truly and completely the image of the invisible God.

What then of the hard cases that are the bane of formulations of the *imago Dei*? First, the human being who appears committed to sustainedly evil actions. Is such a person created in the image and likeness of God? The standard answer would be yes and that this is a restatement of the fundamental equality of all human beings before God.[114] My answer would be more nuanced – such a person is continually being created into the divine image, in being continually offered the opportunity to respond to God, to correspond to God, but continually refuses the offer, refuses the invitation to be conformed to the example of Christ. Such a person is in fact trapped in her or his own negativity, is more imprisoned than conventional prisoners, as we noted in Chapter 4 in discussing Etty Hillesum and her guards.

Second, the human being who seems incapable of relating normally to others because she or he seems to lack the 'theory of mind' to do so. Those who are far into the autistic spectrum are a challenge to relational views of the *imago Dei* since they appear to lack the capacity to relate to other human beings in ordinary socialised ways. But God need not be reliant on mirror neurones, or yet on social norms. There seems to me no reason why people on the autistic spectrum might not be continually receiving

[113] F. L. Shults, *Reforming Theological Anthropology: After the Philosophical Turn to Relationality* (Grand Rapids, MI: Eerdmans, 2003), 138.
[114] Though see Young, *God's Presence*, 173–6, for a nuancing of this view.

love from God, and pouring out their hearts to God, and thus being continually created in the divine image, even though they find interpersonal communication hard.

The same argument might be pursued in relation to human beings with profound learning difficulties, or indeed dementia. Their minds, we must I think believe, are as open to God as that of a normally functioning human being, and we should not write off the possibility that they are responding wholeheartedly, just because that is a response we cannot see, or because their circumstances prevent them from expressing loving relationships with other persons.

So, wherever we see self-giving, costly relating to others for others' sake, I would hold that we see the image of God beginning to develop. One of the few things we know of Neanderthals is that they looked after individuals past child-bearing age who had broken limbs and severe arthritis – here we see, implicitly, signs of self-giving behaviour after the image of God. I conclude more generally that we should not be afraid to see this proto-image in other primates, or indeed in elephants and other animals, resulting, once again, from the continual, moment-by-moment invitation offered by God's own love for creatures.

But our focus here, returning to our text from 2 Corinthians 3, is the response of the Christian, beholding, more and more with unveiled face through the encouragement of the Spirit, the sign of God's love that is the quality of Christ in his life, crucified and risen. A sign always calling for a response. And the response is in turn to reflect that offered love, in all the ways that the New Testament suggests to us: from manifesting some or all of the Beatitudes; to ministering to Christ through the sick, the stranger, and the prisoner; to giving an account of the faith; to acting as the true neighbour in imitation of the Good Samaritan; to keeping the new commandment of love; to manifesting the gifts and fruits of the Spirit. The task of this book is not to explore these responses in detail, but rather to ground them in this semiotic response to glory, which is at the same time transformation *apo doxēs eis doxan*.

I stressed earlier in this chapter the corporate nature of this response. The call on the individual 'beholder' of the glory of the Lord with unveiled face is not just to contemplate that glory, but to reflect it to others, and so to be bound ever more closer with those others, becoming the 'same image'. Paul is confident that this process *is* taking place. The corporate dimension, on which he memorably insists in other places, especially 1 Corinthians 12, precludes the notion that some are to be given disproportionate honour within the fellowship. Christians are formed *together* into a sign of the sign of God that is Christ,[115] the Eucharist being the classic locus of this formation.

I have proposed that the *imago Dei* in humans should be understood as the capacity to respond to the self-giving love of God, and that that capacity is re-created from moment to moment. It is therefore not possession but rather gift. Another way of expressing this is to say that humans are continually being offered signs of the divine reality – most especially in the quality of the life of their Lord. As we contemplate this quality, we have the opportunity to reflect it. Alejandro Garcia-Rivera writes very movingly:

the Glory of the Lord is a community that has caught sight of a marvelous vision, a universe of justice emerging from a community's experience of divine Beauty, the 'lifting up the lowly'. Such a community counts as members the sun and stars, the dead and the living, the angels and the animals, and, of course, the marvelous yet lowly human creature.'[116]

Put another way, it is a community that is learning to attend to the creation, to know Christ through it, like Hopkins with his bluebell (*Gloria mundi*); to see in Christ contemplated *Gloria crucis*, and then eventually to *be Gloria crucis*, to behold and then reflect the quality of utterly self-giving love, to know and inhabit the cost of that love; also to long in true freedom for *Gloria in excelsis*, the state in which all the lowly are lifted up in equal honour, to long for it so passionately that the Kingdom begins to become a reality in the life of that community.

THE IMPORTANCE OF LONGING IN THE BELIEVER'S RESPONSE TO GLORY

Longing is the remaining element to be explored in the human response to glory. A central element in the response of the believer to the divine glory must be a longing to see the *Gloria in excelsis* in full, face to face. Further I suppose that God too longs for this consummation. Therefore, *part of the human response to God is for human longing to conform to the divine longing.*

---

[115] So Gorman: 'This is the essence of believing existence, to "see" the glory of the Lord (i.e., Christ) and be gradually transformed by the Spirit into the image of Christ, the image of God', *Inhabiting*, 120.

[116] A. Garcia-Rivera, *The Community of the Beautiful: A Theological Aesthetics* (Collegeville, MN: The Liturgical Press, 1999), 195.

The theme of longing therefore also conveys something of the way the image of God connotes a conformity to the divine nature. Richard Harries writes: 'Our human longing is first of all to be united with God, to be in deeper communion with him. Secondly, it is to be changed into his likeness.'[117]

So, when we receive God's gift of God's image and likeness, our human longings come to be in the likeness of God's longing for the creation to become what it will ultimately be. Wherever there is a match between creaturely longing and divine longing there is comfort for the creature and the potential for mission, in anticipation of the *Gloria in excelsis*. For Macarius, 'Not his action, but his longing builds man up to be the Church.'[118] To live for the eternal future, Terrien concludes, 'becomes the proleptic vision of the glory.'[119] This longing is ultimately a gift of the Spirit.[120] Or to go back to Hopkins' language, as adopted by von Balthasar, the Holy Spirit is 'stress' within us – comforting, cheering, encouraging, persuading, calling us on.[121] As God longs for humankind to come into that loving relation with God and neighbour Christians call the Kingdom, so humans in their moments of image-bearing should learn to long as God longs.

We could wish that the dimensions of the Kingdom, of God's will being perfectly done, were more clearly defined, and indeed more accessible. But since God has desired that God's will be done in perfect freedom, such prescription of the exact shape of the Kingdom is impossible. We get only glimpses in the Gospels, especially in the Beatitudes, and Jesus' reply to the disciples of the Baptist at Matthew 11.4–6. Christians are to long, then, for the healing of the world in that counter-intuitive mode of which those texts speak. Or to put it another way, they are to long for the full development of the fruits of the Spirit throughout human life. Beyond that, they are to long for what God longs for. Such a longing community is being conformed to the image of Christ, who wept over Jerusalem.

---

[117] R. Harries, *Art and the Beauty of God, A Christian Understanding* (London: Mowbray, 1993), 98.

[118] Quoted in von Balthasar, *GL1* 275.   [119] Terrien, *Elusive Presence*, 477.

[120] So von Balthasar, 'we could not even ascribe to ourselves the power of the longing to escape this state of decay: it is the Spirit who, from within man and the world, groans to God with unspeakable sighs and, by so doing, first of all makes man and his world aware of their fallenness and decay' (*GL1*, 231).

[121] H. U. von Balthasar, *The Glory of the Lord: A Theological Aesthetics*, Vol. 3, Studies in Theological Style: Lay Styles, transl. A. Louth, J. Saward, M. Simon, and R. Williams, ed. J. Riches (Edinburgh: T&T Clark, 1986), 388.

Such human longings are signs of the great sign of God's saving purposes, full of grace and truth.

The previous sections have explored what it might mean as an individual to be transformed into a truer sign of Christ, so that the 'colour' of that life comes closer to his, and as a community to be conformed to his image, according to the dynamics of interdependent gifting that Paul articulates in passages such as 1 Corinthians 12. Among other things, that process involves contemplation of the wonder of the creation, and of human beings as created in the image and likeness of God, and of Christ, the authentic image, in the qualisignness of his life, and especially in his Passion and Resurrection. It involves embracing the already-but-not-yet of Christian eschatology. If the emotion underlying the discussion so far has been wonder *at*, leading as I began to explore in Chapter 1 to wonder *that*, the dominant emotion to be explored in this section is *longing*. If we still see as in a glass darkly (1 Cor 13.12 KJV) and what we will be has not yet been revealed (1 Jn 3.2), if moreover the whole creation 'stands on tiptoe' awaiting the glorious liberty of the children of God (Rom 8.19–21), then believers are necessarily in a state of longing for what has not yet been revealed, not yet been consummated.

The classic locus of the expression of this longing is the Lord's Prayer (in its Matthean form). We are taught to pray the parallel longings: 'Your kingdom come, your will be done' (Mt 6.10). In that parallelism is expressed all the Christian's longing for what we do not yet see. This prayer is a training of the longings, a day-by-day consolidation of the image of God in the believer.

C. S. Lewis, writing about *Gloria in excelsis*, says this about our desire to be with God in a way that transcends our mortal lives:

The sense that in this universe we are treated as strangers, the longing to be acknowledged, to meet with some response, to bridge some chasm that yawns between us and reality, is part of our inconsolable secret. And surely, from this point of view, the promise of glory, in the sense described, becomes highly relevant to our deep desire . . . The door on which we have been knocking all our lives will open at last.[122]

Michael Ramsey also reflects of our longings for God:

[A person] wants God very much, he [*sic*] is hungry and thirsty for God, and perhaps all he is able to tell God is that he has a hunger and thirst for him, though

---

[122] C. S. Lewis, *The Weight of Glory and Other Addresses* (Grand Rapids, MI: Eerdmans, 1949), 11.

even that is very feeble; but he wishes the hunger and thirst were more. And this longing for God when released in simplicity appears to be, not something the brain is doing, but rather something in the depths of the person ... This hungry longing for God leads on to an experience in which the self, emptying itself of its own capacities, finds itself filled by God.[123]

Ramsey also notes that a particular gift of the Holy Spirit is the moment 'when the soul knows itself to be possessed by God to the depths of its existence'. However, 'the Christian mystic does not long for experiences; he longs to love and serve God, and ... to do the will of God'.[124] In other words, longing for God does not simply have its terminus in God in the present, but in the purposes for which the Christian loves and serves God.

The Christian tradition teaches that desire, purified, becomes the desire for union with God, knowledge of God, enhanced relationship with God. It therefore becomes something that cannot be grasped. Purified desire, then, turns into longing. In this perspective *apo doxēs eis doxan* does not look so much like putting on splendour, but putting on the Creator's lament at the incompleteness and frustration of the creative process. Weeping over the Jerusalem that in the Hebrew mind represented the whole cosmos. That indeed *is* the thrust of my project on glory – recognizing glory is not simply dissolving in beauty, but putting on a more and more honest and Christic understanding of the way things really are, and recognizing too that the path to consummation lies through struggle and tragedy.

The human emotion of longing shapes our world in all sorts of powerful ways. Religious longings – for salvation, for holiness, for enlightenment – continue, across the world, to have a huge influence on human behaviour, and are also implicated in many wars that both impoverish and embitter human lives and degrade natural environments. Consumerist longings – to be younger, or older, more perfect, more stylish, more sexy, more mobile – drive much of the world's economy. Much other human activity is driven by the longing for security – for peaceful streets, for reliable supplies of food and water. So it could be argued that indeed longing is *the* human emotion that shapes the contemporary world.

All consumerist desires are eminently understandable in psychological terms in the evolved animals we are. They are brilliantly depicted in the

---

[123] A. M. Ramsey, *Sacred and Secular: A Study in the Otherworldly and This-Worldly Aspects of Christianity: The Holland Lectures for 1964* (London: Longmans, Green, 1965), 37.

[124] A. M. Ramsey, 'The Mysticism of Evelyn Underhill' in *Evelyn Underhill: Anglican Mystic*, ed. A. M. Ramsey and A. M. Allchin (Oxford: SLG Press, 1996), 3–14, at 13.

opening section of James K. A. Smith's *Desiring the Kingdom,* in which he analyses a shopping mall.[125] Smith shows us how consumerist lives have their ritual practices, they satisfy religious as well as hedonistic needs. Reflection on consumerism also shows that much desire is semiotic in nature – we desire one thing out of conviction of its connection to something else. That pair of designer sunglasses we buy is more than anything else a sign, to ourselves and to others, that we are a certain sort of person with a certain sort of life. Maslow importantly showed the hierarchical character of human need.[126] As one goes up the hierarchy, so needs are addressed in increasingly indirect and semiotic ways. I have argued earlier in this chapter that the human vocation is to become a sign, a sign of Christ who is the utterly reliable sign of the character of the divine life. Adorning one's life with other signs can, at its worst, be testament to idolatry.

The primary source for Christian reflection on desire, arguably, is not biblical but the philosophy of Plato. Plato's fascination with desire runs through many of his dialogues and is expressed in two of his most famous myths, that of the two horses in the *Phaedrus* and Aristophanes' account of the origin of love in the *Symposium.* Plato's concern is continually to urge the disciplining and suppression of earthly desires in order that the purer desire for the Good may flourish.

Early Christian thought developed in a climate of middle Platonism and Stoicism. Out of this came the New Testament's exhortations to 'set your hearts on the things from above' (Col 3.1–2), and Paul's fascinating exploration of the pre-Christian's dividedness in Romans. 7. In Evagrius and other Desert Fathers we find sophisticated psychological insights into 'the passions' that distort our authentic longing for God.[127] But the classic Christian heir of Plato on this subject is Augustine of Hippo, who draws movingly on his own biography to express the possibility of the transformation of desire. Our hearts are restless until they rest in God. That reflects our truest and most fundamental longing.[128] The tradition's continuing fascination with desire is indicated by, among other things, the

---

[125] Smith, *Desiring,* 19–25.

[126] A. H. Maslow, 'A Theory of Human Motivation', *Psychological Review* 50 (1943), 370–96.

[127] For a contemporary reading of the passions, see W. Farley, *The Wounding and Healing of Desire: Weaving Heaven and Earth* (Louisville, KY: Westminster John Knox Press, 2005), chapters 3–4.

[128] So desire for something other than for God's sake counts as *cupiditas*: T. J. Oord, *The Nature of Love: A Theology* (St. Louis, MO: Chalice Press, 2010), 61.

many commentaries on The Song of Songs written throughout the patristic and mediaeval periods.[129]

DESIRE AND LONGING

Clearly the terms 'desire' and 'longing' overlap. The main distinction I want to propose is that desire tends to imply a relation to something achievable, even something that may be grasped at the expense of others' well-being, whereas longing for something seems to suggest that the longer cannot grasp the object.[130] Desire, then, can be seen as a wanting to grasp another person or thing while remaining the same, and thus to be in control of that person or thing. Longing recognises that the person or thing cannot be grasped, and that therefore change might be involved in meeting with that person or thing. (Of course, that change may be impossible, as in the longing to see again a person who has died, but that does not detract from the principle.)[131]

For Sebastian Moore, our desire continually finds itself baffled by wanting something that demands a change in the wanting self.[132] This is one of the characteristics of healthy longing. Because we cannot grasp the object of our longing while remaining the self that first experienced that desire, longing invites us to change, indeed to transcend ourselves, so we can be placed in a healthier orientation to the object of our longing. Unfulfillable longings may need to be renounced – as in the (for most) hopeless longing to become a racing driver. They may need to be reframed, as in the longing for someone who is the partner of another. They may need to be endured and kept company with until their strength recedes, as in the longing that accompanies bereavement. Longings may need to be explored because the real object may not in the first instance be clear – as

---

[129] See S. Coakley, *God, Sexuality and the Self: An Essay 'On the Trinity'* (Cambridge: Cambridge University Press, 2013), 127–32 on Origen's treatment of sexuality in relation to prayer.

[130] Indeed, longing may be felt for someone or something that is already in the past, in which case the term 'yearning' perhaps expresses better the pathos of that state.

[131] It might be said that all ten of the commandments in the Decalogue are restrictions on the operation of desire in its grasping or controlling mode. In limiting such grasping, they make space for longing. Here we might discern a helpful overlap with Jan-Olav Henriksen's category of metaphysical desire, and his insistence that God must always be more than we need, and open up a reality beyond what we can contemplate: *Desire, Gift and Recognition: Christology and Postmodern Philosophy* (Grand Rapids, MI: Eerdmans, 2009).

[132] S. Moore, *Jesus the Liberator of Desire* (New York: Crossroad, 1989), 7.

in many cases where someone discerns a vocation to ministry. Or the longing may need to be pursued, but always with an openness to being formed, being changed, as with the longing to know more fully a lover, or a friend, and most notably the longing for God. There is always, then, an element of surrender in the pursuit of a longing, surrender of the past self.[133]

The Christian tradition teaches that desire, purified, becomes the desire for union with God, knowledge of God, enhanced relationship with God. It therefore becomes something that cannot be grasped at or seized.[134] Purified desire, then, turns into longing. I suggest that what T. S. Eliot called 'the purification of the motive in the ground of our beseeching'[135] is a process by which 'desire that' becomes 'longing for', longing for God. Insofar as this remains also a 'longing that', it becomes concentrated on the parallel longings that 'thy Kingdom come' and 'thy will be done', which in themselves are one longing, and are enacted believer by believer as persons of desire become conformed to God's will.

A remarkable characteristic of the most healthily oriented longing is that it desires its own increase. Addiction causes the desire to return, ever more strongly, after it is gratified, yet the sufferer seeks to withdraw from this cycle of compulsion. But holy longing wants to want more, to be ever more open to the infinite riches of the journey with and towards God in God's own longing.[136]

I suspect contemporary Christian commentators on desire and longing are divided between those who draw their inspiration from Augustine, and behind him Plato, and those who take Charles Darwin and Sigmund Freud as their starting points. The former group may tend to see the latter as reductive, and probably inalienably atheistic. The Darwinian/Freudians may tend to see the Plato/Augustine followers as over-spiritualising and unscientific. Darwin and Freud were of course not moral philosophers – they do not seek to tell us what we *should* long for, but their insights and those of their successors tell us a huge amount about why we tend to desire what we do. A great part of how humans behave, and construct societies, may be understood in evolutionary terms, centring on the drives to survive, to reproduce, and to safeguard kin. The work of analysts and

---

[133] Ibid.

[134] Cf. Farley's comments on contemplation as never leading by way of possession (*Wounding*, 123).

[135] T. S. Eliot, *Complete Poems and Plays* (London: Faber and Faber, 1969), 196.

[136] Cf. Moore, *Jesus*, 11. Note the story of the rich young man in Matthew 19, in which Jesus discerns at once what holds back the young man's longing for God.

therapists from Freud onwards has helped us see the strength of those drives, and the pathologies that arise from some types of effort to suppress them. This concern over the unhealthy suppression of desire generates a fault line between the two understandings, the Platonic/Augustinian and the Darwinian, which it is important for theologians to address.[137]

Philip Sherrard's study *Christianity and Eros* depicts in quite a chilling way the effects on understanding sexuality of relying only on the Platonic/Augustinian strand of thought. He gives as example this from Gregory of Nyssa,

'it is in man's investiture with animal sexuality that the most fatal consequences of his fall are evident ... In Paradise, man [*sic*] had an angelic mode of propagation. This he lost with the fall, and he was given in its place a mode proper to animals ... for St Gregory the sexual life is the source of the passions which, when stirred up, lead to sin.'[138]

Marriage, although taught by the Church as a sacrament, was seen merely as an expedient for the bearing of children even in an encyclical of Pope Paul VI dated 1968.[139] Another strange legacy of Plato's mythology is found in the work of Russian thinkers such as Soloviev and Berdyaev, who supposed that humans were first created as androgynes – Sherrard spells out well the misogyny to which such views can give rise.[140]

It is possible to argue that positions that set aside Darwin and Freud and follow Augustine and Gregory of Nyssa do so on the basis of an implicit belief in a prelapsarian perfection. Direct relationship with God was present in the garden in Genesis 2, and that, so such a position suggests, should be our reference point in respect of human desire. But wise as that Eden story is, it misleads us if it makes us suppose that humans ever actually were in that state. Rather a state in which longing for God comes to predominate, among the range of human animals' physical desires, must be an emergent state made possible by millennia of evolution (as well as God's gracious calling to the developing human consciousness).

What else do the insights of evolutionary biology and the psychology of the unconscious contribute to our theological understanding of desire? A full answer to that question would take us well beyond the scope of this book. But here are some initial thoughts. There is a useful link, too little

---

[137] Coakley writes of the 'messy entanglement of sexual desire and desire for God.' *God, Sexuality*, 43.

[138] P. Sherrard, *Christianity and Eros: Essays on the Theme of Sexual Love* (London: SPCK, 1976), 66.

[139] Sherrard, *Christianity*, chapter 1.   [140] Ibid., chapter 3.

explored, between Darwinian insights and the doctrine of original sin.[141] But that doctrine should in my view be turned on its head. It is not that the first humans were fully self-conscious and made an informed decision to defy God, but rather that selfish behaviour, and the assertion of boundaries, were an entirely predictable product of the naturally evolved drives of primates in a competitive and hostile environment. Humans never knew perfect relationship, or pain-free longing. It is the emergence of goodness, generosity, and transcendence of the interests of the self that is the remarkable feature of the evolution of human behaviour, not the ubiquitous presence of selfishness.

There is also a link between psychoanalytic understandings and the sense that we find for example in Dante (but going back to Plato) of the need for love to be refined, purified, in order that it can focus on the truth. We emerge from childhood with a strong sexual energy complicated by certain necessary frustrations to our drives. Healthy adult expression of sexuality is assisted by understanding those frustrations, and sublimating the drives as appropriate – not, notice, by denying their existence or regarding them as part of fallen or incomplete humanity. Such denial can lead to fear and guilt of toxic proportions.[142]

The Bible helps us here because of the inclusion within it of the astonishing erotic poetry of The Song of Songs. But it frustrates us by offering no commentary, or system, by which we can integrate these insights into a Christian life. I suggest that the place of The Song is not, as the mediaeval commentators tended to insist, that it is an allegory of the delight that can exist between Christ and the Church, but to remind us that physical desire is just that, whole-body physical, and does not necessarily need to be denied, or sublimated into the contemplation of the loved face, or her extraordinarily beautiful eyes, in an extension of the sort of pre-adult attraction Dante first felt for Beatrice.

Coakley quotes a beautiful passage from Luce Irigaray on 'communion in pleasure'. Irigaray writes of:

the shared outpouring, ... the loss of boundary to the skin into the mucous membranes of the body, leaving the circle which encloses my solitude to meet in a shared space, a shared breath ... In this relation *we are at least three*, each of which is irreducible to any of the others, you, me and our creation ... that ecstasy of ourself in us.[143]

[141] See D. P. Domning and M. K. Hellwig, *Original Selfishness: Original Sin and Evil in the Light of Evolution* (Aldershot: Ashgate, 2006).
[142] As Moore notes, 'psychoanalysis ... consists in giving permission for desire': *Jesus*, 18.
[143] Quoted in Coakley, *God, Sexuality*, 317–8, emphasis in original.

Irigaray identifies the key theme of self-transcendence, to which I return later in this chapter, but importantly, and at variance with the tendency of so much Christian writing, she recognises that that self-transcendence can be achieved in the context of the physical act, not only through its renunciation.[144] A rounded account of human desire and longing must make space for this possibility.

DIVINE LONGING

The biblical witness contains little direct reference to longing on the part of God. Perhaps this is because of the very strong assertion in the Scriptures of divine power, both in creation and redemption. God's desire is implemented ipso facto, as in 'his' desire to make 'his' dwelling on Zion (Ps 132). But God also desires what God does not compel. God desires, we are told, 'truth in the inward being' (Ps 51.6); 'steadfast love and not burnt offerings' (Hos 6.6). God's covenant-making may be seen as a desire for intimacy.[145] And we also catch hints of divine longing in the language of Hosea 11, and when Jesus weeps over Jerusalem in Luke 19.[146] The moving ending of the High Priestly Prayer in John 17 is Jesus' 'I wish them also to be with me' (17.24).[147]

To take another famous text, 'God so loved the world that he sent his only-begotten Son, that whoever believes in him should not perish, but have everlasting life' (Jn 3.16). God does not compel humans into everlasting life, into the new creation in Christ, but longs for them to turn away from perishing, and come into the full possibilities of their existence.

The picture we receive throughout the Scriptures is that God's attention focuses on particular groups or individuals – they receive callings to fulfil divine purposes, and sometimes signs to reinforce those callings. But God does not, typically, compel the chosen and called groups or individuals to carry out their task. Even Jonah is fenced about but not compelled.

---

[144] As Sherrard notes, this path is fraught with dangers, but so much better than 'pretending to be bodiless or sexless': *Christianity*, 48.

[145] Elmer Martens quoted in Oord, *Nature*, 130.

[146] A bitter longing heightened by the broken grammar of the verse. So S. Voorwinde, *Jesus' Emotions in the Gospels* (London: T&T Clark/Continuum, 2011), 149–50.

[147] For R. E. Brown, S.S., this is a majestic expression of Christ's will: *The Gospel According to John: Chapters 13–21* (London: Geoffrey Chapman, 1971), 772. But that seems to me to neglect the fact that this is a *prayer*, and moreover a prayer set immediately before Jesus' 'hour' of passion. I suggest therefore that Jesus' tone does not soar here into majesty, but rather his prayer to the Father deepens into longing. See later in this chapter for further consideration of this passage.

John 6.66 tells us that many followers of Jesus fell away, and this was re-enacted in the desertion of the Twelve at the Passion itself.

If the God of the Scriptures is a longing God, then the image of God, which we see perfectly in Christ, is an image that also contains longing. More, one could say that it is the purification of humans' longings that would constitute Christlikeness. In the terms I have been framing here, the Spirit is setting the believer free to long only for that for which God longs. That loving longing conveys the loving longing of Christ that all may 'turn to the Lord' (2 Cor 3.16) and know that freedom the Spirit works in those who so turn.

As Coakley indicates, a more explicit articulation of divine longing than we find in the Scriptures comes (perhaps surprisingly) in the neo-Platonic writings of Pseudo-Dionysius.[148] He wrote, 'the divine longing is the Good seeking good for the sake of the Good'.[149] Or again,

the very cause of the universe ... is, as it were, beguiled by goodness, by love, and by yearning and is enticed away from his transcendent dwelling place and comes to abide within all things ... That is why those possessed of spiritual insight describe him as 'zealous' because his good yearning for all things is so great and because he stirs in men [sic] a deep yearning desire for zeal.[150]

For Coakley, indeed, desire 'is an ontological category belonging primarily to God, and only secondarily to humans as a token of their createdness "in the image"'.[151] So the orientation of human desire is necessarily conditioned by divine desire. Coakley goes on to link this to the pneumatological language of Romans 8 – 'Likewise the Spirit helps us in our weakness; for we do not know how to pray as we ought, but that very Spirit intercedes with sighs too deep for words' (8.26). Not that we do not know the mechanics, as it were, of prayer, but that we do not know how to order and focus our longings towards God unless the Spirit involves us in God's own desire. The Spirit comes to our aid through our own longing. Coakley writes of 'deep prayer in the Spirit' that it 'veritably magnetizes the soul toward God',[152] in a way to which human-human sexual attraction is an analogy. Yielding to the sighs of the Spirit shows us that 'prayer at its deepest is God's, not ours'.[153] However, divine longing

---

[148] Coakley, *God, Sexuality*, 295.   [149] Quoted in Farley, *Wounding*, 1.
[150] Quoted ibid., 101.   [151] Coakley, *God, Sexuality*, 10.   [152] Ibid., 13.
[153] Ibid., 115. So also Richard Rohr, 'we must all keep praying "with groans unutterable" (Rom 8.23) until our prayers match the much deeper caring of God, and we discover our own will and God's will are finally the same': *Silent Compassion: Finding God in Contemplation* (Cincinnati, OH: Franciscan Media, 2014), 57.

is, for Coakley, not a manifestation of need or privation, but an expression of the character of the Triune Creator. The desire within the Trinity is as Coakley puts it, 'the perfect mutual ontological desire that only the Godhead instantiates – without either loss or excess. Here is desire not of need or imposition but of active plenitude and longing love'.[154] This divine longing will only fully be consummated when 'God will be all in all' (1 Cor 15.28).[155]

In 2 Corinthians 3.17, Paul tells us that where the Spirit is (and is Lord), there is freedom. There, in other words, is a release from the idolatries that trap human longings, from the false orientations that drain spirits of vitality and capacity for love. 'The freedom of our glory' in Romans 8, then, can be linked to the picture Paul gives us in 2 Corinthians 3, if we think of the human being coming truly into the image of Christ as that human being becoming a sign of the divine life. Such a signification can only be lived out in freedom – the traps of idols and compulsions would distort the image and corrupt the sign. Idolatry, then, takes our orientation away from God, takes our longings away from what God may be presumed to long for.

So it is important to clarify what it is that Christians believe God to long for. We have noted the famous Johannine quotation about God's love of the world, and therefore God's longing for the *metanoia* of the individual, and individuals' acceptance of the gift of eternal life. But at the level of society, God's longing must be presumed to be for the embracing of the values of the Kingdom, such that indeed the prayer may be fulfilled 'thy will be done'. As I noted earlier in this chapter, the signs of the Kingdom are proclaimed in the Gospels in various places, such as Luke 4.18–19 and Matthew 11.5; the response we are called to is perhaps best seen at Matthew 25.31–45 – Jesus both identifies totally with the plight of the hungry, the naked, and the imprisoned, and longs for his servants to serve him through meeting their needs.

---

[154] Coakley, *God, Sexuality*, 333.
[155] The concept of longing not out of need, but out of fullness, is an interesting one. It may be argued that human longing is distorted by the aching need to make up what we lack (or think we lack). So we tend not to long for the good of others with the generous, kenotic giving of our fullness that we find in 'the mind that was in Christ Jesus' (Phil 2.5; cf. also 2 Cor 8.9). So humans' cultivation of that generosity would be a way in which our longings might be conformed to the divine longing.

THE ORIENTATION OF LONGING

Is there not a danger, however, as soon as we talk of desire for God and of God's own desire, of retreating into patristic concepts that fail to do justice to our contemporary self-understanding? The difference in a properly modern approach is that natural human drives are not regarded either as non-existent, or yet evil. Rightly understood, they can take their place within an overall 'web of desire'.[156] But they must take their fundamental *orientation* from those twin petitions in the Lord's Prayer, 'Your kingdom come, your will be done'. A biblical image of oriented longing can be derived from Jesus' saying that 'foxes have holes ... but the Son of Man has nowhere to lay his head' (Mt 8.20). Ultimately, the true human being has no abiding home, but only the fundamental orientation towards God, only the journey of longing, towards the coming Kingdom. An exhortation to this journey comes in Philippians 4.6–7 – desire is to become not anxiety, but prayerfulness. Darwinian and Freudian understandings will insist on the reality of our earthly desires, and that they are a huge part of our energy and identity as creatures. It is not healthy to try to deny these desires their existence, their character, or their power.[157] The issue of right response to God, then, cannot be about the denial of those desires, but it can, I argue, be about their orientation.[158] Part of being conformed to Christ, being 'metamorphosed by the renewal of [our] minds' (Rom 12.2), is the re-orientation of our longings.[159]

Can we say more about what the re-orientation of longing should look like? Can we offer a more contemporary account, more affirmative of the physical animals we each are, without losing the extraordinary insights that Plato, Augustine, and Dante offer us? I have tried to suggest that part

---

[156] E. Stump, *Wandering in Darkness: Narrative and the Problem of Suffering* (Oxford: Oxford University Press, 2010), 7–8.

[157] It is interesting to read of C. S. Lewis, sometimes thought of as such a stern apologist for orthodox Christianity, noting that sexual activity 'reduces the nagging and addictive character of mere appetite'. Lewis,: *The Four Loves* (London: Geoffrey Bles, 1960), 112. What he warns against is rather attempting 'to find an absolute in the flesh' (114). That would be idolatry.

[158] The 'right aiming' of desire, in Gregory of Nyssa's phrase (quoted in Coakley, *God, Sexuality*, 285).

[159] Stump analyses this in terms of second-order desires, the desire in a person that they would desire certain things, and ultimately 'the re-folding of the heart's desires' (*Wandering*, 443–8). Though I prefer the language used here of the orientation of longing, I find her Aquinas-based analysis of the necessary integration of the person in the formation of second-order desires, and the necessity to that integration of relationship with God, very helpful.

of growing into the image and likeness of God, after the example of Christ, through the grace and power of the Holy Spirit, is to come to conform our own longings to the divine longing. Just as Jesus' 'if only' at Luke 19.42 presumably echoes the longings of the Father, so our longing should echo that of Christ.

Thérèse of Lisieux wrote [addressing God] that: 'To love you as you love me, I must borrow your own love – it is the only way which will satisfy my desire'.[160] Farley writes, 'In our thirst we are images of the power that thirsts for the beauty of each existing thing'.[161] 'The divine image gives rise to a flame of desire that burns without consuming'.[162] Dante's famous 'In his will is our peace' (*Paradiso* III.85) is itself a translation of Augustine. Tempered by a twenty-first-century understanding of the horrors of the world, and the elusiveness of the Kingdom for which Christians are to long, we might re-render this, less elegantly, 'Within God's longing we find our wholeness, the true orientation of our own longing.' This is not to say that those desires disappear that go with being the animal that Darwin and Maslow describe. The reality of the longings of physical creatures for food, for healing, and for love is continually affirmed in the Gospels. So we are still faced with the struggle to combine these descriptions of human longing, longing for the finite and longing for the inexhaustible.

Farley calls desire for God the warp against which we weave the particularities of our lives[163] and insists, interestingly, that it would be wrong to orient our desire *only* on God's eternal life.[164] The warp needs weft for a full life. Our other desires may pull in a different direction, but if the desire for God remains strong, the shape of the life will be retained. The stronger the desire for God becomes, the more the life will develop a holy orientation.

Eleonore Stump in her remarkable book *Wandering in Darkness* makes a distinction between propositional desires – desires that such and such might be the case – and desire for a person.[165] Stump supplements her image of 'the web of desire' with the terminology of 'heart's desires'.[166] These are a person's principal longings (almost by definition

---

[160] Quoted in Farley, *Wounding*, 16.   [161] Ibid., 17.   [162] Ibid., 21.   [163] Ibid., 2.
[164] Ibid., 10–11.
[165] Stump, *Wandering*, chapter 3. See C. S. Lewis on the difference between sexual desire that sex may take place, and erotic desire for a person who is sexually loved: *Four Loves*, 109–10.
[166] Stump, *Wandering*, 7.

a heart's desire is not something fully realised, or fully in the person's control). Stump also uses another model, that of the 're-folding' of a heart's desires, as the three-dimensional structure of a protein might refold.[167] One strength of this picture is that it emphasises continual movement – the desiring self is never static, and is continually relating. We are not, as Moore says, isolated monads, but constantly relating to our environment in all sorts of ways. Relation, not isolation, is the default.[168] And desires and longings are, as again the model would suggest, always plural and diverse.

The model would also stress that changes in the patterns of desire are a process, not a once-off change. For Coakley, contemplation is 'a progressive modulator and refiner of human desire'. She continues, 'in its naked longing for God, it lays out all its other desires – conscious and unconscious – and places them, over time, into the crucible of divine desire.' 'Over time' is the key phrase here. Therefore, '[s]exual desire ... is thus drawn into an inexorable tether with all other desires, judged by its approximation, or lack thereof, to the purity of divine desire'.[169]

I do not overstate the power of Stump's analogy with protein folding. I merely point out that for those familiar with the science it is perhaps a more generative one than the two-dimensional picture Farley offers of warp and weft, and also a richer one than that of a web. It is a dynamic one since proteins are always in motion, always interacting with their environment. And it does make imaginative space for the notion that all sorts of desires are natural and understandable, bound to arise in the flexing of the sort of 'molecule' we each are, even if they lead to states that are not all that human flourishing might be.

The divine invitation is not, as the tradition has too often held, that we humiliate those natural desires,[170] but that we reconfigure them radically in an understanding that calls for love even of enemy (Mt 5.44), and sees very understandable efforts to store up security as idolatrous and vain (Lk 12.18f). This surely is the essence of the matter – however we want to picture it – that once the matrix of longings is reconfigured around love, and God's gifts in creation are received as gifts, then the physical desires of physical creatures start to incarnate a life lived towards the divine longing. We begin, while remaining fully ourselves, to transcend the selfishness of those selves. Indeed, it is through this process

---

[167] Ibid., 443.   [168] Moore, *Jesus*, chapters 2 and 12.
[169] Coakley, *God, Sexuality*, 52.   [170] So also Farley, *Wounding*, 32.

of self-transcendence[171] that we open up the possibility of becoming more truly the full selves we are called to be.[172]

Another way of putting this would be to say that much of our creativity stems from sexual energy, and that energy can be focused in a range of ways.[173] Where the self is accepted, so the ego's fears are stilled, the self can be given over out of its fullness for the love of the other, and the Spirit can give 'the increase' of that self-gift (cf. 1 Cor 3.6) The great example, for the Christian, is always Jesus, in whom is the full possibility of the 'self-given self',[174] 'the man of oneness',[175] whose desire is completely oriented by his perfect attention to the Father. But the great problem, for the Christian, is that we are given so little indication of how Jesus handled his sexual energy. (And the other great model of human behaviour, the Virgin Mary, is elaborately protected in the tradition from being identified as a sexual being – *vide* the traditional Catholic denial that Jesus had full brothers.)

Hence, again, the importance of The Song of Songs. As I noted earlier in this chapter in quoting the passage from Irigaray, self-transcendence can in the right context be catalyzed by sexual self-giving. Sherrard, writing of the work of Soloviev, talks of the importance of encountering 'another living being to whom he [*sic*] attributes an absolute importance and who awakens in him an awareness of his own essential nature'.[176] This is a very particular form of encounter, because the other is met as equal and equivalent to the self but yet still other; there are, therefore, particularly rich opportunities for ego-transcendence in such relationship.[177]

---

[171] C. Southgate, *The Groaning of Creation: God, Evolution and the Problem of Evil* (Louisville, KY: Westminster John Knox Press, 2008), chapter 4.

[172] Here my model differs somewhat from that of Coakley and is more anchored in a sense that selves in competition with other selves are intrinsic to biological evolution. Coakley's own exploration of cooperation in evolution (S. Coakley, 'Sacrifice Regained: Evolution, Cooperation and God', Gifford Lectures 2012 available on the Web at http://www .giffordlectures.org/lectures/sacrifice-regained-evolution-cooperation-and-god). predisposes her to her understanding of desire as 'the constellating category of selfhood' (*God, Sexuality*, 26).

[173] Cf. Sherrard, *Christianity*, 78–83.

[174] Southgate, *Groaning*, 71–3; 'Re-reading', 386.   [175] Moore, *Jesus*, ix.

[176] Sherrard, *Christianity*, 56.

[177] 'We all desire to be desired by one we desire, but the fulfillment of this longing involves much dying to ego': Moore, *Jesus*, 104. Which is not to deny the huge problems associated with this path to self-transcending longing. Moore notes 'No desire is as prone to self-deception … as is sexual desire' (ibid., 94.)

Moore explores this theme of ego-transcendence further, noting that a person is continually required to die to self (or rather a particular ego-construction of self) and be reborn at a more profound level. A person longing for a deeper relationship with a lover is always finding themselves anew. Human desires are only liberated when human beings fully realise in whom they 'live and move and have [their] being' (Acts 17.28). 'The liberation of desire is not "getting what I want"' but '"coming to want as ultimately as I am"'.[178] But we dread not needing the things we think we cannot do without – more indeed than we dread not having them. Self-transcendence means deepening trust in a mystery, a trust going beyond what can be known. It therefore involves a kind of death, of reliance on the known.[179]

Moore's view of sin is also striking. He sees it not so much in dis-ordered desire (the familiar view) but in the inertia of the ego, which represses the desire to desire more. Sin may also be understood as an idolatry of the ego at its present state of development, which inhibits the surrender of the self to further possibilities arising out of the longing for God.[180] The advertising industry seizes upon this, offering all sorts of easy fixes to bolster a particular shape of the identity, which is in fact that of 'consumer', though disguised in the trappings of material aspira-tion. Sin, then, can be seen in the absence of the proper fear that attends self-transcendence, in the denial of authentic desire, in 'the arrogance of common sense'.[181] Holy desire, then, will be very attentive to the possi-bility of connecting with and cooperating with others[182] for it is in relationship that we find our true selves.

I return now to my proposal about how human and divine long-ings might become conformed. Coakley points to the importance of Romans 8, very much in accord with my own thinking. In Paul's lan-guage of 'groaning' (Rom 8.22–3), the Spirit conforms itself to Christians' own struggle and sense of incompleteness, and groans with them. Before believers even conform their desire to God, God has awakened that

---

[178] Ibid., 18.   [179] Cf. Ibid., 19.   [180] Ibid., chapters 4 and 5.
[181] Ibid., 34, citing Lonergan. Moore also offers a very interesting reading of the Genesis 3 story, pointing out that part of the disruption the story describes as resulting from the Fall is that the 'higher' nature of human beings ceases to befriend the 'lower', the physi-cal. The human beings in the garden became ashamed of their nakedness. The whole burden of the tradition (much influenced by Augustine) is that the lower fails the latter, by virtue of its disordered lust. Moore says rather that lust is secondary, and results from primordial shame (chapter 10).
[182] Cf. Farley, *Wounding*, 66.

desire, and met it in God's own. And when Christians pray, hardly knowing how to pray, seeking to orient their longings towards God, and summing up their prayer in the words 'Thy Kingdom come, thy will be done', the Spirit catches up their incoherent longings and prays them in our place (Rom 8.26–7). This role of the Spirit is central to both Coakley's model and my own. She writes that the Spirit 'painfully darkens my prior certainties, enflames and checks my own desires, and so invites me ever more deeply into the life of redemption in Christ'.[183]

The activity of the Spirit in respect of God's longings and those of Christians is, for me, beautifully caught in Bianco di Siena's fifteenth-century hymn, translated into English as 'Come down O Love Divine'. The hymn begins 'Come down O Love divine/seek thou this soul of mine/ and visit it with thine own ardour glowing'. 'Ardour' is a fascinating word, connoting as it does not only passionate love, but also the Spirit's longing for communion with the soul of the believer. The last verse begins 'And so the yearning strong/with which the soul will long/shall far out-pass the power of human telling.' The effect of the Spirit's longing love, the hymn tells us, is to take away the power of the passions, to evoke true lowliness of heart, and to evoke in the believer a most powerful yearning, not only, I would suggest, for God but for what God longs for, a radical conversion of hearts.

In putting together these fine phrases I do not suppose for a moment that this conversion of the heart, re-orientation of the longing, is an easy process. 'The purification of the motive'[184] is a lifelong struggle, charac-terised by seemingly endless failure. That is what it means to be a sinner. The virtues, Farley tells us, are the muscles of our spiritual lives – we need their tone, their habits, to keep us moving onwards. Love, which she calls 'the most opulent expression of our power', needs the virtues to keep it balanced.[185] But even the virtues have counterfeits at their elbow.

The language of the orientation of longing can all too easily slide into the language of will mastering emotions. That is not at all the model I want to convey here. The will does have a role, transformed 'by the renewing of our minds' (Rom 12.2), in preventing humans from acting on our own destructive longings. But this is only one role within a complex matrix. I suggest that to recognise and accept the naturalness of our longings, and to perceive that certain desires may be expressions of deeper

---

[183] Coakley, *God, Sexuality*, 56.   [184] Eliot, *Poems and Plays*, 196.
[185] Farley, *Wounding*, 152.

longings, takes a particular fusion of intellect, imagination and emotion, a listening to the self that is much more than analytical.

Because the re-formation of human longings to conform to God's longing is a re-formation of the pattern of the emotions,[186] it cannot be wrought by the will alone, though the will does have a further important role in sustaining a discipline of prayer and worship. But ultimately the re-orientation I am describing is, for the Christian, the work of the Spirit on the emotions themselves, growing in them the fruit that is so beautifully listed in Galatians 5. (Self-control, it should be noted, is one but only one of these fruit, and comes last in the list.) Beyond even these fruit, the work of the Spirit is to strengthen in believers what have been called the three theological virtues, but which are really the three primary longings for what God longs for. Faith is the underpinning of the primary longing, to be one with God. Hope is the essence of the longing for God's kingdom to come, and love is the longing for the full flourishing of other creatures.

JESUS' FINAL PRAYER IN THE FOURTH GOSPEL – BELIEVERS' SHARE IN THE GLORY OF GOD

In our consideration of John in Chapter 2, we bracketed out the High Priestly Prayer in John 17, which might be called the ultimate expression of Jesus' longing, before he and his Father perfect the work of the Incarnation in Cross and Resurrection. For Thomas Gardner, 'To overhear these words would have been like listening in as God spoke to himself about his deepest desires, as taste of the very intimacy to which his Son was even now opening a way'.[187]

At John 17.22–23 we find a thought very close to what we have been exploring in 2 Corinthians:

[22] The glory that you have given me I have given them, so that they may be one, as we are one, [23] I in them and you in me, that they may become completely one, so that the world may know that you have sent me and have loved them even as you have loved me.

Here we see glory derived from the Father, the glory 'beheld' in John 1.14, made available to the community around Christ. This transmission of

---

[186] See also T. Gorringe, *The Education of Desire: Towards a Theology of the Senses* (London: SCM Press, 2001) for an emphasis on the importance of the senses.
[187] T. Gardner, *John in the Company of Poets (Studies in Christianity and Literature)* (Waco, TX: Baylor University Press, 2014), 149.

glory is unifying, it binds the community together 'into the same image', as John might have written. The Johannine imagery is intimately partici- pative; it is not optical as we have been considering in Paul, but the theology is very similar. The sign of God that is Jesus is not accepted by all (1.11); but now 'glory' is shared with the community, they are also to challenge the world to recognise God in Jesus.[188]

In reading John 1.14, one could interpret 'glory as of an only begotten of a father' as connoting not only being-a-sign of all that God the Father means for the world, but also having-the-power-to-be-such-a-sign. That power seems to have existed 'in the beginning with God' (1.2). In John 17, however, if 'glory' is read in this way, the power comes from the love that the Father had for the Son 'before the foundation of the world' (17.24). On this understanding the glory of the Father, transmitted to another to signify the reality of the Father and that Father's love, involves not only the offer of such signification, but the power to effect it. This coheres with what several New Testament authors confess about the work of the Spirit. The opportunity for mission is not only offered by the Spirit, but Spirit empowered (e.g., Acts 1.8, Jn 16.13). And as we have seen, the Spirit is the freedom-begetting energizer of the processes of transformation we learn about in 2 Corinthians 3.18.

So the task of the believer is not only that great task of three-lensed seeing that I have commending in these chapters. It is the task of being with Christ and in Christ in these three modes of his journey, what might be called in a slightly ugly phrase 'three-age being'. Christians are already fully part of the first creation (and part of bearing reality to the full is to appreciate to the full our evolutionary inheritance and that inheritance has shaped our embodiment, the possibilities of our flesh, and the way it shapes our desires and longings). Christians are called, so the Gospels remind us, to take up their cross, or as Paul puts it, be part of the death of Christ for the world. Having the mind of Christ, in self-emptying, is a condition 'costing not less than everything'.[189] Believers then are called to be part of that eternal newness of life that begins for human beings at the Resurrection.

The promise in John 17 seems to go beyond the possibility, opened up in Paul's language, that being found in Christ's death, and therefore being in touch with the newness of life that stems from his resurrection, is to be *kainē ktisis* ('new creation') in the words of 2 Corinthians 5.17.

---

[188] So Brown, *John 13–21*, 778.   [189] Eliot, *Poems and Plays*, 198.

The Johannine vision in 17.22 is that the disciples (and therefore the believers who inherit their role) are *given* the divine glory 'so they may be one'. It is possible to read this semiotically, in the light of the following verse – 'I in them and you in me, that they may become completely one, so that the world may know that you have sent me and have loved them even as you have loved me' (17.23). Jesus, we might say, as the perfect sign and image of God, draws the disciples into that same image (cf. 2 Corinthians 3.18), and in their oneness in him, they become perfect signs of the sign that he is.[190] (Indeed the Greek here, rendered by the NRSV as 'become completely one' is *teteleiōmenoi eis hen*, 'being perfected into one.')[191]

Readers will recall that in the Introduction and Chapter 1, we established that divine glory has to be understood on a spectrum from sign to ontological reality. Glory in John 17 seems to be more about essence, less about sign. This is interesting given the overtly semiotic structure of the first 'book' of the Gospel, which is often called The Book of Signs. Glory is clearly something visible at 1.14, and closely associated with a sign at 2.11. The more 'ontic' character of glory in Chapter 17 accords with the Evangelist's theme there, which is that of the eternal relation of Son and Father, and the everlasting bond of love into which the community is drawn.

So it is also possible to read John 17.22 with verse 24: 'Father I desire that those also, whom you have given me, may be with me where I am, to see my glory, which you have given me because you loved me before the foundation of the world.' Here glory does sound to be more property than signification. Signification was presumably not needed 'before the foundation of the world'.[192] The property concerned is (as again I sought to establish in the Introduction and Chapter 1) nothing other than 'Godness'.

What the Fourth Gospel says here is utterly extraordinary (and a great offence to those who would want to claim that there is no theosis in the

---

[190] Such a merely 'functional' reading of the glory given by Jesus at 17.22, solely in terms of Christ's mission and work, is rejected by Andrew J. Byers, *Ecclesiology and Theosis in the Gospel of John* (Cambridge: Cambridge University Press, 2017), 197–8.

[191] So R. Bauckham, *Gospel of Glory: Major Themes in Johannine Theology* (Grand Rapids, MI: Baker Academic, 2015), 34.

[192] Though I note an intriguing quotation from Eberhard Jüngel, 'the doctrine of the Trinity is the interpretation of the self-interpretation of God': *God's Being Is in Becoming: The Trinitarian Theology of God in the Theology of Karl Barth: A Paraphrase*, transl. J. Webster (Edinburgh: T&T Clark, 2001), 29.

New Testament).[193] Reading back into verse 22, we might now say that Jesus prays that the disciples be given Godness.[194] This reading might be resisted on the grounds that *doxa* is glory in the sense of honour, and that the prayer is for honour (accorded by others) or reputation.[195] But God does not seem to have given that to the earthly Jesus or his disciples. Honour accorded by others is precisely what they have not been given. Rather they have been given a relationship with the Lord so close that even Godness is shared with them, in being one as the Son and the Father are one. That does function as a sign, as is clear from verse 23. It does not (how could it?) identify creatures with God. But it emphasizes the way believers may be drawn into the divine life, and that Christians' experience in Christ is in continuity with that eschatological state in which Godness will be all in all, and sign and reality will be one.

CONCLUSION

We have considered here what it might mean for believers to respond to God's glory. Further, we explored the implications of Jesus' life being considered as a qualisign of the life of God, and the application of that to the writings of Paul – in particular his conviction that the lives of believers can be transformed through progressive degrees of glory. This we proposed as believers contemplating and reflecting the glory of Jesus in such a way as to become more and more truly signs of the great sign of God that is Christ.

We then considered this transformation of believers in relation to freedom in Christ and in relation to Christlikeness in the divine image.

---

[193] For C. W. Morgan, 'Jesus' High Priestly Prayer also reveals that the self-giving and self-exalting triune God draws his redeemed people into the circle of fellowship, mutual blessing, and shared glory': 'Towards a Theology of the Glory of God' in *The Glory of God*, ed. C. W. Morgan and R. A. Peterson (Wheaton, IL: Crossway, 2010), 153–87, at 178. More generally, see Byers for a treatment of theosis in John as 'Jewish, narrative and communal': *Ecclesiology*, chapter 9.

[194] L. William Countryman, 'The unity into which believers are now called is that of the primordial glory, the beauty and power of the godhead, before the foundation of the cosmos': *The Mystical Way in the Fourth Gospel: Crossing Over into God* (Valley Forge, PA: Trinity Press International, 1994), 116.

[195] Indeed that key Pauline text Romans 8.30: 'those he justified he also glorified' could be read in terms of God according honour to believers (so Goranson Jacob and Wright, *Conformed*). Less easy perhaps to read Philippians 3.21 in that way – 'to be conformed to the body of Christ's glory' sounds more like becoming a sign of the Christ whose body was broken in pain, out of love, and then raised, out of power.

This led to the exploration of the theme of longing and the orientation of the believer's longing to the longing of God. Finally, we saw in John 17 that believers might be drawn into the actual Godness of God, through the relationship of the Son to the Father.

That ends our exploration of divine glory understood principally as a sign of the deep reality of God. In the Conclusion, I evaluate the success of using this understanding as a hermeneutical lens to point up God's glory even in the most difficult and paradoxical of contexts.

Conclusion

So, in summary, I have proposed a reading of divine glory in terms of a spectrum of meaning from sign to essence, and the need to interpret events in terms of creation, Cross, and eschaton. This reading brings into particular focus the mystery of God's nature, the identification of that nature with suffering at Christ's Passion, the idea that the whole creation is full of signs of God, and the promise to believers of the possibility of redeemed participation in the divine life.

How would I evaluate this threefold hermeneutical lens with which I have tried to interpret divine glory? I suggest that it offers several advantages:

1. It preserves a sense of the mystery of God, refusing to reduce the character of the God glimpsed in revelation and creation to simple attributes, even the attributes of beauty and goodness.
2. It recognises that what we can know of God is always God's self-communication.
3. It insists, in respect of divine glory, on what Fout calls 'self-referentially communicative dynamism'[1] and brings a more dynamic, revelatory quality to most manifestations of glory than the mere equation of glory with 'honour'. At the same time it allows glory a spectrum of meaning to be interpreted according to context. At the other end of the spectrum from divine self-revelation by the

---

[1] J. Fout, *Fully Alive: The Glory of God and the Human Creature in Karl Barth, Hans Urs von Balthasar and the Theological Exegesis of Scripture* (London: Bloomsbury T&T Clark, 2015), 13.

giving of signs is self-reference, glory as sheer Godness (here the term comes closest to honour). This spectrum of meaning collapses in on itself only at the eschaton, when there will be no more need of signs, for then we shall see 'face to face'.

4. It allows us to face up to, and explore, how the Godness of God is communicated to us through the Passion and Crucifixion of Christ, and thus shows that the other main understanding of divine glory, in terms of splendour or radiance, is also inadequate to do justice to the complexity of the term.

5. Once it was recognised, from reflection on the Passion, that experiences of great complexity, oppression and even apparent God-forsakenness might still include an element of glory, this allowed us to be bold in 'bearing the maximum amount of reality'. We were then able to hunt for divine glory even within the violence of the natural world, and even within situations of great human oppression, or where long spiritual search seems to lead more to a sense of divine absence than presence. Here the concept of 'three-lensed seeing', a willingness always to look for *Gloria mundi* and *Gloria crucis* and *Gloria in excelsis* within the same event was particularly important.

6. The approach opens up the theme of God's glorious self-communication to analysis using Peirce's sign-categories. A semiotic understanding permits us to revisit our foundational texts and to ask questions like: what kind of signification are we seeing here? What is the role of the interpreters of the sign, both in the texts of Scripture and tradition and in other 'reading' of the natural world and of human life? Much more work could be done here in investigating the relation of indexicality to iconicity, in exploring the Christian tradition,[2] and especially in relation to the Eucharist as the particular focus both of believers' contemplation of Christ and their transformation.

7. The understanding of the believer becoming herself a sign of the divine life through being a sign of Christ in turn enables us to ask what kind of sign such a believer's life would be. That transformation 'from one degree of glory to another' we supposed to include conformation of the believer's longing to the divine longing for that time when the Kingdom will come and God's will be fully done.

---

[2] For example, in comparing the Peircean semiotic understanding presented here with Augustine's language of trace, image, and resemblance.

As I indicated when I introduced the concept of a hermeneutical lens, some aspects of a complex 'object' of study will be in less clear focus when others come up 'sharp'. I recognise that the complex, self-communicative understanding of divine glory I have proposed makes less clear a picture of glory as an objective 'thing' to be possessed or acquired, though the Scriptural witness to glory can often be interpreted in that way.

By bracketing out the whole subject of creaturely glorification of God, I took out of 'focus' the whole question of creaturely praise and the use of glory-terminology to describe that praise. In doing so I recognise that I laid very heavy stress on God's communication to human beings at the expense of considering what human responses of praise might mean to God.

I also recognise that divine glory can often be rendered 'splendour' and that to hunt for glory in places of pain and tragedy minimises that important connection. However, here I issue a challenge, as I began to do when I introduced the subject by coming at discourse on glory from the connection to theodicy. At the end of my long search to try and clarify that discourse, I remain convinced that so much Christian thought, and Christian worship, focuses too much on beauty and splendour, and so fails to bear reality, and needs to acknowledge to the full God's involvement in the ambiguity and struggle of creaturely life.

I hope this book finishes on a note that may inspire some readers to think the infinitely challenging thought that their lives might take on, more and more, the 'colour' of Christ's life, as they become more and more truly 'qualisigns' of that life. But I also hope it serves as a challenge not to oversimplify our thinking about God our Creator and Redeemer, and to allow honest exploration of God's involvement even in difficulty, even in pain, even in our apparent abandonment.

Drewsteignton and Exeter   December 2017

Bibliography

Achtemeier, P. J., *1. Peter: A Commentary on First Peter* (Minneapolis, MN: Fortress Press, 1996).

Agamben, G., *The Kingdom and the Glory: For a Theological Genealogy of Economy and Government (Homo Sacer II, 2)*, transl. L. Chiesa (with M. Mandarini) (Stanford, CA: Stanford University Press, 2011).

Alba, A., *The Holocaust Memorial Museum: Sacred Secular Place* (Basingstoke: Palgrave Macmillan, 2015).

Allchin, A. M., 'Emerging: A Look at Some of R. S. Thomas' More Recent Poems' in *Critical Writings on R. S. Thomas*, ed. S. Anstey (Bridgend: Seren Books, 1992), 100–11.

The World Is a Wedding: Explorations in Christian Spirituality (London: Darton, Longman and Todd, 1978).

Allen, D., *Temptation* (Princeton: Caroline Press, 1986).

Theology for a Troubled Believer: An Introduction to the Christian Faith (Louisville, KY: Westminster John Knox Press, 2010).

Allison, D. C., Jr., *James* (London: Bloomsbury, 2013).

Ashton, J., *The Gospel of John and Christian Origins* (Minneapolis, MN: Fortress Press, 2014).

Understanding the Fourth Gospel (Oxford: Clarendon Press, 1991).

Aune, D., *Revelation 6–16* (Nashville, TN: Thomas Nelson Pubs, 1998).

Barbour, I. G., *Religion and Science: Historical and Contemporary Issues* (London: SCM Press, 1998).

Barnett, P., *The Second Epistle to the Corinthians* (Grand Rapids, MI: Eerdmans, 1997).

Barrett, C. K., *A Commentary on the Second Epistle to the Corinthians* (London: A&C Black, 1973).

Barth, K., *Church Dogmatics*, Vol. 2, Part 1, The Doctrine of God, transl. T. H. L. Parker, W. B. Johnston, H. Knight, and J. L. M. Haire, ed. G. W. Bromiley and T. F. Torrance (Edinburgh: T&T Clark, 1957).

Church Dogmatics, Vol. 3, Part 3, The Doctrine of Creation, transl. G. W. Bromiley and R. J. Ehrlich, ed. G. W. Bromiley and T. F. Torrance (Edinburgh: T&T Clark, 1961).

Church Dogmatics, Vol. 4, Part 3, First Half: The Doctrine of Reconciliation, transl. G. W. Bromiley, ed. G. W. Bromiley and T. F. Torrance (Edinburgh: T&T Clark, 1961).

Evangelical Theology: An Introduction, transl. G. Foley (New York: Holt, Rinehart and Winston, 1963).

Bauckham, R., *Gospel of Glory: Major Themes in Johannine Theology* (Grand Rapids, MI: Baker Academic, 2015).

'Joining Creation's Praise of God'. *Ecotheology* 7 (2002), 45–59.

Bedient, C., *Eight Contemporary Poets* (Oxford: Oxford University Press, 1974).

Begbie, J. S., 'Beauty, Sentimentality and the Arts' in *The Beauty of God: Theology and the Arts*, ed. D. J. Treier, M. Husbands, and R. Lundin (Downers Grove, IL: IVP Academic, 2007), 45–69.

'Created Beauty: The Witness of J. S. Bach' in *The Beauty of God: Theology and the Arts*, ed. D. J. Treier, M. Husbands, and R. Lundin (Downers Grove, IL: IVP Academic, 2007), 19–44.

Belleville, L. L., *Reflections of Glory: Paul's Polemical Use of the Moses-Doxa Tradition in 2. Corinthians 3.1–18* (Sheffield: JSOT Press, 1991).

Bentley Hart, D., *The Beauty of the Infinite: The Aesthetics of Christian Truth* (Grand Rapids, MI: Eerdmans, 2003).

The Doors of the Sea: Where Was God in the Tsunami? (Grand Rapids, MI: Eerdmans, 2005).

Berquist, M. W., 'The Meaning of Doxa in the Epistles of Paul' (Ph.D. Thesis, Southern Baptist Theological Seminary, 1941).

Blackwell, B. C., *Christosis: Pauline Soteriology in Light of Deification in Irenaeus and Cyril of Alexandria* (Tübingen: Mohr Siebeck, 2011).

Blake, W., *Poetry and Prose of William Blake*, ed. G. Keynes (New York: Random House, 1946).

Block, D. I., *The Book of Ezekiel: Chapters 1–24* (Grand Rapids, MI: Eerdmans, 1997).

Blumenthal, D. R., *Facing the Abusing God: A Theology of Protest* (Louisville, KY: Westminster John Knox Press, 1993).

Bonhoeffer, D., *Voices in the Night: The Prison Poems of Dietrich Bonhoeffer. A New Translation with Commentary by Edwin Robertson* (Trowbridge: Eagle Pub., 2003).

Bovon, F., *Luke 1 – A Commentary on the Gospel of Luke 1:1–9:50*, transl. C. M. Thomas, ed. H. Koester (Minneapolis, MN: Fortress Press, 2002).

Brenner, R. F., *Writing as Resistance: Four Women Confronting the Holocaust* (University Park, PA: The Pennsylvania State University Press, 1997).

Brenton, Sir L. C. L., *The Septuagint Version in Greek and English* (Grand Rapids, MI: Zondervan, 1970).

Brown, D., *Divine Generosity and Human Creativity: Theology through Symbol, Painting and Architecture* (London: Routledge, 2017).

Divine Humanity: Kenosis and the Construction of a Christian Theology (Waco, TX: Baylor University Press, 2011).

Brown, R. E., *The Gospel According to John: Chapters 1–12* (London: Geoffrey Chapman, 1971).

The Gospel According to John: Chapters 13–21 (London: Geoffrey Chapman, 1971).

Brown, T., '"On the Screen of Eternity": Some Aspects of R. S. Thomas's Prose' in *Critical Writings on R. S. Thomas*, ed. S. Anstey (Bridgend: Seren Books, 1992), 182–201.

R. S. Thomas (Cardiff: University of Wales Press, 2013).

Brown, W. P., *The Seven Pillars of Creation: The Bible, Science, and the Ecology of Wonder* (New York: Oxford University Press, 2010).

Brueggemann, W., *Finally Comes the Poet: Daring Speech for Proclamation* (Minneapolis, MN: Fortress Press, 1989).

Ichabod toward Home: The Journey of God's Glory (Grand Rapids, MI: Eerdmans, 2002).

Brunner, E., *Revelation and Reason*, transl. O. Wyon (London: SCM Press, 1947).

The Christian Doctrine of God, Dogmatics, Vol. 1., transl. O. Wyon (London: Lutterworth, 1949).

Bulkeley, K., *The Wondering Brain: Thinking about Religion with and beyond Cognitive Neuroscience* (London: Routledge, 2005).

Burridge, R. A., *Four Gospels: One Jesus: A Symbolic Reading* (London: SPCK, 1994).

Byers, A. J., *Ecclesiology and Theosis in the Gospel of John* (Cambridge: Cambridge University Press, 2017).

Caird, G., 'The Glory of God in the Fourth Gospel: An Exercise in Biblical Semantics'. *New Testament Studies* 15 (1968), 265–77.

'The New Testament Conception of Doxa' (D.Phil. Thesis, Oxford University, 1944).

Cassuto, U., *A Commentary on the Book of Exodus*, transl. I. Abrahams (Jerusalem: The Magnes Press, The Hebrew University, 1967).

Chase, S., *Job* (Louisville, KY: Westminster John Knox Press, 2013).

Childs, B. S., *Exodus: A Commentary* (London: SCM Press, 1974).

Isaiah (Louisville, KY: Westminster John Knox Press, 2001).

Christianson, E. S., *Ecclesiastes through the Centuries* (Oxford: Blackwell, 2007).

Clayton, P., *In Quest of Freedom: The Emergence of Spirit in the Natural World*: Frankfurt Templeton Lectures 2006, ed. M. G. Parker and T. M. Schmidt (Göttingen: Vandenhoeck and Ruprecht, 2009).

Clayton, P., and Knapp, S. *The Predicament of Belief* (New York: Oxford University Press, 2011).

Coakley, S., *God, Sexuality and the Self: An Essay 'On the Trinity'* (Cambridge: Cambridge University Press, 2013).

'Kenosis: Theological Meanings and Gender Connotations' in *The Work of Love: Creation as Kenosis*, ed. J. Polkinghorne (London: SPCK, 2001), 192–210.

'Sacrifice Regained: Evolution, Cooperation and God', Gifford Lectures 2012, www.giffordlectures.org/lectures/sacrifice-regained-evolution-cooperation-and-god

Cody, A., OSB, *Ezekiel: With an Excursus on Old Testament Priesthood* (Wilmington, DE: Michael Glazier, 1984).

Coetsier, M. G., *Etty Hillesum and the Flow of Presence: A Voegelinian Analysis* (Columbia, MO: University of Missouri Press, 2008).

Countryman, L. W., *The Mystical Way in the Fourth Gospel: Crossing Over into God* (Valley Forge, PA: Trinity Press International, 1994).

Culp, K. A., *Vulnerability and Glory: A Theological Account* (Louisville, KY: Westminster John Knox Press, 2010).

Dales, D., *Glory: The Spiritual Theology of Michael Ramsey* (Norwich: Canterbury Press, 2003).

Dante Alighieri, *The Divine Comedy*, transl. C. H. Sisson (Oxford: Oxford University Press, 1993).

Darwin, C., 'Letter to J. D. Hooker, dated July 13, 1856', Letter No. 1924, www.darwinproject.ac.uk.

   On the Origin of Species by Means of Natural Selection, Or, the Preservation of Favoured Races in the Struggle for Life (London: John Murray, 1859).

Davies, W. D., *Paul and Rabbinic Judaism: Some Rabbinic Elements in Pauline Theology* (Philadelphia: Fortress Press, 1980).

Davis, W. V., *R. S. Thomas: Poetry and Theology* (Waco, TX: Baylor University Press, 2007).

Dawkins, R., *Unweaving the Rainbow: Science, Delusion and the Appetite for Wonder* (London: Allen Lane, 1998).

Deane-Drummond, C., *Christ and Evolution: Wonder and Wisdom* (Minneapolis, MN: Fortress Press, 2009).

   Wonder and Wisdom: Conversations in Science, Spirituality and Theology (West Conshohocken, PA: Templeton Foundation Press, 2006).

De Costa, D., *Anne Frank and Etty Hillesum: Inscribing Spirituality and Sexuality*, transl. M. F. C. Hoyinck and R. E. Chesal (New Brunswick, NJ: Rutgers University Press, 1998).

Dembski, W., *The End of Christianity: Finding a Good God in an Evil World* (Milton Keynes: Paternoster, 2009).

DeSilva, D. A., *Honor, Patronage, Kinship and Purity: Unlocking New Testament Culture* (Downers Grove, IL: InterVarsity Press, 2000).

de Vries, P., *The Kābôd of YHWH in the Old Testament with Particular Reference to the Book of Ezekiel* (Leiden: Brill, 2016).

Dibelius, M., *James: A Commentary on the Epistle of James*, transl. M. A. Williams (Philadelphia, PA: Fortress Press, 1975).

Dohmen, C., 'kābēd' in *Theological Dictionary of the Old Testament*, Vol. VII, ed. G. J. Botterweck, H. Ringgren, and H.-J. Fabry, transl. D. E. Green (Grand Rapids, MI: Eerdmans, 1995), 13–17.

Domning, D. P., and Hellwig, M. K., *Original Selfishness: Original Sin and Evil in the Light of Evolution* (Aldershot: Ashgate, 2006).

Donoghue, D., *Words Alone: The Poet T. S. Eliot* (New Haven, CT: Yale University Press, 2000).

Doron, C.-O., 'The Microscopic Glance' in *Practices of Wonder: Cross-Disciplinary Perspectives*, ed. S. Vasalou (Cambridge: James Clarke, 2012), 179–200.

Dozeman, T. B., *Commentary on Exodus* (Grand Rapids, MI: Eerdmans, 2009).

Dunn, J. D. G., *Christology in the Making: An Inquiry into the Origins of the Doctrine of the Incarnation* (London: SCM Press, 1980).
  The Epistles to the Colossians and Philemon: A Commentary on the Greek Text (Grand Rapids, MI: Eerdmans, 1996).
Edwards, D., 'Every Sparrow That Falls to the Ground: The Cost of Evolution and the Christ-Event'. *Ecotheology* 11 (2006), 103–23.
Eliot, T. S., *Complete Poems and Plays* (London: Faber and Faber, 1969).
  The Letters of T. S. Eliot, Vol. 5: 1930–31, ed. V. Eliot and J. Haffenden (London: Faber and Faber, 2014).
Evans, C. A., *Word and Glory: On the Exegetical and Theological Background of John's Prologue* (Sheffield: JSOT Press, 1993).
Evans, C. F., *Resurrection and the New Testament* (London: SCM Press, 1970).
Farley, W., *The Wounding and Healing of Desire: Weaving Heaven and Earth* (Louisville, KY: Westminster John Knox Press, 2005).
Farrer, A., *The Glass of Vision* (Westminster: Dacre Press, 1948).
Fee, G., *The First Epistle to the Corinthians* (Grand Rapids, MI: Eerdmans, 1987).
Fergusson, D., *Faith and Its Critics: A Conversation* (Oxford: Oxford University Press, 2009).
Ferreira, J., *Johannine Ecclesiology* (Sheffield: Sheffield Academic Press, 1998).
Fiddes, P. S., *The Creative Suffering of God* (Oxford: Clarendon Press, 1992).
  Freedom and Limit: A Dialogue between Literature and Christian Doctrine (Macon, GA: Mercer University Press, 1992).
  Participating in God: A Pastoral Doctrine of the Trinity (Louisville, KY: Westminster John Knox Press, 2000).
  Seeing the World and Knowing God: Hebrew Wisdom and Christian Doctrine in a Late-Modern Context (Oxford: Oxford University Press, 2013).
Finlan, S., 'Can We Speak of Theosis in Paul?' in *Partakers of the Divine Nature: The History and Development of Deification in the Christian Traditions*, ed. M. J. Christensen and J. A. Wittung (Grand Rapids, MI: Baker Academic, 2007), 68–80.
Flanagan, R., *The Narrow Road to the Deep North* (London: Vintage, 2015).
Ford, D. F., *Self and Salvation: Being Transformed* (Cambridge: Cambridge University Press, 1999).
Ford, D. F., and Hardy, D., *Living in Praise: Worshipping and Knowing God* (London: Darton, Longman and Todd, 2005).
Fout, J., *Fully Alive: The Glory of God and the Human Creature in Karl Barth, Hans Urs von Balthasar and the Theological Exegesis of Scripture* (London: Bloomsbury T&T Clark, 2015).
Friesenhahn, J., *Trinity and Theodicy: The Trinitarian Theology of von Balthasar and the Problem of Evil* (Aldershot: Ashgate, 2011).
Furnish, V. P., *II Corinthians* (Garden City, NY: Doubleday & Co., 1984).
Gaffin, R. B., Jr., 'Glory, Glorification' in *The Dictionary of Paul and His Letters*, ed. G. F. Hawthorne and R. P. Martin (Downers Grove, IL: Inter-Varsity Press, 1993), 348–50.
Gallaher, B., *Freedom and Necessity in Modern Trinitarian Theology* (Oxford: Oxford University Press, 2016).
Gammie, J. G., *Holiness in Israel* (Minneapolis, MN: Fortress Press, 1989).

Garcia-Rivera, A., *The Community of the Beautiful: A Theological Aesthetics* (Collegeville, MN: The Liturgical Press, 1999).

Gardner, T., *John in the Company of Poets: The Gospel in Literary Imagination* (Waco, TX: Baylor University Press, 2014).

Gardner, W. H., *Gerard Manley Hopkins: A Study in Poetic Idiosyncrasy in Relation to Poetic Tradition*, Vol. 2 (Oxford: Oxford University Press, 1958).

Garner, D. (ed.), *Antitheodicy, Atheodicy and Jewish Mysticism in Holocaust Theology* (Piscataway, NJ: Gorgias Press, 2012).

Garrett, S. M., *God's Beauty-in-Act: Participating in God's Suffering Glory* (Eugene, OR: Pickwick Books, 2013).

Goranson Jacob, H., and Wright, N. T., *Conformed to the Image of His Son: Rethinking Paul's Theology of Glory in Romans* (Downers Grove, IL: IVP Academic, 2018).

Gorman, M. J., *Becoming the Gospel: Paul, Participation and Mission* (Grand Rapids, MI: Eerdmans, 2015).

Cruciformity: Paul's Narrative Theology of the Cross (Grand Rapids, MI: Eerdmans, 2001).

Inhabiting the Cruciform God: Kenosis, Justification and Theosis in Paul's Narrative Soteriology (Grand Rapids, MI: Eerdmans, 2009).

Gorringe, T., *Earthly Visions: Theology and the Challenges of Art* (New Haven, CT: Yale University Press, 2011).

The Education of Desire: Towards a Theology of the Senses (London: SCM Press, 2011).

Green, J. B., *1. Peter* (Grand Rapids, MI: Eerdmans, 2007).

Grudem, W., *The First Epistle of Peter: An Introduction and Commentary* (Leicester: Inter-Varsity Press, 1988).

Hafemann, S. J., *Paul, Moses and the History of Israel: The Letter/Spirit Contrast and the Argument from Scripture in 2 Corinthians 3* (Tübingen: Mohr Siebeck, 1995).

Harries, R., *Art and the Beauty of God: A Christian Understanding* (London: Mowbray, 1993).

The Beauty and the Horror: Searching for God in a Suffering World (London: SPCK, 2016).

Harrisville, R. A., *Fracture: The Cross as Irreconcilable in the Language and Thought of the Biblical Writers* (Grand Rapids, MI: Eerdmans, 2006).

Hart, K., *The Trespass of the Sign: Deconstruction, Theology and Philosophy* (Cambridge: Cambridge University Press, 1989).

Harvey, A. E., *Renewal through Suffering: A Study of 2 Corinthians* (Edinburgh: T&T Clark 1996).

Haught, J., *Deeper than Darwin: The Prospect of Religion in the Age of Evolution* (Oxford: Westview, 2004).

Hays, R. B., *Echoes of Scripture in the Letters of Paul* (New Haven, CT: Yale University Press, 1989).

Heath, J. M. F., *Paul's Visual Piety: The Metamorphosis of the Beholder* (Oxford: Oxford University Press, 2013).

Henriksen, J.-O., *Desire, Gift and Recognition: Christology and Postmodern Philosophy* (Grand Rapids, MI: Eerdmans, 2009).

Herzfeld, N., *In Our Image? Artificial Intelligence and the Human Spirit* (Minnea-
    polis, MN: Fortress Press, 2002).
Heys, A., *R. S. Thomas and Romanticism* (Plovdiv: Pygmalion Press, 2004).
Hillesum, E., *Etty: The Letters and Diaries of Etty Hillesum 1941–1943*, ed.
    K. A. D. Smelik, transl. A. J. Pomerans (Grand Rapids, MI: Eerdmans, 2002).
    Letters from Westerbork, transl. A. J. Pomerans (New York: Pantheon Books,
    1986).
Hoggard Creegan, N., *Animal Suffering and the Problem of Evil* (New York:
    Oxford University Press, 2013).
Hopewell, J., *Congregation: Stories and Structures*, ed. B. G. Wheeler (Phila-
    delphia, PA: Fortress Press, 1987).
Hopkins, G. M., *Correspondence, Vol. II, 1882–1889*, ed. R. K. R. Thornton and
    C. Phillips (Oxford: Oxford University Press, 2013).
    Poems and Prose: Selected with an Introduction and Notes by W. H. Gardner
    (Harmondsworth: Penguin, 1953).
    The Sermons and Devotional Writings of Gerard Manley Hopkins, ed.
    C. Devlin (London: Oxford University Press, 1959).
Horrell, D. G., Hunt, C., and Southgate, C., *Greening Paul: Rereading the Apostle
    in a Time of Ecological Crisis* (Waco, TX: Baylor University Press, 2010).
Howsare, R. A., *Balthasar: A Guide for the Perplexed* (London: T&T Clark/
    Continuum, 2009).
Huxley, A., *Along the Road: Notes and Essays of a Tourist* (London: Triad/
    Paladin Books, 1985 [1925]).
Jaeger, W., *Early Christianity and Greek Paideia* (Cambridge, MA: The Belknap
    Press, 1961).
Jewett, R., *Romans: A Commentary* (Minneapolis, MN: Fortress Press, 2007).
Jonas, H., *Mortality and Morality: A Search for Good after Auschwitz*, ed.
    L. Vogel (Evanston, IL: Northwestern University Press, 1996).
Jones, D., *Epoch and Artist: Selected Writings*, ed. H. Grisewood (London: Faber
    and Faber, 1973).
Jones, J. R., 'Love as Perception of Meaning' in *Religion and Understanding*, ed.
    D. Z. Phillips (Oxford: Blackwell, 1967), 141–53.
Jones, S., *Trauma and Grace: Theology in a Ruptured World* (Louisville, KY:
    Westminster John Knox Press, 2009).
Jüngel, E., *God's Being Is in Becoming: The Trinitarian Theology of God in the
    Theology of Karl Barth: A Paraphrase*, transl. J. Webster (Edinburgh: T&T
    Clark, 2001).
Kaiser, C. B., *Seeing the Lord's Glory: Kyriocentric Visions and the Dilemma of
    Early Christology* (Minneapolis, MN: Fortress Press, 2014).
Kaiser, O., *Isaiah 1–12: A Commentary*, transl. R. A. Wilson. 2nd ed. (London:
    SCM Press, 1963).
Kelsey, D. H., *Eccentric Existence: A Theological Anthropology*, Vol. 2 (Louis-
    ville, KY; Westminster John Knox Press, 2009).
Kilby, K., *Balthasar: A (Very) Critical Introduction* (Grand Rapids, MI: Eerd-
    mans, 2012).
Kilner, J. F., *Dignity and Destiny: Humanity in the Image of God* (Grand Rapids,
    MI: Eerdmans, 2015).

King, P., *Dark Night Spirituality: Thomas Merton, Dietrich Bonhoeffer, Etty Hillesum: Contemplation and the New Paradigm* (London: SPCK, 1995).

Kittel, G., 'dokeō, doxa, doxazō, sundoxazō, endoxos, endoxazō, paradoxos' in *Theological Dictionary of the New Testament*, Vol. II, ed. G. Kittel and G. Friedrich, transl. G. W. Bromiley (Grand Rapids, MI: Eerdmans, 1964), 232–55.

Köstenberger, A. J., 'The Glory of God in John's Gospel and Revelation' in *The Glory of God*, ed. C. W. Morgan and R. A. Peterson (Wheaton, IL: Crossway, 2010), 107–26,

Kuhn, T. S., *The Structure of Scientific Revolutions* (Chicago: University of Chicago Press, 1962).

Lambrecht, J., 'Transformation in 2 Corinthians' in *Studies on 2 Corinthians*, ed. R. Bieringer and J. Lambrecht (Leuven: Peeters, 1994), 295–307.

Langer, L. L., *Admitting the Holocaust: Collected Essays* (New York: Oxford University Press, 1995).

Larsson, T., 'Glory or Persecution: The God of the Gospel of John in the History of Interpretation' in *The Gospel of John and Christian Theology*, ed. R. Bauckham and C. Mosser (Grand Rapids, MI: Eerdmans, 2008), 82–8.

Leahy, B., 'Theological Aesthetics' in *The Beauty of Christ: An Introduction to the Theology of Hans Urs von Balthasar*, ed. B. McGregor, OP, and T. Norris (Edinburgh: T&T Clark, 1994), 23–55.

Lewis, C. S., *The Four Loves* (London: Geoffrey Bles, 1960).
The Weight of Glory and Other Addresses (Grand Rapids, MI: Eerdmans, 1949).

Lindars, B., *The Gospel of John: New Century Bible Commentary* (Grand Rapids, MI: Eerdmans, 1972).

Litwa, M. D., '2 Corinthians 3.18 and Its Implications for Theosis'. *Journal of Theological Interpretation* 2 (2008),117–34.

Lloyd M., 'Are Animals Fallen?' in *Animals on the Agenda: Questions about Animals for Theology and Ethics*, ed. A. Linzey and D. Yamamoto (London: SCM Press, 1998), 147–60.
'The Humanity of Fallenness' in *Grace and Truth in a Secular Age*, ed. T. Bradshaw (Grand Rapids, MI: Eerdmans, 1998), 66–82.

Loader, W., *Jesus in John's Gospel: Structure and Issues in Johannine Christology* (Grand Rapids, MI: Eerdmans, 2017).

Lossky, V., *In the Image and Likeness of God*, ed. J. H. Erickson and T. E. Bird, (Oxford: Mowbray, 1975).

Louth, A., *The Wilderness of God* (London: Darton, Longman and Todd, 2003).

McCullough, L., *The Religious Philosophy of Simone Weil: An Introduction* (London: I.B. Tauris, 2014).

McDaniel, J., *Of God and Pelicans: A Theology of Reverence for Life* (Louisville, KY: Westminster/John Knox Press, 1989).

McGrath, A., *A Fine-Tuned Universe: The Quest for God in Science and Theology: The 2009 Gifford Lectures* (Louisville, KY: Westminster John Knox Press, 2009).
Darwinism and the Divine: Evolutionary Thought and Natural Theology (Oxford: Wiley-Blackwell, 2011).

Re-imagining Nature: The Promise of a Christian Natural Theology (Chichester: Wiley-Blackwell, 2017).

The Reenchantment of Nature: Science, Religion and the Human Sense of Wonder (London: Hodder and Stoughton, 2002).

McGill, W. J., *Poets' Meeting: George Herbert, R. S. Thomas and the Argument with God* (Jefferson, NC: McFarland & Co., 2004).

McKnight, S., *The Letter of James: The New International Commentary on the New Testament* (Grand Rapids, MI: Eerdmans, 2011),

Macquarrie, J., *A Guide to the Sacraments* (London: SCM Press, 1997).

Principles of Christian Theology (London: SCM Press, 1977).

Maimonides, M., *Guide of the Perplexed*, Vol. 1, trans. S. Pines (Chicago: University of Chicago Press, 1963).

Malina, B., *The New Testament World: Insights from Cultural Anthropology* (Louisville, KY: Westminster John Knox Press, 1993).

Martin, J. N., *Hans Urs von Balthasar and the Critical Appropriation of Russian Religious Thought* (Notre Dame, IN: University of Notre Dame Press, 2015).

Maslow, A. H., 'A Theory of Human Motivation'. *Psychological Review* 50 (1943), 370–96.

Melick, R. R., Jr., 'The Glory of God in the Synoptic Gospels, Acts and the General Epistles' in *The Glory of God*, ed. C. W. Morgan and R. A. Peterson (Wheaton, IL: Crossway, 2010), 79–106.

Merton, T., *New Seeds of Contemplation* (New York, NY: New Directions, 1961).

Messer, N., 'Natural Evil after Darwin' in *Theology after Darwin*, ed. M. Northcott and R. J. Berry (Carlisle: Paternoster, 2009), 139–54.

Meyer, N. A., *Adam's Dust and Adam's Glory in the Hodayot and the Letters of Paul: Rethinking Anthropogony and Theology* (Leiden: Brill, 2016).

Middleton, J. R., *The Liberating Image: The imago Dei in Genesis 1* (Grand Rapids, MI: Brazos Press, 2005).

Midgley, M., *Wisdom, Information and Wonder: What Is Knowledge For?* (London: Routledge, 1991).

Milbank, J., Ward, G., and Wyschgorod, E., *Theological Perspectives on God and Beauty* (Harrisburg, PA: Trinity Press International, 2003).

Mitchell, S., *The Book of Job* (London: Kyle Cathie, 1989).

Moberly, R. W. L., *At the Mountain of God: Story and Theology in Exodus 32–34* (Sheffield: JSOT Press, 1983).

Moltmann, J., *The Crucified God: The Cross of Christ as the Foundation and Criticism of Christian Theology*, transl. R. A. Wilson and J. Bowden (London: SCM Press, 1974).

Science and Wisdom, transl. M. Kohl (London: SCM Press, 2003).

Theology and Joy, transl. R. Ulrich (London: SCM Press 1973).

Mongrain, K., *The Systematic Thought of Hans Urs von Balthasar: An Irenaean Retrieval* (New York: Crossroad, 2002).

Moody Smith, D., *The Theology of the Gospel of John* (Cambridge: Cambridge University Press, 1995).

Moore, S., *Jesus the Liberator of Desire* (New York, NY: Crossroad, 1989).

Morgan, C., R. S. Thomas: Identity, Environment and Deity (Manchester: Manchester University Press, 2003).

Morgan, C. W., 'Towards a Theology of the Glory of God' in The Glory of God, ed. C. W. Morgan and R. A. Peterson (Wheaton, IL: Crossway, 2010), 153–87.

Morley, J., Our Last Awakening: Poems for Living in the Face of Death (London: SPCK, 2016).

Moule, C. F. D., 'Reflections on Triumphalism' in The Glory of Christ in the New Testament: Studies in Christology: In Memory of George Bradford Caird, ed. L. D. Hurst and N. T. Wright (Oxford: Clarendon Press, 1987), 219–27.

Mulhall, S. 'Wonder, Perplexity, Sublimity: Philosophy as the Overcoming of Self-Exile in Heidegger and Wittgenstein' in Practices of Wonder: Cross-Disciplinary Perspectives, ed. S. Vasalou (Cambridge: James Clarke, 2012), 121–43.

Neder, A., Participation in Christ: An Entry into Karl Barth's Church Dogmatics (Louisville, KY: Westminster John Knox Press, 2009).

Newman, C. C., Paul's Glory-Christology: Tradition and Rhetoric (Leiden: Brill, 1992).

Neyrey, J. H., 2 Peter, Jude (New York, NY: Doubleday, 1993).

Nichols, A. No Bloodless Myth: A Guide through Balthasar's Dramatics (Edinburgh: T&T Clark, 2000).

Say It Is Pentecost: A Guide through Balthasar's Logic (Edinburgh: T&T Clark, 2001).

The Word Has Been Abroad: A Guide through Balthasar's Aesthetics (Edinburgh: T&T Clark), 1998.

Nichols, S. J., 'The Glory of God Present and Past' in The Glory of God, ed. C. W. Morgan and R. A. Paterson (Wheaton, IL: Crossway, 2010), 23–46.

Nielsen, K., Incense in Ancient Israel (Leiden: Brill, 1986).

O'Donoghue, N., 'Appendix: Do We Get beyond Plato? A Critical Appreciation of the Theological Aesthetics' in The Beauty of Christ: An Introduction to the Theology of Hans Urs von Balthasar, ed. B. McGregor, OP, and T. Norris (Edinburgh: T&T Clark, 1994), 253–66.

'Theology of Beauty' in The Analogy of Beauty: The Theology of Hans Urs von Balthasar, ed. J. Riches (Edinburgh: T&T Clark, 1986), 1–10.

O'Halloran, N. W., S. J., 'Cosmic Alienation and the Origin of Evil: Rejecting the "Only Way" Option'. Theology and Science 13 (2015), 43–63.

Ó Murchadha, F., A Phenomenology of the Christian Life: Glory and Night (Bloomington, IN: Indiana University Press, 2013).

Oakes, E. T., S. J., and Moss, D. (eds.), The Cambridge Companion to Hans Urs von Balthasar (Cambridge: Cambridge University Press, 2004).

Olley, J. W., Ezekiel: A Commentary Based on Iezekiēl in Codex Vaticanus (Leiden: Brill, 2009).

Oord, T. J., The Nature of Love: A Theology (St. Louis, MO: Chalice Press, 2010).

Peacocke, A. R., 'The Cost of New Life' in The Work of Love: Creation as Kenosis, ed. J. Polkinghorne (London: SPCK, 2001), 21–42.

The Palace of His Glory: God's World and Science (Hindmarsh, South Australia: ATF Press, 2005).

Paths from Science to God: The End of All Our Exploring (Oxford: Oneworld, 2001).

Theology for a Scientific Age: Being and Becoming – Natural, Divine and Human (London: SCM Press, 1993).

Phillips, D. Z., *Poet of the Hidden God: Meaning and Mediation in the Poetry of R. S. Thomas* (London: Macmillan, 1986).

The Problem of Evil and the Problem of God (London: SCM Press, 2012).

Pleshoyano, A., 'Etty Hillesum: For God and with God'. *The Way* 44 (January 2005), 7–20.

Polkinghorne, J., *Faith, Science and Understanding* (London: SPCK, 2000).

'Pelican Heaven'. *Times Literary Supplement*, April 3, 2009, 31.

Reason and Reality: The Relationship between Science and Theology (London: SPCK, 1991).

Potter, D., 'An Interview with Melvyn Bragg' in *Seeing the Blossom: Two Interviews, a Lecture and a Story* (London: Faber and Faber, 1994).

Propp, W. H. C., *Exodus 1–18: A New Translation with Introduction and Commentary* (New York: Doubleday, 1998).

Exodus 19–40: A New Translation with Introduction and Commentary (New York: Doubleday, 2006).

Quick, O. C., *The Christian Sacraments* (London: Collins, 1964[1927]).

Rambo, S., *Spirit and Trauma: A Theology of Remaining* (Louisville, KY: Westminster John Knox Press, 2010).

Ramsey, A. M., *The Glory of God and the Transfiguration of Christ* (London: Longmans, Green, 1949).

The Gospel and the Catholic Church (London: Longmans, Green, 1956).

'The Mysticism of Evelyn Underhill' in *Evelyn Underhill: Anglican Mystic*, ed. A. M. Ramsey and A. M. Allchin (Oxford: SLG Press, 1996), 3–14.

The Resurrection of Christ: A Study of the Event and Its Meaning for the Christian Faith (London: Fontana, 1961 [1945]).

Sacred and Secular: A Study in the Otherworldly and This-Worldly Aspects of Christianity: The Holland Lectures for 1964 (London: Longmans, Green, 1965).

ReManning, R. (ed.), *The Oxford Handbook of Natural Theology* (Oxford: Oxford University Press, 2013).

Ricoeur, P., *Figuring the Sacred: Religion, Narrative and Imagination*, transl. D. Pellaurer, ed. M. Wallace (Minneapolis, MN: Fortress Press, 1995).

The Symbolism of Evil, transl. E. Buchanan (Boston: Beacon, 1969).

Ringgren, H., 'qds' in *The Theological Dictionary of the Old Testament*, Vol. XII, ed. G. J. Botterweck, H. Ringgren, and H.-J. Fabry, transl. D.W. Scott (Grand Rapids, MI: Eerdmans, 2003), 530–43.

Robinson, A., *God and the World of Signs: Trinity, Evolution, and the Metaphysical Semiotics of C. S. Peirce* (Leiden: Brill, 2010).

Traces of the Trinity: Signs, Sacraments and Sharing God's Life (Cambridge: James Clarke, 2014).

Rohr, R., *Silent Compassion: Finding God in Contemplation* (Cincinnati, OH: Franciscan Media, 2014).

Rolston, H., III, 'Disvalues in Nature'. *The Monist* 75 (1992), 250–78.

'Does Nature Need to Be Redeemed?' *Zygon* 29 (1994), 205–29.

'Naturalizing and Systematizing Evil' in *Is Nature Ever Evil?*, ed. W. B. Drees (London: Routledge, 2003), 67–86.

Science and Religion: A Critical Survey (Philadelphia: Templeton Foundation Press, 2006 [1987]).

Rumrich, J. P., *Matter of Glory; A New Preface to* Paradise Lost (Pittsburgh, PA: University of Pittsburgh, 1987).

Rumsey, A., 'Through Poetry and the Call to Attention' in *Beholding the Glory: Incarnation through the Arts*, ed. J. Begbie (London: Darton, Longman and Todd, 2000), 47–63.

Samuelson, N. *Jewish Philosophy: An Historical Introduction* (London: Continuum, 2003).

Savage, T. B., *Power through Weakness: Paul's Understanding of the Christian Ministry in 2. Corinthians* (Cambridge: Cambridge University Press, 1996).

Savran, G. W., *Encountering the Divine: Theophany in Biblical Narrative* (London: T&T Clark/Continuum, 2005).

Segal, A. F., *Paul the Convert: The Apostolate and Apostasy of Saul the Pharisee* (New Haven, CT: Yale University Press, 1990).

Seifrid, M. A., *The Second Letter to the Corinthians* (Grand Rapids, MI: Eerdmans, 2014).

Sennett, J. F., and Groothuis, D. (eds.), *In Defense of Natural Theology: A Post-Humean Assessment* (Downers Grove, IL: Inter-Varsity Press, 2005).

Sherrard, P., *Christianity and Eros: Essays on the Theme of Sexual Love* (London: SPCK, 1976).

Sherry, P., *Spirit and Beauty: An Introduction to Theological Aesthetics* (London: SCM Press, 2002).

'The Sacramentality of All Things'. *New Blackfriars* 89 (2008), 575–90.

Short, T. L., *Peirce's Theory of Signs* (Cambridge: Cambridge University Press, 2007).

Shults, F. L., *Reforming Theological Anthropology: After the Philosophical Turn to Relationality* (Grand Rapids, MI: Eerdmans, 2003).

Sideris, L. H., *Consecrating Science: Wonder, Knowledge, and the Natural World* (Oakland, CA: University of California Press, 2017).

Environmental Ethics, Ecological Theology, and Natural Selection (New York, NY: Columbia University Press, 2003).

Smith, J. K. A., *Desiring the Kingdom: Worship, Worldview and Cultural Formation* (Grand Rapids, MI: Baker Academic, 2009).

Speech and Theology: Language and the Logic of Incarnation (London: Routledge, 2002).

Snaith, J. G., *Ecclesiasticus or the Wisdom of Jesus Son of Sirach* (Cambridge: Cambridge University Press, 1974).

Sobolev, D., *The Split World of Gerard Manley Hopkins: An Essay in Semiotic Phenomenology* (Washington, DC: Catholic University of America Press, 2011).

Southgate, C., 'Cosmic Evolution and Evil' in *The Cambridge Companion to the Problem of Evil*, ed. C. Meister and P. K. Moser (Cambridge: Cambridge University Press, 2017), 147–64.

'Divine Glory in a Darwinian World'. *Zygon* 49 (2014), 784–807.

'Does God's Care Make Any Difference? Theological Reflection on the Suffering of God's Creatures' in *Christian Faith and the Earth: Current Paths and Emerging Horizons in Ecotheology*, ed. E. M. Conradie, S. Bergmann, C. Deane-Drummond, and D. Edwards (London: Bloomsbury, 2014), 97–114.

'God's Creation Wild and Violent, and Our Care for Other Animals'. *Perspectives on Science & Christian Faith* 67 (2015), 245–53.

The Groaning of Creation: God, Evolution and the Problem of Evil (Louisville, KY: Westminster John Knox Press, 2008).

'The Orientation of Longing' in *Issues in Science and Theology: Do Emotions Shape the World?* eds. D. Evers, M. Fuller, A. Runehov, and K-W. Saether (Dordrecht: Springer, 2016), 73–86.

'Re-Reading Genesis, John and Job: A Christian's Response to Darwinism'. *Zygon* 46 (2011), 370–95.

Steenburg, D., 'The Case against the Synonymity of *Morphē* and *Eikōn*'. *Journal for the Study of the New Testament* 34 (1988), 77–86.

Steiner, G., *Real Presences* (Chicago: University of Chicago Press, 1991).

Strong, J. T., 'God's kābôd: The Presence of Yahweh in the Book of Ezekiel' in *The Book of Ezekiel: Theological and Anthropological Perspectives*, ed. M. S. Odell and J. T. Strong (Atlanta: Society of Biblical Literature, 2000), 69–95.

Stump, E., *Wandering in Darkness: Narrative and the Problem of Suffering* (Oxford: Oxford University Press, 2010).

Surin, K., *Theology and the Problem of Evil* (Oxford: Blackwell, 1988).

Taliaferro, C., 'Glory in Human Nature' in *The Ashgate Research Companion to Theological Anthropology*, ed. J. F. Farris and C. Taliaferro (Aldershot: Ashgate, 2011), 319–27.

Taylor, B. B., *Learning to Walk in the Dark* (New York: HarperOne, 2014).

Terrien, S., *The Elusive Presence: Toward a New Biblical Theology* (Eugene, OR: Wipf and Stock, 2005 [1978]).

The Cloud of Unknowing and Other Works, ed. A. C. Spearing (London: Penguin, 2001).

Thomas, M. W., *R. S. Thomas: Serial Obsessive* (Cardiff: University of Wales Press, 2013).

Thomas, R. S., *Autobiographies*, transl. J. W. Davies (London: Orion Books, 1998).

Collected Later Poems 1988–2000 (Newcastle upon Tyne: Bloodaxe Books, 2004).

Collected Poems 1945–1990 (London: J. M. Dent, 1993).

Selected Prose, ed. S. Anstey (Bridgend: Poetry Wales Press, 1983).

Thompson, R., *Holy Ground: The Spirituality of Matter* (London: SPCK, 1990).

Thrall, M. P., *The Second Epistle to the Corinthians: A Critical and Exegetical Commentary*, Vol. 1 (Edinburgh: T&T Clark, 1994).

Tillich, P., *The Boundaries of Our Being: A Collection of His Sermons with His Autobiographical Sketch* (London: Fontana Library, 1973).

Todorov, T., *Facing the Darkness: Moral Life in the Camps*, transl. A. Denner and A. Pollak (New York: Henry Holt & Co., 1996).

Tollerton, D. C., *The Book of Job in Post-Holocaust Thought* (Sheffield: Sheffield Phoenix Press, 2012).

Traherne, T. *Centuries* (London: Faith Press, 1960).

Tuell, S. S., 'Divine Presence and Absence in Ezekiel's Prophecy' in *The Book of Ezekiel: Theological and Anthropological Perspectives*, ed. M. S. Odell and J. T. Strong (Atlanta: Society of Biblical Literature, 2000), 97–116.

Turner, D., *The Darkness of God: Negativity in Christian Mysticism* (Cambridge: Cambridge University Press, 1995).

Van den Brandt, R., *Etty Hillesum: An Introduction to Her Thought*, transl. H. Monkel (Zürich: LiT Verlag, 2014).

Van Huyssteen, J. W., *Alone in the World: Human Uniqueness in Science and Theology* (Göttingen: Vandenhoeck and Ruprecht, 2006).

Vanstone, W. H., *The Stature of Waiting* (London: Darton, Longman and Todd, 1982).

Vasalou, S. 'Introduction' in *Practices of Wonder: Cross-disciplinary Perspectives* ed. S. Vasalou (Cambridge: James Clarke, 2012), 1–15.

Von Balthasar, H. U., 'Another Ten Years – 1975', transl. J. Saward in *The Analogy of Beauty: The Theology of Hans Urs von Balthasar*, ed. J. Riches (Edinburgh: T&T Clark, 1986), 222–33.

Explorations in Theology, Vol. 1: The Word Made Flesh, transl. A. V. Littledale with A. Dru (San Francisco: Ignatius, 1989).

The Glory of the Lord: A Theological Aesthetics, Vol. 1, Seeing the Form, transl. E. Leivà-Merikakis, ed. J. Fessio, S. J., and J. Riches (Edinburgh: T&T Clark, 1982).

The Glory of the Lord: A Theological Aesthetics, Vol. 2, Studies in Theological Style: Clerical Styles, transl. A. Louth, F. McDonagh and B. McNeil, C. R. V., ed. J. Riches (Edinburgh: T&T Clark, 1984).

The Glory of the Lord: A Theological Aesthetics, Vol. 3, Studies in Theological Style: Lay Styles, transl. A. Louth, J. Saward, M. Simon, and R. Williams, ed. J. Riches (Edinburgh: T&T Clark, 1986).

The Glory of the Lord: A Theological Aesthetics, Vol. 7, Theology: The New Covenant, transl. B. McNeil, C. R. V., ed. J. Riches (Edinburgh: T&T Clark, 1989).

Mysterium Paschale: The Mystery of Easter, transl. A. Nichols (San Francisco, CA: Ignatius Press, 1990).

The Glory of the Lord: A Theological Aesthetics, Vol. 6, Theology: The Old Covenant, transl. B. McNeil C. R. V. and E. Leivà-Merikakis, ed. J. Riches (Edinburgh: T&T Clark, 1991).

Theo-Drama, Theological Dramatic Theory, Vol. 4: The Action, transl. G. Harrison (San Francisco: Ignatius Press, 1994).

Theo-Logic: Theological Logical Theory, Vol. 1: Truth of the World, transl. A. J. Walker (San Francisco: Ignatius Press, 2000).

Voorwinde, S., *Jesus' Emotions in the Gospels* (London: T&T Clark/Continuum, 2011).

Walford, E. J., 'The Case for a Broken Beauty: An Art Historical Viewpoint' in *The Beauty of God: Theology and the Arts*, ed. D. J. Treier, M. Husbands, and R. Lundin (Downers Grove, IL: IVP Academic, 2007), 87–109.

Walsh, C., 'The Sacramental Vision of R. S. Thomas' (Ph.D. thesis, Heythrop College, University of London, 2010).

Ward, B. W., *World as Word: Philosophical Theology in Gerard Manley Hopkins* (Washington, DC: Catholic University of America Press, 2002).

Waterman, R., *Belonging and Estrangement in the Poetry of Philip Larkin, R. S. Thomas and Charles Causley* (Aldershot: Ashgate, 2014).

Watson, F., *Paul and the Hermeneutics of Faith* (London: T&T Clark/Continuum, 2004).

Webb, S., *The Dome of Eden: A New Solution to the Problem of Creation and Evolution* (Eugene, OR: Wipf and Stock, 2010).

Weil, S., *Gravity and Grace*, transl. E. Crawford and M. von der Ruhr (London: Routledge, 2000[1952]).

Weinfeld, M., 'kābōḏ' in *Theological Dictionary of the Old Testament Vol. VII*, ed. G. J. Botterweck, H. Ringgren, and H.-J. Fabry, transl. D. E. Green (Grand Rapids, MI: Eerdmans, 1995), 22–38.

Westover, D., *R. S. Thomas: A Stylistic Biography* (Cardiff: University of Wales Press, 2011).

Widyapranawa, S. H., *The Lord Is Savior: Faith in National Crisis: A Commentary on the Book of Isaiah 1–39* (Grand Rapids, MI: Eerdmans,1990).

Wildberger, H., *Isaiah 1–12: A Commentary*, transl. T. H. Trapp (Minneapolis, MN: Fortress Press, 1991).

Wildman, W. J., 'Incongruous Goodness, Perilous Beauty, Disconcerting Truth: Ultimate Reality and Suffering in Nature' in *Physics and Cosmology: Scientific Perspectives on the Problem of Natural Evil*, ed. N. Murphy, R. J. Russell, and W. R. Stoeger, SJ (Berkeley, CA: CTNS and Vatican City: Vatican Observatory, 2007), 267–94.

Williams, D. J., *Paul's Metaphors: Their Context and Character* (Peabody, MA: Hendrickson, 1999).

Williams, R., '"Adult Geometry": Dangerous Thoughts in R. S. Thomas' in *The Page's Drift: R. S. Thomas at Eighty*, ed. M. W. Thomas (Bridgend: Seren: 1993), 82–98.

  Grace and Necessity: Reflections on Art and Love (London: Continuum, 2005).

  The Lion's World: A Journey into the Heart of Narnia (London: SPCK, 2012).

  'Theology in the Face of Christ', unpublished lecture given October 4, 2004, rowanwilliams.archbishopofcanterbury.org

  The Wound of Knowledge: Christian Spirituality from the New Testament to St. John of the Cross (London: Darton, Longman and Todd, 1979).

Wisdom, J., *Philosophy and Psychoanalysis* (Oxford: Blackwell, 1953).

Wolpert, L., *The Unnatural Nature of Science* (London: Faber and Faber, 1992).

Woodhouse, P., *Etty Hillesum: A Life Transformed* (London: Bloomsbury, 2009).

Wright, N. T., *The Climax of the Covenant: Christ and the Law in Pauline Theology* (Minneapolis, MN: Fortress Press, 1992).

'Reflected Glory: 2 Corinthians 3.18' in *The Glory of Christ in the New Testament: Studies in Christology: In Memory of George Bradford Caird*, ed. L. D. Hurst and N. T. Wright (Oxford: Clarendon Press, 1987), 139–50.

Paul and the Faithfulness of God: Christian Origins and the Question of God (London: SPCK, 2013), Parts I and II, 1–605; Parts III and IV, 609–1658.

Young, F., *The Art of Performance: Towards a Theology of Holy Scripture* (London: Darton, Longman and Todd, 1990).

God's Presence: A Contemporary Recapitulation of Early Christianity (Cambridge: Cambridge University Press, 2013).

Young, F., and Ford, D. F., *Meaning and Truth in 2. Corinthians* (London: SPCK, 1987).

Index

Ford, D. F., 104, 219
form (in von Balthasar), 120–1, 126, 205
Fout, J., 5, 11, 13, 20, 30, 52, 67, 70–3,
    206–7, 212, 217
freedom, 14, 150, 193–4, 196, 204, 224–7,
    245
    association with glory, 138, 196, 214,
        219, 225, 245
Furnish, V., 213, 215

Garcia-Rivera, A., 39, 120, 234
Gardner, T., 81, 83, 86, 88, 108, 164, 252
Garrett, S. M., 7, 18–19, 27, 32, 34, 37,
    106, 206, 219, 221
Genesis, Book of
    Chapter 1, 58, 230
    Chapter 3, 112, 250
Gethsemane, 30, 54, 83, 85, 157
Gloria crucis, 14, 39, 46, 90, 99, 106, 115,
    126, 128, 141, 166–7, 173, 194, 196,
    219, 234
Gloria in excelsis, 15, 39, 46, 90, 107, 120,
    128, 142, 152, 166, 171, 175, 196,
    211, 216, 219, 234, 236
Gloria mundi, 14, 39, 46, 106, 128, 130,
    145, 152, 173, 193, 196, 234
glory *see also* contemplation; freedom;
    Gloria; God; Jesus Christ
    as honour, 13, 52, 65–6, 70–3, 79, 255
    contrasted with beauty, 31–40, 49, 69,
        112, 132, 137, 166, 237
    in Etty Hillesum, 182–99
    in R. S. Thomas, 168–82, 194–8
    in the Hebrew Bible, 45–67
    in the natural world, 96–148
    in the New Testament, 74–93
    spectrum of meanings of, 13, 28–30, 47,
        61, 71, 257
God
    absence of, 42, 73, 168, 174–81, 195,
        198, 258
    and mystery, 5, 10, 12, 19, 24, 38, 43, 46,
        55, 60, 71–2, 94, 119, 145–6, 175,
        177, 182, 212
    attributes of, 27–8, 56, 145, 257
    beauty of, 52, 127, 206, 234
    contemplation of, 42
    creaturely praise of, 23, 29, 70–1, 131–5,
        138, 172
    elusiveness of, 170, 174–5, 177, 180, 182,
        197

Godness of, 12, 19, 27, 29–30, 37–8, 46,
    53, 56, 60, 64, 66, 71, 77, 79, 86, 92–3,
    144, 158, 179, 182, 204, 210, 212,
    254, 256, 258
goodness of, 27, 52–3, 115–16, 139
holiness of, 22, 59–62, 119, 213
immanence of, 22, 76, 124, 128, 194,
    202, 222
Kingdom of, 42, 171, 205, 235, 240, 247,
    258
lamenting at suffering, 3, 110, 237
longing of, 142, 198, 243–5
lovingness of, 19, 37, 76, 78, 80, 86, 99,
    111, 118, 120, 193, 211, 216, 224,
    230, 243, 247, 252–3
responsibility for natural evil, 4, 28, 86,
    115, 120, 155
self-giving of, 19–20, 39, 75, 87–8, 111,
    119, 144, 230, 234, 255
sovereignty of, 31, 94, 113, 141, 147, 182
transcendence of, 7, 22, 48, 50, 118, 127,
    188, 207, 244
Godforsakenness, 73
Good Friday, 19, 35, 152, 158, 196
Goranson Jacob, H., 13, 204, 255
Gorman, M., 201, 218, 220–1, 223, 226,
    234
Gorringe, T., 32, 252
Gregory of Nazianzus, 55
Gregory of Nyssa, 152, 176, 216, 241,
    246

haecceitas see particularity
Harries, R., 16, 30, 32, 78, 81, 154, 158,
    177, 235
Harrisville, R. A., 84, 221
Heath, J. M. F., 82, 202, 211, 217–20
hermeneutical lens, 9–10, 13, 15, 17, 46, 95,
    98, 145, 256–7
Herzfeld, N., 227
Hillesum, E., 15, 182–98, 200
Holocaust, the (also the Shoah), 13, 155,
    183, 194
honour *see* glory
Hopewell, J., 189
Hopkins, G. M., 109, 119, 122–9, 136–7,
    151, 187–9, 222, 234–5
    'As Kingfishers Catch Fire', 124, 126,
        129, 187, 222
    'Brothers', 135
    'God's Grandeur', 69, 97–8